The
BOOK OF
ENTREPRENEURS' WISDOM

ALSO AVAILABLE IN THE WISDOM SERIES

The Book of Business Wisdom

Offers 54 essays from such legends of commerce and industry as John D. Rockefeller, Jack Welch, Sam Walton, P. T. Barnum, J. Paul Getty, Andrew Grove, and Henry Ford.

Topics include: the essentials of good management, how to get ahead, and maintaining individuality in the corporate world.

The Book of Leadership Wisdom

Offers 52 essays from such legendary leaders as Andrew Carnegie, Bill Gates, Michael Eisner, H. Ross Perot, Katharine Graham, Akio Morita, and T. Coleman Du Pont.

Topics include: leading revolution, dealing with adversity, and corporate culture.

The Book of Investing Wisdom

Offers 46 essays from such legends of Wall Street as Warren Buffett, Peter Lynch, Abby Cohen, Bernard Baruch, John Moody, John Templeton, Charles Dow, and George Soros.

Topics include: the nuts and bolts of analysis, attitude and philosophy, lessons from notorious characters, and beyond your average blue chip.

COMING IN THE SPRING OF 2000

The Book of Management Wisdom

Offers 50 essays from such legends of business as Jack Welch, Harold Geneen, Carol Bartz, Alfred Sloan, Lee Iacocca, Andrew Carnegie, and David Packard.

Topics include: guiding principles, handling conflict, issues of organization, and the power of technology.

The
BOOK OF
ENTREPRENEURS' WISDOM

Classic Writings by
Legendary Entrepreneurs

Edited by Peter Krass

John Wiley & Sons, Inc.
New York • Chichester • Weinheim • Brisbane • Singapore • Toronto

Contents

Contents

Contents

Contents

Introduction

Gunslinger, explorer, pioneer, thrill seeker—that's the romance of an entrepreneur. Just consider Warren Avis's exaltation: "In popular thought, the independent, high-rolling business person has often been compared to the swashbuckling adventurer epitomized in the Western tales of Owen Wister or Louis L'Amour. This personality type spans generations and historical epochs. On the American frontier, the term was 'gunslinger.' On the high seas, it was 'pirate.' And in Western capitalism, it's 'entrepreneur,'" the founder of Avis Rental Car writes in his essay, "Are You a Gunslinger?", which opens Part II of this collection. However, the idea of leaving behind the comforts of a routine life and plunging into your own business can be nerve-racking, even frightening. Do you have what it takes? Must you be of bold personality? After all, Henry Ford took up race car driving and risked his life to prove he built a better vehicle. So, must you be a gunslinger type with ice water in your veins and a steeley gaze? Just consider that Conrad Hilton took to packing a gun to protect himself from vengeful competitors and disenchanted partners.

Peter Drucker, the business guru and author of *Innovation and Entrepreneurship*, points out that being an entrepreneur doesn't require specific personality traits. He writes, "It is not a personality trait; in thirty years I have seen people of the most diverse personalities and temperaments perform well in entrepreneurial challenges." For him, it's a behavior that can be learned; his own wife, Doris, founded a business at the age of 80! And, Anita Roddick founded The Body Shop because her husband decided to pursue his lifelong dream of riding a horse from Buenos Aires to New York City, a two-year ordeal, and she needed to support herself and two children. So, perhaps the best basic definition is to say that entrepreneurs act a certain way: They start and operate their own businesses. However, even this basic definition must be expanded: Entrepreneurs are inventors who become businessmen by necessity, such as George Eastman, who simply wanted to invent a more compact camera to bring on his vacation, and then suddenly found himself besieged with customers; they are people who buy existing businesses to improve upon them, such as Victor Kiam, who loved the Remington razor so much, he bought the company; and they are visionary business executives who transform companies by invigorating them with the entrepreneurial spirit, such as Thomas J. Watson, who created IBM as we know it.

A brief etymological and historical tour will help bring more meaning to the definition. "Entrepreneur" is taken from the French word, *entreprendre*, which means to undertake. According to Drucker, it was a French economist, J. B. Say, who coined the term "entrepreneur" around 1800. In a paper, Say wrote, "The entrepreneur shifts economic resources out of an area of lower and into an area of higher productivity and greater yield." But there his definition ended. Although Say used it in reference to business, according to the *Oxford English Dictionary*, in the early 1800s, the first *common* use of the word "entrepreneur" in the English language was to define "a director of a musical organization." It's apropos that the term is linked with artists who thrive on imagination and improvisation. Not until the mid-1800s was the term used extensively to define "a person who undertakes or controls a business of enterprise and bears the risk of profit or loss." Etymology aside, the bottom line: Society has always had entrepreneurs, and the definition can indeed be expansive.

Our American tradition is rich with entrepreneurs in all shapes and sizes, beginning with Christopher Columbus, who discovered the Americas and exemplifies Avis's swashbuckling entrepreneur. His story begins with his vision of sailing West to go East to find a shorter route to Asia, thereby making trade in gold and spices more profitable. However, Columbus spent six long years selling his idea to King Ferdinand and Queen Isabella of Spain, before they finally blessed the project and a financial consortium was put together in January of 1492. In June he acquired ships and recruited men, and in August he set sail.

More than 100 years later, the first colonists faced an equally grueling task of finding financial backers to support their endeavors. As Arthur Quinn points out in his book, *A New World: An Epic of Colonial America from the Founding of Jamestown to the Fall of Quebec*, these early adventurers were not escaping religious persecution, but rather seeking wealth from gold, silver, and jewels; therefore, they also provide an early blueprint of what it means to be an entrepreneur, from creating a business plan to obtaining working capital to managing the business. Like Columbus, the colonial leaders had to have a unique vision of how best to tap the new market and then find a venture capitalist, namely the Crown or a trading company, willing to fund their adventure. If you won support, you became both explorer and businessman, facing challenges in an unknown land that included Indian attacks, unpredictable weather, and food shortages, in addition to your primary objective of establishing your business. To say the least, success required innovative thinking and creative solutions.

Not all were successful. In the case of the Jamestown settlement, first established in 1607, only 38 of the original 150 colonists survived as they failed to find the alleged gold, to build a profitable manufacturing base, and to establish trade with Native Americans. Learning from the early disasters, future leaders for the colonies were chosen carefully. Experienced explorers such as Captain John Smith (a Jamestown veteran and featured, with a bit of revisionist history, in the Disney hit movie *Pocahontas*) were even brought in as consultants to help evaluate candidates. The chosen leaders were given stock ownership in the trading company or financial consortium to align their interests with that of their investors—sound familiar? Eventually it worked. In contrast to Jamestown, a Maryland settlement founded in 1630 prospered by being pioneers in the cultivation of a relatively new product called tobacco, which had become a hot commodity back in Europe. Like savvy entrepreneurs, they recognized an opportunity and acted upon it. The same can be said for those who accidentally encountered pods of sperm whales off the coast of Massachusetts and subsequently founded a very prosperous whaling industry.

One hundred years later we begin to encounter the names of America's more widely recognized archetypal entrepreneurs, such as Ben Franklin, Eli Whitney, and Samuel Colt. Whitney exemplifies the hero-entrepreneur who sees an opportunity and seizes the day. After graduating from Yale College, then a liberal arts school that churned out ministers, he went to Georgia to tutor the children living on a plantation. However, there was a dispute about salary and he never took the job. With nothing else to do, he focused on a prevailing problem on the plantation and throughout the South: how to extract the seeds from cotton, which at that time was exceedingly tedious and time consuming. The result: his cotton gin. However, then he encountered a dilemma of his own: manufacturing the machine on a large enough scale to meet demand. Unfortunately, he never did resolve the issue, and farmers with any mechanical inclination began making their own clones of the gin. On the other hand, Whitney went on to make his mark by introducing the concept of interchangeable parts in manufacturing—a critical first step toward mass production that Henry Ford later perfected.

Whitney's cotton gin production problem, however, represents a key management issue successful entrepreneurs must contend with: *growth*. Concerning growth, in the first essay of Part VII, entitled *Entrepreneurial Management*, Alfred Fuller, founder of the Fuller Brush Company and creator of the legendary sales force that became part of Americana, openly admits, "Often I was dizzy, not from excitement but from bewilderment." The details of managing a booming enterprise overwhelmed him, but fortunately he made adjustments and prospered. Not all do.

The reason so many entrepreneurs have difficulties with growth is because they're too busy breaking rules or simply not recognizing them; they're not always disciplined businesspeople with set policies and organizational charts, and quite often there's absolutely no method to their madness. They are innovators first and foremost, as they should be. They take risks, and interestingly, many of those risks are not consciously taken, but a result of ignorance, of not knowing what they're doing or why. In his essay, *Risk Taking*, Richard Branson admits, "The best thing I can do is not to try and rationalise what I, and my colleagues at Virgin, try to do when we are making decisions." One way to limit the downside, he advises, is to "avoid psychological pre-commitments." In other words, you must be willing to walk away from a business, regardless of what you've put in. Another way is to be involved in the nitty-gritty, so you're completely aware of what's happening. Indeed, the great entrepreneurs are people who roll up their sleeves and get their hands dirty; they have intimate knowledge of their trade. Just consider publisher Benjamin Franklin, whose hands were stained with printer's ink from age 12 on, or Domino's Pizza founder Tom Monaghan, who even as CEO of a billion-dollar business, wore pizza sauce on his suit like it was the Red Badge of Courage, or technology wiz Michael Dell, who meticulously upgraded old personal computers in his college dorm room and then sold them.

Entrepreneurs, however, are not just dynamic individuals with a good story to tell about their experiences; collectively speaking, they play a crucial role in the economy, from creating new products to providing new jobs. Like the national economy, entrepreneurialism goes through cycles. Although there have always been innovators such as Benjamin Franklin, entrepreneurs as a force to be reckoned with first exploded on the scene in the 1870s. A primary reason was the rise in banks and bankers, such as J. P. Morgan, who, for example, was willing to finance inventors like Thomas Edison. Wars have always provided great opportunities for entrepreneurs, such as Simon Ramo, who specialized in weapons design and appears in Part IV: "Risk and Strategy." Another critical factor in the tides of entrepreneurship is cultural values. A prime example is the late 1960s when rebellion was in the air and many young people, such as Richard Branson, chose to go their own way rather than the corporate. In the 1990s, the rebellious Generation X, which includes Michael Dell, is providing a surge of entrepreneurship. No doubt, entrepreneurs are rebels, and social events and attitudes bring them out. In contrast, during the height of the Cold War in the 1950s and early 1960s, bigger meant better, so the focus was on creating multinational conglomerates.

Although entrepreneurs come in all shapes and sizes, ultimately they face many similar issues. This book, as with the other collections in the Wisdom Series, is organized in eight parts to effectively address those poignant issues. For the entrepreneur, life begins with the start-up, so this section, appropriately, is first; the collection concludes with a group of personal stories that offer dramatic narratives about the life of an entrepreneur. Each part is introduced with a few lines to summarize its purpose and to define the dominant themes. For example, Part III, entitled "Venture Capital and Going Public," deals with the entire spectrum of financing a venture, from raising seed money to going public, which is for many, the crowning event. One of the major themes in this part is learning the language of a banker and viewing your business through their eyes. As Tom Monaghan warns, if you can't talk their language, you might as well be speaking Swahili. Of course, each entrepreneur has their own distinct opinion, whether it be on financing or branding or management. To put their views into context, each author and his or her respective essay is also introduced with poignant biographical and anecdotal information.

Although these entrepreneurs are deeply involved in their own unique business and industry, some of the common characteristics shared among them include a willingness to take that decisive plunge into a new venture, to sacrifice themselves and even their families, to risk a more comfortable way of life, and to relentlessly pursue their dreams. Most are not swashbuckling extroverts such as Richard Branson, but inside they all have the guts to face the world on their own terms. Like the well-conditioned athlete or the hardened soldier, the entrepreneur must prepare for a grueling battle, and within these pages lies the opportunity to learn from some of the legends. No doubt, these adventurers in capitalism will inspire you to take the plunge.

PART I

The Start-Up

To take the plunge, to start your own company, to shed the comforts of the corporate world, takes guts. However, as Michael Bloomberg states in the opening essay, he'd rather be his own general than a loyal corporate soldier. It also takes more than a bold decision; starting a company requires logical thinking to put together a business plan that involves a series of steps, linking your original vision to acquiring the necessary plant and equipment. However, as Harvey Firestone warns, "The initial product and the initial organization are never right." He should know, he took his business from refurbishing buggy wheels to manufacturing pneumatic car tires—and to accomplish his goals, Firestone had the nerve to stalk the man who would become his most important investor. What can you expect on a daily basis in the early stages? Doris Drucker, who's married to the renowned business guru Peter Drucker, provides a play-by-play analysis of starting her own business—at the golden age of 80! The essays in Part I provide an encompassing look at the mechanics of the start-up, from the initial vision and strategic considerations to the nuts and bolts of actually putting a company together.

MICHAEL BLOOMBERG
1942–

Back in 1981, Michael Bloomberg was terminated as a general partner of Salomon Brothers; today, he runs his own multimedia empire, Bloomberg, L.P., which includes Bloomberg Financial Markets (online financial information) and Bloomberg News (a worldwide wire service), among other ventures. The seed money for the business came from the $10 million that came with his termination. Not too bad for a boy who grew up in blue-collar Medford, Massachusetts, where vocational training was a primary goal after high school. Bloomberg had other plans, even in his youth, becoming the youngest person at that time to ever reach the rank of Eagle Scout. "It was the time," he said, "I learned to be both self-sufficient and, simultaneously, to live and work with others."

Bloomberg attended Johns Hopkins University and then Harvard University for an MBA, finishing in 1966. As graduation approached, he had no career plans; instead, he expected to go to Vietnam, but the Armed Forces rejected him for having flat feet. On the advice of a friend, he interviewed at Goldman Sachs and Salomon Brothers. Both offered jobs and he chose Salomon because they weren't as stuffy. Eventually, Bloomberg was promoted to the equities desk, where he made a name for himself selling large blocks of stock.

In 1973, he was made a general partner; eight years later, however, between a reorganization and a falling out with the powers that be, Bloomberg was suddenly expendable. In 1981, traders were still working with pencils and scrap paper, and he saw an opportunity to capitalize on technology. "I conceived a business built around a collection of securities data, giving people the ability to select what each individually thought the most useful parts, and then providing computer software that would let nonmathematicians do analysis on that information," he said. In *I Love Mondays*, Bloomberg begins by mulling over the fact that budding entrepreneurs expose themselves to the possibility of embarrassing failure. Ultimately, he decides he would rather be his own general rather than a loyal corporate soldier.

I Love Mondays
Michael Bloomberg

I had spent my first twenty-four years getting ready for Wall Street. I had survived fifteen more years before Salomon Brothers threw me out. At age thirty-nine, the third phase of my life was about to start. With whatever values my parents had taught me, $10 million in my pocket, and confidence based on little more than bruised ego, I started over.

A month after the 1981 meeting in Tarrytown,* I realized that Goldman, Sachs, the firm that had offered me my first job in 1966, wasn't going to call and offer me a partnership. If they had, I'd probably have accepted it just for ego reasons. But when they didn't, I had to knock on doors looking for a job, stay unemployed, or start my own company. The prospect of working for someone else wasn't exciting. Perhaps no one would hire me. Besides, I'd already done that. As to retiring, I've always been too restless. I'd go crazy just sitting around. So the last option, chasing the great American dream, seemed all that was left.

Resources weren't a problem. I didn't have to worry about feeding my family. That gave me the luxury of time. I

---

* The announcement of the reorganization took place at this meeting.

had capital to fund a new business (thank you, Salomon Brothers). I knew how to manage and always thought both names on my old business card (Bloomberg and Salomon) mattered. Thus, I could be an entrepreneur rather than an employee if I wanted to.

Did I want to risk an embarrassing and costly failure? Absolutely. Happiness for me has always been the thrill of the unknown, trying something that everyone says can't be done, feeling that gnawing pit in my stomach that says "Danger ahead." Would it be nice not to have uncertainty, to sit back and "veg out?" When the phone rings constantly, when people keep demanding attention, when I desperately need time to myself, it seems an attractive notion just to "chuck it all." But then nobody calls, nobody stops by, and soon I'm nibbling my nails and getting irritable, and I realize that's not what I want. It sounds good. In reality though, I want action, I want challenge.

Work was, is, and always will be a very big part of my life. I love it. Even today, after toiling for thirty years, I wake up looking forward to practicing my profession, creating something, competing against the best, having comradeship, receiving the psychic compensation that money can't buy. Whether you're in business, academia, politics, the arts, religion, or whatever, it's a real high to be a participant rather than a spectator. Not everyone gets the chance. But to have that opportunity and not use it? What a sin! (I was once quoted as saying, "Sunday night was my favorite because I knew when I awoke the next morning, I'd have five full days of fun at the office.")

Did I want to risk an embarrassing and costly failure? Absolutely.

Think about the percentage of your life spent working and commuting. If you're not content doing it, you're probably a pretty miserable person. Change it! Work it out with those next to you on the production line. Talk to your boss. Sit down with those you supervise. Alter what's in your own head. Do something to make it fun, interesting, challenging, exciting. You've got to be happy at your job. Sure, being able to feed the kids is the first focus. But when layoffs and promotions are announced, those with surly looks on their faces, those who always try to do less, those who never cooperate with others get included in the layoffs and miss the promotions. This big part of your life affects you, your family, society, and everything else you touch.

> Happiness for me has always been the thrill of the unknown, trying something that everyone says can't be done, feeling that gnawing pit in my stomach that says "Danger ahead."

So, while finishing my last month at Salomon, I decided to be an entrepreneur rather than an employee. After a decade and a half as a loyal corporate soldier, I'd be my own general. Great. Enough of concept, however. Specifics pay the rent. Unfortunately, until I actually stopped working at Salomon, I didn't have much time to plan my next moves— or even to worry. I worked my usual 7:00 A.M. to 7:00 P.M. twelve-hour shifts right up to the last day and seldom discussed my next career with anyone. The only time I searched for office space in which to start my new venture was on weekends. No one could say I didn't give Salomon my all, even at the end.

Still, I did think about it while running (the time I have my most creative thoughts). What would I do? Since I didn't have the resources to start a steel mill, I ruled out that possibility; in other words, I wouldn't go into industry. Having no musical abilities precluded starting a songwriting business; entertainment was out. Lack of interest in retailing excluded competing with Wal-Mart; Sam Walton's investment was safe. My impatience with government kept me away from politics; all elected officials could stop worrying. Should I start another securities trading firm and compete with my former colleagues? Been there. Done that. Maybe I could be a full-time consultant like so many forced-out executives. No. I'm not much of a bystander beyond watching my daughters Emma and Georgina ride horses. Doing rather than advising others is for me.

What did I have the resources, ability, interest, and contacts to do? The question led me back to Wall Street. It was obvious the economy was changing and services were taking a bigger share of the gross domestic product. My talents, my experience, my financial resources, the momentum provided by the American economy—everything fit. I would start a company that would help financial organizations. There were better traders and salespeople. There were better managers and computer experts. But nobody had more knowledge of the securities and investment industries *and* of how technology could help them.

All I had to do was find a value-added service not currently available. I conceived a business built around a collection of securities data, giving people the ability to select what each individually thought the most useful parts, and then providing computer software that would let nonmathematicians do analysis on that information. This kind of capability was sorely lacking in the marketplace. A few large underwriting firms had internal systems that tried to fill this need but each required a PhD to use and weren't available off the shelf to the little guy.

When it came to knowing the relative value of one security versus another, most of Wall Street in 1981 had pretty much remained where it was when I began as a clerk back in the mid-1960s: a bunch of guys using No. 2 pencils, chronicling the seat-of-the-pants guesses of too many bored traders. Something that could show instantly whether government bonds were appreciating at a faster rate than corporate bonds would make smart investors out of mediocre ones, and would create an enormous competitive advantage over anyone lacking these capabilities. At a time when the U.S. budget deficit (financed by billions of dollars of new Treasury bonds and notes) was poised to explode, such a device would appeal to everyone working in finance, securities, and investments—combined, a very big potential market for my proposed product.

If you're going to succeed, you need a vision, one that's affordable, practical, and fills a customer need. Then, go for it. Don't worry too much about the details.

At great expense, each of the largest securities companies collected data independently. Worse (for them but not for me), they were practically relying on abacuses and slide rules, or the modern equivalents, such as small handheld calculators, to manipulate that information. I could provide a far more sophisticated system at a fraction of the price. Sharing expenses over many users would give me a distinct cost advantage. And if most firms used my data and analysis, I would be creating an industrywide standard, something which, for competitive reasons, the insiders themselves could never accomplish. Equally important, the advantage I had of not being a broker/dealer, of being beholden to no one, would give my product an independence others couldn't possibly claim. And best of all, nobody was currently doing it.

If you're going to succeed, you need a vision, one that's affordable, practical, and fills a customer need. Then, go for it. Don't worry too much about the details. Don't second-guess your creativity. Avoid overanalyzing the new project's potential. Most importantly, don't strategize about the long term too much.

Consider banks and venture capitalists your worst enemies. They create doubt in entrepreneurs' minds with their
insistence on detailed game plans before they lend. They
want five-year projections in a world that makes six-month
forward planning difficult, even for stable and mature businesses, and they insist on "revenue budgeting" when no one
knows what the new product will look like or who'll buy
how much. And worst of all, they think an originator will be
helped by their oh-so-insightful views on how he or she
should run the new business. Often, they kill off what's different, special, and full of potential.

A while ago, one venture capitalist who's on the boards
of two successful companies came to see us. This guy was
one of those self-entitled men who had been born on third
base and thought he'd hit a triple. After telling us that everything we were doing was wrong, that we were too unstructured to survive and were stupid because we were unable to
predict future growth with clairvoyant specificity, he left to
advise his partners not to buy from Bloomberg. The reason?
We didn't show much interest in his views on how to run our
company. He sure was right on that account.

Consider banks and venture capitalists your
worst enemies. . . . Often, they kill off what's
different, special, and full of potential.

I once saw the classic cart-before-the-horse planning error
during a presentation by a would-be competitor. He showed
slides of his new company's shipping department. There were
conveyor belts, packaging machines, truck-loading equipment, and a group of white-coated technicians ready to send
out thousands of units each week. The only minor problem?
They hadn't yet built the first unit. And they never did.

At Bloomberg, we've always built the product first. We
think about accounting and shipping much later in the

process, when those functions become important, at the point where we'd better stop and refocus or get into trouble. Selling is the only process we run simultaneously with development from the start. That gives us feedback as we build — and makes the customers part of the evolution process (they come to believe it's their product). This strategy may not be without risks, but I've always thought it ridiculous to make the wedding arrangements before agreeing to the marriage.

The classic consultant's model for success dictates building in controls at the beginning, but that kind of premature preparation is counterproductive; in fact, it's usually diverting enough to preclude producing anything at all. You don't know exactly what you're going to deliver. You can't predict in what order things will be done. You have no real idea who will purchase it. Why bother gazing into the crystal ball? If you're flexible, you'll do it when it makes sense, not before.

> Selling is the only process we run simultaneously with development from the start. That gives us feedback as we build—and makes the customers part of the evolution process.

In computer terms, doing it whenever needed, on the fly, is working from a "heap," not a "stack" or a "queue." Working from stacks and queues is the rigid, bureaucratized method of operating; it makes you take out things in a pre-described order (i.e., last in, first out for a stack; first in, first out for a queue). But if you work from a heap, where input and output are independent, you can use your head, selecting what you need, when you need it, based on outside criteria that are always changing (e.g., what's needed *now*, such as responding immediately to a customer complaint or getting a gift for your spouse's birthday when that day arrives and you've totally forgotten). Look at your desk. Is everything in order? Or is it in a big pile like mine? Take your choice.

Don't think, however, that planning and analysis have no place in achieving success. Quite the contrary. Use them, just don't have them use you. Plan things out and work through real-life scenarios, selecting from the opportunities currently available. Just don't waste effort worrying about an infinite number of down-the-road possibilities, most of which will never materialize.

Think logically and dispassionately about what you'd like to do. Work out all steps of the process—the entire what, when, where, why, and how. Then, sit down after you are absolutely positive you know it cold, and write it out. There's an old saying, "If you can't write it, you don't know it." Try it. The first paragraph invariably stops you short. "Now why did we want this particular thing?" you'll find yourself asking. "Where did we think the resources would come from?" "And what makes us think others—the suppliers, the customers, the potential rivals—are going to cooperate?" On and on, you'll find yourself asking the most basic questions you hadn't focused on before taking pen to paper.

Don't think . . . that planning and analysis have no place in achieving success. Quite the contrary. Use them, just don't have them use you.

As you discover you don't know it all, force yourself to address the things you forgot, ignored, underestimated, or glossed over. Write them out for a doubting stranger who doesn't come with unquestioned confidence in the project's utility—and who, unlike your spouse, parent, sibling, or child, doesn't have a vested interest in keeping you happy. Make sure your written description follows, from beginning to end, in a logical, complete, doable path.

Then tear up the paper.

That's right, rip it up. You've done the analysis. You've found enough holes in the plan to drive your hoped-for Bentley automobile through repeatedly. You've planned for myriad what-if scenarios. You've presented your ideas to others. You've even mapped out the first few steps.

But the real world throws curveballs and sliders every day, as well as the fastballs you practice against. You'll inevitably face problems different from the ones you antici- pated. Sometimes you'll have to "zig" when the blueprint says "zag." You don't want a detailed, inflexible plan getting in the way when you have to respond instantly. By now, you either know what you can know—or you don't and never will. As to the rest, take it as it comes.

1997

The Firestone tire remains a prominent brand; the company's founder, however, took a while to find his calling. Harvey Firestone wandered through a series of jobs, including that of a traveling medicine extract salesman, before he founded his Akron, Ohio–based tire and rubber company in 1900. Goodyear and Goodrich were already well established in town and did not welcome the newcomer. The unwanted Firestone lost money the first few years and almost folded. Fortunately, Firestone's tire design excelled in an area that was a big issue of the day—keeping the rubber tire fastened to the rim. His big break finally came in 1906 when Henry Ford ordered 2,000 sets of tires, and the next year Firestone sold a total of 105,000 tires.

The two men's relationship soon developed beyond rubber, and beginning in 1916, they went on a series of annual camping trips with Thomas Edison and John Burroughs, the naturalist. While surrounded by these men of vision, Firestone realized that the definition of vision does not necessarily include some mystical quality. Rather, he reflected, vision "is not a dreaming forward. It is a thinking through with the values ever in mind." By "thinking through," Firestone meant developing a practical understanding of what the future would require. By "the values," he meant the best business principles necessary to meet future requirements. His own vision included the building of rubber plantations in Liberia and Singapore, as he anticipated the critical importance of a vertically integrated and globally oriented business.

Like most successful entrepreneurs, Firestone was a man of action. He said, "Ambition is something more than *looking* at the point you want to reach. Ambition is taking off your coat and pulling and dragging your boat up the stream." In *Starting the Company,* he explains how he forged his career and actually stalked the man he needed to finance his business. He also warns would-be entrepreneurs that the best-laid plans can go awry: "The business of any live company has to be revised, but with a new company these revisions have to be drastic."

Starting the Company
Harvey S. Firestone

Having some money in hand, I wanted to go into business for myself. If a man has no capital, it is usually a waste of time for him to start in business on his own, unless he can borrow capital for a long term at low interest. But the chances of success on borrowed capital are slight. It is not possible in beginning a new enterprise to see ahead far enough to discover how much capital really will be needed.

It is unusual, and indeed abnormal, for a concern to make money during the first several years of its existence. The initial product and the initial organization are never right. The first product, no matter how thoroughly it has been thought out, has to be seasoned in the market. An experienced company with ample resources can make extensive laboratory tests, and also tests in use, for a long period before bringing out a product, and can reduce many of the elements of luck and risk. But it cannot know in advance either how the public will receive that product or how it will stand up in actual service. The new company will think that it has taken every precaution. It will think that it has made every sort of an investigation, but really the most searching trials that a new company can make are of small moment, first, because the promoters can never get themselves into the cold, detached frame of mind in which the public approaches anything new, and, second, because the knowledge of what really is a test will be lacking.

The business of any live company has to be constantly revised, but with a new company these revisions have to be drastic. In the exceptional case where the product itself does not have to be revamped, its method of manufacture will have to be changed, and if neither the product nor its manufacture has to be changed, then, most certainly, the human organization—be it three men or a thousand—will prove inadequate.

It is unusual, and indeed abnormal, for a concern to make money during the first several years of its existence. The initial product and the initial organization are never right.

It is difficult enough to pick men in a seasoned business, but then one has at least the advantage of knowing something about the required duties. In starting a new business, although a paper organization may be put down in a small way, the eventual organization will turn out to be something very different. It is always cut and try in business, but in the beginning this cutting and trying have to go on so rapidly that there is not much chance really to make money. It may be possible in exceptional cases to pay the interest on borrowed capital, but unless one strikes a bonanza, any undertaking quickly to pay back borrowed capital is bound to result in failure. It is more than unsafe—it is just a waste of time—to start into business with money that has not been embarked for better or for worse—that is, money which demands no return other than the profits the business can afford—which means money invested in stock and in common stock rather than preferred.

Also, it is exceedingly unwise to hold out any promises of quick returns—although it is human nature to do so. For if a new business does succeed, it will have to be uncommonly careful in the distribution of profits. If you are going ahead, you will need every cent you can lay your hands on to finance operations, and the more of these operations you can finance with your own money, the better off you are. A business which starts off quickly, makes money at once, and seems to be in every respect a gold mine, often does not last long. It is just selling peanuts to the crowd in town for the circus—a once-around affair.

I thought I had money enough to go into business. I had $45,000, and I was strongly advised that it was too much money to hazard in business—that it was a fortune to retire on! At that time it was the desire of every ambitious young man to have his own business. The great corporation had not yet gotten under way, with the exception of the Standard Oil Company, which was thought of more as a mysterious phenomenon than as a type for future business. Today it hardly pays a young man to go into business for himself, unless he has a new idea which he cannot sell to anyone. The rewards of big business today are greater than the individual can hope to achieve alone. Ability is rewarded more highly than it used to be—not because men are more generous than formerly, but because a big concern has to have big management, and big management costs money.

A business which starts off quickly, makes money at once, and seems to be in every respect a gold mine, often does not last long.

In my early days, the head of the concern usually owned most of it and he considered his employees more as servants than as colleagues. Good management is no less personal than ever it was, but in a business of any size a certain amount of judgment and executive duty simply must be delegated, and unless the delegates have pay commensurate with their abilities and responsibilities, they are bound to become time-servers, and the business will go to ruin. . . .

Before I really had a chance to make up my mind about the future, the Kelly-Springfield Tire Company offered me the position of manager in Chicago, and I took it. The sales policy of the company did not prove to my liking. The practice was to charge tires at the cost of material and labour and on top of that a royalty. This seemed to me essentially unsound; the seller ought to make an inclusive price and have done with it. In about eight months I took a vacation, and in Cleveland made up my mind to get out and sent in my resignation. Then I set about the organization of a tire company of my own. I had no difficulty in raising the money and the company would have gone through, but the bankers, who were helping in the promotion, had on their hands a piece of property which they were extremely anxious to get rid of. They insisted that we take it as a factory—in spite of the fact that it was in no way suited for tire making. If the organizers of a corporation cannot agree at the beginning, there is small chance that they will afterward, so I simply dropped the negotiations.

A company in Akron manufacturing twist drills and drop forgings also had a tire department but not a satisfactory tire, so they took license on a tire I had developed and patented and asked me to be its manager. I accepted, but once more the policy did not suit me: this time, instead of resigning, I took an option to buy the department. Akron was the home of the rubber-tire industry. It was a good town for any man interested in tire making, for the big Goodrich, Goodyear, and Diamond factories were there, and also plenty of workmen who knew tires. The tire trade was largely in solid tires and in the single-tube pneumatics used on bicycles. Pneumatic tires were not popular for carriages; they gave easier riding, it is true, but under the extra weight of a carriage their single tubes punctured easily and they were a nuisance. The racing sulky was about the only horse-drawn vehicle that used them.

The prime difficulty in the whole tire trade was fastening the tires to the rims. The clincher principle was popular for a time. In this the rubber was held in a steel channel by converging flanges, but it was not entirely satisfactory. Following the clincher came the circumferential retaining wire idea for holding the tire to the rim. The idea had several variations; the scheme was to imbed wires in the rubber near the base of the tire and clamp to these wires, but the plan was practical only for small sizes and there was a great deal of trouble with the wires cutting through the rubber and permitting the body of the tire to loosen and come off the rim. Each company had its own particular style of fastening, but none was entirely satisfactory.

James A. Sweinhart of Akron had invented a tire which he claimed overcame most of the difficulties of fastening the tire to the rim. His idea was not new to me; I had heard of it in Chicago—although I had never seen a set of his tires. He placed wires crosswise in the base of the tire with the ends projecting through on both sides between the flanges; then he sprung endless retaining wires over the edges of the flanges, catching and binding the ends of the cross wires. This held the tire securely in place. It was much the best device on the market, and it made possible the safe fastening of large tires, whereas all the other devices failed completely in the larger sizes. Sweinhart had several men interested with him. Among them were Dr. L. E. Sisler, the county auditor, M. D. Buckman, one of his deputies, and James Christy, Jr., who was a builder. None of these men knew anything about practical tire making, and they were in no position financially or otherwise to go into the tire business. Sweinhart himself had been a schoolteacher but was then a carpenter building and selling houses on speculation. His real estate transactions brought him in contact with Doctor Sisler, whom he finally persuaded to become interested in organizing a company.

Sweinhart had already been around to most of the rubber people and had been turned down. He was told that his device was not practical — that the jolting would loosen the cross wires and the turning out of the street-car tracks would pull off the tires. Doctor Sisler tried the objections out before he agreed to go in with Sweinhart. He had a tired wheel put under a trip-hammer and pounded for an hour or two, then he bought an old phaëton, had Sweinhart equip it with tires, and had a man driving it around town for a week with explicit directions to turn suddenly out of the street-car tracks whenever he had the chance. The tires stood the tests.

Doctor Sisler did not know me, but he knew a pair of sorrels that I drove and he knew that I was a newcomer in town and interested in tire making. A man used to be judged by the horses he drove, and Doctor Sisler thought mine were a bit better than his — which qualified me as the man to push the patent. He called me on the telephone, introduced himself, and asked me if I should be interested in Sweinhart's tire. I told him I should be interested.

"If that's so, I think we had better get together," he went on.

"All right, make it this evening," I answered.

That evening — it was the twenty-sixth of July, 1900 — I met with Doctor Sisler, Christy, Buckman, and Sweinhart at Christy's house. Sweinhart's patent was about a year old, and its validity had already been tested in a suit by the India Rubber Company for infringement. We had no trouble at all in coming to terms, and signed an agreement that day.

By this agreement we were to organize a company with a capital of $50,000. I put in $10,000 in cash and my option on the tire business of the company for which I received an additional $15,000 worth of stock. The other group put in $10,000 in cash and the Sweinhart patent, and received an additional $15,000 in stock, which gave us a working capital of $20,000. I was to be manager of the company at a salary of $3,000 a year with a bonus of $600 if the company earned 20 per cent or more on its issued capital stock during the first year. Our hopes were larger than our experience; I never got my bonus.

On the third of August, 1900, a charter was issued to us in West Virginia, creating the Firestone Tire & Rubber Company, and we organized according to the terms of the agreement, with James Christy, Jr., as president, J. A. Sweinhart as vice-president, L. E. Sisler, secretary, and H. S. Firestone, treasurer and general manager. The directors were Firestone, Christy, Sweinhart, Miller (my lawyer), and A. P. Cleveland, our first salesman. I did not want to be president, and in fact did not become president until three years later. I have never cared much about titles—it did not bother me who had the title so long as I ran the company.

> I have never cared much about titles—it did not bother me who had the title so long as I ran the company.

I cannot say that the new tire company was particularly welcome in Akron. The big rubber companies thought that there were already enough people making tires, but, at the same time, we were so small that they did not bother their heads much about us—and we did not manufacture. For two years we practically did a jobbing business, having our tires made in Akron, and for a new company we were very successful. In the first year we sold $110,000 worth of tires and in the second year we sold $150,000 worth. This was too much business for a company with only $20,000 in cash, and we were soon ahead of our capital, and to my duties as general manager, general salesman, and general everything I had to add that of stock salesman. We increased our capitalization first to $150,000 and later to $200,000 because it became evident that before long we should either have to do our own manufacturing or go out of business.

It was at this time that S. G. Carkhuff, our present secretary, came with us as a bookkeeper. I hired him myself, persuading him to take a lower wage than he had been receiving from the Washburn-Crosby Company. But as yet we scarcely had an organization. We did not need any. Our only essential equipment was a simple machine for springing the wire bands over the projecting lugs of the tires. We could not afford to carry stocks of any size. We sold to carriage makers and carriage dealers. They sent us their wheels, we fitted them with steel channels to hold the tires, had the tires made, sprung the retaining wires into place, and returned the wheels. There was nothing at all complicated about the business or its finance, excepting that we did not have money enough to swing our volume of operations—and not having enough money is always complicated!

Our margin of profit was very narrow at the best, and at the worst we lost money. For three years we lost money on operations as a whole, but this did not bother me as to the eventual success of the enterprise, because I knew how and why we lost our money. Losing money is not pleasant, but every business must at times lose money. Losing money is really serious if you do not know why you are losing, or if you do know why and cannot help yourself. It was very plain to me why we were losing money. Only a miracle could have taken us out of red.

> Our price was regulated by the merit of our patent—and while it had merit in plenty, it could not command a luxury price. We wanted to sell tires, not jewels.

We had the best tire-fastening device on the market; our tires stayed on better than any of the others. But the very tire manufacturers who were our competitors in the open market were also the manufacturers of our tires. They made ample profits in selling to us, but we in turn could not ask much of a profit from our customers else we should have had our prices far too high. We could not offer a better tire than any one else — that would have been absurd on the face of things, for we were not making our tires — we were buying them from companies which also sold tires. Therefore our price was regulated by the merit of our patent — and while it had merit in plenty, it could not command a luxury price. We wanted to sell tires, not jewels.

That is why it became imperative for us to do our own manufacturing. Against the setting up of a plant stood the financial difficulty. I sold the 6 per cent mortgage of $20,000 which I had designed as a $1,200 annuity for life. My whole $45,000 was soon in the stock in the company, and I was on the hunt day and night for men to buy our stock. It was no easy matter to sell stock in a company that had no assets excepting a patent on which it was losing money. For years I never saw a man with money without turning over in my mind how I could transfer some of his money into our stock. I did some bank borrowing in Akron, Massillon, and some of the smaller towns such as Canal Dover, where either Doctor Sisler or I was acquainted, but it was not bank credit but stock subscriptions that we then needed — money that did not have to be paid back. It would have been sheer suicide to go into a capital extension like a new factory on short-time bank credit.

Losing money is really serious if you do not know why you are losing, or if you do know why and cannot help yourself.

And I did sell stock! The one man in particular to whom I wanted to sell I could not reach, and that was Will Christy. He was the biggest man in Akron and probably the most influential man in Ohio. He was then president of the Central Savings & Trust Company of Akron, and had become very wealthy in the construction of electric street railways. He was among the builders of the first electric railway, and he built the first interurban road in the country—that between Akron and Cleveland. He was just the man to give us financial tone and respectability, and following my old sales policy of going out after the big fellows, I laid my plans to sell Will Christy.

The trouble was I could not get to him. He had a big office and secretaries and all the usual safeguards of a busy man, and I could not get past those guards. The fact that he was a brother of James Christy, who was already in the company, did not help at all. Of course, I might have tried him at his house in the evening, but that would have been poor policy. A man of affairs does not want to be bothered in the evening. A great many salesmen make the mistake of thinking that pestering a man is the same as selling him, and they get their prospects into such a state of exasperation that they would not buy a gold dollar from them at 50 per cent off.

A good salesman will never intrude. . . . No man likes to be panhandled, and some selling comes close to panhandling.

Just getting to a man is not enough—it is when and how you get to him. There are more wrong times to sell a man than there are right times, and if I ever should write a book on salesmanship I should give about one third of the book to the topic "Common Sense." I have been buttonholed thousands of times by salesmen who, if they had just exercised a grain of common sense, would have known that, while the moment might be a very good one in which to make my acquaintance, it was no time at all to persuade me to buy anything. A good salesman will never intrude. In the first place, he will know that intruders do not make sales, and in the second place he will have brains enough to arrange for the right kind of a meeting with his prospect—no man likes to be panhandled, and some selling comes close to panhandling.

I kept tab on Will Christy's plans, and I learned that he was going to California with his wife for a vacation of several months. I found that he was going to stop over at the Auditorium Hotel in Chicago on his way out, and I took a train ahead of his to Chicago, registered at the hotel, made certain that Mr. and Mrs. Christy had registered later in the evening, and made equally certain that they did not see me that evening, for I already knew Mr. Christy slightly. The next morning I was up very early and kept out of sight until I saw Mr. and Mrs. Christy going in for breakfast. Quite by accident, of course, I met them at the door of the dining room.

A great many salesmen make the mistake of thinking that pestering a man is the same as selling him.

We had breakfast together. He inquired about our business. One thing led naturally to another, and before breakfast was over he had bought $10,000 worth of stock. Later, Mr. Christy bought around $50,000 worth of our stock, became our president, and was of immense help to us at a time when we needed all the help we could get.

And he sold himself! All I did was to fall in with him at the right time.

1926

ANDY KESSLER

As cofounder of Velocity Capital Management LLC, an investment firm that specializes in technology and communication companies, and as a regular contributor to *Forbes* magazine, Andy Kessler offers a unique insight into what it takes to start a business in the technology sector. If anyone can decipher and point to the opportunities in the wild and wooly world of technology, he can; his education is steeped in it. Kessler graduated from Cornell University in 1980 with a degree in electrical engineering, and then earned a masters in electrical engineering at the University of Illinois the following year. His first job out of school was with the venerable Bell Labs, where he was a chip designer and programmer.

Kessler's career took a turn when he left Bell Labs to take a job with the Wall Street firm Paine Webber. Next, he worked for Morgan Stanley for five years as a technology strategist and equity analyst, before running a venture fund at Unterberg Harris. Eventually, he struck out on his own, cofounding Velocity Capital, where he specializes in investing in what he calls *out-on-the-edge* technology and communication companies—no easy task. "Technology investing is hard, as hard as Chinese arithmetic," he once wrote. "It is not for the weak at heart. Like those magnificent men in their flying machines, tech stocks go up-up-up, and they go down-down-down."

Entering the rapidly changing technology sector as an entrepreneur can be just as difficult. From his varied experience as engineer, stock analyst, and portfolio manager, Kessler has encountered more than one technology start-up and knows what it takes to succeed. In *Go Ahead—Jump!*, Kessler points to the many opportunities "to build on the shoulders of giants," such as Intel or IBM, meaning today's computer and information craze offers all sorts of niches to get into, from manufacturing to selling components for hardware and software. He gives a rousing charge for anyone interested in starting a business. To those who hesitate, he says ". . . quit whining and do it. The risk is almost all to your ego: the damaging psychological effects of failure. But so what?"

Go Ahead — Jump!
Andy Kessler

Is this a good description of you? You are intrigued by the possibilities of the cheap microprocessors and plentiful bandwidth you've read about in *Forbes ASAP,* bored with your narrow responsibilities, tired of being a company lackey, annoyed that others are making more off of your brilliance than you, tired of begging for a merit raise every year, blah, blah, blah. If so, it's time to poke your head out of your office and look around. There is a harmonic convergence taking place among computers, communications, finance and market opportunity. Certainly you must hear, smell, see, taste, if not touch, all the possibilities in front of you. Well, get that lard out of your chair, storm into the corner office, fire yourself — and start your own enterprise.

There has never been a better time to be an entrepreneur. An enormous infrastructure exists to build or deliver microprocessors, PCs, software, communications equipment and high-bandwidth communications. Opportunities abound to build on the shoulders of giants. Riding the computer wave, you can surely restructure your expertise, whether it be selling, analyzing, marketing, delivering, teaching, managing or, yes, even opinionating (can't leave myself out), to profit your own enterprise.

Heavy machinery, distribution, delivery, communications, clerical help—all terribly expensive not many years ago—are practically free today. A PC with integrated voice mail, scanner, fax and printer replaces even the best secretary; long-distance charges are dropping daily; the nearest superstore can deliver office supplies to you by the hour; you can either rent distribution or, if you are selling bits, get it free; and heavy machinery is so plentiful for information companies (CD manufacturing, semiconductor fabrication facilities, color offset printing) that you need pay for only what you use. It has never been cheaper to be an entrepreneur.

It's time to poke your head out of your office and look around . . . get that lard out of your chair, storm into the corner office, fire yourself—and start your own enterprise.

Now comes the timely part. Today's stock market is the great arbiter, the judge of which businesses should have access to capital and which should be cut off. Clearly the spigot is on for investing capital in technology, as is evident by the number and valuation of the initial public offerings for high-tech companies in 1995. The market has never put a bigger spotlight on entrepreneurs. This truth has been grasped by those who are financing private ventures. Although they're not as generous in valuing companies as the public stock market, on a risk-adjusted basis there is cheap capital chasing the increasing deal flow in private financing. What does that mean? Simply put, in technology, there has never been a better time to be an entrepreneur.

I'm talking about opportunity. Success you must provide. But in setting up your enterprise, no matter what it is, you must find ways to leverage the Internet, the 100 million installed base of interconnected PCs, and to use high-resolution graphics, audio and eventually video across networks. The possibilities are endless, and as an entrepreneur, you have absolutely no baggage, no revenue cannibalization issues, no touchy customers and no strategic relationships to endanger—not yet anyway. Want to offer electronic yellow pages? What do you care if that cuts into printed yellow page ad revenues? Want to deliver real sales information to candy vendors? Why should you care what distributors think about your stealing their added value? Want to sell insurance directly to consumers? Who cares about established insurance agents and their three-martini breakfasts? You are the predator; existing businesses are the fresh meat.

Now, if you are more risk-averse, you don't have to hang out your own shingle and take all the financial, personal and ego risk. You can, of course, join a small, rapidly growing company, already set up and financed by others, that fits your view of where the world is going and that allows you to pursue the business opportunity you envision. But for goodness sake, insist on equity. Stock options and lots of them (in a private company) are the next best thing to doing it yourself.

In either case, quit whining and do it. The risk is almost all to your ego: the damaging psychological effects of failure. But so what? If you don't do this, you may end up in therapy anyway, from boredom or from the nagging coulda, woulda, shoulda nightmares.

On the flip side, the financial risks are mainly opportunity costs, the income you would have earned in your current dull job. You say you're worried about blowing your life savings? If you're any good, you can always get more money by going back to a big company. But remember: You may not always have this opportunity to fire yourself and start up as an entrepreneur.

1996

KIM POLESE
1961–

Kim Polese, cofounder of Marimba, an Internet software maker, was one of *Time* magazine's "Top 25 Most Influential People in America" in 1997 for her contribution to the software industry. From age 9, Polese says, she knew she wanted to be an entrepreneur. "I just didn't know if it was going to be ice cream or software," she said. After earning a B.S. in biophysics from the University of California at Berkeley, she worked as an applications engineer at IntelliCorp. Then she joined Sun Microsystems, where she spent more than seven years; part of that time dedicated to developing Java.

In 1995, Sun released Java, a very flexible language that bypasses a computer's operating system and speaks directly to the microchips. It was an immediate hit. Polese explained, "It jazzed up Web pages and showed what the next step on the Web could be, with live stock tickers and little animations." Wanting to take the software's capabilities to new heights, she and three other key members of the Java team left to found Marimba in 1996. "I decided that I had to be my own mentor, and start talking to smart people, and gather information based on my own thought process," she reflected. "That's when things started turning around for me."

They each chipped in $15,000, rather than chain themselves to a venture capitalist. It paid off, because once they did need financing, they were able to limit the VC firm to only a 17 percent stake, even though it coughed up $4 million. "We wanted to have total independence in the first months to define the product without investors pressuring us," she said. Their Internet software is designed to help connect companies and consumers looking for each other in the great expanse of cyberspace. "We want to ease the pain for people cruising the Internet and for companies doing business there," she said. In *A Tech Dream Comes True,* she explains the need to contain your excitement when starting a new company, and to take a methodical approach, especially when it does come time to seek venture capital.

A Tech Dream Comes True
Kim Polese

Ireally love this job. It is more than I could have hoped for, in terms of its pure fun quotient and enjoyment. I'm the kind of person who likes juggling a lot of different things at one time and dealing with the sort of dynamic environment that a startup situation brings.

I always wanted to be in a small company, always wanted to be an entrepreneur. That was like a dream I'd had since I was a kid. I wanted to run a business. I didn't know what kind of business it would be, but I always thought the idea and the opportunity would materialize.

I grew up in Berkeley, and I actually became involved in science and technology pretty early on. I took a lot of science theory and I went up to the Lawrence Hall of Science, which is a science teaching institute in the Bay Area, and taught programming when I was a freshman in college. I love science and technology, and it was natural to imagine that at some point I would be involved in a technology startup.

Being in the Bay Area helped because there's an expectation that opportunities here are sort of endless, the-sky-is-the-limit kind of thing. You can basically build something from nothing, create a company with some great ideas and some talent and management.

By the end of my time at Sun, we had established a platform for Java. I was feeling gratified that it had gone so well, but I felt it was time to move on. The idea of starting a new company started hatching in my head, and then I happened to have some conversations with a couple of engineers on the Java development team. We converged, four of us meeting between Christmas and New Year's of '95 every day for eight hours, and discussed the company at a café in Menlo Park called Cafe Barroné.

We were very, very excited. We were trying to contain our excitement because we wanted to be very practical and methodical, to make sure that we could prove to ourselves that there was a business and a market opportunity and that we could get financing. This was not, "Let's just go start a company, and we'll figure out what it is later." This was, "Let's really sketch out here what the world needs. What products are missing. What the growth potential of the market is. How we would go about getting the financing."

By the end of January 1996, we left Sun to set up Marimba. Our first office was in the storage room of a defunct stationery store in Palo Alto, which we paid about $2,000 a month for.

Initially, we decided not to accept any kind of financial interest that wasn't our own. Sure, we needed money. But we really wanted to be able to focus. We all felt that if you instantly have $5 million in the bank, you can get pretty lazy. It's de-focusing. None of us are rich, and so we conserved. We each kicked in $15,000 of our own money to fund the rent, software, and hardware and stuff.

But one of the reasons I wanted to start the company was to be exposed to the investment community, the venture capital world. To understand how financing worked and how deals get done, how business plans get executed, and how companies get hatched. I wanted to learn about every aspect of starting a company, especially venture capital, which I found to be fascinating but mystifying. After about five months, we started talking with venture capitalists.

We had a nice, polished, powerful presentation—all the

stuff that you normally would have to pitch to a venture firm. But the difference was that most of the venture capitalists were pitching us. They were impressed with us and would go through their presentations without realizing that we hadn't talked to them about the product. None of them did. They didn't know what we were up to.

Initially, we decided not to accept any kind of financial interest that wasn't our own. Sure, we needed money. But we really wanted to be able to focus. We all felt that if you instantly have $5 million in the bank, you can get pretty lazy.

We chose Kleiner Perkins as our venture capital firm because we were impressed with the breadth of strategic relationships and partnerships Kleiner had in the industry. It was important because we were building a product that really required having strategic relationships with big companies. You know, Marimba is not just a little disk backup system or something. This is about Internet services management—managing the complex infrastructure required for companies who want to deliver powerful, compelling services across the Net. We wanted to build strong industry partnerships. And I wanted a venture capital firm that could help us make those connections.

Our experience with Kleiner Perkins has been terrific. As first-time entrepreneurs, we couldn't have wished for better backing.

1997

NORM BRODSKY

Having been featured on CNN and CNBC, as well as having writen for *Inc.* magazine for years, Norm Brodsky is a respected voice for entrepreneurs. Since the early 1970s, Brodsky has funded start-ups and has also run a number of his own companies. A lawyer by training, he dove into the world of entrepreneurship when he started Perfect Courier, a message service and trucking company. Another venture, CitiStorage, which stores and retrieves archives, is considered a leader in its field. Brodsky contributes his success to building the business from the ground up as opposed to buying an existing concern. "For one thing, it's harder to learn a business if you haven't been with it from the start," he said. "You miss out on all the trial-and-error education that happens in the early stages." Also, he warns that you can never be sure as to what exactly you're buying.

As for his role as a venture capitalist, he said, "Usually I like to be the only investor. That way I can keep control until I get my capital back." When looking over an entrepreneur's business plan, some of the problems he often sees include: not telling investors how much of a return they should expect and how they will eventually cash out; too much money going to fixed assets such as office furniture; too much money going to officers to repay money they originally put into the business. The plans should be customized for the potential investor, too. "You need to find out as much as you can about potential investors—what they want, how they evaluate a deal—before you ever ask them for money," Brodsky said.

On the other hand, Brodsky advises funding your own start-up, if possible, without others' money. "My advice to you is if you have enough dollars to start the company, do it and raise dollars after you have a track record," he says. Brodsky warns investors that "your business plan must also include your life plan." Toward that end, he includes his wife in his work; they both oversee the companies from their Brooklyn office. In *The Three Criteria for a Successful New Business,* Brodsky offers what would appear to be contrary advice, such as, "I never want to be first in a market, and I always like to have a lot of competitors."

The Three Criteria for a Successful New Business
Norm Brodsky

So you have an idea for a revolutionary product in a business that doesn't even exist yet? Unless you're Thomas Edison, you'd better pass.

People get so much bad advice about going into business that I sometimes wonder how anyone survives. You often hear, for example, that to be successful you need a unique product or service, something nobody else has. Or that you should choose a business with as little competition as possible, that you're better off having a market to yourself.

My advice is exactly the opposite. I never want to be first in a market, and I always like to have a lot of competitors. Yes, I want to be different from them, but the more people who are making money in an industry, the better I feel about going into it. There are actually three simple criteria I use in evaluating every new business I start. I suspect they'd work for about 80% of the people who are going into business for the first time.

Number one, I want a concept that's been around for 100 years or more. OK, maybe less than 100 years. The important thing is that it's an established concept, one that everybody understands. It's not something new and revolutionary. Why? Because there is nothing more expensive than educating a market.

I found that out the hard way when I took my delivery business to Atlanta in the early 1980s. At the time, companies there handled deliveries by putting a secretary in a cab and sending her off with a package. The secretaries didn't want our service — they liked having time out of the office — and the companies didn't know they needed it. We had to do mailers, run ads, develop a whole public-relations campaign. And it was a delivery service we were educating people about, not some radical new technology. I'm telling you, it was very, very expensive, and we took a beating. Me, I'd rather be in the biggest, most competitive market in the world and go head-to-head with a hundred other companies.

Of course, if you're going to compete, you have to be able to differentiate yourself with customers. Which brings me to the second criterion: I want an industry that is antiquated. I don't necessarily mean "old-fashioned." I'm talking about a business in which most companies are out of step with the customer. Maybe the customer's needs have changed and the suppliers haven't paid attention. Maybe they're not up-to-date on the latest technology. In any case, there has been a change, and the industry hasn't followed it.

My storage company, CitiStorage, is a good example here. When I first looked into the business, about six years ago, I noticed that, except for a couple of big players, records-storage companies were asleep. They had ancient warehouses designed to store dead files for customers. Meanwhile, the industry had completely changed. Real estate had become so expensive in major cities that customers were looking to store active files — that is, files they still had to get at from time to time. The records-storage business was turning into the archive-retrieval business, and almost nobody seemed to notice. The two big exceptions were Iron Mountain and Pierce Leahy, which recognized the change and built huge, modern archive-retrieval facilities out in the countryside. They became the driving force of the industry.

I sensed an opportunity here, but there was something I didn't understand. How could the other guys stay asleep? Why were they still in business? Why hadn't they lost their customer base? The answer, I discovered, was that some of the biggest customers wouldn't move their files. Why not? Because they didn't want their records to be so far out of town. What if they needed a particular file in an hour?

That gave me my third criterion for a successful new business: a niche. I would build a huge, modern facility in the city. I'd distinguish myself from the old records-storage companies by designing the facility specifically for archive retrieval, using the latest technology. I'd distinguish myself from the giants by my location. The customers would be close to their records.

In fact, having a niche is critical to every start-up, but not for the reason most people think. It has to do with those high gross margins you must have to make sure your start-up capital lasts long enough for your business to achieve viability. If you're the new kid in town, you can't compete on price, because you'll go out of business. On the other hand, you do have to get customers. That means offering them more value at the going rate.

But how do you offer more value without increasing your direct costs, cutting your gross margins, and running through your start-up capital? The answer usually lies in the niche you've selected. I realized, for example, that the latest archive-retrieval technology allowed me to cut my direct costs by building a facility with much higher ceilings than my competitors have. I now get 125,000 boxes in 10,000 square feet, whereas those guys are getting 40,000 or 50,000 boxes in the same space.

So those are my three criteria for starting a successful business: a 100-year-old concept, an antiquated industry, and a niche. I know some people are thinking, "If everybody followed those criteria, we still wouldn't have the wheel." Well, they're right. I don't mean to discourage the visionary geniuses out there. I'm all for advances in technology and the creation of new industries. If you're another Thomas Edison, Fred Smith, or Bill Gates, forget my criteria. Go right ahead. Change the world. . . .

1996

DORIS DRUCKER

Every student of business knows Doris Drucker's husband, Peter, the management guru and author of many notable books; however, few know that at the age of 80, Doris Drucker embarked on an entrepreneurial adventure of her own. She grew up in Cologne, Germany, which was then a village where sightings of cars and zeppelins was exciting stuff. When World War I broke out, her father entered the army, and the rest of the family went to live with her mother's parents in Mainz. "Sometimes the sounds and sights of war came closer; for us children they were nonthreatening and even interesting diversions," she wrote. Of course, when the allies' blockade of Germany cut off food and other supplies, life became more serious.

Although many girls quit school after eighth grade to begin working, Drucker's mother kept her enrolled at a convent school. She went on to study at universities in London and Paris, before returning to Frankfurt to work on her doctoral thesis in international law. While there she met Peter Drucker, who was conducting a seminar. They married in 1937 and after a brief visit with Peter's parents in Vienna, they moved to the United States. Shortly thereafter, the Nazis annexed Austria. Over the next decades, she followed her husband as he taught at Sarah Lawrence, Bennington, New York University, and Claremont Graduate School, and traveled around the world as a consultant to governments and businesses.

When listening to her husband speak, she often couldn't hear and had to shout, "Louder!" After years of frustration, she came up with the idea for VISIVOX, a visual feedback device that monitors the volume of a speaker's voice, so that they can make adjustments. "I invented VISIVOX because so many public speakers, including my husband, Peter F. Drucker, need a monitor that lets them know whether they can be heard," she said. Her invention is also used by speech pathologists who help people modulate their voice. In the following selection, Drucker depicts the many obstacles involved in a start-up, including prejudice against a grandmother, and her triumph, eventually being awarded a patent.

Mrs. Drucker Starts a Business
Doris Drucker

For years my role as the wife of a professional speaker was to sit in the last row of an auditorium and shout, "Louder!" whenever my husband's voice dropped. I decided that there had to be a better feedback device, and if there wasn't, I was going to invent one. Then I decided, at the age of 80-plus, that I would start a business to sell it.

My children thought I'd gone off my rocker. Friends were more tactful, but I resented their sometimes patronizing comments. ("Marvelous that you can still do it!") Of course, the reactions weren't surprising. Though start-ups have become our national pastime, they're considered a young person's game — certainly not an appropriate activity for senior citizens.

But starting a business at 80 is really no different from starting one at any age. The only prerequisites are that you are still alive, in good physical and mental health, and the owner of a vast reservoir of energy. One's sense of urgency is a plus: if not now, when?

My product was going to be an electronic device: a microphone receiving the speaker's voice would transfer changes in volume to a visual display in which lights of different colors would indicate different loudness levels. The device had to be inexpensive and economical to use. It would take the place of a lot of elaborate audio equipment and reduce the need for the routine services of an audio engineer in an auditorium.

Starting a business at 80 is really no different from starting one at any age. . . . One's sense of urgency is a plus: if not now, when?

To convert my brainchild into a marketable product, I looked for help. Several consulting engineers turned me down — perhaps they didn't think much of having an old lady as a client. Others I turned down because they wanted too large a piece of the action. A former business associate suggested a 75-year-old retired engineer, Obie O'Brien, in Rescue, Calif. Obie and I met a few times, discovered that we could work together, and formed a corporation called RSQ, after his hometown. Obie calculated the future production costs for the units we were going to build (which turned out to be an accurate forecast), the price we would have to charge, and the number of units we would have to sell to come out ahead. That was our business plan.

Any investor would have been aghast at the informality of it. But at our age, we couldn't have attracted a venture capitalist anyhow, so why bother to be more specific?

A grandson designed a logo on his computer for the company, and in November 1995 Obie and I signed the documents establishing our limited-liability company. Obie built prototypes, one after the other, which we showed to prospective users. We incorporated their suggestions for improvements into successive models till we had the functional product we had envisioned.

The microphone and all the electronics were built into a chassis; light-emitting diodes in the shape of light bars were mounted in a separate holder, which was to be plugged into the circuitry. That way, the light signals—showing a speaker how loud to talk—could be displayed anywhere within the speaker's line of vision.

The prototypes, primitive though they were, got us some orders for the finished product as soon as it would be ready. Encouraged, we decided to build a few "real" samples to test the transition from a homemade product to a manufactured one. Or rather, we decided to have them built because we didn't have the resources to manufacture anything ourselves. I figured it wouldn't be a problem to buy the chassis and the electronic components and find an assembler to put them all together.

> To convert my brainchild into a marketable product, I looked for help. Several consulting engineers turned me down—perhaps they didn't think much of having an old lady as a client.

Well, how dumb can you be? It took me months, working full-time, to get those samples built. Decisions, decisions: Plastic chassis or metal ones? Cost versus weight. Practicability versus appearance. We needed a box that could be opened and shut by the user. What kind of cover should it have? Sliding? Fitted? Hinged? Nothing was available to meet our dimensions and specifications. I let my fingers do the walking through the yellow pages, culled the names of 10 or 12 chassis makers within an arbitrary radius of 30 miles, and drove from one to the next. Some calls were unproductive—the quoted prices were too high, or the quality standards were too low. Finally, I found a small sheet-steel fabricator with which I placed the order for the chassis. The owner, a retired navy man in his seventies, seemed to like working with other seniors.

Obie and a young electronics specialist whom he had co-opted had made out a parts list of 70 or 80 items, including the manufacturers' parts numbers. With that list in my pocket, I prowled through electronics stores, discounters, and surplus outlets, RadioShacks and Home Depots. It was no use going to manufacturers—they sold parts only in lots of hundreds or thousands. From dusty bins I scooped out capacitors and resistors, Schott and Zener diodes, jacks, plugs, clamps, whatnot.

Any investor would have been aghast at the informality of [our business plan]. But at our age, we couldn't have attracted a venture capitalist anyhow, so why bother to be more specific?

Next I had to find an assembler, but I had no idea how to go about it. On a Saturday morning, as I raked leaves on my front lawn I asked my next-door neighbor, an engineer, who was also working in his yard, whether he knew an assembler who could put my device together. He did. He had worked for one some years ago, a really good guy.

On Monday morning I went to see Lee Hoffman at JDF Enterprises, in Placentia, 28 miles south of Rescue. The shop was well organized and had up-to-date machinery. Hoffman said he could put our project together. "But," he asked, "who is going to provide the two circuit boards per unit, according to your design?"

"I thought you would!" I said.

"No, we do only the assembly, connecting the boards to the microphones, the other components, and the controls on the outside."

"But who does the boards?"

"Steve. He has a lab in Corona, 40 miles to the southeast. I'll give him a call and tell him that you want to talk to him."

At 8 the next morning Steve arrived at my office. He looked at the drawings and agreed to build the boards. "But who is going to do the layout?" he asked.

"I thought that was part of *your* job!"

"No, like I told you, I build the boards, but I have to have a layout."

"Then who does the layout?"

"Helen. Would you like me to call her for you?"

I started to get the impression that this game of "I'll call X and say that you want to talk to him or her" was going to go on forever, but Helen, fortunately, happened to be the last in line.

I went to see her in Chino, only 10 miles away. She had a nondescript house in a nondescript neighborhood; only the tightly drawn black shades of the front windows hinted at the high-tech setup inside. Helen, an elderly lady in sweats, led me into her lab. Yes, she would do the layout for the boards but not right away. She was busy with a major project for another customer, and besides, she worked professionally only in the afternoons. Mornings she worked for her church.

She looked like such an unlikely techie that I asked her how she'd gotten into this kind of work. She used to be a teacher, she told me, till she took early retirement because of arthritis. She spent six months doing crossword puzzles and other busywork. One day she sent for a do-it-yourself radio kit—and then for another and another. Suddenly, it hit her that she could do a much better job of designing the kits, and so she developed a business for which there is more demand than she can fill. A thoroughly competent and conscientious designer, she did an excellent job for us.

While I was waiting for her layout, I wrote a patent application. Then I started to apply for a trademark. A lawyer recommended a professional search to find out whether our provisional name for the invention was available. The search, at $600, showed that it wasn't. Because we couldn't afford to spend that much searching for every other word we might come up with, I went the Lexis-Nexis route myself. A made-up word, *Visivox,* appeared to be available, and we applied for it as a trademark.

All that took much longer than we'd thought, even though we'd expected delays in the development process. One factor was that unlike the engineers of Tracy Kidder's *The Soul of a New Machine,* Obie and I couldn't devote body and soul to our project. Each of us had families, family crises, obligations, and other priorities with stronger claims on our time.

Still, we got the first five sample chassis built and painted, with the legends on right and all the parts put in. We agonized over the costs—sample building is expensive but essential to forestall potentially large errors.

Now we were ready to order our first run of 100 units, but we were not done yet. Every day there was some unexpected problem. The spray painter—24 miles to the south— would get on the phone, saying that all 100 chassis delivered for painting were faulty. The manufacturer had miscalculated the hinge clearance; after the paint was applied, the chassis lids wouldn't close. The 100 chassis had to go back to the manufacturer, who took each one of them apart to fix the problem. He wanted me to inspect the finished work, and the painter wanted me to inspect *his* work. Some days I would drive up to 200 miles just making the rounds.

I also had to think about marketing tools. Ideally, we would have had the brochures produced professionally, the copy as well as the graphics. But we were operating on a shoestring, and so we tried to do as much as we could with the help of family and friends. One of them reviewed the text I'd composed and remarked, "You'll never make it as a copywriter for Campbell Soup." I shrugged—what did soup have to do with it? I ordered a photograph of a Visivox from a professional photographer and looked for somebody to lay out and print our brochures. The first designer, who had come highly recommended, reproached me for waking her with a 9 A.M. call—she needed her beauty sleep, she said. I struck her off; I needed somebody with more get-up-and-go. Number two did beautiful work—I wished we could have afforded him. Number three, an all-woman outfit, was competent; we assigned our work to it.

So they'd stand out among all the direct mail, we had the brochures printed on orange-yellow stock. Envelopes of the same color cost a mint. In the yellow pages I found a manufacturer located in what I knew was a scary neighborhood. Unexpectedly, his was a modern building, and I bought 1,000 envelopes at one-fifth the price asked by a local retailer.

The next foray was to the post office to get a permit for the return-postage-paid postcards that were to be attached to the brochures. The local post office and that of the neighboring community quoted widely divergent prices. I drove to the one with the lower quote, only to find out that the one person authorized to issue the permits had already left for the day. At 2 P.M.? Sure, he worked from 4 A.M. to noon. The next morning at 9, I went to yet another post office, where, I had been assured, the permit issuer would be on duty. That was misinformation: it was two days before Christmas, and the man had gone home at 8. The fourth trip, however, was successful: the post office accepted a check for $100 in return for the permit.

There were still a few minor things to attend to, such as buying shipping cartons, bubble wrap, shipping labels, and sealing tape, but U-Haul and the discounters were glad to oblige.

Now we face another challenge: to introduce and sell a new product. Our initial efforts made the product look like a success. Whenever I have demonstrated the product, I've made a sale to corporations that use Visivox for their internal seminars; to colleges, churches, and debating societies; and to well-known professional speakers. But now I have to organize national distribution.

My husband, the management guru, has watched all this with astonishment. People ask, understandably, if being the wife of the fellow who all but created management science has affected how I think about starting and growing a company—and they're a little disbelieving when I tell them it hasn't. He does my taxes (and I bless him for that; I hate doing them). But otherwise, he has no idea about start-ups. "I wouldn't know the first thing about a small enterprise like yours," he says to me. All the practical steps that consume so much time—they have nothing to do with him.

When Obie and I stand back now, we ask ourselves whether we would have started the venture two years ago if we'd known how difficult it was going to be. The sleepless nights. The worries about how to get around the next roadblock.

And the answer is yes. I got to know and work with a lot of people I would never have met otherwise—people my own age and people 40 or 50 years younger. When I talk electronics to a supplier—when I talk about the negative tip orientation of a charger cable or the type of pot (that is, *potentiometer* in the lingo) — I'm just another professional customer, not an old lady. I'm not just the standard figure expected by our ageist society.

Yes, I'd start a business again. Of course, I still have a long way to go with this one.

1997

PART II

The Maverick Element and Other Qualities

This section addresses the question: Who makes a good entrepreneur? Warren Avis, founder of Avis Rental Car, provides his list of five prerequisites, from having an unencumbered personal life to having good judgment about people. However, do you have to be a gunslinger as he suggests? Sure you need courage, but both Wally "Famous" Amos and Lillian Vernon rank commitment and passion pretty high on their lists, which can very well mean having that unencumbered life because there'll be no time for family and friends. On top of enthusiasm and other personal, emotional, and psychological considerations, the entrepreneur must also be a jack of all trades when it comes to running a business. In other words, the key elements also include being an accountant, an administrator, a handyman, a manager, and even a gofer. As Mark McCormack, founder of the powerhouse agency IMG and whose first client was Arnold Palmer, reminds all entrepreneurs, you must be flexible in every way to capitalize on all opportunities.

WARREN AVIS

Warren Avis first conceived of his rental car business while serving as a captain in the Air Force during World War II. As he traveled all over the United States and Europe, flying transport and combat missions, he discovered that the greatest problem was not enemy fire, but rather finding ground transportation once they landed. Avis and his buddies soon took to carrying motorcycles in the bomb bays, so they could escape the often isolated air bases. Once he reentered civilian life, Avis knew what he had to do: Establish a car rental agency that operated out of airports. "The big entrepreneurial idea is likely to arise from some big public need. With the Avis system, we saw the need for car rentals at airports, and we rushed in to satisfy it," he said.

The Hertz rental agency, already well established in cities and convinced this young entrepreneur's idea would fail, chose to watch from the sidelines as Avis attempted to build his airport car rental business. Failure was not on Avis's mind. Indeed, one of his favorite axioms is, "Ignorance is bliss. If an entrepreneur knew all the pitfalls he might stumble upon, he'd never get started." With $10,000 of his own money, and $75,000 borrowed, he set out, signing exclusive contracts with airports and networking with the airlines. In 1954, he sold the company for $8 million. With more than 20 businesses under his belt since that magical first, it can safely be said that Avis embodies the spirit of the American entrepreneur.

Avis devoutly believes entrepreneurs will always be the true pioneers of business, comparing them with the gunslingers of the Old West. He asserts that he "embarked with total abandon" on his own personal adventure in free enterprise. However, a definite and pragmatic formula lays behind his success. For example, while he compares himself with a gunslinger, Avis understands that the lone ranger type makes for a lousy entrepreneur. He wrote, "The entrepreneur who tries to operate alone, without advice, help and support of others, will surely stumble and fail . . ." In *Are You a Gunslinger?*, Avis outlines his prerequisites for becoming a successful entrepreneur, which include an unencumbered personal life—in other words, spouses beware.

Are You a Gunslinger?
Warren Avis

The dramatic flair and rugged individualism of the old-time gunslinger, frontiersman or explorer have always had the power to pique the imagination. In fact, fantasies of such personal freedom may run wild among modern-day, desk-bound corporate employees who long to escape their humdrum daily schedules.

At one time or another, most workers have felt strongly that they need to shake free of the system; they want to stretch their wings and break away from the constraints of the boring conventions of business-as-usual.

But what kind of personality does it take to strike out on your own —*and* make a success of it?

On one level the answer to this question focuses on the gunslinger myth. In popular thought, the independent, high-rolling business person has often been compared to the swashbuckling adventurer epitomized in the Western tales of Owen Wister or Louis L'Amour. This personality type spans generations and historical epochs. On the American frontier, the term was "gunslinger." On the high seas, it was "pirate." And in Western capitalism, it's "entrepreneur."

Of course, there is some truth to the myth. The best entrepreneurs have some similarities with the old-fashioned adventurers of earlier history. Like the gunslinger, pirate or explorer, the entrepreneur is often unconventional. He's not bound by tradition. He — or she — will tend to come up with a new idea and then run with it in some unexpected, exciting way. He's also willing to put his way of life on the line by taking unusual risks.

> The independent, high-rolling business person has often been compared to the swashbuckling adventurer epitomized in the Western tales of Owen Wister or Louis L'Amour.

At the same time, however, some distinctions have to be made. For one thing, the pirates and gunslingers operated completely outside the law; the entrepreneur, in contrast, must function within the legal system. (Unfortunately, however, our present legal system leaves a lot to be desired. It often permits unethical conduct, if not outright piracy!)

There are some special personal *and* business traits and conditions that distinguish the entrepreneurial personality from all others. These prerequisites ... certainly don't represent an exhaustive list. Many entrepreneurs may possess other qualities or benefits which, for them, are equally important. But still, if these conditions are present in your life, you're more likely to strike pay dirt as an entrepreneur. First, we'll consider in some depth the "personal prerequisites" for success; then, we'll turn to the specifically business-related traits.

Personal Prerequisite #1:
An Unencumbered Personal Life

Because of the overwhelming obligations and commitments that accompany starting a new venture, many successful entrepreneurs are unmarried. You're just not going to find many successful gunslingers with five or six children and an accumulation of family responsibilities. (In fact, in most home circumstances like this, it would be irresponsible to venture out on your own for the first time—unless you're an extremely unusual and gifted person.)

The best entrepreneurs have some similarities with the old-fashioned adventurers of earlier history. Like the gunslinger, pirate or explorer, the entrepreneur is often unconventional.

In those situations where entrepreneurs are married, their spouses often work. In almost every successful case, the spouse is as committed to the venture as the entrepreneur. Otherwise, there's a great danger that the marriage or the venture will fall apart. In short, it is essential that your family, friends and business associates pull you toward and not away from your business goals.

A friend of mine had just outfitted his yacht, and I must say, he had done a beautiful job. But then his wife took one look at what he had done and began to criticize every single thing. As she continued for a while in this vein, I asked, "Don't you realize what you're doing?"

She hadn't the slightest idea. She was destroying her husband without being aware of it. And I knew she had done the same with some of his business ventures. Certainly, he was a success by most standards. But he could have achieved much more and been happier, if only she had built him up instead of tearing him down.

Constant criticizing will often eventually destroy all confidence, whereas a supportive attitude will achieve much more happiness and success. That same principle applies to both men and women, of course. Whether male or female, the victimized spouse always ends up one step farther back in the race to have a successful life, marriage or business.

Personal Prerequisite #2:
A Severe Case of Monomania

The best entrepreneurs have a one-track mind.

One classic new entrepreneur was willing to live in a one-room, cold-water flat by himself. He walked up four flights, spent practically nothing on himself in the way of luxuries and worked eighteen hours a day. In short, he lived and breathed his company. And well he might. This man eventually made it, but only about one in five new ventures succeeds. The others go defunct, regardless of the best intentions and efforts.

Because of the overwhelming obligations and commitments that accompany starting a new venture, many successful entrepreneurs are unmarried.

So the person who is the inspiration behind a venture must have something extra in the way of personal commitment. It's been said that the successful American business person loves business first, family second, and sports and other things third. There's a lot of truth in that.

In a special report on entrepreneurs published by *The Wall Street Journal* (May 20, 1985), the creator of a successful water-ski company said that he often is preoccupied by business matters, even when he and his family are off somewhere on an outing.

His wife will say, "Talk to me," but instead, he'll pull out a pocket tape recorder and begin dictating some new concept that has come to mind.

"Sometimes, he treats us like workers instead of family," his wife said.

And when asked whether he values family above work, this super-successful entrepreneur replied, "Well, that's a tough one. Of course, you have to say family."

The best entrepreneurs have a one-track mind.

A major corollary to entrepreneurial monomania is the entrepreneur's tendency to take charge of situations outside of work. Entrepreneurs tend to be obsessed with an independent life, and they often chafe under any sort of authority. So whenever there seems to be a vacuum of authority, an entrepreneur will most likely step into it and begin to pull strings, order people around and generally try to take control of the situation.

This can be both a great strength and an obnoxious weakness, as I discovered during one social outing with a friend. We had both been invited to the same social event, and when my friend learned I was staying at the Beverly Hills Hotel, he said, "I'll pick you up, and you can go down with us."

When he pulled up to the hotel, he was sitting in the front seat of a limousine, and the other three of us in the group were in the back. In my typical style, I ordered: "Hey, get out and get in back with us!"

My pal then remarked to the other two, "You see I told you, when Warren arrives, he starts running everything!"

He said it in a nice way, with a nice smile, but it made an enormous impression on me. So I now watch that I don't always tell people what to do. And I've learned that 90 percent of the time if I keep my mouth shut or just make a mild suggestion, what needs to be done gets done anyway.

Certainly, an entrepreneur should try to unwind and enjoy himself when he's not working. But it's not always easy to assume a completely different role when you've been charging ahead with some project, living and breathing it and tossing commands around like some field general.

> During the early stages of a venture, you *have* to be willing to dedicate a good portion of your life to your concept if you hope to make it successful.

In fact, during the early stages of a venture, you *have* to be willing to dedicate a good portion of your life to your concept if you hope to make it successful. Otherwise, you're a dilettante; and dilettantes simply aren't competitive in our fast-moving, hard-selling economic environment. It may be true that anybody can create a successful business—but only if there's a willingness to make a near-monomaniacal commitment.

Personal Prerequisite #3:
Plenty of Staying Power

Building a successful business *always* takes longer than the entrepreneur expects. He or she typically believes that the big time will arrive tomorrow. But it's never tomorrow. It's always the day after tomorrow, or the day after that.

I'm that way. Like most entrepreneurs, I always expect to finish a project faster than the time it really takes. I'm firmly convinced it's going to be finished tomorrow. Yet it always takes longer than expected. Even after building a number of successful enterprises, I'm *still* having to learn I have to wait longer; to persevere; to have more patience.

How long can you reasonably expect it will take to turn your business idea into a successful, thriving, profit-producing enterprise?

Typically, it will take between three and five years, from the start of the business to success — though some companies, such as high-tech enterprises, which may turn a huge profit almost immediately, are exceptions to the rule. If you make it big in much less than five years, you're lucky. If you're still struggling after five, maybe you should try another idea or another field — or reassess your management style.

Building a successful business *always* takes longer than the entrepreneur expects. He or she typically believes that the big time will arrive tomorrow. But it's never tomorrow.

Now, I realize this may seem to be a massive commitment of your life — to put in as much as five years to achieve an entrepreneurial goal. But that's what it takes. You simply have to be in place for a minimum number of years for your idea to build momentum and have a chance to turn a substantial profit. There seems to be some sort of mystical law of the marketplace which requires an input of time, as well as creativity and energy.

This has been a hard lesson for me to learn because I get impatient. I want to see results now — or even better, yesterday. But super-successful gunslinging in any field just isn't like that. Can you imagine Wyatt Earp walking out on a dusty street the first day he ever held a pistol and hitting his target in the center? Of course not! It takes years of practice to perfect the fast draw and the dead-eye aim. And the same principle applies with entrepreneurial gunslinging.

But there's still a temptation in all of us to want to hop over the hard work of preparation and reap all the benefits immediately. Over the years, I've come to realize that my greatest weakness is my unwillingness sometimes to stay with a job as long as necessary to achieve optimum results.

After I have launched a company, I tend to turn to new opportunities. To compensate for this personal trait, I've started to concentrate more on hiring top managers, at attractive salaries and bonuses, to take over when I decide to go on to new ventures. My guess is that I could be worth a hundred times more money if I had just learned to do this years ago. With experienced, competent managers, I can run a company very successfully without being involved in the daily management.

Personal Prerequisite #4:
A High Energy Level, Nurtured by Periods of Relaxation

Because I'm a very intense person, I need plenty of time off to maintain my staying power year after year. If I didn't pace myself and take good care of my physical and emotional needs, I'd quickly burn out—and I might well run into various health problems.

I've come to realize that my greatest weakness is my unwillingness sometimes to stay with a job as long as necessary to achieve optimum results.

I began to understand this principle a number of years ago, during one of my first entrepreneurial ventures as an independent sales representative. At the time, I worked for only one company, and the management looked at me as another employee. But there were a number of key differences: For one thing, I worked much harder than the company's average employee. Also, I operated independently—often at unusual hours—and I was paid only by commission.

My inclination to throw myself body and soul into various sales challenges made it necessary for me to pull back periodically to recoup my energies. So from the very beginning, I always gave myself generous vacations.

But when I told a top company executive one year that I planned to take a month off at Christmas, he exploded: "Nobody working with this company ever takes more than two weeks off! And here, you say you're going to take a month!"

"That's right," I said—and I pointed out that unlike many companies we did little business in December anyway.

Money is no good if you have to work so hard for it you don't have time to enjoy it. If you make twice as much, but don't have time to spend it, what good is it?

"Hey, you're *almost* fired!" he said. But he said it with a smile. After all, I was one of his best sales reps. As long as I produced, he really couldn't argue with the month's vacation. But still, he urged me not to mention our little arrangement because it might be bad for company morale, and I agreed.

Unbeknownst to the company, in addition to regular vacations, I also took off plenty of time during the rest of the year as well. So I might put in a sixteen- or eighteen-hour day when going full steam with a project. But then I'd always intersperse my hard work with play and relaxation. Money is no good if you have to work so hard for it you don't have time to enjoy it. If you make twice as much, but don't have time to spend it, what good is it? At least, that was my philosophy. Many people fail to savor life while they're still young, and I certainly didn't want to be like that!

In any case, this company didn't argue with my success. But to live by a "relaxed" philosophy *and* maintain an outstanding sales record, it's necessary to get extremely well organized—and work like hell when the time for work has arrived!

Specifically, my approach was to really work hard for about three weeks each month, and then take the rest of the month off. But during that three weeks, it was necessary to go at top speed, day and night.

I'd get in my car, and drive through Indianapolis, St. Louis, Kansas City and then through other cities in Missouri. The whole itinerary was very precisely laid out; I knew exactly who to see and when to see them. Evenings and lunch hours would be devoted to various clients. It was an extremely packed, intense schedule, but I work best that way.

What's the source of this kind of energy? In part, it helps to be born with it. Many entrepreneurs have enjoyed a healthy level of inner drive and ambition since childhood.

But there's more to it than that. Even after the passing of several decades of entrepreneurial efforts, my energies have waned hardly at all. I attribute this to my ability to have fun and relax, but also to my habits of eating reasonably well and exercising regularly. In some ways, I suppose you might say I'm a health nut.

When on one of my frequent vacations or holidays, I don't just sit around or loll about over snacks or big meals. Rather, my tendency is to stay so busy with either work or leisure activities that I forget about eating.

In fact, I naturally tend to eat only one meal a day—and that's always been the evening meal. But I've learned over the years that I should always plug in one more small snack of fresh fruit each day just to keep my energies up.

Typically, I skip breakfast. But then, I'll make it a point late in the morning to eat some high-fiber, low-cholesterol dish, like All-Bran with skim milk—mainly to provide energy and to reduce the risk of cholesterol or colon cancer. Then, I may have a little fruit around 4 P.M. Finally, when the evening rolls around, I'll usually have fish or some other low-fat dish.

As for exercise, I do a lot of swimming, wind-surfing, jumping horses and water-skiing. The water-skiing may not sound all that strenuous, but it burns up the calories the way I do it: I'll get behind a boat on one ski and sweep back and forth over the wake for as long as an hour. Also, I find some comfort in an old saying that "you won't get arthritis if you water-ski"!

Yet even though I've developed a few personal and health routines, I can't lay out my life in a predictable, exact, evenly spaced way, day after day, month after month, and year after year. I do organize my time effectively; but it's organized according to my special emotional and physical metabolism. I have to go at something very intensely for a short period and then take time off to recoup my energies and interest.

It was quite natural for me to develop this sort of approach at the outset of my career because I was an unfettered bachelor. I had total freedom to go anywhere I wanted and stay with any client or prospect for as long as I felt was warranted.

Of course, it was quite boring on the weekends in many of those towns. That's why I always tried to line up sales meetings on the weekends if I possibly could. I've always hated bars and living alone in a series of boring hotel rooms. But I found I could put up with anything for three weeks at a time. And that was all I needed to reach the top level of sales with this particular company.

While spending a lot of time in Europe, I've come to realize that the approach to life I developed years ago coincides with what might be called the European view. On the Continent, there's an attitude that making money isn't the ultimate end of all endeavor. Business is just a part of one's existence.

But the typical American loves business. Even when the business person retires—and this is especially true of the executive—he often wants to go back to work. That's because when you're a manager in American business, you have great power over other people; and controlling other people can become a powerful narcotic. Also, if you've never learned to relax and enjoy other things, you get bored.

When the top-level business executive who is an employee, is forced into retirement, he loses a major part of his identity; and that's when the big health problems often begin. Heart attacks often occur soon after retirement, but these people don't just die of a normal heart attack. They die of a broken heart. The phone stops ringing. They're no longer in demand. They failed to make friends apart from their business associates. Also, those goals they had striven for are no longer a possibility for them. And their lives, at least in their view, become worthless.

That's the value of the entrepreneur's way of life. You never have to retire if you're in business for yourself. You can begin to pull back from your responsibilities and time commitments as you get older. But as long as you learn how to develop some staying power, you never have to withdraw completely from the work you love—at least not unless you really want to.

Personal Prerequisite #5:
Good Judgment about People

One of my major problems as an entrepreneur has been my failure to hire the right people to handle enterprises that I begin or buy into. On a number of occasions, it's been too easy to become enchanted by the inspirational sales talk of young business gunslingers, and to trust their thin managerial background—against better business judgment. And more than once, I've lived to regret it.

For example, one obviously intelligent, impressive young hotshot in his mid-twenties had a great idea for a manufacturing project—though it was clear right at the beginning that he needed some "gray hair." In other words, he needed older managers with considerable experience to run the production and financial departments in the company. Unfortunately, he thought he knew it all, and he went broke.

Underlying this is a basic principle of building a successful entrepreneurial venture: You need hard-charging, creative young people (or the classic, Billy-the-Kid-type of gunslinger) *plus* stable, experienced older managers. Without the gray hair, you're often doomed to failure. I wish I had learned this lesson much earlier because I could have avoided many mistakes by including relevant clauses in contracts. All I would have had to do was to require inexperienced partners to hire experienced people where they were needed.

One of my major problems as an entrepreneur has been my failure to hire the right people to handle enterprises that I begin or buy into.

Against my better judgment, another young entrepreneur also talked me into forgetting the experience that goes with the gray hair. So he chose unqualified young friends of his for those experience-related jobs.

Unfortunately, the lack of experience once again quickly began to show. The company almost fell apart with cost overruns and other inefficiencies until experienced people were hired.

I've gotten better at orchestrating the managerial makeup of various companies in recent years—but only after working very hard at improving my lack of good judgment in hiring the right people. With our venture capital operation, it's almost an automatic procedure for us to judge prospective entrepreneurs according to the qualifications of the people they have hired or want to hire. If we don't reach a "meeting of the minds" on this issue, we don't invest.

Specifically, there are five personal features we look for

in any prospective business associate: appearance, personality, intelligence, integrity and status.

Appearance. If a person is sloppy, unkempt or otherwise physically unpresentable, he'll immediately have one strike against him. Half of success at any business is getting your foot in the door. And you'll never get your foot in *any* door if you somehow just don't look right.

Two young men approached an investor to get money to finance a venture which was designed to disseminate specialized business information. One of the would-be entrepreneurs was trim and sharply dressed. He *looked* successful. The other, however, was overweight; his top shirt button was open; his tie was askew; and he always seemed to be perspiring and out of breath.

To make a long story short, the investor made a separate appointment with the sharp entrepreneur and suggested, "This is a good idea you have, but why don't you go into this on your own? This other guy is going to hold you back."

> Half of success at any business is getting your foot in the door. And you'll never get your foot in *any* door if you somehow just don't look right.

In fact, the disheveled young fellow knew more about many of the technical aspects of the venture than his partner. But the investor wouldn't be convinced; and eventually the deal fell through because the sharp entrepreneur insisted on remaining loyal to his untidy cohort.

The moral to this story? Do a devastatingly honest evaluation of your own appearance, and clean up your act before you try to launch any new venture.

Personality. An essential asset for any entrepreneur is a good personality. "Good personality" means the personal quality that makes another person appreciate being around you. People with good personalities tend to be sensitive to the feelings and needs of others, and to be able to communicate their concern effectively. In addition, this involves several "not-beings": *not being* abrasive; *not being* rude; *not being* sarcastic; and *not being* late.

One woman, a boutique owner, has a very sharp wit—and she uses it far too often to poke fun at others, or to make jokes at their expense. She's obviously intelligent and has many other fine qualities. She's also quite attractive—in fact, she spends more than an hour a day making herself look just right. Unfortunately, she doesn't spend even a minute trying to improve her personality by reflecting on her negative effect on other people.

Because she projects a rather unpleasant aura to others, most people prefer not to be around her very long. She's certainly not the first one they think of to do business with or to ask out to social affairs. As a result, she's often unable to attract business contacts who could be a great help as she tries to build her business. In addition, her personal life suffers.

Intelligence. This concept doesn't just refer to IQ or native genius, though certainly, the best entrepreneurs are rather shrewd and bright. Rather, the type of intelligence that really helps a person make a go of a new business is one that involves (1) an ability to communicate, and (2) a capacity to think straight and logically.

In other words, if you have a group of people of only average intelligence and below-average education, they can still put together a thriving enterprise—*if* they can just talk to one another, and to their prospective customers. By communicating effectively, they are in a position to solve their problems more constructively. Also, they'll be better able to work productively together and make effective, joint decisions.

Also, the kind of intelligence that characterizes a successful entrepreneur is one which enables the person to set proper goals and focus on key priorities. One of the major weaknesses among young, inexperienced, would-be entrepreneurs is their inability to narrow their objectives. They tend to be "all over the lot," because they fail to mass their energies and resources to achieve precise objectives.

One very bright young man in the nonprofit field wanted to set up a new religious ministry, but he had many ideas that fascinated him—and he became intent on trying to put all of them into effect. Of course, he lacked the time, ability and financial backing to do everything that interested him. As a result, he accomplished nothing for several years. His career was a total disaster.

Finally, however, he opened his ears to the advice of a couple of friends who had been telling him he needed to focus his considerable skills on one or two things. When he took this approach, he suddenly found his organization growing by leaps and bounds.

So it's not enough just to have a high IQ. You also have to learn practical ways to marshal your brainpower to achieve limited entrepreneurial objectives.

Integrity. You should be able to trust anyone you plan to work with—and they have to be able to trust you. If you tell colleagues or clients you've done something when you haven't, and they find out about it, that's going to erode their trust. Or worse, if you cheat a business associate, you could ruin your reputation in an entrepreneurial field forever. Dishonesty is something that usually throws up an impossible barrier to a working relationship.

One woman was starting off a job search firm which seemed to have tremendous potential, both for herself and for a couple of employees who had gotten in on the ground floor with her.

One Friday, one of the employees, a seemingly bright and promising young man, was given the assignment of mailing a very important package by overnight mail to an important client. But he got involved in some personal business that afternoon and failed to get the package in the mail until the following Monday.

Unfortunately, when he was questioned by his frantic boss that Monday, he lied. He said he had mailed the package as instructed on Friday, and he assumed it must have been lost in the mail. But of course, his lie was uncovered the next day when the package arrived and the client examined the date of mailing which was written clearly on the mailing slip.

This man's employer, the woman who had started the business, seethed for several days about this dishonesty. Finally, she realized she couldn't work with the young man under these circumstances, so she let him go.

The young man ended up missing out on a great opportunity. His other co-worker went on to a responsible and well-paid position as the firm grew. And there's every reason to believe he might have achieved the same level of prestige—if only he had shown some integrity. Unfortunately, most people never realize how much a lack of integrity can cost in the loss of friends and of business success.

Status. This is a tough quality to talk about because when you even raise the issue of status, many people in our egalitarian society think you're trying to be an elitist. But still, I think it's important for an entrepreneur to understand that if he comes across as being of the wrong social status in certain company, he's going to place himself at a decided disadvantage.

What exactly is status?

Having the right status doesn't necessarily mean appearing to be someone who might be in the Social Register. Rather, it just means knowing how to position yourself socially in the group you're trying to influence.

Relatively high status may accompany your education or profession: Doctors, lawyers and others with professional graduate degrees automatically enjoy a high status in most business gatherings. Titles also tend to raise a person's status—president, professor, executive vice president, executive director, chairman, or in Europe inherited titles like duke, count or whatever.

Furthermore, having a significant amount of money—or *appearing* to have money—may add to your status. Also, various achievements, such as honors received, awards earned, or books written, may mean higher status.

Even the town or neighborhood you live in may confer status. In New York, for example, a Park Avenue or Fifth Avenue address will convey more status than one in the outlying sections of Brooklyn or Queens.

None of these things are essential to enable you to fulfill your aspirations to become a successful entrepreneur. But they can certainly help. If your status is perceived as far too low, for example, you may be considered a loser. You'll find yourself always on the outside looking in.

One young entrepreneur had been invited to a party— part-business, part-pleasure—with some high-brow, old-money types. He was looking for supporters for a new venture he had proposed, and he seemed to have everything going for him—sharp looks, a winning personality, obvious intelligence and a reputation for sound integrity. But it quickly became apparent that the young woman he had brought along as a date didn't fit in at all.

During the evening's conversation, she consistently murdered the English language. She made one faux pas after another. Soon, the damage had been done. The young entrepreneur now had a strike against him in the eyes of these investors because his date's social inadequacies had caused his own status to be lowered a notch or two.

It's not necessary to be an elitist—just be realistic! Status is a factor that people use, consciously or subconsciously, in evaluating the business potential of others. And in this particular group, the requirements for status were more stringent than they would be in many other situations. Because this entrepreneur didn't realize this fact, he hurt his chances to get financial backing for his project.

The basic principle here is rather simple: Know the mentality of the people you're dealing with and use common sense. Obviously, bankers don't wear open-neck shirts; so don't wear sloppy or casual clothes to see a banker if you want money from him!

Of course, in some cases, a snooty suggestion of "high status" might hurt. I've run into many situations where it was necessary to project an earthy, good-old-boy image to get potential clients and investors on one's side. In such circumstances, any suggestion of an Ivy League background could hinder rather than enhance your chances.

So when you're thinking of hiring someone, taking on a partner or otherwise evaluating a person, try this five-point evaluation process: Focus on appearance, personality, intelligence, integrity and status. By using this approach, you'll be more likely to exercise sound judgment about people. You might even give yourself the same test periodically, to see how you measure up in the eyes of others. The main idea is to identify your greatest personal weakness, and then try hard to improve it.

1986

In the world of entertainment, Barry Diller's name is synonymous with innovation. He worked at ABC in the 1970s, and while there, he introduced the miniseries concept and "Movie of the Week." Diller's next stop was Paramount Pictures, where he produced such hit movies as *48 HRS* and *Raiders of the Lost Ark*. Also, it was Diller who launched the Fox network in 1985, changing television forever by offering an alternative to the three long-established networks. That's not bad for a college dropout whose first job was working in the mailroom at the William Morris talent agency.

Finally, in 1992, Diller struck off on his own, leaving Fox with a severance package that amounted to about $140 million. After spending $5 million on a Gulfstream jet, he started searching around for business opportunities. His first venture involved becoming a partner in QVC, the home shopping network. Many entertainment people questioned what they viewed as a step backward. His response: "You just have to try to say to yourself that what you based your decisions on is sound, and it doesn't matter what anybody says." He was enamored with the entrepreneurial spirit found in the cable industry: "Talk to the cable people, as opposed to senior people in the news-gathering business, or at the TV networks, or in the studios. Just line them up, and you find that people in the leadership of cable are students of technology and spend vast amounts of time and capital thinking issues through."

After two years, Diller left QVC and formed his own company, Home Shopping Network (HSN). More recently, he won control of USA Networks, which includes the USA and Sci-Fi cable channels. Money and spirit is what you need to start a business, Diller says, and when evaluating a business you have to be careful. Why? Bluntly put, "Because if you don't have enough cash to pay what you owe, your throat will get ripped out by somebody." Whether it be taking on the major networks or forging new ground in interactive media, Diller said, "I function best in a skeptical environment." In *The Discomfort Zone*, he explains why conventional wisdom will get you nowhere.

The Discomfort Zone
Barry Diller

In my experience, one of the secrets to success is to embrace failure.

Now, I'm not talking about the kind of failure that's psychological, a state of mind. Nor am I talking about setting low expectations. I'm talking about real failure. Failure so close you can taste it, so strong that your clothes reek of it—the kind of failure that makes people pretend they don't know you. That sort of failure is the best thing that can happen to you if you want to run your company creatively.

In my experience, one of the secrets to success is to embrace failure.

I learned that lesson when I was 23. I had a great job: I was assistant to the head of programming at ABC, and I ran the whole department while my boss was out creating new shows like *The Flying Nun.* I was sure my career would always be in administration. I would work for this talented guy, and as he moved onward and upward, I would follow him, happily making everything neat and clean so that the creative types could thrive. Never, did I imagine that I could become one of them. Even though the programming department was the exciting place to be in television, it was much too scary on that side of the hall.

It seemed so much better where I was: I felt so comfortable, with so much power already at such a young age and with nothing ever to risk. My fear of putting myself on the line—of risking the inevitable ridicule when you put forth new ideas—prevented me from even thinking I might be qualified for creative work. The loftiest goal I would permit myself, my top fantasy, was that I'd be the best damn clerk in the world.

I discovered the secret to success: Plunge into the uncomfortable; push, or be lucky enough to have someone push you, beyond your fears and your sense of limitations.

One fateful day, though, my boss threw me a script and said, "Read this and tell the producer what you think." I was terrified. That producer was the emperor of television—he had something like 11 shows on the air.

I studied the script. I hated it. When the producer cornered me, I croaked out my opinion—an inarticulate, incompetent response. The guy let me have it, up one side and down the other. But thank God, I'd gotten my feet wet. I was in the water—hardly courageously, but in there nonetheless, barely able to breathe and trying to defend my opinion with whatever ideas I could come up with. And I didn't drown. That's when I discovered the secret to success: Plunge into the uncomfortable; push, or be lucky enough to have someone push you, beyond your fears and your sense of lim-

itations. And that's what I've been doing ever since, overcoming my discomfort as I go along.

From ABC I moved to Paramount. This time I started at
the top, as chairman of the board. But I was still the under-
dog, the first person at the studio to have come from the perceived ghetto of television. The man who ran Paramount's
parent company, who had taken such a risk in hiring me, was
being pressured daily to get rid of me. Outsiders said that
Paramount was the last stop for scripts and new material,
seventh on a list of seven companies—until we did *Saturday
Night Fever*, which propelled Paramount from seventh to first
place.

What all my experiences have had in common
is a battle, a holy war if you will, between
process and expertise.

I learned many things at Paramount, but one lesson
stands out: Maybe it's a good thing not to be the first stop,
getting what everyone else thinks is the best material. Maybe
nobody really knows what's best. Maybe the best comes
from making your own choice, on its merits, not its blood-
lines. Maybe it's better to be uncomfortable, and to be left
alone to believe in what you can put together based on your
own judgment.

I took that lesson with me to Fox. This time when outsiders predicted failure, I welcomed it. All they knew was
that fourth networks had always failed before and that even
the Big Three were suffering a depressed ad market at the
time. What they didn't know, what they couldn't know, was
that we weren't interested in creating fourth network. We
were inventing an alternative.

They based their conclusion on one set of expectations.

Meanwhile we were free to operate on another. But we didn't find our voice immediately. The truth is, our first shows were horrible. We were losing, just as everyone had expected. But we were also working it out, figuring out a process as we went along.

What all my experiences have had in common is a battle, a holy war if you will, between process and expertise. Expertise is a pack mentality that concludes something can't be done, or that it must be done this way. It's a mentality that relies too heavily on conventional wisdom. It has to. Because the awkward alternative would be to accept that a new thing can't be fully known or comfortably understood. Conventional wisdom, by definition, favors that which has come before, that which is known. That's great if you're building a house or flying a plane. But it's useless, and much worse, dangerously misleading, in creative positions.

The absolute best time for me is always that period just before the victory when you know the work is good and it's your secret.

Process, on the other hand, is ignoring the doomsayers and optimists alike. None of them matters. Process is fundamentally a human function. It can't be duplicated or automated. It's about finding a grain of an idea and following that through to its conclusion. And process can't be forced or rushed. It works for everyone, not just the four or five real geniuses out there. For them, God bless them, instinct is enough. For the rest of us, there's process.

What is this process? If I could put it clearly, I would. But I can only point to it. I know it when it happens, and you do too. It's a kind of tough yet tender anarchy. Creativity always starts off with new, half-baked ideas, with half-coherent musings.

Expertise is a pack mentality that concludes something can't be done, or that it must be done this way. It's a mentality that relies too heavily on conventional wisdom.

And for me, at least, the fun is in the process. I never find great joy once the work is finished and everyone else starts cheering. Sure, victory is sweet. But it's just a moment. The absolute best time for me is always that period just before the victory when you know the work is good and it's your secret. Even that is just a moment. When you're in the process, in the groove of the work itself in all its twists and turns, its mess, its mistakes, the nightmare days and anguished nights when you're working it through—that's sustainable excitement. It's the journey. No one remembers myths for their endings—we remember the epic adventures along the way. When you're propelled by curiosity and the claims of a self that dares to fail, that's the process.

1995

WALLY AMOS
1936–

This baker of premium cookies opened his first store in 1975, received the President's award for Entrepreneurial Excellence, lost it all, then resurrected himself, now baking and distributing muffins under the Uncle Noname brand name. It's been some "cookie trip" for Wally "Famous" Amos, who was born in Tallahassee, Florida, but at age 12 moved to New York to live with his Aunt Della, who later turned him on to homemade chocolate chip cookies and was his inspiration. In New York, he survived a mugging and the gangs, and he worked odd jobs. To escape the streets, he joined the Air Force in 1953, in hopes of seeing the world—first stop: Biloxi, Mississippi, although he did make it to Hawaii and Guam.

Amos's first big break came in 1961 when a friend helped him get a job at the William Morris talent agency's mail room. Not long after, he became a secretary, and when the agency created its music department to handle rock-and-roll acts, Amos positioned himself to become a full-fledged agent. The first big act he brought in was Simon and Garfunkel; unfortunately, the duo signed with another agency. Amos made numerous friends and contacts that came into play when he launched his cookie company. By 1974 he had wearied of the "show business treadmill," so he decided it was time to start his venture. The next year he raised $25,000 and opened his first store in Hollywood.

"Anyone who believes that what happened to me came easy, or overnight, is terribly incorrect. . . . [M]y day-to-day, night-in-and-night-out concerns were about Famous Amos continuing until the next batch of money came in from somewhere, anywhere, and from anyone." To secure that stability, in 1985, Amos sold a majority stake to the Bass family, who then sold their share to another investor group, who then sold it to a Taiwanese food conglomerate. Meanwhile, Amos lost control and the use of his name as a brand. Part of the problem, according to Amos: "I didn't always listen to others. I thought I was invincible; my ego got a little too big for me." One thing he never lacked was enthusiasm. In *The Power in Commitment,* he gives a highly charged rallying cry for what it takes to see an idea through.

The Power in Commitment
Wally Amos

T o commit or to procrastinate? That is the question. Whether to make a decision to create a rich abundant life filled with the desires of your heart or to live a life of defeat and lack? Why is it that some people are successful and others never attain their goals? What do you suppose is the secret ingredient that pushes some over the top while others never even begin the climb? The largest obstacle between you and your goal is a lack of *total commitment*. Often we use phrases like, "I'll try," "I guess I can," "I hope I can." But commitment is expressed in two words: I WILL.

My personal struggles and experiences over the years have proven without a doubt that commitment gets the job done. Commitment is what separates the achievers from the sustainers. It was my unwavering commitment to open a store selling chocolate chip cookies that enabled me to give birth to the Famous Amos family of cookies.

Before going any further let me share with you a writing by the great German writer, Goethe. It is titled "The Power of Commitment."

Until one is committed, there is hesitancy, the chance to draw back, always ineffectiveness. Concerning all acts of initiative (and creation), there is one elementary truth the ignorance of which kills countless ideas and splendid plans: that the moment one definitely commits oneself, then providence moves too.

All sorts of things occur to help one that would never otherwise have occurred. A whole stream of events issues from the decision, raising in one's favor all manner of unforseen incidents and meetings and materials assistance, which no man could have dreamed would have come his way.

Are you in earnest? Seek this very minute, whatever you can do, or dream you can, begin it. Boldness has genius, power and magic in it. Only engage and the mind grows heated, begin and then the task will be completed.

Why is it that some people are successful and others never attain their goals? . . . The largest obstacle between you and your goal is a lack of *total commitment.*

If you have never taken inventory of your life, now might be a good time to do so. How many times have you tried something without successfully completing it? What was your attitude at the time? Did you doubt your ability to perform? Did you doubt the credibility of your idea? Did you check with friends and relatives for their approval? What was your level of commitment? These are all symptoms of a person who has not made a total commitment to a goal. Perhaps you even said "yes" and then later decided it was a foolish idea or too risky. The point is, you never gave birth to your idea, and I'll bet you dollars to cookies a lack of total commitment played a big part in causing you to fall short of your goal.

I saw a series of illustrations entitled: "It Was Just an Idea," which further illustrate how crippling procrastination or lack of commitment can be. Immediately below the title were nine squares, each with a picture of a light bulb and a quote above each bulb.

1. The first square contains a brightly glowing bulb with the quote "I have an idea."

2. The bulb in square two has lost some of its glow and says, "A word of caution."

3. Square three has a dimmer bulb with the words, "A little too radical." Can someone really determine if something is too radical for you? Isn't that a decision only you can make?

4. In the fourth square the bulb continues to fade with the quote, "I like it myself but." "But" is one of the smallest words in the English language, yet it has become the biggest obstacle for so many people. "But" has probably killed more great ideas than any other word in the English language. Do yourself a favor, eliminate "but" from your vocabulary. You will achieve a lot more.

How many times have you tried something without successfully completing it? What was your attitude at the time?

---

5. The fifth square shows the bulb darker yet and reads, "We tried something just like that once." They tried something just like that *once*. When you are committed, you make the effort over and over again. Commitment is the foundation on which determination and perseverance are laid. It's also important to realize that you have a different energy, spirit and creativity than anyone else. Even though many may have attempted and failed at an idea, *you* might succeed because the idea was just waiting for the right mixture of

energy, spirit and creativity that you bring to the table. Don't let anyone talk you out of pursuing your goals or acting on your ideas.

6. The sixth square sees almost all the light gone from the bulb and the quote says, "Let me play devil's advocate." Beware of people who play devil's advocate, my friend, because they tend to be negative thinkers and nine times out of ten they will talk you out of doing whatever it is you're attempting. Also, people who play devil's advocate are out to show you why something *will not succeed*. You want to focus on *how you can succeed*. Maybe you should only hang around with angel's helpers.

7. In the seventh square, the bulb is ever so faint and the quote says, "It's just not us." How do you know until you've made the attempt? Oftentimes it takes many efforts to find out who you are anyway. Each attempt gets you closer to your goal and also to discovering just what and who you really are.

Even though many may have attempted and failed at an idea, *you* might succeed because the idea was just waiting for the right mixture of energy, spirit and creativity that you bring to the table.

---

8. The eighth square shows only a slight trace of the bulb and says, "I wish it were that easy." Let me tell you a secret. It's as easy or as hard as you decide it's going to be. Nothing is anything until you say so. And today with so much technology—with so much information at your fingertips and so many people to assist you with whatever you wish to do—it's easier than it's ever been in your lifetime. Quit saying you *wish* it were that easy and know it *is* that easy. It's as easy as your attitude determines it will be.

9. In the ninth and last square the bulb has completely disappeared and the final quote says, "Oh, it was just an idea." IT WAS JUST AN IDEA!

"But" is one of the smallest words in the English language, yet it has become the biggest obstacle for so many people.

Everything that is, ever was or ever will be started as an idea in someone's mind. The right to ideas is a right that cannot be taken away from you. Always believe in yourself and your ideas.

1988

ANDREW CARNEGIE
1835–1919

Andrew Carnegie is the model Horatio Alger story. Born in Scotland, he immigrated with his family to the United States when he was 12 years old. His first job was as a bobbin boy, earning $1.20 a week. At 16, Carnegie became a telegraph operator for the Pennsylvania Railroad, where he moved up the ranks for 12 years. While there, he realized that the traditional wooden bridges were obsolete, so he struck out on his own and started the Keystone Bridge Works in 1865. Beginning in the early 1870s, he concentrated on steel production, founding the company that J. P. Morgan would organize into U.S. Steel in 1901. Upon reflection, Carnegie wrote, "And here is the prime condition of success, the great secret: concentrate your energy, thought, and capital exclusively upon the business in which you are engaged."

Besides being focused, Carnegie also attributed much of his success to the men around him. At one point, he wrote an epitaph for his grave that read, "Here lies one who knew how to get around him men cleverer than himself." Of course, he was a tough operator whose idea of conciliation with competitors was their complete surrender to his demands. As an employer, he squeezed all that he could from his employees, offering them wage packages that, in effect, amounted to "tails I win, heads you lose." During the Homestead Steel Works' strike of 1892, Carnegie remained at a safe distance in Scotland while 300 Pinkerton guards were hired in an attempt to crush the workers. The conflict ended in a bloody battle, and remains a black mark on Carnegie's legacy.

On the other hand, Carnegie was considered a saint for giving away more than $325 million to charitable causes before his death, including 7,000 church organs. Carnegie, along with John D. Rockefeller, was the first to make philanthropy big business. He also cared for America's youth, endowing libraries and universities for their education. That interest is apparent in *The Crucial Question,* as he advises young people on how to become business owners. Sometimes that means accepting "what the gods offer."

The Crucial Question
Andrew Carnegie

W e often hear in our day
that it is impossible for young men to become owners,
because business is conducted upon so great a scale that the
capital necessary reaches millions, and, therefore, the young
man is doomed to a salaried life. Now there is something in
that view only so far as the great corporations are concerned,
because an interest in these is only attainable by capital; you
can buy so many shares for so many dollars, and as the class
of young men I address are not willing to remain forever
salaried men, but are determined sooner or later, to become
business men upon their own account, as masters, I do not
believe that employment in a great corporation is as
favourable for them as with private owners, because, while a
young man can look forward to a large salary in their service, that is all to which he can aspire. Even the presidents of
these corporations, being only salaried men, are not to be
classed as strictly business men at all. How, then, can a
young man under them be anything but a salaried man his
life long?

Where to Look for Opportunities

Many a business which has long been successful as a partnership is put into a joint stock concern, and the shares are offered in the market, and professional men, guilelessly innocent of business, and, sometimes, women of a speculative turn, and, I am sorry to say, many times clergymen, and artists, are deluded into purchasing. The public buys the business, but they should have bought the man or men who made the business.

You remember the Travers story? A friend called Travers in to see a dog that he wished to buy to clear his conservatory of rats, and when the dog-fancier undertook to show him how this dog demolished these pests, one great, big old rat chased the dog. Travers's friend said to him:

"What would you do?"

Travers replied: "B-b-b-buy the rat."

The public often buys the wrong thing.

It would be an excellent study for you to read frequently the stock-lists of miscellaneous companies. You will find some of the newspapers give the list, and then note the par value of the shares and the price at which you may purchase them. It may be said that this par value is upon fictitious capital. That is so only in some instances; in manufacturing companies especially I think the reverse is the rule. The capital does not fully represent the cost of the properties.

But there are many corporations which are not corporations, many instances, of partnership in which the corporate form has been adopted, and yet the business continued substantially as a partnership, and comparing such institutions with the great corporations whose ownership is here, there, and everywhere, we find a most notable difference. Take, for instance, the great steamship lines of the world. Most of these, as those of you who read well know, fail to make returns to their shareholders. The shares of some of the greatest companies have been selling at one-half and sometimes one-third their cost. These are corporations, pure and simple, but if we look at other lines engaged upon the same oceans, which are managed by their owners and in which, generally, one great business man is deeply interested and at the head, we find large dividends each year and amounts placed to the reserve fund. It is the difference between individualism and communism applied to business, between the owners managing their own business as partners, and a joint stock concern of a thousand shifting owners ignorant of the business.

> Begin, if necessary, with a corporation, always keeping your eye open for a chance to become interested in a business of your own.

The same contrast can be drawn in every branch of business, in merchandising, in manufacturing, in finance, in transportation by land as well as by sea. It is so with banks. Many banks are really the property of a few business men. These soon become the leading banks, and their shares are invariably quoted at the highest premium, especially if the president of the bank be the largest owner, as he is in many of the most remarkable cases of success. In such partnership corporations there is every opportunity for the coming business man to obtain ownership which exists in pure partnerships, for the owners of both manage affairs and are on the constant watch for ability.

Do not be fastidious; take what the gods offer. Begin, if necessary, with a corporation, always keeping your eye open for a chance to become interested in a business of your own. Remember every business can be made successful, because it supplies some essential want of the community; it performs a needed office, whether it be in manufacturing which produces an article, or in gathering and distributing it by the merchant; or the banker, whose business is to take care of and invest capital.

There is no line of business in which success is not attainable.

A Secret of Success

It is a simple matter of honest work, ability, and concentration. There is no question about there being room at the top for exceptional men in any profession. These have not to seek patronage; the question is, rather, how can their services be secured, and, as with every profession, so in every line of business, there is plenty of room at the top. Your problem is how to get there. The answer is simple: conduct your business with just a little more ability than the average man in your line. If you are only above the average your success is secured, and the degree of success is in ratio to the greater degree of ability and attention which you give above the average. There are always a few in business who stand near the top, but, there are always an infinitely greater number at and near the bottom. And should you fail to ascend, the fault is not in your stars, but in yourselves. Those who fail may say that this or that man had great advantages, the fates were propitious, the conditions favourable. Now, there is very little in this; one man lands in the middle of a stream which he tries to jump, and is swept away, and another tries the same feat, and lands upon the other side.

Examine these two men.

You will find that the one who failed, lacked judgment; he had not calculated the means to the end; was a foolish fellow; had not trained himself; could not jump; he took the chances. He was like the young lady who was asked if she could play the violin, she said she "did not know, she had never tried." Now, the other man who jumped the stream had carefully trained himself; he knew about how far he could jump, and there was one thing "dead sure" with him, he knew he could, at any rate, jump far enough to land at a point from which he could wade ashore, and try again. He had shown judgment.

Prestige is a great matter, my friends. A young man who has the record of doing what he sets out to do will find year after year his field of operations extended, and the tasks committed to him greater and greater. On the other hand, the man who has to admit failure and comes to friends trying to get assistance in order to make a second start is in a very bad position, indeed.

1896

It's a pretty good bet that the Lillian Vernon catalog has reached your mailbox. Her tale is one of survival and triumph. She was born in Germany, where her father had built a prosperous lingerie business; however, when Adolf Hitler was elected Germany's chancellor in 1933, everything changed for this Jewish family named Hochberg. After Vernon's older brother was attacked by Nazi thugs, the decision was made to emigrate to Amsterdam and then to New York City in 1937 to escape the impending war. After the war (her brother was killed fighting for the United States), Vernon went to college for two years and then married.

Pregnant in 1951, the soon-to-be mother felt she had some greater purpose in the working world, but it was very unfashionable for women to work at that time. Regardless, with $2,000 of wedding gift money, Vernon founded her mail-order business. To create an appealing image for her customers, she called the company Lillian (her first name) Vernon (after a waspish-sounding town in Westchester County, New York); then, she also renamed herself Lillian Vernon. Her first venture was to offer a monogrammed purse and matching belt via an ad in *Seventeen* magazine. It brought in $32,000 in sales. In 1954, Vernon mailed out an eight-page black-and-white catalog to 125,000 potential customers.

In the early 1960s, the company diversified, making their own line of products and opening a wholesale business. Sales exceeded $1 million in 1970; the company went public in 1987; and today, lifetime customers number about 20 million. As the company grew, Vernon felt the pressure and occasionally exploded. "Risk brings entrepreneurs close to their emotional edge, and they find themselves beset with anxieties." The growth was also like a double-edged sword, and she brought in MBAs to solve management issues, but found they were focused on "analysis to the point of paralysis." In the following selection, Vernon warns that entrepreneurs must be prepared to do it all, from gofer work to the financials—MBAs and accountants can't be relied upon.

The Successful
Entrepreneur's Toolkit
Lillian Vernon

F
rom my years of experience
as an entrepreneur in the mail-order business, I have formulated my own guidelines for successful ventures. And I'm
pleased to pass my hard-earned insight on to others who are
thinking of starting businesses of their own—mail order or
not. All innovations originate with an idea—a vision. And
every idea that led somewhere was supported by solid
research and hard work. The successful entrepreneur learns
to be a practical visionary. In the following pages, I share
with you what I've learned about starting a business that
thrives and endures.

Are You an Entrepreneur?

If you're thinking of starting your own business, here are ten
questions you should ask yourself before you begin. Your
answers should help you make your decision.

1: Do you have the necessary commitment? To succeed,
you must feel passionate about the work you have cho-

sen. Lukewarm enthusiasm will not sustain you through the challenges you will face in a start-up business.

2: Are you prepared to work extremely hard? Launching your own business demands long hours of labor. Are you sure you want to give up a good part of your social life: your weekends, golf games, and vacations? For your developing business to succeed, you will need to focus all your energies on it.

3: Are you sure you have the mental stamina and concentration to meet the demands your project will impose on you? If your attention flags, you may jeopardize your venture.

4: Do you accept new ideas easily? Do you treat other people's ideas with respect? Are you able to make decisions right away? An entrepreneur must be open-minded, flexible, and able to respond to new ideas.

5: How do you deal with problem solving? Are you prepared to spend time analyzing a problem and finding a solution? Or do you just close your eyes and hope for the best? No matter how carefully you plan, you are bound to run into an unforeseen problem now and then. Be prepared to cope with such a situation.

6: Are you ready to commit to the long term? A company's success is never an overnight miracle. That is one reason you must be absolutely certain that you love your work—there will be a lot of it.

7: What back-up resources do you have? Banks and other financial institutions seldom lend money to start-up businesses. Will family members or friends invest in your company or tide you over during a rough patch?

8: Are you good at concentrating on detail? Often, no one but you will be able to take care of small items. An entrepreneur's life is not one of ideas alone.

9: Are you ready to sit down and write a careful analysis of your business prospects? Without a best case/worst case scenario to guide you through the first years, you may be in for an unpleasant surprise or two. Be aware and be prepared.

10: Are you by nature an optimist? Mistakes and setbacks are bound to occur. Can you—without getting derailed or discouraged—learn from your mistakes?

Keep It Simple

Visionaries that they are, entrepreneurs easily fall so in love with their ideas that they inadvertently neglect the practical steps that will get their businesses going. Until you have some experience, it's wise to tame your ambitions. If you're going into mail order, limit your first product list to two or three items. By starting on a small scale, you will find it simpler to define your product and its potential market and, consequently, to budget your costs. Don't distract yourself with unnecessarily complicated goals.

Let's suppose, for example, that you have been making leather skirts and vests as presents for your family and friends. Over the years, you have accumulated all the necessary equipment for what has essentially been a hobby. After years of sewing these leather products, you have mastered the skills, and you think you can turn your hobby into a real moneymaker. Should you stick with skirts and vests or should you branch out into other leather goods, which you have never before attempted? My answer to you is: concentrate on what you know you can do.

Learn the Numbers

Learn to read balance sheets and income statements. You don't need an MBA from Harvard or Stanford. Local community colleges often offer accounting courses that are great for business beginners. You may think you can sidestep accounting ABCs by hiring an accountant you trust. Wrong. Your accountant can calculate the figures, but you must interpret them so that you can respond quickly and appropriately. The numbers will tell you how a product is selling, but it will be up to you, as the owner of the business, to decide whether to increase production, change your advertising, or even drop that product.

Visionaries that they are, entrepreneurs easily fall so in love with their ideas that they inadvertently neglect the practical steps that will get their businesses going.

The tasks that face a new entrepreneur range from the ridiculous to the sublime, but they cannot be ignored. Other business courses provide instruction on how to incorporate your company, fill out business tax forms, and comply with regulatory requirements. For instance, if you want to market cosmetics, you need to know that the cosmetics industry is heavily regulated by federal agencies. And as far as forming your company is concerned, you will need to decide whether to incorporate or register as a sole proprietorship in your own name. If you use a different name for your business bank account, you will file a DBA (Doing Business As) form with your county clerk. When you learn how to calculate expenses and income, you will have to be ready to lay out a realistic budget. Some entrepreneurs are really uncomfortable with the nitty-gritty of balance sheets and income statements. Their strengths lie in their inventiveness, and they have trouble focusing on outlays and income. But those whose businesses survive and prosper are the entrepreneurs who learn how to read such barometers of progress.

In addition to night-school courses, such business magazines as *Inc.*, *Income Opportunities*, and *Small Business Opportunities* are great sources of timely help to many entrepreneurs.

Research Your Market

Before you take any large steps, you should certainly have examined the market for your product or service. Is there a need? Is the market near saturation? Assess your competition. Make sure you are offering something different from the rest. Is your product unique or sufficiently unusual to fill a neglected niche in the market?

Newspaper and magazine ads and mail-order catalogs can help you determine what's on the market. If you notice that the same ads for the same products appear consistently, you can be sure that there is a receptive market for them. Can you find room in that market alongside your competitors?

If there is a place for your merchandise, you should focus your investigation. If, for instance, you plan to sell to teenagers, then you need to research the demographics of the geographic area you wish to target. What is the average age of the population? Is it a high- or low-income area? SCORE—the initials stand for Service Corps of Retired Executives—is an organization whose members can probably give you good, solid advice. Its members are experienced businesspeople who can guide you to sources for the information you will need. SCORE's members aim to be mentors to entrepreneurs. Another good source of help may be your local bankers. It is their job to keep tabs on the local economy, and they can often help you figure out your best market.

Money! Money! Money!

A few people are lucky or smart enough to have money set aside for their new ventures. Others keep working at their salaried jobs until their new businesses can support them. There are still others, however, who can raise enough cash to support the start-up phases. You will need a realistic budget to show potential investors that you are a professional. When you are raising money, you are not only selling your business idea, you are also selling yourself. Banks and venture capitalists are not usually fertile sources of funds for new businesses or entrepreneurs with scant experience. A good track record is what makes the difference. As a beginner, your best bet is to persuade friends or family to help you out. You might approach the Small Business Administration about a loan guarantee, but that can develop into a long, drawn-out project. You might also find a partner with cash to invest, but entrepreneurs, as the originators of a business, often find it difficult to share decision making. So make absolutely sure that you can work together, and put everything in writing. . . .

Be a Miser

Do not spend your hard-earned cash on anything but true necessities—stylish office furnishings and the like are peripheral to the ultimate success of your business. Good letterhead and business cards, however, are worth the investment: they link you to the outside world.

There are bound to be cash crunches, and if you aren't sufficiently established to borrow money, you may be forced to close. At first, take only the bare minimum out of the business. An expensive vacation or a new car may be tempting, but the needs of your fledgling company must come first. Remember, without a cash reserve you probably won't survive. Inadequate cash is the chief cause of business failure.

Know Your Customers

Your customers are the key to the survival of your business. Their responses will keep your company afloat. Therefore, woo them with all your creative energies.

In a world filled with so many products of average quality, a good entrepreneur understands the value of well-made products. Most people are willing to pay a little more for a product that endures.

Your customers are the key to the survival of your business. . . . Therefore, woo them with all your creative energies.

Above and beyond every other consideration, be honest with your customers. The mail-order business once suffered badly from the dishonesty of some of its practitioners. Today, its reputation is good. Unless your customers trust you, they will certainly leave you. Your ads should never exaggerate. If your product is first-class, you certainly don't need to embellish it or try to mislead your customers.

Listen to your customers: they—better than most—can help you define your product. If people don't buy what you offer, you'd better recognize that you're on the wrong track. Response to a product is mail order's most reliable market research. If your product flops, redesign or drop it.

As your business grows, you will find it helpful to set up focus groups. They provide a direct approach to customer relations. Certain companies make a business of assembling focus-group meetings. You, the entrepreneur, sit, invisible, behind a one-way mirror through which you can observe—and videotape—the group's conversation. The group leader presents your product to the group and the participants react to it—for or against. Their comments may be revealing and should help to guide your merchandising. . . .

Remember, You Must Do It All

Here is where some entrepreneurs fail. They are filled with creative juices and total commitment to their business, but too often they don't understand that they must also be managers, administrators, even gofers—at least for a while. Some entrepreneurs do understand the art of management. As administrators they have to make sure that daily activities function smoothly. As gofers? Well, that includes everything from wrapping packages to making trips to the post office and brewing coffee. To run a fledgling mail-order company, the entrepreneur must curb his or her enthusiasm for expansion, learn to keep an analytical eye on the bottom line, and be prepared to undertake any job, no matter how menial. At the same time, entrepreneurs must never allow details to obstruct their overall vision for the business.

Growth Is a Two-Edged Sword

Suddenly your company takes off. You're enjoying a gratifying response to your catalogs; revenue is pouring in. Can you now sit back and simply let success happen? The answer is a firm no. Paradoxically, it's just at the moment of explosive growth that a mail-order company teeters on the brink of disaster. Rapid growth eats cash. You must hire staff to deal with the increase in business. You may have to make a significant investment in an up-to-date computer system. If fulfillment of orders lags because your system cannot handle the jump in customer orders, you really have no other choice.

This is the moment when a cash infusion is imperative. If your books show that you have run your company carefully, your cash flow can support interest payments, and you understand good business practices, your chances of getting a bank loan are good.

Focus, Focus, Focus

Peter Drucker, the father of modern management, has written that "concentration is the key to economic results." That's advice every entrepreneur should heed. Is the business on track? Has it deviated from its original purpose? Concentrate on the products you know how to sell and on the market with which you are familiar. Stay in the business you know. Develop short-term and long-term goals, but concentrate on present priorities.

By nature, entrepreneurs are optimists, but there is danger in a rosy, unrealistic assessment of a company's financial status and management. Self-confidence is a necessary character trait for someone starting a new business, but you must temper that enthusiasm with an ability to look at a situation with complete honesty and gritty objectivity. A strong streak of realism in the founding entrepreneur is key to success, especially in the early stages of business. Don't ignore flaws or mistakes, and never pretend that a false move wasn't important. Correct it. Self-deception can cover weakness only temporarily. Cold, dispassionate appraisals ward off future failures and lead instead to a flourishing business.

1996

In 1990, *Sports Illustrated* named Mark McCormack "The Most Powerful Man in Sports." Not bad for a guy who in 1960 founded his talent agency, International Management Group (IMG), with about $500 in start-up money. After attending William and Mary, and then Yale's law school, he was a mere associate at a Cleveland law firm when he started representing an unknown golfer named Arnold Palmer. Since then, he has reached out to represent more than just athletes with his roster including: Itzhak Perlman, Robert Dole, Lauren Hutton, among such sports stars as Chris Evert, Joe Montana, and Tiger Woods.

McCormack also became a pioneer in sports marketing, merchandising, licensing, and television programming, realizing early on that sports sell cable and satellite systems, not movies. One of IMG's subsidiaries, TWI, is the largest nonnetwork producer of sports programming, and IMG now has some 74 offices in 30 countries. The key, he says, is to stay on the cutting edge. "You go through fads. It happens with any product. In autos, you go through a speed phase, then through a safety phase, then through a style phase. It's a question of being where the consumer is going." Although McCormack would reap financial rewards, he has no interest in taking his company public. "Impressing Wall Street has become the Great American Corporate Pastime," he once wrote. "Long-term gains are sacrificed for short-term benefits. . . . It may just be too hard to try and run a company and keep the stockholders happy at the same time."

McCormack wrote the bestseller, *What They Don't Teach You at Harvard Business School.* In this book, he points to three qualities that champions, whether businessmen or athletes, are imbued with: "The first is the champions' profound sense of dissatisfaction with their own accomplishments . . . as a spur to greater ambition. . . . The second is an ability to peak their performances, to get themselves up for major tournaments and events. . . . Finally, it is their ability to put their opponents away." In *Starting Your Own Business,* he also advises that to be a winner you must commit to quality, stay in control, and be unconventional to be a winner.

For Entrepreneurs Only
Mark H. McCormack

Oone of the most dramatic cultural shifts over the last thirty years has been a redefinition of the Great American Dream. People are no longer content to work for two cars in the garage and a house in the right school district. Today the enjoyment of the job itself may be even more important than the enjoyment of its tangible rewards.

A lot of people are convinced that they will never achieve total job satisfaction by working for someone else. Given the choice of becoming chairman of their company or owner of their own small enterprise, they would opt for the latter. Starting a business has become the new Great American Dream.

As someone who started his own business, I can testify it is everything it is supposed to be. However, as John Mack Carter, editor-in-chief of *Good Housekeeping* magazine, once said to me, "Ninety-nine percent of the people in the world should be working for somebody." . . .

If everyone who has talked about starting a business actually went out and did it, the whole nation would be self-employed. But most people would rather fantasize about it than actually try to make it happen.

The first thing you have to do is examine your motives

and, in doing so, determine whether you are a dreamer or in the 1 percent.

If everyone who has talked about starting a business actually went out and did it, the whole nation would be self-employed. But most people would rather fantasize about it than actually try to make it happen.

If you want to be in your own business because you are "sick and tired of being told what to do," because you want more "freedom," or because you are unappreciated or under-valued, forget it. These are not reasons for starting a business; these are reasons for running away from your present job. If you want to "make a lot of money," that's probably not a great reason either. That is a fine and worthwhile goal, but if it is your prime motivation it is not going to be enough to get you through the lean years.

Before starting our company I was a lawyer with a prestigious Cleveland firm, but I knew I didn't want to spend the rest of my life practicing corporate law. I loved negotiating contracts, not drafting them, and the security of the paycheck wasn't going to be enough to keep me at the firm. I was cautious and apprehensive, but I was more intimidated by the thought of wasting my time and energy building a career I wouldn't enjoy. I couldn't afford not to give this new venture a try.

This, I believe, is at least part of the motivation of most people who successfully start a new business: a feeling that if they never tried they would always regret it. It is what gives you the momentum to get out the front door, to cut the corporate umbilical cord, and what makes it possible to keep going, even when everything else makes you feel like turning back. Starting a business is a financial and professional commitment. But even more, it is an emotional one.

I have a friend who, five years ago, started what has become a very successful apparel manufacturing firm. He told me recently that if he had known then what the first two years were going to be like he would have never gone through with it.

We never had it that rough, but I could relate to what he was saying. There are so many moments in starting a new business when the negatives outweigh the positives that any feelings of satisfaction are very small compensation. There are times when it is the emotional commitment alone that keeps you going.

Ask Hard Questions

Starting a new business is no time for self-deception, yet it is quite tempting to get caught up in your own notes, business plans, and prospectus, in the romance of your own words and numbers.

You should be able to "state your business" clearly and succinctly. Is it a "hard" idea (a new product or one that fills a clearly defined void) or a soft one (certain consulting businesses, an already crowded industry, or an idea that isn't all that indistinguishable)? The danger, at the beginning, is that everything is still fiction and that fiction can block your ability to ask the right questions and provide the necessary hard-core answers:

What Are the Connections?
How does the idea connect to the market, to the time, and ultimately to the people who will have to buy it? What edge does it have over existing competition?

I have seen many new consulting businesses go under because the idea wasn't very good in the first place. In fact, it amazes me how often people think someone will pay for their expertise when theirs is not an essential expertise to begin with and when they have no monumental personal success stories to convince potential customers otherwise.

If I were starting IMG today in the same way as I did twenty years ago, I'm not all that sure it would work, and I'm almost certain it would not have worked to the degree that it has. Arnold Palmer was the right person to represent at a time when the sport of golf was growing by leaps and bounds. A decade later, with our representation of Laver, then Newcombe, and then Borg, we were able to repeat this success in tennis, and now, again ten years later, we are positioned to do the same thing in running, though no stratospheric superstar has yet emerged in this sport.

In the first two instances, however—golf and tennis— while there is a sizable core market, there has been a flattening out of the growth curve.

If I were forced to repeat IMG's initial success today, I would have to wait for the right combination of factors—the connections—to come along: an emerging new participant sport; one with seeming whirlwind growth potential; and a superstar who embodied the essence of that sport.

Why Won't It Work?
What are the immediate problems likely to be encountered? Are they insurmountable, and if they aren't, how do I go about solving them?

What Makes Me Think I'm the One to Make It Work?
The new businesses that are most likely to succeed are the ones that have some relation to what you are already doing for someone else. In my case, IMG was not so much a new business as an extension of what I was already doing for a law firm.

Several years ago a friend of mine started a very successful photo reproduction business, which he later began to franchise. One of his franchisees, whose background was in lithography and design, was in trouble. After meeting with him in an attempt to straighten out the problem, my friend told me, "Just because our product is twice the quality at half the cost of our competition, he didn't think he had to go out and *sell* it. When I pointed this out to him, he said, 'Oh, but I'm not a *salesman!*' "

The new businesses that are most likely to succeed are the ones that have some relation to what you are already doing for someone else.

The dream of opening a restaurant, a frequent new business fantasy and a project with one of the highest mortality rates, is an example of why businesses fail because of the wrong aptitudes of their founders.

Restauranteering is a margin business which demands shrewd buying and a head for numbers. One should also be naturally gregarious and have a fondness for people and a willingness to work incredibly long hours.

Yet I have known a number of people who talked about opening a restaurant because they wanted "to do something different" and their sole qualification was that they were good cooks or liked to eat.

What Is the "Doability" Quotient?
We were once presented with a proposal for a World Air Race to coincide with the 1984 Olympics. The initial investment was around $3 million, and it was already partially funded. The concept was quite detailed and well presented. The only problem was that its execution required the cooperation of half the air forces in the world and an equal number of permissions to use air space.

Needless to say, the "doability" of this project was absurdly low. A good idea requiring reasonable expenditures may still be wrong because it is next to impossible to do, or, even if it can be done, the time required to execute it is far too high. Projects like this can have you working for fifty cents an hour.

Start Small and Keep It Simple

Many new venturists are preoccupied with all the money they are going to make rather than how they are going to go about making it. Set realistic goals by setting realistic steps—discrete, "doable" actions, each of which connects to the next one in some logical progression.

At some point you have to walk through the wall to get to the other side. But don't just "do it" until you have a good idea of what you do next. If you can't get "there" from "here" in a number of very specific steps, then you probably don't have a business yet.

I am a great believer that the more up-front money a new business requires the less chance it has of ever getting off the ground.

I'm prejudiced, of course, having started my own business with capitalization of less than $500. I am also aware there is a whole industry of venture capitalists who do nothing but fund new businesses. But the mere existence of this industry has created a kind of entrepreneurial myth—that there are all these people standing in line waiting for the opportunity to give you money and that you just haven't met any of them yet.

If and when you do, you will probably find that they aren't as eager to part with their capital as you might have anticipated, or, if they are, they will want to extract a large piece of the business in return for their faith.

Many new businesses never get off the ground, not because they were bad ideas, not because the people were wrong, but because the fund-raising efforts failed. Yet many of these new ventures, I believe, didn't actually require the capital the participants convinced themselves that they did.

If they had been willing to start small, to go back a few steps and start from further back, they could have given themselves a fighting chance.

Many of the great American success stories emerged from humble beginnings. If you are selling a service, a skill, or an expertise, how much more do you really need than a desk and a phone?

I can't overemphasize the importance of starting small and keeping it simple. When I began it would have been very easy to convince myself that it simply couldn't be done on any less than a million dollars. How could I represent the top three superstars in the booming sport of golf without a staff of seven or eight and at least a token presence in England and Japan? A million dollars, in fact, would have been helpful and certainly convenient. But it wasn't necessary.

Many of the great American success stories emerged from humble beginnings. If you are selling a service, a skill, or an expertise, how much more do you really need than a desk and a phone?

Be Flexible

Just as it is essential to know what business you're really in, it is equally important to be aware of what new business you *might* be in—of new directions and other opportunities which present themselves in the course of your doing business.

If you are tuned in and appropriately flexible, you may find that your original business is the tail and the new business it suggests is the dog. I have an acquaintance whose business is lecturing to corporations on effective writing techniques. He discovered that many companies were so impressed with his course they were willing to pay whatever he asked to write their corporate brochures for them. This has become a far more lucrative business for him than lecturing.

As I have mentioned, new divisions in our company grew out of our flexibility—the most obvious example being our marketing consulting division. We discovered in selling the services of our clients to various corporations that often our ideas as to how those clients should be used (how to position a particular athlete, what kind of campaign to structure, and so forth) were as valuable as the individual services themselves.

Share Your Success

In any business, new or otherwise, the idea is to take in more than you spend, but this is most painfully obvious when running a small, new operation.

Pay the people working for you as little as possible and sell them on yourself, on your vision, and on their future and the promise that as the company grows and becomes successful they will make more than they could ever make elsewhere. I don't think there is anything whatsoever wrong with this as long as you keep your end of the bargain.

If someone working for you makes a substantial contribution to the company, he or she is entitled to considerably more than the satisfaction of a job well done. In business, one's income acts as a scorecard. And while the company's overall profitability must be taken into consideration, that is going to matter a lot less to that executive than it does to you. Whether such tangible financial proof comes in the form of a raise, a bonus, or additional perks, it is important that people feel they are participating directly and commensurately with their contributions to the company.

Double Your Overhead

Several years ago I asked a friend who was starting a new business what he anticipated his overhead would be for the first year. He was starting small and financing it himself, and he replied in the neighborhood of $75,000. I told him at the time that he would be advised to double that amount.

People fail to take into account all the hidden costs in starting a new operation. It probably stems from a subconscious overzealousness to make the numbers work (or at least make them palatable). In any case, it's easy to forget about withholding and social security taxes when you've become accustomed to having them automatically deducted from your paycheck. Pens and pencils don't cost much, but supplying an office—even a small one—for a year adds up. Most businesses require some travel and entertainment, and that gets expensive. Utilities are extremely easy to underestimate. Last year our phone bill alone was over a million dollars. Over the years I've discovered that if you double the hard operating expenses you originally budgeted you'll end up with a reasonably accurate projection figure.

Recently I ran into the friend to whom I had given the advice. He told me that at the time, since I knew very little about his initial operation—what his rent and personnel were going to cost, and so on—he felt that it had been a fairly arrogant thing for me to say. "But when I closed the books at the end of the first year," he said, "the total was almost exactly $149,000."

Double It but Don't Triple It
Many people who want to start a new business but can never seem to get out the front door have convinced themselves

that it is just a matter of waiting until they have enough money saved up. For these people $10 million would be just short of what they need.

No amount of money in the bank is going to compensate for the loss of security that accompanies the loss of a paycheck.

In working out your business plan, if you find yourself allowing for the maximum conceivable amount in every expenditure column, your plan will probably never be more than a mental exercise.

Income First/Organization Later

Good organization is essential to any successful operation. But there is something nonsensical about a brand-new corporation sporting an impressive five-year plan before it has even earned its first dollar. It's one thing to know where you're headed (or where you'd like to be headed). It's another thing entirely to practice "cart before the horse" planning.

Prospectuses versus Real Life

I would be quite happy if I never saw another prospectus. The only ones who end up believing them are the people who write them.

The vast majority of the prospectuses I have been shown or invited to finance reveal a warped time perspective. It's amazing how many people forget to consider the importance of cash flow in planning their first year. If the first sale is made during the first week of business, very often the proceeds from the sale won't be collected for ninety days, and so on for the second and third sale, the result being, of course, that the initial float required for the business is actually a multiple of what's been projected on paper.

No amount of money in the bank is going to compensate for the loss of security that accompanies the loss of a paycheck.

It is also amazing how blatantly obvious people are in padding their numbers. Allowing for a reasonable margin of error in the numbers is one thing; assuming stupidity on the part of the person reading them is another. I've seen proposals for business ideas which I thought had merit but which have so turned me off by the projected income and expense numbers that I lost faith in the people doing the proposing. I suspect that these people don't believe in the business themselves and are merely trying to con someone into financing a big expense account.

I have also seen prospectuses in which I knew the principal had factored in a salary for himself that was more than he was presently making as an employee. I don't think asking someone to finance a $2 million proposal is a very effective or efficient way to go about getting a $50,000 raise. I know for sure I don't want to be the one giving it to him.

Motion versus Accomplishment

Being self-employed is the purest form of capitalism and the best way I know of getting paid what you are truly worth. It also demands a different mind-set, including an awareness that the number of hours you put in is only meaningful in terms of what you do with them.

Most successful entrepreneurs spend twenty-four hours a day either working or thinking about their business. But it is how they fill those hours that makes the difference between success and failure. The cliché is, "Don't work hard, work smart." The truth is, "Work hard, work long, *and* work smart."

On the positive side, in the beginning, when you are not having to deal with meetings and memos and all the other internal corporate time-takers, you can add, literally, four or five hours to every day. But if you don't spend them productively, not only will the difference be "deducted from your pay"; you might as well spend them writing memos to yourself.

Don't Have Partners

Not enough people examine their motives for taking on partners as carefully as they should. Often it is a safety-in-numbers factor. Naturally it is comforting to know that the buck doesn't necessarily stop at your desk. However, the problems of any partnership are likely to be a lot greater than the degree of security partnership is presumed to provide.

Obviously there are situations in which the strengths and weaknesses of each partner are well balanced and the business benefits from them. But the odds are a lot greater that the partnership itself will become the business's worst enemy, if only by limiting its flexibility. It is probably not an accident that some of the greatest entrepreneurial successes have been solo acts.

1984

PART III

Venture Capital, LBOs, and Going Public

"Bankers are the keepers of the keys to success for an entrepreneur," announces Domino's Pizza founder Tom Monaghan in the opening essay. He strongly advises establishing a relationship with local banks that is built on appreciation, which includes doing nice things for them even if you don't currently do business with them. As he warns, one bad word from a banker can kill your business. Another key, especially when starting a business, is to find banks that are used to dealing with private companies. Whether a start-up looking for seed money, or an existing business desiring to recapitalize, a common theme of all the authors is that you must think like a banker when approaching a banker. To understand what excites venture capitalists, the essays by Arthur Rock, who funded Intel's start-up among many others, and by Henry Kravis, whose firm was featured in the renowned business book *Barbarian at the Gates*, are must-reading. For example, Rock is looking for the would-be entrepreneur who asks, "How can I make this business a success?"—not "How do I make a fortune?" For many entrepreneurs, going public is a crowning event after years and decades of toil. However, as An Wang, founder of Wang Laboratories, warns, you must decide on your priority: money or control? The authors in Part III provide the pros and cons of the various ways to finance a company, which is so critical because cash flow is the life blood for every business.

TOM MONAGHAN
1937–

With no college education and no prior business experience, Tom Monaghan opened his first pizza joint at the age of 23. As of 1998, Domino's Pizza was operating over 6,100 stores around the world. Not bad for a kid who grew up in a Catholic orphanage and was kicked out of seminary school. However, while at school he read about Abraham Lincoln's life, which inspired him to dream big. Monaghan joined the Marine Corps in hopes of getting some college education paid for, and while there, he learned the importance of discipline, responsibility, and self-motivation. Unfortunately, an (ex)friend swindled him of his savings, so college remained a distant dream.

Instead, in 1960, he and his brother borrowed $500 to buy Domi Nick's Pizza. Again, he wanted to use the income to pay for college, but when his brother quit after a few months, Monaghan had to handle the store full-time. He reflected, "In that instant, I made the decision to commit myself heart and soul to being a pizza man." In those early years, Monaghan constantly visited the competition, and in one three-year period, he visited some 300 stores. In 1965, Domi Nick's became Domino's; in 1967, he issued his first franchise license. The next year a fire destroyed his commissary, almost wiping out the business, but he persevered, working 18-hour days, seven days a week.

"To me, the real substance of life and work is the constant battle to excel," he wrote. "I am determined to win, to outstrip our company's best performance and beat the competition." To do that Monaghan preached teamwork, and always looked to promote people who "have pizza sauce in their veins." If Monaghan was inspecting a store that happened to be shorthanded, he wouldn't hesitate to jump in. "A spot of pizza sauce on your suit during store inspections isn't a sign of bad grooming at Domino's; it's a badge of honor." Finding the funds to grow his empire has made Monaghan an expert in dealing with bankers. In *Bankers Are the Keepers of the Keys*, he makes it obvious as to why entrepreneurs have to be able to speak the bank's language to procure a loan; otherwise, you might as well be "speaking Swahili."

Bankers Are the Keepers of the Keys
Tom Monaghan

Bankers are the keepers of the keys to success for an entrepreneur. They can help you more than anyone else. They can also hurt you most, because all creditors and potential creditors check with the bankers first. A negative word from a banker can block all your plans. In times of trouble, it's doubly important to have a good relationship with your bank, because you must be able to write checks to stay in business.

But bankers speak the language of accounting and finance, and if you haven't been schooled in those mysterious tongues, as I was not, you can talk yourself blue in the face and they won't understand you. My inability to communicate with bankers was enormously frustrating to me. I always felt they were creating unnecessary barriers, trying to limit me.

Why? The only reason I could see was that I was too honest with them. I'd tell them what my problems were. I thought they'd appreciate my candor. My first inkling that this was not necessarily the case came after Doug Dawson joined us as chief financial officer and went with me to talk about arranging some financing. I told the banker the background of Domino's . . . To my surprise, after we left the man's office, Doug asked, "How come all you talked about was all that negative company history?"

109

109

"I didn't think it was negative," I said. "I think the fact that I was able to get out of trouble is positive. Bankers always think, What's he going to do if we loan him money and he gets in trouble? They are trained to think about the worst that can happen, and the message I was trying to get across to him was that if we do get into trouble, we're going to make a lot more effort than others would to get out of it. We're not going to throw in the towel."

It's important not to take bankers for granted when times are good. We work hard at letting bankers know we appreciate them and at keeping them abreast of what's going on in the company.

I still feel that way, but Doug's reaction certainly underscored the fact that I might have had an easier time getting money in the past if I'd not bothered to bring up a discussion of our problems. But I couldn't do that. I wanted to make sure the bankers understood that our company was honest, that the Golden Rule really was our operating philosophy.

I told Doug I wanted him to be sure and tell bankers the down side as well as the up about Domino's. I consider the truth cheap insurance. If we have problems, our banks won't be taken by surprise or panic on us because they lack information.

It's important not to take bankers for granted when times are good. We work hard at letting bankers know we appreciate them and at keeping them abreast of what's going on in the company. We have Bankers' Days, to which we invite a lot of bank officers; they come to Ann Arbor to play golf, tour our plant, and review our financials. Many of them represent banks we've never done business with, but we want a lot of banks out there to be familiar with us in case we need them. We pump them full of knowledge about Domino's.

The low point of my banking relationships was that time in 1970 when the president of the National Bank of Ypsilanti swore at me on the telephone and used barracks-room language to order me over to his office. I'd learned to use that lingo myself in the Marine Corps, and I gave it back to him in spades. That was a mistake because the resulting blot on our relationship was difficult to erase.

Part of the problem with my approach to bankers, I think, was that I was always begging for money. I'd go hat in hand, which probably gave them the impression I was weak. I can remember a humiliating discussion with another Ypsilanti bank president back in the early sixties. I wanted to borrow $250 to buy a used refrigerator for my DomiNick's store. I asked for the money in a very humble way.

"Nope," he said.

I begged and pleaded, but he just leaned back in his big leather swivel chair and tossed his head from side to side for emphasis as he slowly repeated, "Nope . . . nope . . . nope."

He gave me a long lecture about all these ratios, and what it amounted to was that I had to have $500 in the bank in order to borrow $250.

"If I had five hundred dollars," I asked, "why would I want to borrow two hundred fifty dollars from you? Why don't you take that refrigerator I want to buy as collateral?"

"Nope."

Needless to say, I switched banks at the first opportunity.

I couldn't help thinking of that Ypsilanti banker early in 1985, when Charles T. (Chick) Fisher III, chairman and president of NBD, the National Bank of Detroit, and his senior vice-chairman, Richard Cummings, came to my office and asked me to sit on NBD's board of directors. As I accepted, I thought, This is my revenge for being turned down on that refrigerator loan, and as Jackie Gleason used to say, "How sweet it is!"

Even as late as 1973, after we had recovered from the Crash and Operation Surprise was whittling away at our old debts, I was denied a bank loan. I'd been paying off notes with interest and hadn't borrowed any new money—I paid cash for everything. But I wanted to get two new Gremlins as delivery cars for $8,000, and I figured I could put half down and borrow the rest. So I explained my proposal to a vice-president of the bank, and his response was: "We don't need that kind of trouble." When the bank president found out about it, he called me up and got very diplomatic. He had good reason: Our average weekly balance was $100,000, and we were probably his bank's best customer. "You shouldn't be buying delivery vehicles with car loans," he said. "You should be buying a fleet of cars at commercial rates." I thanked him for his advice and paid cash for the two cars.

The financial guru who spoke the mysterious language of bankers and acted as my interpreter to them was John McDivitt, now president of TSM, Inc., and its divisions.

I met McDivitt in 1977 through a mutual friend who had retained his Financial Intermediaries, Inc., as a financial consultant. McDivitt's list of clients included some of the wealthiest people in Michigan, and I was impressed with his command of figures and the swift, aggressive way he dealt with issues. He was younger than me by about thirteen years, but we felt we had a lot in common, not the least of which was a strong religious background—my years in the orphanage and his growing up in a strict Irish-Catholic family. Anyway, we clicked, and John said he would help me figure out a better approach to financing Domino's operations. It must have been quite a contrast for him to leave the offices of a powerful industrialist in Detroit and walk into my Quonset-hut quarters. My desk was rickety, one leg propped up on a milk crate. I had a swivel chair with one caster that would pop out from time to time and drop me down with a jolt.

I'm not sure what John thought of Domino's potential, but I was fascinated by his response when I explained the hard times I'd had in dealing with bankers. He told me that when a company has difficulty raising money, it often means it has structural problems. Domino's certainly had such problems, and I was then in the midst of trying to sort them out. John helped solve one of these difficulties by recommending Doug Dawson. But his principal contribution was a penetrating financial analysis of our business and a presentation of it that allowed bankers to understand, for the first time, what a dynamic company they were looking at in Domino's.

John constructed an economic model of our business, demonstrating its organization from a single working unit, a store, through all the various levels of consolidation we had at that time. He analyzed the variable costs at the store level, showing how they changed and related to each other at differing volumes of business. These models became templates to overlay reports from the stores so we could interpret what was happening in them. I was fascinated by the logic of this exercise and how it clearly demonstrated the economic functioning of our stores as if they were machines with observation windows cut into them to show their working parts.

John then drew a numerical picture in which he channeled the cash tributaries produced by all our operating units into a single stream. Collectively, this grew into a broad river of money. I wasn't surprised. I knew what a powerful cash producer Domino's was, but this was the first time I had seen it depicted so objectively. Now I understood what John meant when he talked about explaining our business in economic terms.

No wonder bankers had failed to appreciate my passionate appeals for money. I might as well have been speaking Swahili, because the words I was using to describe our business simply weren't meaningful to them. The persuasive power of John's economic model was immediately self-evident.

1986

CONRAD HILTON
1887–1979

The founder of the Hilton Hotels Corporation knew both poverty and glamor. Conrad Hilton grew up in New Mexico in the same "primitive adobe" that housed his father's general store and five spare rooms rented to transients. He later married and divorced Zsa Zsa Gabor and became the proud owner of the Waldorf-Astoria. From early on, Hilton set high goals; for example, he hoped to attend Dartmouth, but the financial panic of 1907 nearly destroyed the family business and he found himself at the New Mexico School of Mines for two years. Hilton's first business venture was managing the Hilton Trio, a group of musically inclined ladies (including his sister), but it flopped. He then worked for a bank and took over management of his father's store in 1915.

His father, however, kept meddling. Hilton reflected, "Perhaps that is why, in later years, when I had carefully selected a man for a job I left him completely alone, knowing that I had either been right in my selection or I had been wrong." After a stint in the Army during World War I, Hilton desperately wanted to be an independent banker, so an old friend advised him to seek his fortune in Texas. When Hilton tried to find a hotel bed his first night in Cisco, Texas, he couldn't, and he knew immediately what to buy—that very hotel. The owner, who was half-crazed to get into oil, gave him one week to come up with $40,000. Feverishly, Hilton scraped up money from friends and relatives, and spent his first night as a hotel owner sleeping in the office and dreaming of a chain.

"The Mobley in Cisco, my first love, was a great lady," he wrote. "She taught us the way to promotion and pay, plus a lot about running hotels. She was indestructible, the ideal hotel to practice on." By 1921, he had added two more hotels. Then in 1924, he broke ground on building his first million-dollar hotel. Finding the funds was just as tricky as when he bought the Mobley, and in *A Million-Dollar Mountain and a Red Hat,* Hilton provides both a dramatic and humorous story of how he raised the money. "There is nothing tame about raising a million dollar building from a standing start," he said.

A Million-Dollar Mountain and a Red Hat
Conrad Hilton

A man's first million dollar deal may come under the heading of Big Business. To me it spelled Big Adventure — comparable to sailing around Cape Horn, or climbing Mount Everest. Anyone who brushes business off as a tame occupation revolving around a conference table and poring over figures with corpulent gentlemen, is just plain wrong.

There is nothing tame about raising a million dollar building from a standing start.

If you climb Mount Everest, no matter how carefully you plan, anything can happen. Your ice axe slips, your oxygen gives out. A concealed crevasse swallows you up. Well, that's about the way it was building my first Hilton Hotel.

I hung over precipices, gained a promontory only to have my rope break, got within sight of the top and, before I could plant my flag, all but perished for lack of money, the lifeline used to build my mountain ahead of me, one floor at a time.

Story by story, I fought my way toward the summit — and there was never a dull moment.

Halfway up I met a girl, *the* girl this time, and all but lost her when it looked like I'd crash to the bottom, pulling my self-made mountain down on top of me.

No, if you want the dull, tame life, if you have no compelling dreams or head for excitement, stay on the ground, away from big business.

This first mountain I decided to climb is a pretty good example of the high adventures that have gone on, one after another, in my business life.

I began with some long talks with St. Joseph, that Patron of Builders, and then I went around and talked to a firm of architects. The exact spot for my new dream girl stood on the corner of Main and Harwood in the Dallas business district and I had optioned it from the owner, George W. Loudermilk, onetime liveryman and undertaker, now real estate rich.

Anyone who brushes business off as a tame occupation revolving around a conference table and poring over figures with corpulent gentlemen, is just plain wrong.

The architects estimated they could put my new hotel on that site for exactly the sum I had foreseen, one million. I do believe that under his breath the man may have said, "or more." I now know all estimates have that inherent possibility. But I wasn't listening.

"Go ahead with the blueprints," I ordered. And then I set out to raise a million dollars.

It wasn't easy.

My first move was positively naïve. An advertisement in a New York paper caught my eye: "Need money? See us. We will finance you." So off I went to New York. The company sold me an insurance policy and lent me exactly nothing.

Back in Dallas I decided I'd better do a little more thinking and a lot more praying. I was around the impressive cathedral on Ross Avenue so much I suspect Father Diamond thought I was permanently unemployed. I figured I could probably realize $100,000 on my own, one-tenth of what I needed, and two-tenths more from my regular backers. But what was three-tenths of a million? And there was nothing to invest it in at this point but a wild dream. If I raised the money and gave it to Loudermilk I'd have nothing left to erect a building.

The more I thought, the more I decided that Loudermilk was the key man in this deal. I had an idea, a startling idea, but it was worth a try. I worked the whole thing out in my head, and then carefully thought up all the possible objections. Loudermilk was known as a difficult fellow and old-fashioned in his ways. My idea, while beginning to be accepted in the East, would be brand new to him. And Porter Lindsley, Loudermilk's real estate advisor, was a hard man to do business with. I'd need all the answers.

When I thought I had them, I broached Loudermilk.

"I'm going to pick up that option," I announced, "and build a million dollar hotel."

Loudermilk beamed. He allowed Dallas needed a new hotel. That was just the sort of talk I wanted to hear.

"Of course a hotel like that is going to tie up all my capital, so instead of buying your land, I want to lease it. . . ."

Loudermilk beamed no longer. He snorted. "You're crazy. You're not about to build anything on land I own."

"Lease it," I continued, "on a ninety-nine-year lease. It's really a sale in installments. . . ."

"I'm not Methuselah," Loudermilk shouted. "I won't *live* ninety-nine years."

"And you go right on owning the land. If I don't pay, you get the land back. . . ." My man was beginning to look interested, so I gave him my biggest gun. "And my building, too."

"I'd own the land . . . and the building, too," he repeated. He thought a minute. "I'll talk it over with Lindsley."

Lindsley had heard of the ninety-nine-year lease practice. He worked out a figure of $31,000 a year, a total of some three million dollars, all of which would be protected by my hotel.

Loudermilk decided he'd been very clever. I agreed with him. Then I discharged a cannon. "I'd just like that lease to have a clause authorizing me to float a loan on the real estate," I said quietly.

You could have heard Loudermilk's yelp out on the Panhandle. But eventually I got it. Not enthusiastically, I'll admit. I recall his saying something about getting rid of me while he still had his gold cuff links, but I got that all-important clause.

I had something now to build my mountain on and I began stringing the lifeline that would carry me to the top. I had the land. I still needed the million. I went to St. Louis where W. L. Hemmingway, president of the National Bank of Commerce, agreed to lend me $500,000—to be paid in installments as each story of the building was finished, but with the understanding that at all times I must have enough money on hand to finish the building or they would stop advancing money.

Hemmingway was talking turkey. But I was thinking positively. I was halfway home. So far, so good. I picked up another $50,000 from my friend Bob Thornton, who was now with the Mercantile National Bank. When it came time to accept bids on the building, I borrowed another $150,000 from the contractor. Seven-tenths of a million. Now that three-tenths I figured I could get, would lasso the top for me.

I put up my own hundred thousand first. Harry Siegel, one of the partners from whom we had originally gotten the Waldorf, bought it back as sole owner-manager. Cisco was returning after her boom years to the cowtown she originally was and we let the Mobley go. I raised my hat in salute to my first and most gallant "dowager." In the fashion of businessmen I have been true to her, for I've used everything she ever taught me. But I had a new love now and that hundred thousand represented everything I had, plus all I could safely borrow on existing hotels.

Once my capital was up, I was in a position to invite my friends in. I have never once in my life asked anyone to follow me financially into an adventure when I was not willing to take the lead. And I did then exactly what I do today. I wrote to or talked with people I knew were interested in investing and told them what I had to offer. The $200,000 of venture capital I needed came in quickly. There were old backers among them, including my mother and Ira Casteel.

On July 26, 1924, for the first time, I spaded up a bit of earth and threw it over my shoulder, breaking ground for a Hilton Hotel.

1957

IRENE SMITH

No, Irene Smith is not Henry Ford or Lillian Vernon, but she did parlay her $2,500 in seed money into a $500,000 business five years later, which is nothing to sneeze at. Smith is the typical entrepreneur, fighting it out in the trenches, that most will relate to, and as author of *Diary of a Small Business,* in which she takes a candid look at her experiences, she provides a clear voice for all entrepreneurs. Back in 1977, she founded The Business Center, which provided indispensable services such as word processing, copying, graphic design, printing, and more to other businesses. Her education, however, gave little hint of her becoming an entrepreneur: an English degree from Barnard, and a masters in history from the University of Madrid. Then, in 1977, at age 43, she was fired as an executive secretary and was out of a job for the first time ever. She reflected, "During the last ten years of my working life, I had fought an all-encompassing sense of futility."

Before founding her company, Smith conducted her own informal market survey by looking in the yellow pages and walking around her neighborhood to find potential customers. Then she surveyed the potential competition to see what services they offered and how they handled their customers. From her research she developed a concise mission statement: "My business is designed to be flexible, providing entrepreneurs, small retail and service businesses, and restaurants with fast, professional support services and access to the advanced technology that these small businesses could not make cost-effective themselves." The next step was to estimate start-up expenses and a 12-month budget.

After only four months, she actually almost went under from too much business. She was so busy selling that she hadn't focused on the company's infrastructure to handle the volume. Therefore, she convinced her husband to take two weeks' vacation from his job to help out. "Starting a business is fun; managing it is hellish," she said. The same is true for financing it. She advises finding a bank that works regularly with small businesses. In the following selection, she illustrates some tricks to funding a start-up without a bank, and she explains why phenomenal growth can hurt your chances to win more financing.

Money: The Truth about Financing a Growing Small Business
Irene Smith

When you are in business for yourself, you think about money all the time; if you can sleep, you dream about money, when you are awake, you worry about money.

Businesses don't fail for want of money; they fail because their owners lack the management skills to find money and use it as a creative tool for the growth and health of their businesses. If you tackle the problem when you are first planning your business and deal with it in a realistic and informed way from the beginning, you will have won half the battle.

When you are in business for yourself, you think about money all the time; if you can sleep, you dream about money, when you are awake, you worry about money.

When my business was two-and-a-half-years old, I realized that I needed additional working capital. As a total neophyte in the area of finance, I grasped at the most obvious straw and assumed that a Small Business Administration loan would be relatively easy to obtain.

I gathered all the necessary information together (a staggering accomplishment) and made an appointment with my local bank to present the application. I was under the naive misconception that the growth and survival of my business demonstrated a certain management ability on my part.

The bank manager flipped immediately to the section of my application containing financial statements covering the complete life of my business. It took about thirty seconds and a little head shaking before he handed the whole mess back to me and informed me that it would be a waste of my time and the bank's to process my loan application. "What you need, Irene, is a substantial capital investment, not debt financing," he said. "We would be taking an enormous risk in lending your company money . . . and, though I know you find it hard to believe, we would probably be doing you a disservice."

I was furious. I had accomplished a miracle through faith, iron determination, and incredibly hard work. I believed that I had the nucleus of a multimillion-dollar, nationwide service industry. I was well aware of my need for additional capital. But seeking outside investment is a lengthy and expensive process—and I needed working capital now!

I decided to approach the First Women's Bank of New York, believing that it might be more receptive to a woman entrepreneur. How wrong I was. The meeting was unpleasantly similar to that with my own bank manager. The loan officer immediately opened my application to my financial statements, took a look at them, and proceeded to tell me the financial facts of business life in a manner that was clear to the point of brutality.

In fact, I *had* accomplished a miracle. My financial statements reflected a business that had been grossly undercapitalized from the day of its birth. They reflected a business that had experienced phenomenal growth. They showed excessively high labor costs, a very low gross-profit margin, and current liabilities that outweighed current assets by a margin of four to one. In short, they reflected an undercapitalized business, growing too rapidly, with insufficient controls—a business that could go right down the drain at any minute; a business to which nobody would risk lending money.

That experience marked the beginning of my education in business finance. As I crept out of the First Women's Bank, disappointed and humiliated, I felt desperate. It was clear that the odds of borrowing money for the short-term working capital needs of my company were exactly zero.

The next day, after I'd slept off my pessimism, I sat down with my bookkeeper to draw up a battle plan. I knew that, in addition to the immediate problem of survival, we were going to have to manage a lot more tightly before anyone else would be interested in lending to, or investing in, the company. At the same time, we were going to have to use the resources presently available to us to increase revenues to keep us going.

The lessons we learned, while bitter, were invaluable. It was then I realized that, of all the gaps in my knowledge, my ignorance of the world of banking and business finance was the most threatening to the future of my business, and I set about to remedy the situation.

One of the facts of business life that the loan officer at First Women's Bank pointed out was that my financial statements showed that the business had experienced a small loss every year. She further stated that she assumed that my accountant had deliberately structured these losses to lessen the amount of corporate income taxes we had to pay (she was right). She went on to say that she saw this situation all the time and, of all the mistakes a small business owner and an accountant can make, this is probably the most foolish. The savings thus effected are a high price to pay for the negative results—you have financial statements that demonstrate conclusively that you cannot manage your business for profit. Once those financial statements are issued by your accountant, they are, for all practical purposes, irrevocable.

The realization dawned, as I assessed my meeting at the First Women's Bank, that I would have to work hard for at least another year and possibly two before I would be able to produce acceptable proof, via my financial statements, that I could manage my business profitably. (That's when I fired my accountant.) Until I could do so, it was very unlikely that I would be able to obtain working capital from any outside source. I almost gave up at that point. The alternative, how-ever—having to go back to work for someone else—made me decide to stick it out.

Of all the gaps in my knowledge, my igno-rance of the world of banking and business finance was the most threatening to the future of my business.

I began then to do what I should have done before. I started the long process of learning about business financing and how to obtain it. It was then that my own financial state-ments became meaningful to me, and I realized the vital importance of generating timely management information from my own records.

I came to the conclusion that seeking outside financing, whether debt financing (borrowing money) or equity capital financing (the sale of stock), is not a simple business prob-lem. It is a marketing problem. Just as you must market your product or service to make it appealing to your poten-tial customers, you must present your business to potential lenders or investors in a way that will make it an attractive investment for them. You must speak eloquently in a lan-guage to which they will respond—and that language is profit.

What, in the eyes of a lender, makes your business cred-itworthy?

- You as owner or manager must demonstrate good character.
- You must show ability to operate a business successfully.
- You should have invested enough capital in your business so that, with the loan, the business can operate on a sound financial basis.
- You must show that the proposed loan is of such sound value, or that it can be fully collateralized, as to assure payment.
- You must show that the past earnings record and future prospects of the firm indicate ability to repay the loan and other fixed debt, if any, out of profits.
- You must be able to provide, from personal resources, sufficient funds to have a reasonable amount at stake in the event of possible losses, particularly during the early stages of a new venture.

Seeking outside financing, whether debt financing (borrowing money) or equity capital financing (the sale of stock), is not a simple business problem. It is a marketing problem.

When you approach your banker, the Small Business Administration, or any other potential source of debt financing, equip yourself to speak their language. Have a copy of your business plan available (if you don't have a business plan, you have already demonstrated your ineptitude as a manager). Be prepared to give substantial proof that the money they loan you can be repaid and demonstrate how it will be repaid. People who are in the business of lending money are in business to make a profit, just as you are. They will not hand over their stock-in-trade (money) without reasonable assurance that the transaction will be profitable, any more than you would supply your customers with goods or services without reasonable assurance of payment.

True entrepreneurs are innovative in their approach to obtaining capital for their businesses. Department of Commerce statistics show that only 10 percent of new business start-ups are financed with venture capital. The other 90 percent are financed by the guts, creativity, and faith of their founders. Some of my customers have used various sources to obtain seed capital for their new companies.

If you don't have a business plan, you have already demonstrated your ineptitude as a manager.

Credit cards. While working as an executive for a brokerage firm, one of my customers decided that she would go into business for herself. Still employed at a fairly high salary, she proceeded, with malice aforethought, to push her credit rating as high as she could. She obtained bank credit cards from several different banks and proceeded to use them lavishly, always charging slightly more than her approved credit limited and always repaying promptly. She took out a bank loan she didn't need, and repaid it in a timely manner. Then she took out another, larger bank loan, and repaid that. Over a period of a year, she was able to expand her credit so that she had immediately available sources of cash amounting to $100,000. Supplementing this were her charge cards (not good for obtaining cash, but available for the purchase of furniture, office equipment, and supplies).

My customer was then ready to start her business. She drew on her available sources of cash as needed, using (and successfully repaying) about $75,000. She charged all furniture and office fixtures (about $25,000) and repaid that money over a period of two years. Unorthodox, but it worked for her!

Personal collateral. Another customer, in the banking business, stumbled across an opportunity to acquire the patent for an improved process for performing certain kinds of blood tests. Convinced that a fortune awaited her if she could manufacture and market the process, she bought the rights to the patent. After developing her business plan, she went to her bank with a copy of the patent, her business plan, and a list of her assets. She was able to obtain a personal loan sufficient to provide the seed money she needed to start up, fully collateralized by her own assets. However, she obtained an agreement from the bank that, as soon as she could demonstrate to the bank's satisfaction that the business was established and on its way to profitable operation, the loan would be transferred to her new company.

Within twelve months she was able to do that, and when her company had successfully repaid the loan, she obtained another loan for expansion, this time without any collateral other than the assets of her company and her record of success as its manager.

Bankers are human too, and a banker who has been given ongoing information about the state of your business is much more likely to have developed a favorable bias toward it.

This new business owner, because she came out of the banking field, was particularly well-equipped to speak the language of the lender whose money she needed. She admits that she orchestrated her whole approach in order to (a) get the seed money she needed by borrowing, (b) free up her personal assets as soon as possible, and (c) quickly establish a record of creditworthy performance for her new company that would enable her to finance continued growth by being able to borrow money when she needed it.

The bank is not particularly interested in the success or failure of your business. The bank's concern is whether the money it is lending is safe and will be repaid.

She feels that it is very important to establish an ongoing relationship with the bank where you do business, informing the manager about the state of your company and your plans for it. If you are a good enough manager to meet your own forecasts and fulfill your plans, and you have let your bank manager know this, you have encouraged the executive who makes the recommendations for or against loan applications to respond favorably to your requests. She stresses that bankers are human too, and a banker who has been given ongoing information about the state of your business is much more likely to have developed a favorable bias toward it.

This woman also stresses the importance of understanding your banker's point of view. The bank is not particularly interested in the success or failure of your business. The bank's concern is whether the money it is lending is safe and will be repaid. Even when this ability to repay a loan is demonstrated, the bank will require some kind of protection in the form of collateral — either your own assets or the assets of your business.

Financing the start-up of one business by generating revenues from another business. One of my favorite customers is a tiny brunette dynamo, having qualifications she knew she could apply successfully as a consultant. Her problem was that she didn't want to be in the consulting business. She wanted to start a specialized publishing company and write books, magazine articles, and columns (preferably syndicated) about the area in which she was both vitally interested and especially qualified—gourmet food. Unfortunately, she had almost no tangible personal assets—no stocks, bonds, real estate, or other investments, and only a minuscule savings account.

Nevertheless, she is on the way to achieving her goal. She is supporting herself and raising initial financing for her future publishing company from her current consulting-business income. She simultaneously formed two separate companies: a sole proprietorship for her restaurant-consultant business and a corporation for her embryonic publishing company. She formed the two companies on the advice of her accountant for two reasons: because a greater tax liability is involved in the publishing venture than in her consultant business and because monetary returns from her publishing venture are relatively remote.

1982

Who better to get a perspective on the entrepreneurial adventure from than one of the greatest venture capitalists. Arthur Rock grew up in Rochester, New York, where his father owned a candy store. After graduating from Harvard University, he joined an investment banking firm in New York. In 1957, a new business proposal from eight disenchanted engineers (who happened to include Gordon Moore and Robert Noyce, the future cofounders of Intel) came to his attention—they were looking to start their own semiconductor company. Rock peddled it around, looking for money, and found a supporter in Fairchild Camera and Instrument Company, who put up $1.5 million.

In 1961, he cofounded the Davis & Rock venture capital firm; today, it's simply Arthur Rock & Co. In 1968, Moore and Noyce again entered the picture and Rock helped them finance the founding of Intel, which, needless to say, became a major bonanza. Another winner was Apple Computer; in 1978, he bankrolled Steven Jobs and Steven Wozniak for a mere $57,400—two years later his investment was worth $14 million. When helping fledgling companies, Rock always makes sure stock options are spread around to keep the young talent on board. He not only invests money, but becomes active in the company's management; for example, he served as a director for Intel and Apple. By the mid-1980s, Rock was worth more than $200 million, but he said, "I don't like to count my money. That isn't what turns me on."

Rather than take on numerous clients, Rock has invested mostly his own money in start-ups so he remains free to do as he pleases. He searches for ideas, people, and products that are key to new industries with lots of potential. "I want to build great companies. That's how I get my kicks. I look for people who want the same thing." Toward that end, he finds the most important section of a business plan to be the resumes, not the financial projections; for, as he writes in the following selection, "Frankly, how anyone can figure out what sales and earnings and returns are going to be five years from now is beyond me."

Strategy versus Tactics from a Venture Capitalist
Arthur Rock

As a venture capitalist, I am often asked for my views on why some entrepreneurs succeed and others fail. Obviously, there are no cut-and-dried answers to that question. Still, a few general observations about how I evaluate new businesses should shed some light on what I think it takes to make an entrepreneurial venture thrive and grow.

Over the past 30 years, I estimate that I've looked at an average of one business plan per day, or about 300 a year, in addition to the large numbers of phone calls and business plans that simply are not appropriate. Of the 300 likely plans, I may invest in only one or two a year; and even among those carefully chosen few, I'd say that a good half fail to perform up to expectations. The problem with those companies (and with the ventures I choose *not* to take part in) is rarely one of strategy. Good ideas and good products are a dime a dozen. Good execution and good management—in a word, good *people*—are rare.

To put it another way, strategy is easy, but tactics—the day-to-day and month-to-month decisions required to manage a business—are hard. That's why I generally pay more attention to the people who prepare a business plan than to the proposal itself.

Another venture capitalist I know says, somewhat in jest, that the first thing he looks at in a business plan is the financial projections. Frankly, how anyone can figure out what sales and earnings and returns are going to be five years from now is beyond me. The first place I look is the résumés, usually found at the back. To me, they are the essence of any plan. (Maybe no one reads the middle section!)

Good ideas and good products are a dime a dozen. Good execution and good management—in a word, good *people*—are rare.

I see the plan as really an opportunity to evaluate the people. If I like what I see in there, I try to find out more by sitting down and talking with the would-be entrepreneurs. I usually spend a long time on this. (Unless their first question is "How much money am I going to get?" Then the interview is very short.) I don't talk much during these meetings; I'm there to listen, I want to hear what they've got to say and see how they think.

Some of the questions I ask have little to do directly with the particular business under discussion: Whom do they know, and whom do they admire? What's their track record? What mistakes have they made in the past, and what have they learned from them? What is their attitude toward me as a potential investor—do they view me as a partner or as a necessary evil? I also ask specific questions about the kind of company they want to develop—say, whom do they plan to recruit, and how are they going to do it?

I am especially interested in what kind of financial people they intend to recruit. So many entrepreneurial companies make mistakes in the accounting end of the business. Many start shipping products before confirming that the orders are good, or that the customers will take the product, or that the accounts are collectible. Such endeavors are more concerned about making a short-term sales quota than about maximizing the long-term revenue stream.

Granted, the pressure on new businesses to make sales quotas is strong. And that's precisely why the company needs a very, very tough accounting department. Otherwise, it will get into trouble. I always ask what kind of chief financial officer the entrepreneurs plan to bring on board. If they understand the need for someone who will scrutinize the operation closely and impose appropriate controls, they are more likely to be able to translate their strategy into a going concern.

I usually can tell the difference between people who have that fire in their stomachs and those who see their ideas primarily as a way to get rich.

This may go without saying, but I also look at a person's motivation, commitment, and energy. Hard work alone doesn't bring success, of course, but all the effective entrepreneurs I've known have worked long, hard hours. And there's something more than the number of hours: the intensity of the hours. I think of two software entrepreneurs I know who are going at 110 miles per hour, 18 hours per day, 7 days a week. And they have instilled their intensity and their belief in the business in all the people who work for them.

Belief in the business, clearly, is critical. If you're going to succeed, you must have a burning desire to develop your idea; you must believe so firmly in the idea that everything else pales in comparison. I usually can tell the difference between people who have that fire in their stomachs and those who see their ideas primarily as a way to get rich. Far too many people are interested in building a financial empire instead of a great company.

I want to build great companies. That's how I get my kicks. I look for people who want the same thing.

At a presentation I gave recently, the audience's questions were all along the same lines: "What are the secrets to writing a business plan?" "How do I get in touch with venture capitalists?" "What percentage of the equity do I have to give to them?" No one asked me how to build a business! And here's a question that both amused me and bothered me: "How do I get rid of the venture capitalists after they've made their investment?"

I'm looking for entrepreneurs who ask, "How can I make this business a success?"—not "How do I make a fortune?" And I prefer someone who *wants* me to play a role in the enterprise's decision making. Obviously, when they come to me entrepreneurs are interested in getting my money. Many have the attitude, "Uh oh, is this guy going to want to come to staff meetings and open his big mouth?" But they should realize that I can be a resource for them in more ways than one. I've been around for a long time; there just aren't many business problems that I haven't seen before. And most entrepreneurs can use all the help they can get in developing and implementing the tactics that will make them successful in the long run.

When I talk to entrepreneurs, I'm evaluating not only their motivation but also their character, fiber. And the issue I set the most store by is whether they are honest with themselves. It's essential to be totally, brutally honest about how well—or how badly—things are going. It's also very difficult.

Too many businesspeople delude themselves. They want so much to believe that they listen only to what they want to hear and see only what they want to see. A good example is a top executive in the parallel-processing industry; he believed his engineering people when they told him the product would be ready on time, and he believed his marketing people when they told him how much they could sell. So he developed a sales staff and doubled the size of the plant and built up inventories before he had a product to sell. The computer was late because of some last-minute bugs, and he was stuck with it all. The first 98% of designing a computer is easy; the bugs always come up in the last 2%. Fixing the problems took time, which ate up all kinds of overhead. And when he was finally ready, he couldn't meet the company's forecasts—which had been unrealistic from the beginning.

I'm looking for entrepreneurs who ask, "How can I make this business a success?"—not "How do I make a fortune?"

This story illustrates well my thesis that strategy is easy, execution is hard. The company's product was two years ahead of its competition. Execution of the idea, however, was terrible. That the strategy was good is obvious now; several other manufacturers have entered the field and are doing very well. But the company has lost the competitive advantage it would have enjoyed if its management had been better.

I can cite a similar example, also from the computer industry. The three people who started the company were the president, the manager of the software division, and the manager of the hardware division. The two managers kept telling the president that things were going swimmingly, and he wanted to believe what they said. Then one day, faced with an order the company couldn't fill, the software division manager called the president, who was out of town, and let forth a blast that in essence said, "We've been making a lot of mistakes we haven't told you about. We're at least a year behind."

Now, that's a ridiculous situation; the president should have known the status of product development. He had enough background in the field, and he knew the managers well enough that he shouldn't have been caught by surprise. But he didn't look closely enough, and he didn't ask the right questions. In the meantime, the business had a rather large marketing and sales force. Then the question became whether to keep the sales force (which by this time was fully trained but doing nothing) or to let everyone go and wait for the software to be finished. If the latter, they'd have to hire and train a new sales force—a no-win situation either way.

Failure to be honest with yourself is a problem in any business, but it is especially disastrous in an entrepreneurial company, where the risk-reward stakes are so high. As an entrepreneur, you can't afford to make mistakes because you don't have the time and resources needed to recover. Big corporations can live with setbacks and delays in their "skunkworks"; in a start-up situation, you'd better be right the first time.

After being honest with yourself, the next most essential characteristic for the entrepreneur is to know whom to listen to and when to listen, and then which questions to ask. Sometimes CEOs listen only to what they want to hear because of fear of the truth; in other cases, it's because they are arrogant or have surrounded themselves with yes-men/women. A lot of managers simply will not accept criticism or suggestions from other people; they demand absolute loyalty from their subordinates and call disloyal anybody who tries to tell them something they don't want to hear.

It's usually easy to spot this trait by the way someone talks with outsiders about the organization. If an entrepreneur says, "This guy's lousy and that one doesn't know what she's doing, but I saved the company"—or if he or she explains how brilliantly he or she performed at his last job, in spite of being fired—I get wary. That kind of attitude is a red flag, like the statement, "I'll be honest with you": you know you're not getting the whole story.

To be sure, there's a thin line between refusing to accept criticism and sticking to your guns. Good entrepreneurs are committed to their ideas. In fact, I knew one company was in trouble when the CEO accepted almost everything I told him without argument or question. But some people have an almost perverse desire to prove to the world that their way is the right way—and the only way. I remember one CEO who had a great strategy—an idea for a unique computer architecture—but who refused to accept any advice on anything from anyone, including potential customers. He ended up with a product that had to be totally re-engineered and a weak staff. The company is now under new management and may be able to make something out of what is still a good idea, but the CEO's tunnel vision sure stalled it at the starting gate.

After being honest with yourself, the next most essential characteristic for the entrepreneur is to know whom to listen to and when to listen, and then which questions to ask.

Another important quality—one that also has to do with taking a hard look at oneself and one's situation—is to know when to bring in skills from outside and what kind of skills.

As I see it, a company's growth has three stages. During the start-up, the entrepreneur does everything himself: he or she is involved in engineering the product, making sales calls, and so on. After a while, the company grows and others are hired to do these things—a vice president of sales, a vice president of engineering—but they report directly to him, and he or she still knows everything that's going on.

The company reaches the third stage when it hits, say $100 million to $200 million in sales. At that point, it's just too large for the president to be involved in all the doings. More management layers are in place and a fleet of executive vice presidents, and it now calls for entirely different skills to run the company than it did during its infancy. The president has to get work done by delegating it to other people and get information through two or more organizational layers.

The ideal would be a president who could manage a company at all three stages, starting the business from scratch and staying involved until retirement. Alfred Sloan at General Motors and Tom Watson at IBM were able to do just that, and the leaders of Teledyne and Intel have done it more recently.

But not all entrepreneurs can manage a large company. And many do not want to. Some people who relish business start-ups are simply not interested in running a formal, multi-tier organization. After Cray Computer grew to a fairly good size, for example, Seymour Cray wanted to get back to designing computers. Similarly, Apple Computer's Steve Wozniak and Steve Jobs (at least in the early stages) recognized that their genius was technical and promotional, not managerial, and that they needed experienced, professional managers to oversee their company's growth.

Other entrepreneurs have been less aware of their own limitations. Consider the experience of Diasonics and Daisy. Both flourished when they were small enough that their founders were able to control all aspects of the business. But they grew too fast, and the managers didn't realize that they now needed a different style of management and control. In both cases, a resounding initial success turned into an ignominious mess. As a result, both enterprises were reorganized.

Sometimes problems arise because the entrepreneur doesn't grasp the importance of strong management. I know of one young company that has already gone through two CEOs and is looking for a third. On the plus side, the men who founded the business acknowledged that they were engineers, not managers, and they went out and looked for a CEO. They considered their strategy so brilliant, though, that they figured anyone could carry it off. The first man they hired talked a good game but had been a disaster at two other corporations; eventually they had to let him go. He just

138

couldn't manage the company. Then the directors hired another CEO who lasted only a few months. The company's product is still a good one, but without equally good leadership it may die in infancy.

The point of these examples is simple. If entrepreneurs do not have the skills required to manage the company, they should bring in an experienced professional. And they should never settle for someone mediocre by telling themselves that the business is such a winner that it doesn't need the management and controls that other companies do.

I look for an entrepreneur who can manage. A conventional manager isn't risk oriented enough to succeed with a new venture, while an entrepreneur without managerial savvy is just another promoter.

A great idea won't make it without great management. I am sometimes asked whether there is an "entrepreneurial personality." I suppose there are certain common qualities — a high energy level, strong commitment, and so on — but there are as many different personal styles as there are entrepreneurs. Henry Singleton of Teledyne, for example, reminds me of Charles de Gaulle. He has a singleness of purpose, a tenacity that is just overpowering. He gives you absolute confidence in his ability to accomplish whatever he says he is going to do. Yet he's rather aloof, operating more or less by himself and dreaming up ideas in his corner office.

Max Palevsky, formerly at Scientific Data Systems (SDS), is, by contrast, a very warm person. At SDS he'd joke around with his employees and cajole them into doing what needed to be done. His very informal style was evidenced by his open shirt and feet up on the desk.

The CEO's personality is extremely important because it permeates the company, but there's no one style that seems to work better than another. What *is* important is to *have* a style. An "average Joe" won't inspire others and lead a business to success.

I look for an entrepreneur who can manage. A conventional manager isn't risk oriented enough to succeed with a new venture, while an entrepreneur without managerial savvy is just another promoter.

Good entrepreneurs are tough-minded, with themselves and with their teams. They can make hard decisions. They have to be able to say, "No, that won't work," to colleagues who come to them with ideas, or to say, "That's a good idea but we can't do it because we have other priorities." To make such professional judgments, managers should ideally be well versed in the technology on which the company is based.

There are exceptions, of course. John Sculley at Apple Computer comes immediately to mind. When Apple was looking for someone to fill the top slot, it instructed the executive recruiter to find a CEO with a technical computer background. But the recruiter asked Apple to consider someone from left field (from the soft-drink industry), and I need not point out that the results were excellent. It was a lucky fit. In fact, as far as the "secrets of entrepreneurial success" go, it's important to recognize that a little bit of luck helps and a lot of luck is even better.

Another company I know, formed by two young, inexperienced men, benefited from a lucky break. Though very knowledgeable, they seriously underestimated how long it would take to write the 1,500,000 lines of software code they needed to launch their product. Consequently, they were two years late in bringing the product to market. But the market was also slow in developing. If the product had been ready on time, the company probably would have gone bankrupt trying to sell something for which the market wasn't ready. As it turned out, the market and the product were ready at the same time, and the company could exploit the product without competition. Many business success stories are due at least in part to simple good luck.

I emphasize people rather than products, and for good reason. The biggest problem in starting high-tech businesses is the shortage of superior managers. There is too much money chasing too few good managers.

Many business success stories are due at least in part to simple good luck.

I have always preferred to wait and have entrepreneurs come to me, to approach me because they have a great desire to build a business. Now with all the megafunds available, it's often the venture capitalist who goes out to start a company and looks for people who can head it up.

Those who call us "vulture capitalists" do have a point; some venture capitalists lure away a company's best people, thus hampering its growth. How can an enterprise develop and thrive when its top executives are always being pursued to start new companies? Unfortunately, in the high-tech industries, more and more businesses are being formed simply to make a buck. As for myself, though, I will continue to look for the best people, not the largest untapped market or the highest projected returns or the cleverest business strategy.

After all, a good idea, unless it's executed, remains only a good idea. Good managers, on the other hand, can't lose. If their strategy doesn't work, they can develop another one. If a competitor comes along, they can turn to something else. Great people make great companies, and that's the kind of company I want to be a part of.

1992

Henry Kravis earned his place in history as cofounder of Kohlberg, Kravis, Roberts and Company, and for his pivotal role in the takeover of RJR Nabisco, immortalized by the bestselling book, *Barbarians at the Gate*. From day one he was groomed for success, attending the best prep schools in New England. Kravis majored in economics at Claremont Men's College in California, and then attended Columbia for his MBA. While there in the late 1960s, he almost dropped out because he disliked the heavy antiestablishment atmosphere. "I left it to my liberal friends to get arrested. I had my mind on business," he said. After graduating in 1969 and going through a couple of dead-end jobs, Kravis joined Bear Stearns on the advice of his cousin, George Roberts, who was working under Jerry Kohlberg.

Under Kohlberg's tutelage, Kravis learned the art of the leverage buyout. When it came to seeking opportunity, they were hawks. "We were always looking. We had the attitude that if you throw enough stuff on the wall, something will stick," Kravis said. After several disputes with upper management, Kohlberg decided to leave Bear Stearns and convinced his two underlings to join him in their own venture. Kohlberg put up $100,000 for a 40 percent share, and the other two put up $10,000 each. They opened for business on May 1, 1976. Kravis once reflected, "I always knew that someday I'd want to do my own thing. I've always liked small organizations. I like shopping in small stores. . . . I'd rather be a big fish in a small pond."

Their buyout formula: They find an undervalued company; put up about 10 percent of the purchase price; use junk bonds to finance the rest; install a management team to reorganize the company, to cut costs, and to make it attractive for a new buyer. In *LBOs Can Help Restore America's Competitive Edge*, Kravis, who has plenty of detractors, delivers a spirited sermon on how leveraged buyouts reinstill the entrepreneurial spirit in companies and what he looks for in a good management team. It also becomes clear why he despises the maxim, "Go along to get along."

LBOs Can Help Restore America's Competitive Edge
Henry R. Kravis

Now, more than ever, we need to rediscover our entrepreneurial traditions in order to face the new economic challenges. But I believe that, as corporate bureaucracies expand, entrepreneurial attitudes become nothing but mere memories. Accounting skills, for example, are valued above production prowess; management types force out the entrepreneurs. Indeed, bureaucracy always fights against the intrusion of new ideas, against novel ways to approach problems. It revels in routine, then slips into stagnation. In such an atmosphere, the entrepreneurial energy is not only lacking, it is simply not wanted anymore. Creative thinkers are viewed suspiciously. And when, as often happens, such thinkers cannot live by the bureaucratic maxim, "Go along to get along," they find themselves getting out—either by choice or by termination.

I suppose that this march toward ever larger and more dominant bureaucracies—at the expense of creativity, innovation and flexibility—would have continued completely unabated, were it not for the simultaneous trend toward globalization, and the fear by management that stagnation would lead to an unwanted takeover. Suddenly, exposed to stiff competition from abroad, corporate bureaucracies stood revealed for what they were—gridlocked organizations that were dragging the US economy down the drain.

As corporate bureaucracies expand, entrepreneurial attitudes become nothing but mere memories.

Slow moving, unalert and narrow-minded, American industry by the late '70s and early '80s looked as if it could not build competitive products unless it were shielded by Government regulation from more flexible economic adversaries. Corporate bureaucracy was interfering with progress. A sad thought indeed, for a nation built by the unfettered individual talents of millions of people, great and small, from the early industrialists to the immigrant shop owners.

We have not yet conquered the problem of bureaucracy. But I believe that in the last ten years, we have discovered that Americans—natives and new immigrants alike—have a wellspring of entrepreneurial energy and individual initiative within themselves. Ten years ago, we forlornly asked: "Where are the inventors, the innovators and the organizers? Where have they gone?" Today, we proudly answer: "They are still here." And they are America's secret weapon against suffocating corporate bureaucracy at home, and our edge in the economic competition abroad.

Building on this native strength, US companies have significant advantages as they meet today's competitive challenges. But alone, this is not enough. Companies also need carefully reasoned strategies as they compete in the global economy. Allow me to suggest some strategic directions which, I believe, can ensure American pre-eminence in the coming century.

- **First:** We need companies that are highly flexible and able to adapt rapidly to changes in the global marketplace. This means that corporate bureaucracies must be tamed. Companies must get closer to their customers and markets. Creative thinking must be unleashed—not only in small enterprises, but in the largest corporations, as well.
- **Second:** We need to take the long-term view of our businesses and to encourage that view among shareholders, managers and employees. This means that we must find ways to reduce the intense pressure on managements to perform on a quarter-to-quarter basis. Companies have to stop sacrificing their futures on the altars of the great God of immediate profit.

Bureaucracy always fights against the intrusion of new ideas, against novel ways to approach problems.

- **Third:** We need to increase capital investment and investment in our people. This means that our position among the major industrial nations as the laggard of capital investment must be improved, and that we must be committed to making the necessary investments in the education of our work force.
- **Fourth:** We must put incentive in the right place for management and employees. Today, too many American CEOs have become what I call "renters of the corporate assets"—not owners. Managers move through the ranks, and eventually—for political reasons or otherwise—reach the top of the corporate hierarchy, never risking any of their net worth in the ownership of their company—not options! Too many feel it is a God-

given right to be in their position, and so they feel quite comfortable living off the corporate assets, wasting and abusing those assets. Where are the Carnegies, the Mellons, the Morgans and the Vanderbilts of today? They were, in their day, the owners and builders of corporate assets, not mere renters.

It is, in my opinion, important to put real accountability into the corporate system—an accountability that requires shareholders, Boards of Directors and management to have the same objectives and goals. Too often, this is not the case. Boards of Directors do not hold management accountable as they should. Nor do most institutional and individual shareholders, none of whom have any real control over the actions of the company. If they are not happy with the results, instead of holding the Board accountable, they merely sell their investment and go on to something else.

Creative thinking must be unleashed—not only in small enterprises, but in the largest corporations, as well.

I believe that companies that pursue these four general strategic directions are properly positioning themselves to compete—now and in the future—in the global economy. Some companies may do so as private entities; others as publicly held corporations. But one thing is certain. Pursuing these strategic directions requires that a company constantly re-evaluate its businesses, its management techniques, its work force, its capital-spending plans, its products or services, its position in the market place and its success in motivating managers and employees. It may even require the restructuring of the company itself. And this is where a Leveraged Buy Out, as one possible alternative, may be of considerable benefit.

Henry R. Kravis

Increase Competitive Position

I see LBOs as one tactic, among others, to free US business from the paralyzing clutches of hidebound corporate bureaucracies and to increase our competitive position in the world economy. First of all, let's not forget that LBOs are a financing technique, not a type of business. So accurate generalizations about them are not easily made. It is important to keep in mind that, as a financing technique, an LBO should not be an end in itself. In my view, an LBO should be a means to accomplish a particular objective for a specific company. And that objective should be to enable the company to compete more effectively in its market place by making it more efficient and profitable.

Very recently, KKR, along with Deloitte Haskins & Sells, undertook a survey of 17 companies that we acquired through LBOs in which we still have an ownership position—companies such as Beatrice, Safeway, Owens Illinois, Fred Meyer, Malone & Hyde and Houdaille Industries. We examined the results before and after the LBO for comparison. The study demonstrated that we were able to achieve our general objective of creating more competitive companies. And it also shed some light on other controversial issues that often swirl around LBOs.

> I see LBOs as one tactic, among others, to free US business from the paralyzing clutches of hidebound corporate bureaucracies.

Some members of the press, academicians, public officials and businessmen cannot resist the temptation to generalize about LBOs. They argue, for example, that when an LBO is completed, all R&D stops. Capital expenditures are curtailed. Employees are terminated for no good reason. And, they say, it's most alarming that Government is subsidizing all of this by allowing the interest deduction on the acquisition debt. Of course, all of these supposed cutbacks are in the name of interest payments and debt amortization, not good business judgment. These allegations make great headlines, but they just are not supported by the facts.

Avoid the Common Trap

The key to successful LBOs has been to give management an ownership stake. This puts control, ownership and management of a company on the same level. And that creates an incentive to maximize the long-term value of the enterprise. The fact is that LBOs do result in more efficiently run companies. Management ownership, for example, avoids the common trap of bigness for bigness sake, of making acquisitions for their own sake—just to increase assets, sales and short-term profitability.

Going private also releases management from the unhealthy necessity of focusing on short-term performance for the sake of satisfying security analysts and certain institutional investors. Long-term planning can become a real company goal. Under such circumstances, it is quite common to witness the dramatic reduction of corporate overhead simply by eliminating waste. For example, at Beatrice, we found a $60 million, four-year contract that plastered the corporate name on Formula One racing cars. But the company did not make any products that used the corporate name as its brand. It is very difficult to imagine that a person, sitting in the stands watching a car with the name Beatrice on it going around the track, will be influenced by the spectacle to buy a bottle of Wesson oil, Hunt catsup, Tropicana orange juice or a Playtex brassiere.

Needless to say, we canceled that contract. Furthermore, we found an annual advertising budget of $975 million, $75 million of which was not even spent to promote products, but simply to publicize the Beatrice corporate name — an ego builder for the CEO. Again, no products sold under the Beatrice label: "Just Beatrice. You've known us all along."

Going private also releases management from the unhealthy necessity of focusing on short-term performance for the sake of satisfying security analysts and certain institutional investors.

Discipline of Debt

When companies are not publicly traded management can make tough decisions that would otherwise be avoided because of a potential negative short-term effect on the stock price. In a non-public situation, there is no incentive to carry non-productive assets and operations. On the contrary, the discipline of debt encourages management to allocate more efficiently all company resources and to view non-productive assets with a clear eye. Return on investment becomes the key criteria — not more management perks at the expense of shareholders.

So LBOs generally result in more efficient, flexible companies with downsized bureaucracies and managers with a long-term view. That's an important step in the direction of making US companies more competitive in today's global environment. Equally important, however, companies must invest for the future in both people and equipment. Despite claims to the contrary, the Deloitte study of our companies demonstrates that capital spending, for example, remains strong after LBOs, increasing, in fact, over 14% from the first year after the buy outs to the third year. In R&D,

another critical area of investment for future competitiveness, the story is pretty much the same. On the average, in KKR-owned companies in the years subsequent to the buy outs, R&D spending was 15% higher than in the period preceding the LBOs.

But even if the harshest critics of LBOs were to concede that LBOs do indeed contribute to making companies more competitive, efficient and long-term oriented, they are sure to ask: "But at what price? After Leveraged Buy Outs, don't companies just terminate employees without rhyme or reason?"

Increase in Employment

Generally speaking, LBOs do not, because of the debt alone, result in employee layoffs. That does not, however, mean that there are no initial layoffs. This has occurred—and will occur—in certain areas and in certain companies, for good, purely business reasons. Very often, previous managements had encouraged untrammeled overgrowth—big for bigness sake. However, on the whole, in our own companies, excluding our most recent acquisition of RJR Nabisco, employment has increased from 276,000 employees in the year preceding the buy outs to 313,000 three years later. And we almost doubled the average annual rate of growth in employment from 2.3% before the buy out to 4.2% after.

Now, on the surface, this fact may be surprising. But when you look more closely at the rationale behind LBOs, it becomes quite an expected development, because over the long term an increase in profitability is likely to lead to the creation of more jobs and increased man hours. For example, in 1984, 100 million man hours were used to operate 1,273 Safeway Stores. In 1988, four years later, after the sale of a number of stores, 118 million man hours were used to operate 1,155 stores. This is because we are 40% more profitable on $13 billion in sales than we were at $20 billion when the company was acquired.

Thus far, I have been talking about re-establishing the competitive position of American business by, in effect, drawing upon our powerful traditions of invention, innovation and risk-taking. These were characteristics that set America apart in the eyes of observers the world around. And they are the characteristics that will, I am convinced, carry us through the next century, as the continued envy of the world.

Our nation has another strong tradition: An idealism, a concern for ethical and moral behavior, that makes us seen as the hope of the world.

I believe that we must call upon these two traditions — entrepreneurial spirit and idealism — as we face the challenges ahead. Business leaders must embody both, for embracing one exclusively will only distort, beyond all recognition, the value of the other. Entrepreneurship without ethics cannot lead to greater economic good, but only to a dead end that will benefit no one.

1989

An Wang's story is one of survival. The man who was a pioneer in calculators and word processors was lucky to survive his youth in China, which included the civil war in the 1930s and Japan's brutal occupation in World War II. His mother, father, and eldest sister were victims. Of this embittered early life, Wang said, "I learned to negotiate my way in unfamiliar territory. I became a loner by circumstance, not by choice, but the discovery that I could survive and even thrive on my own gave me confidence." Wang came to the United States in 1945 as a university student in a two-year fellowship program and he eventually earned a Ph.D. in applied physics from Harvard.

Deciding to remain in the United States, Wang took a research job at Harvard and pioneered work in electronic memory storage. "My innovations with memory cores had given me the status of an expert in digital electronics, and with that reputation, I thought I might have the credibility to start my own business." So, he founded Wang Laboratories in 1951 as a one-man show. As for the name: "I used the plural, laboratories, rather than the singular because I thought the company would expand over the years, and I wanted a name that would accommodate growth." His capital: $600. And not a customer in sight, although he soon found them at various research facilities.

In 1964, he invented the basic processing unit for the calculator, and by 1967, it was a huge success, generating over $4 million in revenue. That same year, Wang went public, with an initial public offering of $12.50 a share, which equated to a reasonable 25 times earnings. However, Wang was warned that the market might discriminate against his stock because of his name. "I continued to hear people argue that I should change the company name to avoid discrimination long after we went public," he wrote. To Wang's relief, the first public trade came in at $38. Whether or not to go public is a dilemma many successful entrepreneurs must deal with, and in the following selection Wang describes his decision process. His greatest fear: the loss of control. He wrote, "So long as I am in control, I have a stake in whether I'm right or wrong."

Going Public
An Wang

Going public has long been a rite of passage for entrepreneurial high-tech companies. In recent years, more and more companies have been going through this corporate adolescence at ever younger ages. In the early 1980s, it was not uncommon for computer firms to go public long before they had earnings, and in some cases, even before they had sales or products.

The late 1960s was also an exciting time for high-tech companies. The period has been called the Go-Go Years, and it was marked by inflated valuations much like those that characterized the new issues market in the early 1980s. It was in this market that I decided to take Wang Laboratories public. We needed capital to retire short-term debt, and to finance our growth, and I recognized that the mood of the times presented a great opportunity for the company. I also recognized that this mood might pass.

Unlike a number of companies that went public on the promise of great things in the future, when Wang Laboratories went public, we had solid earnings, very rapid revenue growth, and sixteen years' history as a private company. Since some other companies were going public with scarcely more than a letterhead, we looked extremely good in this environment. Going public was therefore a very happy and exciting event for us. It also turned out to be a very lucky event. About a year and a half after we went public, the Go-Go Years came to a grinding halt, and the new issues market all but died. Eventually a recession brought shareholders face-to-face with the reality that prices on the stock exchange were far higher than anything that might be justified by the prospects for earnings of the companies being traded. Stock prices collapsed, and although there have been speculative binges since then, the Dow Jones Industrial Average in constant dollars has never been as high as it was back then. Had we not gone public when we did, the capital markets might well have been closed to us for the next eight years, and our finances extremely stretched.

My decision to go public was based on our extremely rapid growth. I was not trying to cash in on the overheated new issues market. I was not interested in increasing my own net worth. Unlike many other entrepreneurs who look at going public as payday, I have never sold any of my Wang stock. Frankly I would have been happy if Wang Laboratories had remained private. However, the investments necessary to meet the demand for the calculators forced us to the limit of our credit with the First National Bank of Boston.

In fiscal year 1967, we sold $4,259,000 worth of calculators. This was eight times the sales volume of calculators during the previous year. At this point, calculators comprised nearly 62 percent of our sales. In anticipation of this demand, we doubled our work force to four hundred people and expanded our facility in Tewksbury by about 150 percent. It is a fact of life of business that you have to spend money for staffing and building before you reap the rewards of increased sales, even if people are begging to buy your products. We kept going to the First National Bank of Boston for additional short-term loans. By early 1967, we had already borrowed over a million dollars at a time when the net worth of the company was only about a million dollars. Our contact at the bank was Ernest Stockwell (who subsequently became a board member of Wang Laborato-

154

ries). Peter Brooke, who was (and is) on our board, had earlier left the bank and was now involved in venture capital with the investment banking firm of Tucker, Anthony & R. L. Day. At the First National Bank of Boston, Mr. Stockwell was getting a little nervous because of the size of our borrowings in relation to the net worth of the company. In early 1967, he suggested that we go public as a means of raising capital so that we might reduce our debt burden.

One of the reasons I founded Wang Laboratories was that I like to take my own risks. So long as I am in control, I have a stake in whether I'm right or wrong.

For me, the crucial issue in going public was entirely distinct from the relative merits of debt and capital. Of most concern to me was the issue of management and control. I had already diluted family control of the company by the earlier alliance with Warner & Swasey. While James Hodge of Warner & Swasey had been a very positive presence on our board, I did not want to lose control of my company to an outside board of directors.

One of the reasons I founded Wang Laboratories was that I like to take my own risks. So long as I am in control, I have a stake in whether I'm right or wrong. I have never advocated venture capital because I do not want to be hamstrung by outside investors. Even if the outside investors are absolutely compliant, the fiduciary responsibility implicit in dealing with other people's money makes the CEO of such a company more conservative. This does not mean that I do not want to listen to other opinions. Indeed, I place great importance on communication within and outside the company. Nor does it mean that I do not feel responsible for the well-being of those who are affected by the fortunes of the company. It simply means that as CEO of a company that I

155

founded, I want to be the final authority on any matters that affect its destiny. Furthermore, so long as I have control, I can never be tempted to abandon the business.

Apart from these personal considerations, I feel that there are other, practical arguments for individual control, if not ownership, of a corporation. For one thing, a CEO who does not have to answer to outside directors for quarterly performance can lead the company with his eye focused on its long-term interests. This is important today since it takes a strong leader to balance the market's obsession with quarterly performance against the long-term positioning of a company. The CEO with control can also be more decisive and move much more quickly to take strategically important action than can the CEO who is second-guessed by directors and investors. Later in my career, there were a number of instances in which I was able to make such crucial decisions quickly, precisely because I had *both* the responsibility *and* the power to do so.

It takes a strong leader to balance the market's obsession with quarterly performance against the long-term positioning of a company.

There is, of course, a converse to these arguments: a CEO answerable to no one but himself can destroy a company with impunity. Still, that is the risk of any corporate endeavor, and it is also self-corrective. Diversity in a free market economy acts to limit the damage that can be done by the incompetent or irrational CEO with total authority. People can leave a company and find work elsewhere, and customers have the option of buying from an alternative supplier. There are, of course, stories of abuses inflicted by privately held companies on communities they monopolize. But Boston is an economically diverse community, and high technology is a highly competitive part of that community. In this environment, the power-mad CEO would only hurt himself.

Every company has a set of goals. When I founded Wang Laboratories, my goal was for the company to serve its community and its customers, both through technology and through the positive economic dividends of its growth. I feel now, as I did in 1967, that I can best ensure that the company continues to pursue those goals through control of its policies.

A CEO answerable to no one but himself can destroy a company with impunity.

Today, there are innumerable stories about founders of high-tech firms who find themselves ousted by dissatisfied shareholders. The question of whether or not these founders should be removed for the good of the company is moot, but it is certain that once a founder loses control of his company, he can no longer direct the company toward whatever goal he set for it.

This philosophy also influences the way I view the larger question of family control. As the founder, I would like to maintain sufficient control so that my children might have the chance to demonstrate whether they can run the company without fearing to take a risk or two. But the question of how far one should go to maintain family control of a publicly held company is a delicate one. All other things being equal, my children should be more highly motivated than a professional manager because of their substantial stake in the ownership of the company. On the other hand, I do not want to make that decision for my children. Nor do I rule out the possibility that a professional manager might prove to be the best steward of the company's future.

Today, both my sons work for Wang, and I have given each a different opportunity to learn about the way the company runs. Fred, who is now executive vice-president, has worked in a number of different divisions and has had a chance to see how every facet of the company works. Courtney has taken a very different route. He has asked for permission to form and control a small semiautonomous division of the company called Wang Communications, Inc., where he has the opportunity to show his entrepreneurial skills. Because Fred is the oldest son, he has a six-year lead in any effort to prove himself, and I am pleased that Courtney recognizes this. Juliette is still in college, and she has not yet decided what to do after graduation.

Beyond this, I have tried to educate my children as to my style of management, which is to lead by example rather than to dictate, and to leave room for individual initiative rather than to spell out every step of how a job is to be accomplished.

I want my children to have the opportunity to demonstrate their skills at management. In fact, I consider it their obligation—rather than their privilege—to do so. While I hope they succeed ultimately, the continued ability of Wang Laboratories to grow and serve its community is more important to me than who controls it after I retire.

It was with these considerations in mind that I weighed the question of going public. While lack of voting control may not automatically hamstring a CEO, given the choice, I preferred not to have to put that proposition to the test.

1986

PART IV

Risk and Strategy

Risk is synonymous with entrepreneur, and this section is dedicated to addressing the various strategies that limit risk's downside and enhance the prospects for success. Richard Branson, although a flamboyant showman, is all too conscious of the risk he faces, stating, "Risk taking is something I am very well aware of 'at a gut level' . . . but I find it extremely difficult to describe in the abstract." Scott McNealy, cofounder of Sun Microsystems, loves to take risks and challenge conventional wisdom, but he protects the downside by using a business model built around developing alliances with customers, suppliers, and the local community among others. Another strategy is to study trends, which both Simon Ramo, a technologist who cofounded TRW and brought us the intercontinental ballistic missile, and Dave Thomas, a restaurateur who founded Wendy's and brought us the spicy chicken sandwich, used to determine the focus of their business. Other strategic considerations the authors address include pricing, buying, and manufacturing. Steve Case, founder of AOL, gives his 10 commandments for success, concluding with "Thou Shalt Build a Medium That Improves the Lives of All People and Benefits Society." Improving the lives of people has to be the ultimate goal of all entrepreneurs.

RICHARD BRANSON
1950–

The title of Richard Branson's 1998 autobiography, *Losing My Virginity,* pretty much sums up this entrepreneur's flair for promotion. British-born Branson, the founder of Virgin Records and Virgin Atlantic, among other ventures, begins his autobiography with the following childhood memory: "My mother was determined to make us independent. When I was four, she stopped the car a few miles from our house and made me find my own way home across the fields. I got hopelessly lost." Apparently, Branson became not only independent, but a bit naughty, too; while at prep school, he was beaten for poor grades, and decided to skip college all together. And, it was none other than the Sex Pistols, whom Branson signed in 1977, that put Virgin Records on the map.

Unfortunately, the bankers forced him to sell his beloved recording company in 1992 to raise cash to support his other renowned start-up, Virgin Atlantic, which today is one the most successful airlines in the world. It left a bad taste in his mouth, and since then he has relied on joint ventures with wealthy partners as opposed to going to the bank for a loan. For example, he put up a mere 1,000 pounds and his brand name for a 50 percent interest in a cosmetics business, Virgin Vie, while his partner put up 20 million pounds. As of 1998, this uber-entrepreneur had created an empire of some 200 companies with sales revenue of $4 billion. "I want Virgin to be as well known around the world as Coca-Cola," he said.

So far, he's had the golden touch in most of his ventures, which he attributes partly to intuition, a trait he developed in his youth. "Perhaps my early problems with dyslexia made me more intuitive: when someone sends me a written proposal, rather than dwelling on detailed facts and figures I find that my imagination grasps and expands on what I read," he said. His P. T. Barnum–like promotional stunts have helped, too—Branson has cross-dressed, driven an army tank in Times Square, and attempted to circumnavigate the world in a balloon, among others. In *Risk Taking,* however, Branson presents some down-to-earth ideas on how to reduce risk when taking on a new venture.

Risk Taking
Richard Branson

R isk taking is something I am very well aware of "at a gut level," when I am actually taking decisions, but I find it extremely difficult to describe in the abstract. There is such a temptation to rationalise past decisions; so that all the successes can be described as examples of measured and systematic risk taking, but all the failures can be written off to events that could not possibly have been identified at the time the decision was made.

One example of a decision that I would like to claim full benefit for would be our acquisition of the first Boeing 747, which came just before a rapid upturn in the secondhand market for 747s. On the other hand, I would like to blame the fact that *Event*—the magazine we started up some years ago in competition with *Time Out*—failed, not because we did not plan it or manage it carefully enough, but because something completely unexpected happened. (*Time Out* managed to improve its editorial policy when a left-wing group of staff resigned to form yet another competitor magazine, *City Limits*).

The best thing I can do is not to try and rationalise what I, and my colleagues at Virgin, try to do when we are making decisions. Instead, here are some practical "dos" and "don'ts" for when you are taking decisions, so that your strike rate might be a bit higher and your return on the investment substantially higher.

Know the Business

The biggest risk any of us can take is to invest money in a business that we don't know. Very few of the businesses that Virgin has set up have been completely new fields. Admittedly, I started fresh—"a virgin"—in the mail order record business on the back of the abolition of retail price maintenance. Since then, however, the development of the Group has been through a linked series of investments, which I gather the business schools call "vertical integration," but which I just call common sense. From the mail order business we went into retailing records, from the retailing of records we went into record production, through the setting up of the Virgin record label. We soon found that it was possible to negotiate music publishing rights as well as record rights with the same band, so we set up a music publishing company. Once we got past the very early stages, we realised that we were spending an awful lot of money on recording costs so we got into the recording studio business. When music videos became a necessary part of the marketing of records, we did not just make them and waste them, but began to distribute them ourselves. This got us into the video distribution business and it was a natural move to begin to acquire other products for video distribution. Another good example is when we noticed the increasing importance of film soundtracks: now it is almost worthwhile for us to get into a film for the soundtrack rights only. So, behind the Richard Branson "whizzkid, entrepreneur" image there lies—I believe—measured growth from the initial business of mail order through to the core of the Virgin Group as it is today.

So, Know the Business

These linkages do not happen without hard work and, in almost each case, I have devoted my time to the new business and have got completely immersed in it before making any significant investment.

I have not depended upon others to do surveys, or a lot of market research, or to develop grand strategies. I have taken the view that the risk to the company is best reduced by my involvement in the nitty gritty of the new business.

So, Get Involved, Don't Stand Back

That in turn means that I have got to depend a lot on the management of the divisions I leave behind when I become totally immersed in a new area. Risk management, which I suppose is what we are talking about, depends a lot on not risking your core business; and you do that by having a good management team in your core business before you embark on any risky venture in a new business. *So, don't depend* on others to do the diversification and to take the risk. *But do depend* on others to do the job they know.

I have not depended upon others to do surveys, or a lot of market research, or to develop grand strategies. I have taken the view that the risk to the company is best reduced by my involvement in the nitty gritty of the new business.

Avoid Psychological Pre-commitments

It is important not to become so entranced by a business area that you become forced to invest at a particular rate or in particular market sectors before you are ready. This I think is often a flaw in corporate plans and strategies. The plan itself becomes the reason for the investment and the risk taking. Because a team of people or a managing director have said that they like a particular market and intend to invest heavily in it, it becomes extremely difficult for them not to invest. The danger then is that they invest at too high a risk. *So, always be prepared to walk away.*

It is wonderful how the knowledge that you are in a position to do that can improve a deal. A recent example has been in our negotiation for the financing of a second 747. Had we been an airline like British Caledonian or British Airways, who "have to be in the business," then the bankers would have asked for all sorts of security and they would have got it. However, because we were able to say to the bankers "you are either going to lend us money without recourse to the rest of the Virgin Group or we are not going to bother buying a second aircraft" they have lent money just to the airline and enabled us to reduce the risk enormously. *So, being prepared to walk away from a deal almost always has the effect of reducing the risk you run.*

A further point on this is "remember there is always another deal." Deals are like London buses—there is always one coming. And it is surprising how often the next deal is better than the one you have, with great reluctance, had to give up.

Remember there is always another deal.
Deals are like London buses—there is always one coming.

Under this rather strange heading of avoiding psychological pre-commitments there is another general point I would like to make. A lot of companies are very greedy about how they share the benefits from risk taking and investment. We in the Virgin Group are often seemingly very liberal with the way we give managers minority shareholdings and participation in new ventures in new markets. It is the sort of policy that is very easy for accountants and bankers to look at and say "that is extremely expensive." The fact is that they can often only count the cost and fail to see its value. The commitment and participation of senior executives in new ventures is often one of the best ways of reducing risks for the company. If there are people within the company who are capable of becoming millionaires if they set up on their own, we want them to stick with the company and become millionaires.

Limiting the Downside

This is my overriding concern. Perhaps it is because we have been a private company and I have often been extremely short of cash that I have never wanted to put the company on the line. However, in retrospect I think it has also been a very important part of getting a good return from our investments. We limit the downside in a number of ways, some of which can seem to be expensive when looked at coldly.

The first way is through the financing structure of a new investment. We will, typically, set up a new company which will employ all the people involved and on whose performance their future will rest. Now, of course, we very rarely walk away from a subsidiary and let it go bankrupt but nevertheless this practice does help focus the minds of the people involved. In addition, we always attempt to arrange the financing of this company so that, as far as is possible, any borrowings or liabilities are without recourse to Group funds. I have mentioned the airline already and it is perhaps the best example. There, we have the banks lending on the basis of the airline's performance and the value of the aircraft themselves. The Group's only obligation to the banks is to provide leadership and management to the team at the airline. This may seem fairly obvious but I can assure you it is not something we see in other companies.

Another example is the entertainment business. There are significant differences between investing in new bands in the music division and investing in a film. Most people see music, films and entertainment generally as being all highly risky business without really understanding how it is possible to manage the risks involved. We invest very heavily in new artistes but not very heavily in films. The difference is that our commitment to new artistes is limited — usually to an initial advance and the marketing and promotional costs of their first few singles and an album. This might commit us to, say, £300,000. If that first album is a success or meets certain criteria, then we go on to a second album and so on, up to eight or nine albums. So, over a few years, our commitment to an artiste might be £3–4m. However, the risk of losing £3–4m has been limited. In contrast, however, if we invest in a film, although its success is no more or less certain than an artiste on the music side, the situation is different. It is not the practice in the film business to contract with talent for anything more than one film. In other words, if a film is successful we have no rights to the future services of the producer, director or cast. An example I know of is Hugh Hudson who was the director of *Chariots of Fire*. His fee for the film was some £200,000. It was of course an enormously successful film and some months later when the production company wanted to have him direct their next film, they found that they had nothing other than a weak moral hold on him and were facing a likely fee level of over $1m. That sort of thing just does not happen in music; therefore we invest heavily in music, not in films.

The second method of limiting the downside is the obvious one about reducing the scale of the risk through joint ventures. Of course joint ventures often actually increase the *degree* of risk in a venture because it adds another variable — e.g. how can two or more people work together satisfactorily? However, it certainly reduces the *scale* of the risk. A good present example of this is our investment in Music Box. This is pan-European television programming based on the hugely successful MTV network in the United States. The total investment required was way beyond the resources of the Group. However, being convinced that this was a good product in a rapidly expanding market, we found a way of going ahead in partnership with Thorn EMI and Yorkshire Television.

The third point to mention is the need to *have a way out* of a high risk venture. Very often you will find that one of the greatest risks in investment is lack of flexibility. You get halfway through a project after a year, you get to the point where the only way forward, even if you are then way above budget, is to invest more money—because at that point the marginal decision always seems to encourage ploughing on. That will always be the case unless you have structured the deal so that there is a way out. Again, our best current example is from the airline. We went into the airline business on the basis that we could get out after a year or two so, (using the "walk away" rule) we said to Boeing that we were not going ahead unless they gave a commitment to buy back the 747 during the first three years of its life at a fixed price. They agreed, so we were able to embark on the airline business, knowing that the downside was very limited. Equally, on the music side of the company, we typically have the right not to proceed with an artiste's contract. On our retail side, we make sure that all of our leases or freeholds are easily realisable so that we are not trapped into lossmaking shops.

Keep It Small and Cheap

A little while ago, the *Economist* ran an article on us and identified one of the Group's strengths as its corporate structure. It made a number of points—all of which are relevant to a discussion of risk, and which I would group under the heading "small and cheap."

First, keep overheads low. We run about 16 small offices in Notting Hill, which are miles in style from the high-rent corporate headquarters of the City or West End. Staff numbers are kept small, and we insist they work in small units — I think our largest is about 120 people.

Second, as businesses grow, watch out for management losing touch with the basics — normally the customer. We set out to avoid any one subsidiary being in any way large. For example, music is our biggest business and rather than let Virgin Records (150 staff and £150 million turnover) grow into an EMI (10,000 staff and £300 million turnover), we've split it up and set up new labels.

There is one overriding point I would like to make. Having done the evaluation of an investment . . . *do not pussyfoot around. Go for it!*

Thirdly, this "keep it small" rule enables us to give more than the usual number of managers the challenge and excitement of running their own businesses. It is, I think, the only way to encourage entrepreneurship from within the company, and then only if it is coupled with substantial personal incentives in terms of minority shareholdings or profit sharing. Throughout the Group, we are prepared to set up as many new businesses as our employees have marketable ideas. Lastly, under this heading, we are able to accept a "buy, don't make" strategy. We see ourselves primarily as publishers of entertainment in all its forms. This makes us extremely flexible to change in taste or consumer spending patterns — a good example being how we've survived the bloodbath in the computer games business by just having programmers and marketing staff — and all of them on short term contracts. It also helps our low overhead policy enormously.

We do not have record pressing plants or record distribution systems. This means that we have no fixed plant and depreciation charges and no large overhead in buildings and staff that are very insensitive to volume. Incidentally, it also has another advantage in that as technology and consumer tastes change, we can continue to publish in whatever medium the public wants—black vinyl, cassettes, compact discs—without having record plants with reducing utilisation, or heavy start up costs in new disc plants.

Conclusion

There is one overriding point I would like to make. Having done the evaluation of an investment and having applied all the rules I have listed and any others that you find particularly helpful in your markets, and having decided to make an investment, *do not pussyfoot around. Go for it!* In reality, one of the biggest risks that a lot of British industry takes is the lack of commitment to new projects and new ventures. They do not put enough energy, personal commitment or leadership into them. The fact that they are risky often taints them as second best. I try to avoid that by getting involved in new ventures more than in the mainstream activities of the company. This gives them a high status, an importance and my experience! It makes the probability of success that much higher. So, in conclusion, having decided to take a risk, do not run further risks by not committing yourself fully to your decision.

1985

Scott McNealy, cofounder of Sun Microsystems, had a privileged childhood. His father was vice chairman of American Motors Corporation, and the younger McNealy found himself playing golf with such celebrities as Lee Iacocca and attending a fancy prep school where he became captain of the tennis team. He attended Harvard to study economics, but ended up playing a great deal of golf (he was team captain) and swilling a good amount of beer. After graduating, McNealy took a foreman position in a Rockwell International factory located in Illinois, where he remained for two years. Then it was on to Stanford for an MBA specializing in manufacturing and more goofing-off: "I minimized hours per grade point," he concluded.

Then came the twist of fate in 1982; a former Stanford classmate invited him to join in the founding of Sun, with McNealy in charge of the manufacturing. "I love the factory," he said. "That's what business is all about. Making things. Not this Wall Street stuff, not this consulting stuff, not this lawyer stuff. None of that adds value. You gotta make something." When one of the other founders left, McNealy, whose motto is "Kick butt and have fun," became president and CEO shortly thereafter. In 1986, Sun went public. More recently, McNealy has cultivated a bitter rivalry with Microsoft founder Bill Gates, attacking what he calls "Bill Gates' centrally planned economy." Incidentally, McNealy's known for shooting from the lip.

The successful 1995 introduction of Sun's Internet software, Java, has fueled both the battle with Gates and Sun's revenues. It's not the first time McNealy has grappled with success. Back in 1988 sales boomed to $1 billion, and like many other young companies that experience explosive growth, Sun found itself in trouble, posting its first quarterly loss, and in need of a reorganization. McNealy trimmed back the product lines and pushed responsibility down, creating what he calls planets, or product groups. His latest vision for a business model is depicted in the following selection, in which he explains the importance of a "leveraged alliance business model" to keep the entrepreneurial spirit alive.

A Winning Business Model for the 1990s
Scott McNealy

The companies that succeed in the years ahead will be the ones that challenge and change conventional wisdom—not just on the fine points of doing business, but on the fundamentals of being a business. And that means adopting a new business model that will satisfy the needs of customers, suppliers, and governments while still allowing the company to make money.

It is clear that the traditional business model, at least for the computer industry—vertical integration, proprietary product lines, direct selling—just isn't working any more.

I believe the business model pioneered by Sun Microsystems more than 10 years ago can provide some useful insights for companies—in the computer industry and other fields—that are interested in positioning themselves for success for the remainder of the 1990s. Sun's approach, considered radical just a decade ago, has proved its merits in this era of increased global competition.

In 1982, Sun Microsystems had a staff of seven and was headquartered in offices that were rented by the day. Today, analysts forecast Sun's revenues at $6 billion and the company is in the top half of the Fortune 500, with 13,000 employees and offices around the world.

In the early days, we succeeded because we had revolutionary products. Andy Bechtolsheim and Bill Joy, two of Sun's co-founders, launched the concept of open systems with the Sun-1, a computer made from standard off-the-shelf components and running the Unix operating system. Unix was powerful yet easy to "port," meaning that it could run on many different types of computers. This, combined with Sun's Unix-based Network File System (NFS), gave customers several important new capabilities. They could create networks of supercharged desktop computers, called workstations, which could share information. They could make every resource on the network available to anyone else on the network — from any physical location on the network. And they could integrate newer technologies with existing systems, allowing them to take advantage of emerging technologies without sacrificing their previous investments.

For other computer vendors, open systems had an equally significant impact: it threatened to break their strangleholds on prized markets. Vendors of proprietary products had grown accustomed to enjoying what amounted to an unregulated monopoly. They had little competition, so they commanded high prices and set low standards for ongoing innovation. The advent of open systems introduced a new dimension of competition. We all know what happens when competition escalates: prices tumble, innovation soars. Consider, for example, the effect of cloning on the capabilities and pricing of IBM-compatible personal computers.

Initially, Sun's business model was no different from that of its rivals. We wanted to beat our competitors, grow internally, build manufacturing plants, create new distribution channels, acquire promising startups, and so on. What happened was that we realized we couldn't do it all alone. The market was vast, our competitors were huge, barriers to entry in some segments were overwhelming, we didn't have enough cash, and the pace of change in the industry was too fast.

Pure Instinct

What we did was purely instinctive. We reached out to other companies that could help us. We leveraged their expertise and specialty products by forming strategic alliances.

Our first partner was Fujitsu. We wanted to produce special high-capacity hard drives for our workstations, but found that the idea of manufacturing them ourselves was not realistic, given our small size and lack of credit history. We approached Fujitsu and found that they were willing to make the drives for us. The alliance worked so well that we looked for other opportunities. Soon we had a partner that could produce printed circuit boards for us. And another partner that could supplement our service offerings. Then ComputerVision, one of Sun's early customers, approached us with a partnership proposal whereby we would supply our workstations for resale by ComputerVision, allowing them to focus on software product development. We agreed.

So Sun's leveraged alliance model was born of necessity, not ingenious foresight. But we allowed it to continue evolving, and for that we can take credit. Initially, the alliances focused on manufacturing and service agreements, but gradually they expanded to include product development, marketing, distribution—practically every element of our business.

Today, strategic alliances are the very heart of our business. We have alliances with more than 3,500 software vendors, who have created more than 10,000 solutions for our computer systems. We outsource much of our manufacturing and assembly to multiple companies throughout the world. We buy and sell through a multitude of channels, including value-added resellers, systems integrators, consulting companies, other OEMs, even direct mail. And we maintain separate alliance programs for many areas of technology, including networking, systems integration, hardware, systems management, service, and more.

Now, with the benefit of 20/20 hindsight, I believe I am
able to explain why the leveraged alliance model works so
well by showing you in more detail how it works at Sun.

Adding Value to Core Competencies

The central premise of the leveraged alliance model is that
no one can do it all alone any more. On the other hand, every
company has to do something. How does a business determine what to do internally and what to outsource?

The first step is to ask a very tough question. What is the
company really good at? What technology, resource, or
capability does the company provide that gives it a true competitive advantage? The answer to this question is the company's core competency. This is the platform on which to
build—the foundation on which to add value by leveraging
the expertise of third-party specialists.

For example, Sun's core competency is open network
computing: integrating heterogeneous resources into a single, powerful network environment. While Sun itself offers
hardware, software, and networking products in support of
this core competency, we depend heavily on our partners to
add value to the Sun foundation.

In the software development market, for example, Sun
provides the high-performance programming tools that most
developers need to write powerful applications, and forms
development partnerships with third-party vendors whose
products enhance the Sun development platform.

Each company is able to do what it does best, so redun-
dancies and inefficiencies in product development are minimized. The vendors leverage each other's strengths and take
advantage of synergies to address customer requirements.
Similarly, Sun produces and sells the operating environment
that customers need to run their powerful applications, but
most actual software applications are created by our worldwide network of independent software vendors.

On the service side, alliances allow Sun to provide outstanding service for products that weren't manufactured by Sun. Our alliance with Amdahl, for example, complements Sun's service offerings with full third-party hardware support, so customers can take care of all their service requirements through a single vendor.

Worldwide Market Development

Sun's implementation of the leveraged alliance strategy has helped the company enter and succeed in new markets both at home and overseas.

Our operations in Japan provide a good example. Unlike other computer vendors that have attempted to do business in Japan by simply extending their vertically integrated business model to the Japanese market and muscling in on Japanese customers, Sun's approach has been to enter Japan through Japanese partners.

First, we established a local presence with staff and office facilities. The local staff then went about investing in strategic business relationships with Japanese suppliers, distributors, and manufacturers—who of course have a great deal of experience with local expectations, requirements, and culture. As opposed to the traditional "direct sales" model favored by other computer vendors, Sun sells into the Japanese market with assistance from its partners. In addition, rather than setting up its own manufacturing plants, Sun purchases many of its workstation and server components from Japanese firms—some of whom are also Sun customers. The larger of these companies—such as Fujitsu and Toshiba—are potential sources for multiple products, including microprocessors, memory, power supplies, keyboards, and so on.

Buying from suppliers who are also customers yields several positive results. First, it strengthens the business relationship between the companies. Second, it allows for the possibility of more attractive purchase terms on both sides. Negotiations do not have to center on cash-only transactions. Hence, currency risks on both sides can be hedged to some degree. Third, it makes the market more competitive by increasing the number of competitors.

Sun's leveraged alliance approach has created a mutually beneficial relationship between Sun, its partners, its customers, and the Japanese economy. Sun is able to take advantage of Japan's advanced R&D and manufacturing bases; partners have the freedom to create the industry's most innovative leading-edge products; customers can find a solution that fits their business requirements; and Japan benefits from the resulting increase in business. Today, Nihon Sun is one of the most successful foreign enterprises in Japan. In the Japanese workstation market, Sun is now the dominant force, with approximately 40% of the market in 1994. In fact, Sun is the only foreign company in Japan with a number-one share in a key computer segment.

The leveraged alliance model works equally well in European countries. Throughout Europe, Sun regional offices are staffed by both U.S. and local employees who are charged with creating demand for Sun products. The staff forms alliances with local companies to adapt products to meet specific local requirements, or to supply components to specific geographies.

Another Winner: Local Economies

Clearly, Sun's leveraged alliance model can yield large benefits for corporations. What is frequently overlooked is how local economies also benefit from this approach. Obviously, local economies are always beneficiaries of increased volumes of business. More workers have jobs, more companies have customers, and more taxes flow to local coffers. But consider the types of jobs Sun's leveraged alliance model produces. In contrast to companies that simply take advantage of low wage rates to build factories that employ minimally skilled workers, Sun helps encourage the development of an information technology infrastructure—a workforce of highly trained, well-paid people.

For example, in China, Sun's vertically integrated competitors have built factories that take advantage of low-cost labor. These factories create low-wage, low-skill jobs. In contrast, Sun has set up four offices in China that are incented to create alliances with other local companies—even to encourage the formation of new companies that can provide specialty products and services—to satisfy the requirements of local customers. In addition, Sun provides training for its reseller partners, allowing individuals to build their personal levels of expertise, which in turn results in a more skilled workforce. In China, all of this has led to the development of a thriving microeconomy that simply didn't exist previously. Sun has many similar examples throughout the world.

Redefining the Supplier Relationship

In the old business model, corporations maintained "arm's length" business relationships with their suppliers. Sun is redefining this relationship by viewing its suppliers as integral partners in the company's business. This fosters a closer relationship in which both Sun and the supplier work together to make each other more competitive.

The cornerstone of Sun's new approach to supplier relations is its Supplier Management Model, unique in the computer industry. Under this model, Sun assembles cross-functional teams to develop and execute strategy for the purchase of each core commodity: chips, mass-storage subsystems, displays, batteries, and so on.

The leaders of these teams, called Global Commodities Managers (GCMs), develop a strategy road map three to five years ahead, taking into account new developments in technology, product shipment forecasts, supplier capacities, etc. Every six months, the GCM meets with individual suppliers to discuss the latest long-term strategy and compare it against the plans of the supplier. As a result of these meetings, suppliers are clear about Sun's expectations and any investments they may be required to make to accommodate those expectations, and Sun is clear about the supplier's ability and willingness to conform to its strategy.

Loyalty Rewarded

Sun in turn rewards suppliers that are able to comply with a high level of loyalty. More than 85% of Sun's expenditures to suppliers last year went to the company's top 20 suppliers, an indication that Sun provides major volumes of business to companies that meet its criteria. In 1994, the total of that expenditure was approximately $2.5 billion, or almost 60 cents on the dollar of Sun's worldwide gross revenue.

The redefined supplier relationship has proven to be a win/win situation for Sun and its supply base. For Sun, the benefits are quite tangible. Sun's inventory turns—a metric that depends heavily on good relations with suppliers—are approximately 11 per year, double the average for other computer vendors. Sun has also achieved remarkable gains in productivity through good supplier relations: Revenue per employee is more than $400,000, much higher than the industry average. For suppliers, the new model has resulted in increased productivity and competitiveness, and a closer working relationship with a very large customer.

Clearly, the traditional organization chart doesn't mesh well with the leveraged alliance business model. A centralized, top-down bureaucracy crushes the entrepreneurial spirit and responsiveness that the alliance model creates.

Over the past few years, Sun has been experimenting with and refining an organizational structure that is completely novel in the computer industry. We have formed several discrete operating companies to focus on developing and marketing the company's core technologies independently. For example, Sun Microsystems Computer Co. (SMCC) manufactures and markets SPARC workstations and servers; SunSoft focuses on selling software products, such as operating and development environments, networking and network management products, and multimedia

178

software applications; SunService provides consulting services, education and system support; and SunExpress offers quick, easy ordering and delivery of selected Sun products.

New Ways to Win

Each of the companies is operated as a separate business, run by a general manager who has decisionmaking authority and profit-and-loss responsibility. Each develops its own product lines. And each implements the company's leveraged alliance strategy in its own way, forming partnerships with other technology vendors, suppliers, customers, and competitors as necessary to meet customer requirements.

The new structure has brought Sun Microsystems Inc. closer to its customers, and has made the company more responsive and dynamic than ever. As separate entities, the business units have the flexibility to pursue new alliances, markets, and customers for Sun at their own pace.

For example, by breaking out service as a separate business, Sun is now able to offer its customers a broader range of service options. As an independent business, SunService is free to create service alliances on its own terms with a large number of third-party companies, who provide specialized services under the Sun name. This helps Sun create a critical mass for itself in the service arena while also cutting market development costs.

By using strategic alliances creatively, Sun encourages innovation and competitiveness. All around the world, Sun partners—ISVs (independent software vendors), resellers, suppliers, distributors, customers, and even competitors— are actively looking for new ways to win business by forming alliances that leverage each other's core competencies. In a world where the pace of change is scorching, this approach opens up new opportunities for forward-looking companies to create a competitive edge.

1995

Few have contributed more to the United States than inventor and entrepreneur Simon Ramo, who was awarded the Presidential Medal of Freedom by Ronald Reagan, and whose initial R is in TRW, the company he cofounded. Interestingly, the violin paved his way. As a senior in high school in 1929, he spent all his savings on a top-of-the-line violin for a competition he hoped to win—the prize would pay for college. "Many years passed after that first deliberate gamble before I realized I had become a hybrid of scientist, engineer, and entrepreneur. Risk-taking, I understood well by then, was a major factor in my life." He won, and earned a Ph.D. in electrical engineering and physics from the California Institute of Technology.

Ramo then took a research job with General Electric, and by age 27, he was recognized as the preeminent expert in radar technology; however, he found the GE bureaucracy stifling, and in 1946 he joined the fledgling Hughes Aircraft Company "to institute high-technology research and development." It was perfect because Howard Hughes, the owner, was a recluse, so Ramo had both funding and free reign. To keep the entrepreneurial spirit alive, Ramo said, "We would have a weekly 'town meeting' where the scientists and engineers could voice their ideas about how to cut administration red tape and maintain close communication and mutual stimulation to achieve the full benefit of each other's talents."

As Ramo and Hughes Aircraft gained recognition in developing weapons such as air-to-air missiles, the U.S. government became worried about the increasingly bizarre Hughes being in control and threatened to pull the plug. So Ramo and his friend Dean Woolridge left in 1953 to found the Ramo-Woolridge Corporation (to merge with Thompson Products in 1958 and become TRW). Their first project: overseeing the development of the intercontinental ballistic missile (ICBM). Whether anticipating military or commercial needs, the entrepreneur must define his market and its potential. Toward that end, in *The Technique of Anticipation,* Ramo lists six steps for taking the mysticism out of vision, which he likens to driving on a fast, bumpy road.

The Technique of Anticipation
Simon Ramo

W e are unlikely to be very effective in guiding the society of the future if all we do is respond to unanticipated events after they occur. The beginning of action toward the superior utilization of science and technology for society is to anticipate changes before they take place.

Everyone occasionally daydreams about how nice it would be to be able to predict what will happen and then go about exploiting this knowledge in advance of the events and in advance of others. But it need not be just wishful thinking. It is possible — on a sound, professional, and effective level — to anticipate change and to benefit from such anticipations.

Of course, all predictions of the future are bound to be incomplete and of questionable and limited accuracy. Thus they are potentially misleading and, in the wrong hands, even dangerous. But this is where the discipline of professionalism comes in.

At the outset, we must recognize that prediction as such has a bad "image," as it is called these days, particularly among those who are the most necessary participants if this sort of prediction is to be done well. Industrial leaders are inclined to shy away from anything that sounds like the dreaded "planned economy." Political leaders like to associate themselves with the "pragmatic" approach. Both groups prefer to profess that the world is too complex for one to look ahead and base serious plans on what one thinks will happen. Instead, the safer course is to "tackle each problem as it arises." The academic community especially shudders at the thought of prediction and anticipation. Such activities are associated with crystal balls and horoscopes—at best, guessing, and at worst, an activity for charlatans.

All of us whether in our family activities, businesses, professions, schools, or government, are engaged in predicting the future and choosing what we do in substantial part based upon those predictions.

Yet all of us are engaged in doing it, and our efforts are necessary and serious. A scientist will choose an area of research in which he thinks the probability for discovery is high, basing his selection on his existing knowledge and what seem to be favored directions for the future. Economists are now expected to produce not only analyses of the past but specific future figures, and the consequences of their estimates are significant. Industrial concerns have to plan ahead, even though, too often, when a planning group is set up it soon gets isolated from the chief executive's office.

All of us, whether in our family activities, businesses, professions, schools, or government, are engaged in predicting the future and choosing what we do in substantial part based upon those predictions. We do this often without articulating how we do it, without consciously analyzing the available facts and possibilities and consequences. And we do it without any commitment to the idea that we should spend some of our energies improving our ability to look ahead and act on what we see.

Now, in a world in which things change slowly, in which one can easily shift courses with no noticeable loss, it would not be very important to pursue this subject further. But our civilization is changing rapidly as a result of accelerating technological advance without balanced social progress. Our world is so dynamic, in fact, that more things happen *to* us than *because* of us. If you are going ten miles an hour in broad daylight on a straight road with little traffic, it is sufficient to look ahead for only a few feet. But on a bumpy road with fast vehicles, traffic congestion, fog, mud, impatient or drunk drivers, and surprising intersections and obstacles, you had better look well ahead and learn how to translate what you see into appropriately timed steering wheel, accelerator, and brake activities.

Since we are engaged in prediction in any case, why don't we set out to do it right? Can we do it professionally, even scientifically? Can we find methods for anticipation that will give us enough warning so that we can plan, prepare, and take timely action to attain our objectives? I submit that we can. By the systematic use of an orderly technique, we can do an effective job of anticipating the major technological events that will have significant impact on our society.

Six Key Steps

First, list the major technological changes that can be anticipated.

Second, order the list by relative importance; reorder the list as to probability of occurrence; then reorder it again as to time of occurrence if the events do occur.

Third, for those listed events which have a strong enough combination of importance and probability, try to describe the potential impact on society.

Fourth, for each such event, separate possible consequences into "good" and "bad."

Fifth, analyze and plan how to maximize the benefits and minimize the dislocations.

Sixth, organize to implement this plan.

It is obvious that these six steps constitute both a tremendous oversimplification and an overly ambitious effort to arrange that science and technology be used to the fullest on behalf of society. We are not in a position, with the social structure of our time, to carry through these steps completely. Nonetheless, we can come a great deal closer to proceeding effectively along these lines than a superficial first contemplation might suggest.

As an example, consider the "Technological Probe," an experiment of TRW Inc., one of America's largest and most highly technological corporations. For that company's future, it is extremely important that major technological advances be anticipated, if at all possible, in order to permit effective planning for the maximum use of the resources of the corporation.

In principle, the "Probe" is a simple exercise. The subtleties and pitfalls are in the execution and utilization of the results. Some one hundred fifty scientists and engineers are carefully selected for a combination of wisdom, imagination, and proven ability to accomplish well-above-average results in the application of advanced science and technology. They are asked to set down their guesses of significant changes on the technological front that might occur in the future—just possibilities, not absolute predictions of what will necessarily happen. Their opinion is also asked as to the probability that the event will really occur and, if so, when.

All the events listed are then circulated to all participants. After editing and refining the descriptions of the events, a total of a thousand to two thousand key items remains. Typical ones are 3-D color television in millions of homes, a manned landing on Mars, multichannel educational TV programs direct from satellites to rooftops, fuel-cell operated automobiles, supersonic planes in daily use, computer-controlled traffic in large cities, electronic teaching aids in most schools, a tenfold improvement in weather prediction, and hospitals designed by the systems approach.

At TRW, it was found necessary to computerize the information-flow process. Consider that there are events numbering thousands and, for each, numbers for probability of occurrence and for description of the time period, each of these in turn to be designated by each of hundreds of participants, to which are also added, as the Probe proceeds, a group of company-pertinent criteria like society's demand for the product, TRW's ability to handle the development, and the strength of competition.

This system produces more than a record of the feelings of a large number of experts. A stimulation process is set up that acts on everyone, and promotes searching by the individual with regard to the reasons for his particular estimates. For example, when one person differs significantly from the majority of his peers, this discrepancy is pondered and discussed. The over-all analytical process thus brings the series of listed possibilities to a jell, which would yield rewards even if the exercise were to go no further.

A private corporation, of course, cannot totally determine its future . . . Its ability to capitalize on early recognition of changes depends upon numerous factors beyond its control, including political, social, competitive, and broad economic considerations.

The next step is to arrange this list in order of the importance of the potential impact of these events, should they occur, on the company, so that both opportunities and negatives become apparent (the latter, for example, because the direction of technological change could cause some profitable product areas to disappear). The list is also ordered as to likelihood of occurrence. If an event is either extremely important, even with only a small probability of occurring, or fairly important, but with a high probability of occurrence—and especially if it is both—TRW then takes some follow-up action.

A private corporation, of course, cannot totally determine its future, even if it anticipates to perfection the major technological advances which might bear upon the product and services from which it makes its living. Its ability to capitalize on early recognition of changes depends upon numerous factors beyond its control, including political, social, competitive, and broad economic considerations. Yet with competent effort at anticipation, a company can prepare itself for potential consequences, and thus be in a far better position to benefit from the changes as they occur, and to minimize what otherwise might be severely negative impacts. . . .

The Elephant Department

Can we really claim the possibility of being *scientific* about anticipation? Of course, there is more than one meaning to "science"; what the physicist means when he uses the word may be a little different from what the political scientist or the sociologist might mean. But we can start applying this term to our technique of anticipation if, for one thing, we go about it in a logical and objective manner, because that is part of what it means to be scientific. We should try to understand what is behind the results we get, and that, again, is being scientific. But more especially, there are certain scientific techniques which we can apply. We can use *feedback* to compare actual with predicted results. Where there is a difference, we can use that difference to improve our approaches, our models, our estimates of trends, and our system, whether clear or vague, of giving weight to various aspects of our procedures for reaching our list of possibilities and probabilities.

Thus, for example, TRW's planning anticipated there would be a NASA, before Sputnik, by a combination of extrapolation of the technology and a model or theory we had of the pattern of decision-making and organization by the federal government when it comes to the handling of new major technological efforts. Our model was intended to cover this kind of situation: an activity has to be managed by the federal government; it is new; no agency is clearly the natural one to take it on, and there are instead a group of agencies which seem only in part well-matched to this new issue. According to TRW's postulate of the general pattern of federal government behavior, a new agency will be set up. The theory did not say this always happens. It did say that it has a high probability of happening.

This is an example of a theory we can go back and check. If over a period of time we find that this pattern does not happen often, and that we have been listing a possibility as reasonably likely when it appears to be unlikely, then we should change the theory. This is, again, one of the basic approaches of the scientific method.

We can particularly emphasize short-term items selected for expected importance and probability, and then plan to revise all forecasts frequently enough to accomplish two purposes. First, we want to have the most effective possible description of the future. That means updating and revising, making use of new information as a continuous process. But we also want to be scientific in the sense that we want to improve our ability to do predicting and anticipating. So we want to evaluate what we have done against the actual truth as the future becomes the present. Our plotting of the trajectory of change, our predictions, should hopefully, on the average, lie increasingly closer to the actual as time passes, or we are not making progress.

If we have surmised, for example, that there are only four routes to a certain destination, and events show that there are fourteen, and the destination is not so certain, then we should go back and review what it was about our thinking, or about the available facts, that led us to such wrong conclusions. We should ask whether anything has happened that affects us seriously and that we did not list as a possibility. The scientific approach is not limited to natural physical phenomena, where it is possible to keep a record with utmost precision of what happens in controlled experiments planned to pin down a theory, or to find a basis for a theory that will cover the fundamental relationships involved. The scientific method can also be used where we cannot hope to capture and understand all the facts and interrelationships, and where we are satisfied with only a partial and not wholly accurate picture.

In summary, we can do the first of the six steps we outlined earlier. We can list ahead of time many of the important technological changes that will face us in the years to come, that is, if we put our minds to it. But can we go on to the other steps? Will we be able to order the possibilities by importance, separate the anticipated benefits from the impairments of our society that result from these postulated events? Can we go on to plan and implement action to maximize the good and minimize the bad?

It is submitted that for virtually any private operation, it should be entirely feasible to do something practical on all six steps. Of course, we have to worry that we will estimate a mouse to be an elephant occasionally. Even this is not too penalizing if we avoid setting up an expensive ivory marketing organization well ahead of time. We should plan to carry on our regular operations just as before, using whatever approach we have been using (even if it is just hunches by a chief executive who has been successful in the past, or fast response on an opportunistic basis to an event when it does happen). We ought to put the anticipation effort on top of the present activities, as something to do in addition that ought to be profitable. When it comes to step six, organizing to implement the plan to maximize the good and minimize the bad, we should not commit our operation to one or another anticipated event so fully that if wrong we are irrevocably lost on a dead-end road. We must keep in mind that any given happening might not happen, or might not happen as anticipated. In fact, such a disappointment is obviously one of the things we should anticipate.

We will not get through these six steps at all unless we understand our objectives and can set down criteria of what is good or bad for our operation. We need a basis for comparative tradeoff analyses. This is a key aspect of the systems approach, whether we call it by that name or not. It will do very little good to anticipate what might happen, and to plan to take advantage of these anticipations by appropriate early action, if we have too little understanding of what we are trying to do, or of relationships with the outside world. It can be said, naturally, that if we have serious shortcomings in these respects (and all activities do), then the anticipation exercise is worthwhile for this reason alone. It is part of what should be a high-priority plan of action to remove these deficiencies in management.

We have to worry that we will estimate a mouse to be an elephant occasionally.

These six steps should be broadly useful in virtually every business and industry, because we assume that there is still in the United States considerable justification for using the words "private" and "free" for private, free enterprise operations. There is usually quite a lot of action that such operations are free to take without waiting for outside approval.

1970

DAVE THOMAS
1932–

Any connoisseur of fast food knows Wendy's and the founder's wry television commercials, especially the "Where's the beef?" campaign from the 1980s. Back in his youth, Thomas ate many a meal in cheap restaurants (wondering that very question about the beef), and it was then he decided to be a restaurateur. During the Korean War, he volunteered and attended the army's Cook and Baker School. According to Thomas, feeding 2,000 hungry soldiers a day taught him "some important skills about the big picture of feeding a lot of people." After the army, he worked as a short-order cook for a man who happened to also own four Kentucky Fried Chicken franchises. Luckily for Thomas, the franchises were failing, so his boss offered him a deal: If he could turn around the KFCs, he would give Thomas 45 percent ownership.

One of Thomas's first moves was to install air-conditioning to attract customers, but the bank refused him a loan. He now advises, "When you pick a banker, don't go after the one with the fanciest computer system or the slickest brochure. Pick a bank with experience in dealing with small businesses and a banker with a good sense of business judgement." Eventually, Thomas made good, then cashed out for $1 million in 1968 and started Wendy's with his proceeds. He emphasized a homey feeling in his restaurants and fresh burgers that didn't sit under heat lamps.

Both quality and image were key, for as Thomas explained in his autobiography, "Food is a personal thing, and it's tied closely to family life. People want to know the values of the person ladling it out." He doesn't hold those who focus just on the financials in high regard. "Today, too many MBAs make a lot of money BEFORE they're thirty, and all they know about business is how to read profit-and-loss statements." Part of business is gut instinct, which is how he came up with the name, Wendy's. In *The Secrets of Sniffing Around* Thomas explains how the name came about, and how he tapped into the antiwar sentiment during Vietnam, using social trends to find the right market.

The Secrets of Sniffing Around
Dave Thomas

When my daughter, Melinda Lou, was born, neither her brother nor her two sisters could pronounce her name. They started calling her Wenda, which then turned into Wendy. Her cleanly scrubbed, freckled face was it. I knew that was the name and the image for the business: "Wendy's." And I knew "Old Fashioned Hamburgers" had to be part of the image because that's the type of hamburger we'd serve. With the name WENDY'S and the logo of a smiling, wholesome little girl, my restaurant would be the place where you went for a hamburger the way you used to get them, with fresh, pure American beef. My experience with the Colonel[*] taught me the importance of image and of having a personal identity tied to the restaurant.

Wendy's was born at a time when nostalgia was sweeping the country. I wanted to offer a warm but simple family atmosphere, with upscale overtones, so the interior of any store featured carpeting, Tiffany lamps, hanging beads, old-fashioned advertising on the tabletops, and bentwood chairs. The crew was dressed in traditional "whites," which gave the feel of cleanliness and tradition.

[*]See Colonel Harland Sanders' essay on page 309.

The women wore white dresses and scarves, and the men wore white pants, white shirt, a black bow tie, and chef's hat. Everyone wore white aprons.

The menu for Wendy's would be limited and simple. A single hamburger would go for 55 cents, a double for 95 cents, and a triple, with ¾ pound of meat, for $1.35. Thick and meaty chili cost 55 cents, a creamy, smooth Frosty, 35 cents, french fries, 30 cents, and assorted beverages ranged from 15 cents to 25 cents. My angle was that at Wendy's you could get hamburgers served the way you liked them because of the many ways you could mix the condiments. The customer could come up with hundreds of combinations, but the meal itself was super narrow. The only item on the original menu that we got rid of was sugar cream pie at 40 cents a slice. Why? Because I kept on eating it all, and we'd forever be running out for the customer.

Wendy's stuck with my original menu for ten years, but it was a fight to keep it that way because there was always pressure to add more items. I'd come up with ideas. Everyone else would, too; but we hung tough. To this day, I believe that most entrepreneurs—especially in the restaurant business—get into trouble by making their menus too broad and offering too many products.

Before we opened, my biggest worry was the view held by serious business people that the fast-food industry was saturated, and the last thing that America needed was another hamburger restaurant. Every day, there'd be articles in *The Wall Street Journal* or some other business publication about new fast-food places. To me, hamburgers made to order and made from fresh meat made all the difference. My friends Len Immke, Ron Musick, Kenny King, and Bob Barney—who hooked up with me at KFC—supported me 100%. Wendy's would work, I knew, if the product was made fast enough and costs were controlled.

I always preach about having a plan, but, ironically, I really didn't have a plan for Wendy's when I started out. What I had was a concept and plenty of operating experience, but there was no five-year plan with a restaurant-opening schedule or a financing program. There was nothing like that at all. For the sake of drama, I wish I could tell you that it was more complicated than that, but it wasn't.

I believe that most entrepreneurs—especially in the restaurant business—get into trouble by making their menus too broad and offering too many products.

On November 15, 1969, I did a lot of praying. That was the day we opened the first Wendy's. We had three full-time employees. Gloria Ward Soffe, who still works for me today, was bookkeeper, chili maker, and register operator.

A crowd of Columbus dignitaries—including the mayor—and a number of suppliers came to the opening party. The hit of the evening was little eight-year-old Wendy. Lorraine made her a long blue-and-white striped dress, and styled her hair, sprayed it, and put pipe cleaners into her pigtails to make them stick out. On the end of each pigtail, Lorraine tied two blue bows. About midway through the party, I felt a tug on my jacket. Wendy looked at me, pigtails drooping, and said, "Daddy, I've been smiling so much, like you told me to, that my mouth hurts now."

From that first day forward, Wendy has been a great spokesperson for the company. When she was sixteen she gave a speech to fifteen hundred people at our annual convention. She's lost some of her privacy because she's been tied so closely to the company. While in school at the University of Florida, she got plenty of letters from guys who had hopes, she says, "of marrying her dad's wallet." (Relax, guys. Wendy and Paul are happily married, have a youngster, Amanda, and now have a Wendy's franchise.) Because some people still take her for the official company spokesperson, sometimes she hedges speaking her mind. I don't blame her.

The first day we opened our doors for business, customers were lined up down the street, and the business caught on right from the start. Like Len Immke said, the time was right. But why? Because the market was ripe for the business. The opening of Wendy's wasn't backed up with fancy market research, but I had a nose for trends in the restaurant business. (Research isn't everything. Not long after we started, Burger King paid a lot of money for a research study that explained why Wendy's wouldn't work.) Now, I can look back and tell you what those trends were. Back in 1969, those were feelings in my gut. They would have been tough to put into words then, but let me try now.

The Secrets of Sniffing Around

1. *People wanted choices.* This was the time of Vietnam. People were rebelling against everything. Some big segments of the population were tiring of a prepackaged world, including the stuff they were getting at McDonald's. They wanted some influence over what they were buying. Also, people were doing a lot of experimenting. They wanted something new.

I always preach about having a plan, but, ironically, I really didn't have a plan for Wendy's when I started out.

---

2. *People were fed up with poor quality.* There was a big drive for things natural and wholesome, the way people remembered them being before World War II. Today's baby boomers were then just becoming young adults and discovering their taste buds. They wanted better alternatives.
3. *People were adjusting to a new, more complicated way of life.* So many changes were going on—the Vietnam war, comput-

194

ers, the stress of modern-day life. The young adults were after something that was "totally radical," while their parents just wanted the kids to turn down their stereos and stay in school. The parents wanted a simpler time and traditional values. In a funny way, the old-fashioned decor and the Tiffany lamps provided a novelty for the young adults and nostalgia for the older generation at the same time.

Research isn't everything. Not long after we started, Burger King paid a lot of money for a research study that explained why Wendy's wouldn't work.

---

4. *People were on the move.* That's why the Pick-Up window was so important. Drive-ins had lost popularity, and nobody had figured out how to deliver a custom sandwich through a pick-up window. It's interesting that this is one part of the business that we didn't perfect right away. At first, Wendy's succeeded as a restaurant, not a carryout spot. However, when we got the pickup right, it was such a powerful advantage that it allowed us to franchise the business fast.

5. *People were ready for an upscale hamburger place.* Plenty of people were like me. They grew up loving hamburgers, but they didn't like what they got at most fast-food places, where the food was designed for kids and teenagers who really didn't care what they were eating.

Knowing these five trends allowed Wendy's to focus on the right market. My bet is that if you looked at any successful business, you would find factors very much like these behind that business's success. If you're going to bet your bankroll on a business concept, you had better be able to understand those forces. If you can't describe them, you have to feel them so clearly in your gut that you *know* you're right.

1991

J. C. Penney's first independent venture, a butcher shop, failed because he refused to supply meat to hotels that sold liquor (Penney's father was a Primitive Baptist preacher and a Missouri farmer with 12 children). In 1902, he started working for a dry goods store in Kemmerer, Wyoming, and was eventually allowed to buy into one-third of the business for $2,000. He then opened two more stores before buying out his partners for $30,000 in 1907. Several years later he owned 13 stores, calling them the Golden Rule Stores (Penney insisted his employees never touch tobacco or alcohol). In 1913, the name of the stores was changed to J. C. Penney, and by 1917 he was operating 175 stores.

The rapid growth and financial success was achieved in part by requiring the store managers to own 33 percent of their store, an early form of franchising. The arrangement provided Penney with financing, and provided the managers with a stake in the businesses' success, the importance of which Penney had learned back in Kemmerer. To find those worthy of a partnership in his store, Penney looked for very particular qualities in the people he hired, even paying close attention to their body language during interviews. In 1918, he personally interviewed some 5,000 applicants and hired about 100. "One of the first tests to which I put an applicant is to make our offer just as unattractive as possible," he said. Penney also believed in studying the applicant's face: shifty eyes suggested furtiveness; tight, thin lips suggested mean spiritedness; and so on.

Penney's most ingenious revolution was the creation of a central warehouse and corresponding inventory control system, which greatly increased buying power and reduced overhead costs. Inventory turnover was key: "No article that seems likely to impede the speed of the turnover either because of its price, or its novelty, is purchased." In the following selection, Penney provides a blueprint for his buying, selling, and inventory strategies, among other management principles that any entrepreneur selling merchandise should have stamped on their business plan.

Why a Buyer's Market Hasn't Changed Our Plans
J. C. Penney

Nineteen years ago out in Kemmerer, a little Wyoming town, stood on the main street a roomy, sturdily built general store. The proprietor was well rated and carried stock which on an average, he took pride in saying, was worth $100,000. He sold on credit—mostly long credit—and was known to do a business running to $150,000 a year.

He bought entirely from salesmen and never bothered to visit the big city markets. He bought also on credit—mostly long credit. His half-dozen or more clerks had been with him a long time; they were experienced and they intended to stay on as clerks; they knew the stock and the high and low prices for each item. They knew something of human nature— enough, anyway, meticulously to bargain.

It was the custom in those parts then to dicker over all prices. That was an established store, one of the few landmarks of Kemmerer. Anybody who was anybody for miles around owed the proprietor money.

Around the corner from the big store there stood a weatherbeaten old 1½ story shack with a 25-foot front and a depth of 40 feet. It strikingly resembled a none too carefully put up construction camp. Into it one day came a man and his wife and set up a general dry goods store with a stock of staple goods that were worth about $6,000. The couple slept in the bare half-story room over the main floor and their furniture was wholly made from packing boxes and crates. They were itinerants in property but residents in intention. What little they had they kept very clean and not only was their sales stock fresh, new, and good, but also their prices were far below those of the big store. They had bought it directly in the big markets and for cash. However, they sold only at one price and for cash; they would not shade a price for a large buyer or give credit to the richest man in the country.

The people did not like that way of doing business; their intelligence was insulted by the notion that the newcomer expected them to pay the first price asked and their integrity was assailed by his refusal to open books. But the prices were attractive and so whenever they had money to spare they bought at the new store. When they needed time they bought at the old store. The shack did a business of $29,000 that first year.

The big store is still there — but it is no bigger than when the little store started. The little store is now a big store, but it is guided by exactly the same principles as was the shack. It is known as the "mother store" of a chain of 312 stores that last year did a business of about $50,000,000!

My wife and I were the couple who started that little store. We honeymooned cheerfully among packing cases. I was the manager and she was the clerk. Out of that store grew other stores and out of them grew still other stores, and out of them more stores, until we have the many stores of today. But I did not start all of the stores and do not own them. I did not start that first store on my own money; I had only a third interest at the beginning — two other men held shares. My third interest had been gained by work and saving.

Just as I was a partner in that store, so other men became partners with me in later stores and then they in turn took partners. All of them gained their interests by work and saving. No man ever came in because he had money to invest. The only money that ever counted with us was that which represented the margin of earning over spending by men who worked so hard that their time for earning was great and their time for spending was small. Thus the chain made its own links and they were human, not money, links. . . .

When a Man Earns Something He Really Appreciates It

A third interest in a small store, for we fixed the capital of the early stores at from $6,000 to $9,000 each, was as little as might reasonably be expected to offer full compensation for effort and as large as a man could easily pay for out of his own effort. For our men have almost wholly earned their partnerships — no partnerships are given. They are all paid for either in cash or by note.

Many of these men began as clerks at Kemmerer and there learned our principles of business. In this way the Kemmerer store became known as the "mother store." As the head of the organization I managed the finances of all the stores and at the end of each day they all turned over their cash receipts to the mother store.

This eliminated bookkeeping in the various stores and also concentrated the cash with the central buying power. It might seem that this policy was evolved out of a lack of confidence, but that is not the case; the new partners in each store are the distributing end of what came to be a central buying organization. The force of that cooperation would have been impaired by the introduction of individual fiscal policies. It is easier to teach a man merchandising than it is to teach him finance. The individual stores have no need for money, while the central buying store has, so it has proved better policy to centralize bookkeeping and finance. Thus we have the force of a great corporation and the initiative of individually owned stores.

There you have the idea behind what is now a great chain of stores. They are not stores—they are individually owned distributing stations formed on the power of human association and in the exposition of these broad policies.

The most splendid of merchandising organizations will not function without men of the right kind. The men put the plans into effect; they are the foundation. Possibly the right kind of employees can be hired, but a hired man is never so useful as a man who has a sense of property—a substantial money interest in the result of his own effort. Such a man might not alone be able to make his own business pay—the wastes of individual effort and the struggles of small capital against large capital often take away the profit that would otherwise accrue. He finds himself handicapped by lack of training, by lack of capital, and, if he is only an average man, struggles to a bare existence, or else fails utterly.

It is not that the man is incompetent. The average man has a measure of success within himself. He is simply never able to buy the proper tools. He is personally more efficient as a proprietor than as an employee; but so seldom can he make proprietorship worth while, that commonly he must look forward to being always an employee. Everyone recognizes as perhaps the largest of our industrial problems the matter of gaining the initiative of proprietorship and still availing oneself of the economies of massed capital. That is what we think we are accomplishing.

Our scheme is to give to the man who proves that he has the ability, the tools of proprietorship and to admit him as an individual unit to the advantages of large organization. Naturally, every man is not qualified for this larger opportunity, but there are men in plenty with all of the qualifications; the thing is to search them out.

That thing we do by taking away every one of the better-known qualities of a "good job." We have no "berths" or "snaps" to offer. "Easy money" is something we are always out of. No man will join our forces or, if he does join, will stay with us unless he is willing to work for tomorrow rather than for today. We give only the opportunity to prove worthy. We do not offer money—as a matter of fact, we consistently try to make the starting salary so far below the market rate that the salary itself can be no inducement whatsoever.

Take a typical case in Salt Lake City. A man there named Hawke was a salesman in a clothing and men's furnishing store making on an average $50 a week including commission. He was married and apparently needed all that he earned. I happened to know him and I offered him a position at $90 a month without a bonus. We have no bonus or commission arrangements. Accepting the offer involved closing his house and moving to a little mining town. The future held the possibility of becoming a partner, but I never promise any man a partnership within a stated time or at all. The partnership is ahead only for the man who can get it. This man accepted. That was in 1912. Today he is a partner in three stores and the hundreds that formerly made up his income have been replaced by thousands. We have dozens of similar cases.

Until recently I personally interviewed all applicants for positions. Some of these men come with recommendations, others come because they have heard of us, and others come in response to an advertisement that we usually keep standing in a number of newspapers. This is the most repelling advertisement that we know how to frame. Its general form is:

Men Wanted: Well-established mercantile concern operating 312 retail stores offers:

1. Long and continuous hours of work.
2. The work itself, hard, ceaseless, trying, testing.
3. The work-drive unrelenting, day in and day out.
4. And for it, a small living salary: perhaps less than you are getting now.

This very unusual advertisement draws plenty of answers. Some come out of curiosity—to see if the writer were not joking. To them a job with work possesses the interest of a freak exhibit. They come to look—and go away shuddering. Out of every several hundred applications from all sources, I get about one prospect. I found my choice upon the man's desire for work and his capacity, as far as I can judge it, to work.

What Is the Best Way to Pick Good Men?

The interview goes on the basis of what he has to offer—not what we have to offer. I never bid for him, I never hold out any hopes, and if I find the man is looking for a job instead of for an opportunity we go no further. The salary is especially low, often lower than it need be, because only by this course can the possibility of getting a floater, a chronic job-hunter, be eliminated.

Once a man is selected he goes to a store for training. If he proves he is worthy he will be sent on to manage a tryout store, and then if he has saved his money and further proves he is competent, he will have the opportunity to open a store with a one-third interest and be in line for the regular chain development.

I usually select young men, because the older man is apt to have become set in his ways—to have gained too intimate an acquaintance with a rut. The older man who is alive and wants to get out of his rut is just as good material as the younger man and we have many partners who started when well past 40 years of age.

All our men have come to us on this basis. It is an absolute rule with us never, under any circumstances, to bid for men or to bother with men who want to be bid for. If a man does not think he will have a better chance with us than outside, then outside is the place for him. We want him to

start with us at a lower wage than he has been getting elsewhere and to end with a larger income than he could get
elsewhere.

One selects partners with care. They will make or break
the partnership. So they must be personally acceptable to
the dominating spirit of the whole organization. This dominating spirit is moral and Christian; we feel that *morale*
comes after morals. We do not require religious affiliations,
but we think a man is the better for having them. He may
choose his own denomination. And we will not have men
who drink, smoke cigarets, or gamble.

Thus we gain a homogeneous body and we have practically no turnover at all in our sales force. The competition for all kinds of labor that lately the country has been
passing through did not touch us. Our people did not come
for wages and likewise they would not leave on that
account.

We have never had to make a readjustment on the
human side; the process of man-building has been steady
and uninterrupted. And we consider ourselves first as a
man-building and secondly as a merchandising organization.

The original merchandising plan of the original shack at
Kemmerer is still the plan under which we operate. We
never rent a store in what is supposed to be a good location
and at a high rental. We try to locate in a fairly central position in a town, but rarely on the main street. We want low
rents. We take to a side street and if the side streets are
expensive then we go to the edge of the business section or
wherever the rents are cheap. We find that people will come
to our stores to buy without regard to location; if we paid
high rents, we could not sell at a profit and keep within the
line of our small mark-up. So we pay no attention at all to the
number of people who habitually use a street on which we
plan to open a store. If 1,000 people a day pass one point and
the rental is high we should not hesitate to go to a street
where only 50 people pass in a day—if the accommodations
are good and the rental low.

How We Manage to Keep Expenses Low

We do not go in for large stores—a small store may grow into a large one, but it starts small. That initial capital does not give much leeway for a splurge; it has to go into stock. We do not need warehouses nor even much storage space, for a store in our system is not a reservoir of goods. It is a distributing point. The store begins with a staff of five people, including a cashier. One store now has 40 employees, but the average is only 7 with extra people in for Saturdays.

These stores do not advertise extensively and the entire expense of doing business must keep within the line of absolute necessity; of course, it is to the manager's interest to keep expenses down both on account of his own profits and for the record of the store. It is easy to keep this expense down because of the character of the organization; the managers receive small salaries and depend upon their profits for real money; the most important clerks have small wages and are working ahead to become managers. And the clerks who are not in line for partnerships find themselves in such an atmosphere of work that those who want to shirk go elsewhere quickly. I cannot imagine a less agreeable place to loaf than in what is known as a "Penney Store."

I had been taught the value of direct cash buying and quick cash selling in that first store at Kemmerer. That principle rules our every store. When we had fewer stores I did all the buying, coming East very frequently and especially in nervous markets, for it has never been our policy to buy far ahead. As the chain grew larger we established a main buying and accounting office in New York in order to be right in the center of the trade. We established branch offices at St. Louis, both to buy shoes and to distribute to our stores in the Southwest, and another branch at St. Paul to serve the Northwest. The whole idea is to provide a sort of pipe line from the sources of supply direct to the distributing stations.

J. C. Penney

A Successful Policy for Buying and Selling

Our policy is to buy frequently and for cash. We hold that it is no part of the merchandising function to speculate in goods value. We might make large future contracts on a rising market and profit by the increased value of the goods. But on the other hand, future contracts would be losing ventures in a falling market. We should have to alter our principle of merchandising to sell the cheaply bought goods at the market instead of at cost, while the goods bought in a falling market could not be sold at cost over a long period. So instead we buy frequently, get the goods out instantly to the stores by express and sell at cost plus our mark-up. Our stores turn their stocks on an average of five times a year, so by the time any large change in price has reached the retail market we are buying and sending out at the new price.

Neither the branches nor the stores carry inventories above what might be termed current needs. With our fingers always in the primary markets and with cash in our pockets, we are content with hand-to-mouth buying and permit the other man to do the guessing on price.

We do not gamble against the market; we buy what we need and not what the other man wants to sell to us. In the end we obtain our goods at a lower price than the average buyer who attempts to get the better of the market and we are never stuck with great lots of high-priced goods. Therefore we have no special sales of any kind throughout our whole chain and never have to go through the operation of adjusting our inventories. A man with cash can always buy what he needs.

We buy only staples; we do not carry fancy or unusual goods of any kind. Our appeal is to the middle class that wants honest merchandise—dry goods, men's and women's ready-to-wear clothing and shoes, men's furnishings and general dry goods. We will not depart from the staple colors or the staple sizes; for instance, in shoes we do not carry

"AA." We would not go into furniture—we have frequently been asked to—because furniture moves slowly and requires storage space. We want the bulk of our goods to be right on the store shelves where they can be sold with a minimum of handling. No article that seems likely to impede the speed of the turnover either because of its price, or its novelty, is purchased.

We do not want the whole trade anywhere; we want only that trade to which we can promise to give the largest value for the dollar. That we have always done, but we could not continue to do it if we experimented with styles or laid wagers against the course of prices.

We buy only staples; we do not carry fancy or unusual goods of any kind. Our appeal is to the middle class that wants honest merchandise.

If we wagered against prices, customers would lose while prices were going up, and we should lose when they were going down. We are distributors of merchandise, not speculators, and during our 19 years of business life we have never had to take a serious loss on merchandise.

How Can You Control the Work of Your Managers?

Our purchases are in a way standardized, but the individual store stocks are standardized only to the extent that the store manager must select from the stocks of the buyers. A store in Texas will not carry the same kind of a stock as a store in the Dakotas. The buyers go out several times a year to convenient points and there the managers of the district gather, inspect the samples, and give their orders. The managers are supposed to be able to judge the wants of their customers and about how much they will sell, but they, too, are encouraged in hand-to-mouth buying, and, with the express delivery service, they cannot gain by buying ahead. If a man did try to buy out of proportion to his sales, the central office buyer would advise with him. But the thorough training that a man receives before he becomes a partner avoids the danger of overstocking.

These stock selection meetings are supplemented by sectional conferences for both social and educational purposes and the whole staff receives monthly a house organ that not only acquaints them with what is going on throughout the organization, but also contains articles by the buyer, on market conditions, articles from managers explaining how they have met specific problems, and articles from the executives conveying whatever general messages seem apposite. This magazine is now being supplemented with a regular business training course.

Most business problems arising out of the change from post-war to normal conditions analyze down to adjusting hours, wages, and inventories—to the adjusting of values—human and material.

Because out of the 2,800 people who are in our organization the most important men—the key men—in each store are partners or on their way to being partners, we have not had matters of wages, or hours, to deal with. A man who is working for himself does not bother about his wages or hours. Because we distribute goods at the market price plus the price of our service, we have no inventory problem.

1921

VICTOR KIAM
1926–

Victor Kiam is, of course, the man who said in his renowned commercials, "I liked it (the Remington electric shaver) so much, I bought the company." At the time of the 1979 purchase, Remington was on the skids, but he used his entrepreneurial drive to turn it around. He cut positions, perks, and prices. "My actions were very psychologically oriented because they were designed to make the company more entrepreneurial . . . ," he said. In fact, Kiam defines entrepreneurs as being people "who understand there is little difference between obstacle and opportunity, and are able to turn both to their advantage." His first solo venture was a Coca-Cola stand on the sidewalk outside his grandfather's house in New Orleans; his latest, Travel Smart, a travel company which, in part, markets EarPlanes, a product that relieves ear pain while flying.

Before pursuing his own course, Kiam graduated from Harvard Business School in 1951 and promptly joined Lever Brothers as a management trainee. For four years he found himself selling cosmetics to backcountry pharmacists, who had a habit of mixing up cold medicines in their basement that "had the kick of low-grade bourbon." In 1955, he left for Playtex, where he found undergarments more interesting and was known to rent a monkey, so customers were sure to remember his sales pitch. He reached the position of executive vice president, but then in 1968, he attended a conference that included a panel discussion on entrepreneurship. Kiam was so enthralled with the speakers that he quit Playtex that same year to pursue his own interests.

As Kiam developed his entrepreneurial and management skills, he recognized, "I couldn't always outthink or outplan my competitors. Who can? But I could sure as hell outwork them." However, making the commitment to being an entrepreneur requires more sacrifices than just sweat equity. Kiam warns that you must be prepared to accept a much lighter wallet in the beginning, and to lose friends, lovers, and even spouses. In the following selection, Kiam provides a blueprint for how he turned around Remington by focusing on one product, the razor, and by tackling the problem of never ending styles.

Remington's Marketing and Manufacturing Strategies
Victor Kiam

W hen I first took over Remington in 1979, the company was mired in the doldrums. This had not always been the case. Sperry-Rand, the international conglomerate, had bought the organization in the late 1940s. It had wisely chosen to retain Remington's founder as president after the acquisition.

During his tenure, Sperry stayed pretty much apart from Remington's day-to-day operations. There wasn't any reason for it to do otherwise; Remington had long been a leader in the electric shaver industry. The company had earned a well-deserved reputation for manufacturing a product of the highest quality. With its founder in charge, Remington continued to prosper.

In 1967, the company was struck by an inevitable but, nonetheless, severe blow: The original owner retired. This was not thought to be a tragedy at first. A company the size of Sperry had the luxury of being able to choose a new Remington president from a large cadre of able executives. Unfortunately, the company, having always placed an emphasis on high technology, appointed a fellow with an engineering background. This proved to be an error. Remington was a consumer products company; more than anything else, it needed a marketing person to guide its fortunes.

The new team in charge was more than capable, but they didn't know how to sell shavers. Realizing this, they brought in marketing experts from Sperry and the outside. This would have been a fine solution, except that none of the people brought in had ever been involved with anything that even remotely resembled the shaver business. Under this well-intentioned, but misguided, administration, the company went into a 12-year slide. It found itself in danger of slipping out of the marketplace.

Kiam's Homework

I was aware of Remington's problems before I bought the company. Naturally, a large amount of homework had been done before the purchase was attempted. Part of the research I did is well known due to the Remington commercials. Before 1979, I had always been a blade man; I had never used an electric shaver. When I told my wife I was interested in acquiring Remington, she went out and bought one of its shavers, and insisted I try it. It gave me the best shave I had ever had.

> Remington was a consumer products company; more than anything else, it needed a marketing person to guide its fortunes.

The day after that shave, I conducted my own market research test. I purchased the top shaver models of each of the leading brands. I would stage a competition each morning. For example, I would shave half of my face with the Remington and the other half with a Sunbeam. The following morning, the Remington would match up with a Norelco or a Schick. It took on all comers. By week's end, I believed Remington was the best electric shaver on the market.

Those tests convinced me that Remington could be a marvelous acquisition. I have always believed that for a product or service to thrive, it must deliver quality. A fine product or service is its own most impressive selling point. Once I took over the company, my task would be to get the public to share my enthusiasm for this great shaver.

The Sperry-appointed management had failed to do that. Instead of developing a top-notch marketing program, it had placed too much emphasis on creative design. Every six months or so, the engineers would introduce a new Remington shaver model. Sometimes the model-to-model changes were so subtle they were barely perceptible. Despite this, each new wrinkle compelled the company to drop its prior model. The result was chaos in the marketplace.

> I have always believed that for a product or service to thrive, it must deliver quality. A fine product or service is its own most impressive selling point.

Retailers hated the never-ending innovations. Who could blame them? Shavers they had purchased only six months earlier could become obsolete overnight. Store owners and buyers were naturally leery of keeping a heavy Remington inventory. They were afraid of getting stuck with the merchandise.

This had a dreadful impact on the company. Our research disclosed that Norelco, which rarely changed its styles, outsold Remington four to one. You know what else it showed? Retailers were stocking ten times as many Norelcos as Remingtons. That made sense; they were being forced to go with the more stable product. When consumers came in looking for an electric shaver, they often found that Remingtons were out of stock. You can bet they weren't going to wait for the next Remington shipment to arrive.

> Every six months or so, the engineers would
> introduce a new Remington shaver model. . . .
> The result was chaos in the marketplace.
> Retailers hated the never-ending innovations.
> Who could blame them?

The ever-changing styles were only part of the shaver's image problem: It also suffered from a hazy identity. When I first arrived at Remington, models were identified by numbers. The top shavers were called the XLR-3000 and the XLR-4000. Other models bore the letters PM and a number. When I asked one of Sperry's marketing people to explain the codes, he replied, "PM is an internal nomenclature. It means Professional Model. XLR is a popular automobile, so we thought it would be a good name for a shaver."

Well, pardon me, but the logic of that escaped me. Experience had taught me that a product's name must be attractive, and that it must also tell the consumer something about the merchandise. PM and XLR were not attractive names. More importantly, they didn't tell consumers anything about the shavers. They might just as well have been named Laurel and Hardy. Come to think of it, that would have been a vast improvement. At least it would have garnered some attention.

We looked at the USP (unique selling proposition) of each shaver in order to develop new product names. The XLR featured a system that shaved you as close as a blade. It became the Remington Microscreen Shaver. The PM, about to be streamlined into a lower-priced model, had three heads. *Voila!* The Triple Shaver was born. Later, it would become the Triple Action Shaver because it shaved three ways. These new names made a tremendous difference in how we were perceived by the public. Now our shaver names set off an immediate mental image in the public mind. Every time they were mentioned, our USP was automatically driven home.

A product's name must be attractive, and that it must also tell the consumer something about the merchandise.

Remington shavers also had been undermined by a faulty pricing philosophy. Actually, the problem was that it wasn't a philosophy at all. Whenever the competition raised its prices, Remington followed suit. When I asked a marketing director about this approach, he explained, "There are only so many electric shavers sold in the United States. The idea, therefore, is to sell as many shavers as we can at the highest possible price." That had to be one of the craziest theories I had ever heard.

Big Changes

As soon as I took over Remington, I began to implement some changes. I was assisted in this endeavor by a small team made up of people I had worked with at Playtex and Lever Brothers, and executives I had retained from the prior Remington/Sperry administration. There were few of the latter. We had to clear out nonproductive areas of the company. For instance, Remington had at one time been involved with a number of diverse products. Now it had only one product: the shaver. Yet it was still carrying five product managers. This meant we had four product managers too many; they had to go. Similarly, those ever-changing styles had handicapped the shavers with retailers. We solved this problem, in part, by getting rid of most of the engineers who had done the tinkering.

With Remington now streamlined for speed and efficiency, we worked on company morale. Many employees, positive we could not succeed where Sperry had failed, left us. Those who did not take part in the exodus were working in fear. This situation could not continue. To reverse it, we opened the lines of communication between our employees and management. We told them all our plans for the company, and convinced them that, with their help, we could revive Remington. Incentive programs were established for every employee, and the perks that separated management from the rest of the company were abolished. Everyone was given a personal stake in Remington's revival; each employee was made to feel a part of the Remington family.

A marketing director explained, "The idea is to sell as many shavers as we can at the highest possible price." That had to be one of the craziest theories I had ever heard.

While this was being done, we kept a good part of our focus on the shaver. Its latest version was festooned with chrome and fancy trimmings. It came packaged in a metal case that seemed heavy enough to give Arnold Schwarzenegger a good workout. We looked at this and asked ourselves: Did any of these adornments at all contribute to the shaver's performance? The answer was no. All they contributed was about $3 to our manufacturing costs. These accoutrements were consigned to shaver heaven, and the savings were passed on to the public.

We then decided—despite what that now-former marketing director had believed about selling shavers for as much money as possible—to introduce a lower-priced Remington. Those PMs, now unadorned and rechristened the Triple Head Shaver, were retailed for $19.95. At the time, the lowest-priced Remington had been selling for $34.95.

We could not have picked a better time for the move. The country was in a recession, and the shaver industry had been particularly hard hit. Old products and ideas weren't selling, and retailers were famished for anything that might stimulate the market. Knowing this, we went at them aggressively. Retailers were told how the new management was going to revitalize the company; more importantly, they received our assurances that our lines would be stable. Distribution, another problem under Sperry, also would be vastly improved. We told retailers that we would ship our orders within 24 hours of their receipt. These promises combined with their interest in the Triple Head Shaver to produce a necessary excitement for our product. Before very long, retailers who had shied away from all things Remington were solidly behind us. The Triple Head Shaver sold more than 500,000 units in the first year, which helped lead the way for Remington's resurgence.

With the retailers supporting us, we had to find a way to get Remington greater exposure on the selling floor. Retailers were reluctant to keep shavers out on the counter because they were easy to steal. In lieu of hiring armed guards, they displayed the models behind glass and under lock and key. This made it impossible for customers to just pick up the shaver and bring it to the check-out register—they had to wait until a clerk was available to assist them. This wait was costing us sales, so we developed a box that was just large enough to make it difficult to steal. With the shavers safely inside, the package was shrink-wrapped. This posed an obstacle for the would-be thief, who was now unable to pry open the box easily to get at the merchandise. With their fears calmed, retailers put our shavers out on the counter. The result was a dramatic increase in sales.

Strategic Marketing

One of our more well-known marketing strategies came as a response to a rival shaver's campaign in Great Britain. This company had instituted a trade-in policy: A consumer could bring in an old shaver of any brand and get a five-pound discount on the company's latest model. Always ready to go one better than our competitors, we came up with the no trade-in trade-in. If you were satisfied with our shaver, you kept it and continued to get a magnificent shave. If you were not pleased, the shaver could be returned for a full refund. This campaign evolved until it was introduced in America, making the Remington shaver the one "that shaves close as a blade or your money back."

It met with great success in the United States. Consumers recognized that our claims about the quality of our shavers were more than words; its performance was guaranteed. I am proud to say that less than 0.5 percent of our customers have returned their shavers. The quality of the product was the key element of the campaign. If the shavers had been unable to deliver as promised, the result would have been a catastrophe.

Without a hard-working crew or an excellent product, no market strategy ever devised would have been able to save Remington.

The Remington commercials featuring some unknown actor named Kiam grew out of talks with our advertising agency in Great Britain. They were fascinated that "a bloke like you could walk in off the street and buy a large company like Remington. That sort of thing just doesn't happen here." When I explained how I negotiated the purchase, the agency representatives seemed fascinated. They were especially taken with the part of how my wife bought me my first Remington. Their interest convinced us to build our new commercials around that part of the purchase. I believe these commercials have proved popular for one reason: They represent something almost everyone would like to do. How many of you have watched a television commercial and thought, "Gee, I could do that better than he can." If you were watching one of my commercials you were probably right. I went out and fulfilled my fantasy with the purchase of Remington, and I think it touches the Walter Mitty in many of the commercial's viewers. I'm an average-looking fellow who is not exceptionally gifted. Viewers correctly perceive that if I can live my dreams, so can they.

In closing, let me add one thing. Nothing we accomplished would have been possible without the best efforts of every Remington employee, or if the shaver hadn't been of the highest quality. Without a hard-working crew or an excellent product, no market strategy ever devised would have been able to save Remington.

1987

FRANKLIN A. SEIBERLING
c. 1860–1955

The Goodyear Tire and Rubber Company is named after the man who invented the vulcanized rubber process, Charles Goodyear; however, the man who founded the company is Frank Seiberling, otherwise known as the "Little Napoleon" of the tire business. The entrepreneurial spirit was in his veins; his father established several companies in the Akron, Ohio, area. After a brief stint at an Ohio college, young Seiberling worked at his father's farm-implement factory and later managed the Akron Electric Street Railway, in which his father had a controlling interest. Unfortunately, the panic of 1897 wiped out most of the family's business, so Seiberling struck out on his own.

In 1898, he bought a vacant cardboard plant for $13,500 and converted it into a rubber plant, intent on making tires and other rubber products. For his logo, he chose the Winged foot of Mercury, the Roman messenger of the gods. The first year, he had 13 employees manufacturing bicycle and carriage tires, horseshoe pads, and poker chips, which generated $500,000 in revenue. Within a few years, they were also making automobile tires, and Seiberling contributed to the industry by designing a tire-building machine and a straight-sided tire with a detachable rim, and by constructing a 21,000-acre rubber plantation in Sumatra, Africa.

By 1916, Goodyear was the world's largest tire company. However, economic trouble struck a second time: In 1920, the rubber market collapsed and Seiberling was stuck with some very expensive inventory. At age 61, he was forced out of the company in a reorganization and suffered a personal loss of $15 million, but the very next year he founded the Seiberling Rubber Company, where he remained chairman of the board until 1950. He was driven, no doubt, and was even renowned for never stopping to eat lunch. "Work hurts no one. Food does," he said. In a timely essay written shortly before the rubber market collapsed, Seiberling presents his strategic view on *Buying or Selling—Which Counts Most?* In founding his business, he said the key was learning who to buy supplies from and how best to make a product; once that's accomplished, the customers "will beat a path to your door."

Buying or Selling—
Which Counts Most?
Franklin A. Seiberling

U nless you happen to be born in a business way with a silver spoon in your mouth, probably your first buying problem will be to get someone to trust you. Our company had no silver or any other sort of spoon at birth; everything that we had was the result of money that we borrowed from those who had confidence in us and of money from the sale of stock to friends who thought we were worth taking a chance with. Because we had so little money we learned how to buy.

We had no general credit of any kind during those first critical years.

We did, it is true, succeed in inducing one machinery maker to trust us for a little additional equipment after we had been going about six months, but hardly were the machines in place before our creditor regretted his recklessness and wanted cash. Cash was out of the question, so we offered him a choice of all his debt in promissory notes, or half in stock and half in promissory notes. He chose the notes as the lesser of the two evils. He had no confidence that we would pull through. We paid the notes, but if he had taken stock and notes, that block of stock would today be worth more than his entire plant and equipment! We offered stock and notes rather freely in those days; for we financed on half a shoestring. And this is our record: No one who took a promissory note from us or trusted us on a book account ever lost money—unless he got nervous and sold out to someone at a discount. Those who, however reluctantly, took stock are today independently wealthy from the stock alone. All of which has nothing in particular to do with buying, but does go to show that sometimes it pays a seller to take a chance.

Whether you are a manufacturer or a retailer, and whether you have a big business or a little business, it is the kind of stuff that you buy which determines the kind of business you will do. You may be the most expert manufacturer in the world; but if the only buying sources which are open to you supply poor stuff, then the best that you can hope to build is a cheap and shifting trade, for you will not be able to hold these customers who buy on performance, and they are the only customers who are worth holding.

There are three ways of doing business. The first is to make and sell the cheapest article on the market regardless of quality. This is a poor and unstable sort of business that can never grow very large, for your customers will not return to buy a second time unless they can find no goods elsewhere; and, in any event, they will hardly be people of sound financial ability.

The second way of doing business is to make the finest article possible regardless of price and sell only to those "ultra" people who have the price. This is almost a luxury market and is not big enough to permit the economies in manufacture which come from volume production.

The third way, and the one that we settled on in the very beginning, is the middle course—to make the very finest article that can be sold at a price which the mass of the people can pay, pressing for volume production to raise the quality to a point where it will equal the quality which might be obtained under "ultra" quality production. Today, for instance, if we should change our policy and decide that price did not matter and that all we cared for was quality, we could not turn out a better product than we do already, watching both price and quality.

The fact that in the beginning we had to buy our raw materials for cash, no matter from whom we bought, allowed us to pick and choose. Cash makes the world your buying market. We bought from local supply people rather frequently, simply because we needed instant supplies in order to keep the place running and could not afford the time to go out into the market and buy on personal inspection.

Had we bought on credit in all probability we very shortly should have run into debt and have been compelled to take whatever was handed to us, for when a supply man tells you, although perhaps not in so many words: "The stuff I am sending to you is all right. If you don't like it pay my bill and quit buying." Then if you cannot pay the bill you have either to take the goods that he offers or his alternative to quit buying. Quitting buying means shutting up shop.

The independence which was literally forced upon us in those early days is one which we soon came to value and I regard it as one of the prime causes of our success. For it will be remembered that 15 or 20 years ago the predominant idea of the business world was selling, and a great deal more attention, generally speaking, was paid to making sales of goods rather than to making the goods. The sales manager was usually the king, the production manager a low commoner, and the purchasing agent a slave.

Looking around at various kinds of business, and especially those which had to do with the automobile, I notice that the concerns which gave their first attention to selling and thought that once an order was sold then the work was done, are today either out of business or running under reorganized management.

Take the selling in our own business today. Our business is not so very different from any other business, for a man demands pretty much the same sort of value from a tire that he does from a hat, or a suit of clothing, or a typewriter, or a desk, or in fact anything excepting a luxury article such as a piece of jewelry or a coat of arms. What he demands is the greatest amount of service in return for each dollar of investment.

In a tire, that service includes safety, ease of riding, and durability. Therefore, we no longer sell just a tire. Instead, we sell an amount of performance and it is the function of the salesman to be sufficiently expert in tire engineering to see to it that the purchaser gets the kind of tire which under the conditions of use will give the greatest performance.

If you do not know how to buy the right goods at the right price, all your refinements of design, of manufacturing, and of selling will be lost.

Here, in the factory, we design and make a tire to do certain things under certain conditions. We know that under those conditions, these tires will do what we say they will do; but, also, we know that a tire which is designed for one set of conditions and is a splendid tire for the purpose will probably be a very poor tire under another set of conditions. For that other set we have designed another kind of tire. Also, we know that if the tire be exactly suited to the conditions but be improperly treated, it will never have an opportunity really to perform. Therefore, we would much rather not sell a tire than sell the wrong one or have the right tire wrongly treated.

A shoe dealer with a salesman who insisted upon putting number 8 shoes on number 10 feet or number 10 shoes on number 8 feet would not be likely to build up a clientele of satisfied customers. That is the way we feel about salesmen. To our mind the biggest part of salesmanship is seeing that the right article goes to the right place—which is a very different matter from merely disposing of goods.

Getting the right article means good manufacturing. That means good buying. The buying is the beginning of the whole process, and hence if you do not know how to buy the right goods at the right price, all your refinements of design, of manufacturing, and of selling will be lost. The old saying that you cannot make a silk purse out of a sow's ear holds absolutely in business. My own personal experience teaches me that the really sound business is founded primarily on buying and manufacturing. It is perfectly true that if you know how to buy and to make, the world will beat a path to your door. We use selling and advertising to widen that path into a road.

There are several ways of buying. They are:

1. To buy everything that you use from a single jobber or broker.

2. To buy not from a single jobber but from the smallest possible number of supply men, it being tacitly understood that each of these men has practically a monopoly for the line that he handles.

3. To shop around, buying as closely as you can and trying to see to it that the man who sells to you does not make any money.

4. To shop around on a give-and-take basis, making sure that you get your goods at a fair price on which you can make money and at which the seller will not lose money.

5. To endeavor either to control or to own the sources and therefore make yourself independent of the market.

6. To make or control the source of only a part of your essential supplies.

If you know how to buy and to make, the world will beat a path to your door. We use selling and advertising to widen that path into a road.

The first method has nothing at all to recommend it. It is the lazy way of buying and also the lazy way of selling. More than that, it is the most dangerous method I know of, for what you are really doing is acting merely as an agent for the jobber or broker. Without the necessary competition of the market it is not human nature for you as a buyer fully to keep abreast of the latest developments; and if the seller is certain of your trade, no matter how conscientious he may be, he too will hardly keep at the same point as he would under the stimulus of competition. You have no accurate check upon price or quality. Suppose you have testing laboratories (they are absolutely necessary in a well-managed business) and you find the quality running down; you will not, unless you know the market, be able to answer the seller's excuse that the quality he is sending you is the best that is obtainable on the market. This is especially true today. Exactly the same thing applies to price.

But more important than all, you are really building on an outside individual whom you do not control; and thus your own investment is continually in jeopardy because the failure of the connection may leave you temporarily stranded. You are afloat on the business sea in a ship that has no water-tight bulkheads. An accident that would only inconvenience a protected ship will send such a ship to the bottom in a very short time.

A Danger to Guard Against Because Production Is Complex

Practically the same criticism applies to the second method of giving what amounts to a monopoly to some supply man in each line of your business. It is less dangerous than the first method simply because all of your supplies cannot be shut off at once. But since the absence of a single article in a manufacturing business may close down operations as effectively as though there were no supplies at all, the result is about the same. For instance, in our early years a coal company did grant us a short credit. Then suddenly they shut off that credit and gave orders that no coal was to be delivered without the money. If that company had not known we were solely dependent on them, they would not have been quite so ready to withdraw our credit.

Later when we got on our feet and could do more or less what we liked, we bought a coal mine of our own. Operating a coal mine was not enough. Once we had the coal on the surface, we had to get it to the works and then we ran up against a shortage of coal cars; so we bought our own coal cars.

We prefer to have the man who sells to us make a fair profit; and we continually stimulate him through competition to giving us the very best stuff that he can find or make.

The third method of buying which I have set out is that of the "keen" buyer—the man who thinks that he has struck a good bargain when he has bought at a price which he knows will result in a loss to the seller. That is not the kind of buying which makes for stable business; such a policy should naturally be avoided.

It may be well enough for the job-lot dealer or for anyone who is selling exclusively on price, but buying in such fashion bears precisely the same relation to legitimate buying as selling at whatever price the market will stand bears to legitimate selling.

It is a principle of salesmanship that the man who buys from you must get his money's worth, which means that he must get full value and service and be able to build up a trade for himself. The connection must be worth while. Conversely, if the man who sells to you loses money, he will sell only when he has no other more profitable customers. And if he is human he will devote more thought to trying to "stick" you than to giving you the best that he knows. Dealing with a man at arm's length, without a considerable degree of frankness is really worse business than giving to him a supply monopoly at whatever price he chooses.

We prefer to have the man who sells to us make a fair profit; and we continually stimulate him through competition to giving us the very best stuff that he can find or make. Thus we build up such a relation of confidence that he would no more think of trying to put anything over on us than he would think of flying to the moon.

The market lives, as a rule, only for the day.
A manufacturer must live in the tomorrow.

That sort of relation does not preclude careful inspection and analysis — both of quality and of price. Rather it tends to make those investigations cooperative and entirely to banish the take-it-or-leave-it notion of salesmanship.

Those who sell to us are in constant consultation with our purchasing department. In that way our men are of great service to the sellers because, seeing the market probably as broadly as the sellers, they are frequently in a position to give expert counsel that helps the seller with his other customers.

This cooperation is particularly useful because then you can have these supply men working ahead with you and they will be in a position to meet your future as well as your day-to-day demands. When we first began business we made only bicycle and solid buggy tires. But all the while we believed in the future of the automobile and for six years we carried on the development and sale of pneumatic automobile tires at a financial loss, just so that we might be ready to supply these tires when the boom which we felt sure would come actually got under way. Some years ago when people generally were burying the automobile we were extending our tire factories!

We felt the same way about the aeroplane, and, for half a dozen years before the war, maintained at a considerable annual loss a department for the development of aeronautics and for the making of balloons and of parts for aeroplanes. We were ready in that department when the war came. And our sources of supply were ready.

But one who buys in large quantities and with a long program in mind cannot depend wholly upon a market; for sometimes in spite of all efforts the market will not respond. The market lives, as a rule, only for the day. A manufacturer must live in the tomorrow. A seller of raw materials can sell to someone else if he cannot sell to you, and it makes no difference to him what the price is so long as he gets the profit. You as a manufacturer or as the seller of some reputation-making article are dependent upon what may be only a small fraction to the other man's business. A refinement of quality or a slight change that may mean everything to you, may mean nothing to the other man. Hence, buying may become a matter of directing and not merely of accepting supplies. . . .

This whole problem of buying is immensely intricate, and it develops in individual fashion according to the size of the business and its requirements. Some of our developments do not have a great deal in common with those of the small or moderate-sized business; but it is to be remembered that every one of our policies is a growth from small business. Because when we were small we planned our buying ahead—that is one of the reasons that today we are large.

1920

Since founding the company that would become America Online, Steve Case has hit his share of glitches. In 1987, for example, the company's board wanted to fire him for spending millions with no profit to show for it; when they went to a flat rate for unlimited access in 1997, a surge of users crashed their system twice, resulting in the company nickname America Onhold; and the Internet is always threatening to render AOL redundant. "I remember reading that the Internet was going to undermine AOL," he once said. "That was back when we had about 500,000 users." As of 1998, AOL had some 14 million members—so much for his detractors.

Case grew up on the island of Oahu, Hawaii, where he and his brother were budding entrepreneurs as kids, graduating quickly from selling lemonade to hawking watches. While attending Williams College, he also started a few small enterprises such as an airport shuttle. Then he joined the corporate ranks, working for PepsiCo, Procter & Gamble, and Pizza Hut. Meanwhile, as a hobby, Case bought a personal computer with a modem that allowed him to connect with Compuserve, the online service. "There was something magical about the notion of sitting in Wichita and talking to the world," he said. In 1983, Case quit the corporate world to join a start-up company, Quantum, that shipped Atari video games over telephone lines. Unfortunately, its capital dried up shortly thereafter. Not willing to give up, Case then built an online bulletin board for Commodore 64 computer users and grew the membership from a few thousand to 100,000. In 1991, Quantum became America Online.

Case's mission includes making the Internet central to people's lives like the television or the telephone and keeping the screen format, or interface, as user friendly as possible. "We want to offer the most magical service possible. We'll use the technology as a means to an end, but we've gotten here because we figure out what the customer wants, not what the technologists think," he said. In the *Ten Commandments for Building the Medium*, his number one is: "The Mass Market Consumer Is Thy Master."

Ten Commandments for Building the Medium

Steve Case

Y ou know the song: "What a difference a day makes?" Well, in our business, the song we sing is more like "What a difference a nanosecond makes."

It's no secret that this is an industry for the vigorous, not the faint of heart. The technological, social, political and economic forces swirling around the emergence of the Internet, and the challenges those forces present to us are fierce.

What I'd like to do today is give you some of my most recent thinking about where we are as a medium, where we're going, and how we should go about the business of setting priorities in this swirling environment. But first, let me give a little status report from the front lines. The number of people jumping online every day is staggering. At AOL alone, we grew from 10 million to 11 million members in almost three months. That's an extraordinary story about a truly extraordinary trend.

But the trend that we're finding is every bit as significant—more significant in many ways—is what those millions of people are doing once they're connected. In just over a year, on average, we've seen our members more than triple, yes, more than triple, their use of the service. Now, granted, a big piece of that has to do with the transition to unlimited

229

pricing. But frankly, our research tells us that the more significant driver of usage is the integration of interactive features and functionality into people's daily lives. These numbers and trends defy the establishment of any but the crudest predictions. They break every model. They represent a rate of public adoption of a new service that has no precedent. Still, there are those who can't help themselves from making predictions. And I can't help myself from quoting them. Jupiter finds that nearly 50 million people were online by the end of 1997. And it predicts that number will increase to 63.3 by the end of this year. And reach 87.3 million by the year 2000. And these figures refer to the United States only!

I don't know about that. What I do know is that those of us in the Internet community have found ourselves on a mission. It's a mission to make this new medium as central to people's lives as the television and the telephone, and even more valuable.

And perhaps the most important thing for all of us to remember about this mission, in order for us to succeed, is how far away we still are from realizing it.

The fact is that the Internet has so much mindshare right now, we've created such a big amount of noise, that it's beginning to feel like we've arrived. I compare us to a moon-bound rocketship. Yes, we've had our count-down and we've achieved a spectacularly successful lift-off, but we haven't left the earth's atmosphere yet, much less started walking on the moon.

Perhaps the most important thing for all of us to remember about this mission, in order for us to succeed, is how far away we still are from realizing it.

Or, for those of you who are metaphorically challenged . . . we're at the top of the 2nd inning.

When I focus on how many people are still not online, on how far we still have to go to reach the mass market, some people say, "Steve, you just can't see this glass as anything but half empty." And, I respond, "No, with 11 million members, we've definitely got a half-full glass. Problem is, we need to fill the whole damn swimming pool."

Recently, I've taken to using what I call the "Fifty, Twenty, One" model to describe where we are. That is, there are those who say AOL has more than 50% of the market. Well, that may be true of home PC users who are online in the United States. But if you look at us against all us Internet users, we're just at about 20 percent. Or if you look at us against all homeowners of PC's, we're only 20%. And, if you compare us to usage of the cable TV, to the major media and telecommunications companies, our marketshare diminishes quickly to less than 1%. Fifty, twenty, one.

I was in Davos, Switzerland, last month on a panel about Internet policy moderated by Eli Noam, and he summed things up very well from my perspective. "Remember," he said, "when you add up all of the people around the world who have access to the Internet and interactive services, you are still hovering at around 4 percent of the global audience of Bay Watch."

The Ten Commandments

The question comes down to how do we get where we want to go from where we are? And the answer I always give is: Stay in touch with the consumer. I've said this so much that people have been sending me emails advising me to talk about something else for a change.

So I've decided to change my tack somewhat today. It occurred to me that, well, the Ten Commandments are something that everybody knows, and yet provide a pretty good basis for discussion when starting a civilized society. And for four thousand years, nobody's criticized them for being tiresome or repetitive.

So let me share my Ten Commandments for building an interactive medium that's central to people's day-to-day lives.

Commandment Number One? What Else?
The Mass Market Consumer Is Thy Master.
In reference to this commandment, those who focus only on the fastest, most high-tech, most powerful technologies may find that they are worshiping an idol.

Technology is critical, and at AOL we're using it to allow members to send photos in email, send instant messages, and to personalize their experience, but ultimately technology is an enabler, a means to an end, and not the end in itself. It, too, should serve the mass-market consumer.

The fact is, today, technophobes outnumber technophiles by several orders of magnitude, and it's the technophobes we need to make this new medium truly mass market. The technophiles are already aboard. Which means that "easy-to-use, fun, useful and affordable" will win every time.

Ultimately technology is an enabler, a means to an end, and not the end in itself. It, too, should serve the mass-market consumer.

And we are making significant progress. Ten years ago, when we started, we were 90 percent male and 10 percent female online. Today, I'm very pleased to report that AOL members are 52 percent female, and 48 percent male, roughly identical to the consumer population as a whole.

Of all of the numbers and statistics about our service and our membership and usage, that's the statistic that best illustrates the true future potential of this medium to reach the true mass market.

The Second Commandment Is:
Thou Shalt Not Take Thy Competition for Granted.
There is no more competitive business than that of this emerging interactive medium. And this competition is occurring in an environment that is simultaneously wrenched by both an extraordinary pace of technological innovation and a dramatic convergence of powerful industries, including computing, entertainment and telecommunications. All of this means that the competitive landscape can, and does, change quickly and mercilessly.

Look at the emergence of Yahoo!, Excite and Lycos from unfunded good ideas to heavily capitalized forces in an unheard of period of time. That can happen in this environment and I expect it will happen many more times before the industry settles down.

People today compare AOL with MSN, Prodigy and Earthlink. In that pond, we're pretty big—we have more than 50 percent marketshare. But remember my 50/20/1 rule. Our little pond is merging with some pretty large rivers, lakes and oceans.

We don't look all that big when we're compared with The Walt Disney Company, NewsCorp, Time Warner, IBM, AT&T, Deutsche Telecom, SBC, Sony, and TCI. And, make no mistake, all of those companies and all of their competitors have only just begun to focus on their consumer Internet strategy, and all of them will come after their share of the market.

So anyone—in any piece of this emerging industry—who takes for granted either who their competition is or the ground rules that define that competition is making a fatal error. The competitive winners will be those with the greatest agility, the greatest ability to be flexible and opportunistic, and, of course, the best ability to envision the effect on the underlying experience of consumers.

The Third Commandment Is:
Remember the Day Thou Learned Economics 101.
This commandment could just as easily have read: Thou Shalt Consolidate.

233

Economics 101 tells us that when you have a whole lot of enterprises competing for the same consumers with products that are not significantly differentiated, you will see the total number of companies shrink, and the size of the individual companies increase.

So anyone—in any piece of this emerging industry—who takes for granted either who their competition is or the ground rules that define that competition is making a fatal error.

Remember when this happened just ten years ago in the PC industry? We're seeing all of the same signs today.

The fact is the period of consolidation is only beginning. We will see it continue and we'll see it accelerate. The only question is who will be the consolidators and who will be the consolidatees.

The Fourth Commandment Is:
Honor Thy Parents, Families, Teachers and Communities.
There are many different ways to judge the ultimate impact and success of a new medium. Clearly one of the most important is the role that the medium plays in expanding opportunities for our children, supporting families and empowering communities.

This is an area that our medium collectively must pay more attention to. And we'd better listen to parents and teachers. They tell us in no uncertain terms that they expect their children to be safe online. The bottom line is that these demands are reasonable. In fact, if Internet online services can't live up to those expectations, we don't deserve to be a mass market medium.

Here, too, we're making good progress. Last December's child safety summit was enormously gratifying for the breadth of participation from the Internet community.

Leaders from entertainment, technology, politics, government, and the private sector all came together to make children's online experiences safer and more rewarding.

As a next step, you'll see this September a major back-to-school public education initiative called America Links Up that will draw national attention to the issues associated with children online.

At AOL, we've also been giving a lot of thought to how we can best use the medium to strengthen civic discourse within our communities and to increase the participation by young people in political discussions.

Frankly, democracy in this country could use a boost. And this medium is tailor made to provide that boost. At AOL we are planning to use the 1998 election cycle to experiment in leveraging the medium to do four things: expand issue education; strengthen one-to-one communications between voters and elected officials and candidates; boost election turnout, particularly among young people; and develop workable models for putting political advertising in context.

Then, I believe you'll see that the year 2000 signals an arrival of the Internet in our political culture that is every bit as powerful as the emergence of television was in 1960.

The Fifth Commandment Is Particularly Relevant Today: Thou Shalt Not Spam.
Along with the online consumer, we're fed up with spam and we're not going to take it anymore. Today, in fact, I can share some news with you about how we're stepping up our anti-spam campaign.

We are adopting a "block and tackle" strategy against spammers. That is, we're going to block as many of their emails at the gateway as we can, and we're going to tackle them in court.

And, we're making some headway on the legal front. We have sent more than 500 cease and desist letters to spammers in just the last couple of months and have followed up with lawsuits against many of them.

Today, we're announcing that we've just won two more legal victories against spammers.

Once we bring the legal guns to bear, we have been getting some telling results. One spammer claimed the Fifth Amendment in his deposition. Another literally threw his computer into a swamp to destroy the evidence. Still others are telling us just how little money they have in their bank accounts and saying they want out of the business. Well, the more spammers we can get out of the business the better.

Which is why, today, AOL is releasing a "Ten Most Wanted List" of the worst current spammers. These are the ones we have in our sights. They include such lovely enterprises as:

- The notoriously nasty spammer
- Love-toys-online
- Lose-weight.org

Together, the spammers on our "Ten Most Wanted List" represent a severe impediment to the growth of the medium and are causing a significant depreciation of the experience of the average consumer. We look forward to taking them on one at a time.

Ultimately, however, it may be that a complete solution to the problem of spam may only come about through legislation, and we are actively pursuing that course, too.

The Sixth Commandment Is:
Thou Shalt Not Launch Before the Market Is Ready.
There are few more critical questions in the interactive services industry than how and when we will see the emergence of broadband. Broadband technology will enable an even more powerful and magical online experience that can help

us reach a wider audience. So, it is a critical personal focus of mine.

Still, let me go on record here and say two things about broadband. First, it won't come as quickly as most people seem to think. And, second, when it does come, it will be available over many more platforms than most people expect.

That doesn't mean we should take our eye off the ball now. In fact, now is when we should be laying the groundwork to ensure that, when broadband gets here, it is easy to use, ubiquitous and inexpensive.

Still, we expect that the availability of broadband will segment the market in the short term. Many customers will prefer to stick with a lower-priced service that is narrowband at a lower cost while heavier or more committed users will pay extra for more speed.

So, we're experimenting with all kinds of new technologies to deliver greater speed, flexibility and ease-of-use for our consumers, from wireless to cable to mindmorphing. And we're watching the equation carefully to understand when speed, platform, and price are in all in alignment for the consumer.

The Seventh Commandment Is:
Thou Shalt Not Fail to Take the Business of the Internet Seriously.
Many businesses do not yet understand that their core franchise is dependent on the emerging interactive medium. This underscores a fairly significant cognitive dissonance that persists among many very large companies who see the phenomenal growth of the Internet as something they need to experiment with, rather than as a make or break development for their entire business.

TV viewership is on the decline, for the first time in my lifetime, in proportion to the time being taken up by online activities. And TV audiences are fragmenting among the increasing number of channels. We believe that a significant reassessment of how traditional mass marketers do business is already underway.

Yet, there are still a lot of companies dabbling haphazardly with Internet advertising when they should be preparing for the full-scale transition to interactive marketing and E-commerce. These companies still have a grace period before they significantly disadvantage themselves by missing the trend, but not a long one.

Many businesses do not yet understand that their core franchise is dependent on the emerging interactive medium. This underscores a fairly significant cognitive dissonance that persists among many very large companies.

I predict that by the year 2000 we will see several examples of large, complacent companies that no one associated with the Internet suddenly in jeopardy and struggling to catch up in the face of competition that emerged seemingly from nowhere.

The Eighth Commandment Is:
Thou Shalt Not Deal with Washington Lightly.
Over the next five years, the future of our emerging medium will be influenced more by the decisions in the area of public policy than by technological development.

In addition to hotbutton issues of pornography and privacy, we've got a cacophony of issues to wrestle to the ground, including encryption, spam email, copyright, advertising standards, hate speech, universal service, access fees, tax issues and many more.

There's a simple statistic that vividly illustrates the amount of attention this medium is beginning to get from legislators. In the 103rd congress, 25 bills referenced the

Internet. So far, in the 105th congress, that number stands
at 151.

We, the entire Internet community, have a critical set of
questions to answer about how we want to govern ourselves
in the next century. But, as I'll describe when I get to the
tenth commandment, we should strive to do more than fend
off legislation, taxation, rule making, and litigation. Our goal
should be to fashion an age worthy of ushering in—not just
a new era, or a new century, but a new millennium.

To do that we have to be proactive and aggressive. If we
put our head in the sand, we will lose a unique window of
opportunity to make this medium something special.

The Ninth Commandment Is:
Thou Shalt Not Compromise Thy Neighbor's Online Privacy.
I've already mentioned that privacy is a critical issue for us
in Washington, DC. It's also a critical issue for us internationally, especially in light of the European privacy directive
which threatens to dramatically affect standard online business practices.

But privacy is one of those issues that transcends the regulatory and legislative challenges and even rises above the
public policy discussion.

The ability to build experiences that are highly personal-
ized and valuable for individual members is what gives this
medium its power. But that very power of personalization
can raise difficult issues of privacy.

The principles that should govern the industry's privacy
policies and standards are no big secret. But we must be
committed to following them.

They include providing consumers with full notice about
how their information is being used and giving them the
opportunity to make informed choices.

The privacy of communications like email, instant messages and chat should be uncompromised, and all of these
policies should be reinforced with state of the art internal
controls, employee training and enforcement procedures.

Finally, special attention should go to protecting children's privacy, including giving parents the absolute right to choose how information about their children is used.

I would hate to look back forty years from now and find that we have developed a plaything for the well-to-do.

I know there are those who worry that standards of privacy for the online world are higher than those for the offline world. They probably are. And they probably should be.

And the Tenth and Final Commandment Is:
Thou Shalt Build a Medium That Improves the Lives of All People and Benefits Society.
History tells us that when steam technology was first developed, both the French and the British had it around the same time.

The French, focused around their system of absolute monarchy, used the new technology initially to create toys for the children of their royalty and to pump water to the fountains of royal palaces.

The British could have chosen to use this power exclusively for their royalty too. But the British chose instead to use steam technology to power what would become the Industrial Revolution, the end of one phase of civilization and start of a new one.

I would hate to look back forty years from now and find that we have developed a plaything for the well-to-do.

Likewise, I would hate to look back and find that the Internet tagged as the television industry has been, perhaps unfairly—as a "vast wasteland." We are at an incredibly unique point in the development of this medium, it's big enough to be relevant, still young enough to shape.

The ways that this medium could benefit society are still emerging. I already mentioned the potential benefits to children and education. The medium also has the ability to elevate and expand civic discourse, including becoming a force for democratization and globalization, and also including healing the communications breakdown between citizens and their elected representatives.

It is not even too much to say that this medium could serve to provide solutions for economic, cultural, geographic disparity. It certainly can bring communities closer together and build greater communications and respect between people.

However, these things will not happen by themselves. It will require vigilance and determination to remain true to the meaning and potential of this medium to build a better, more connected society.

I sometimes feel like I'm behind the wheel of a racecar. I need to keep my eyes on the horizon, but I also need to keep my attention on the rear-view mirror to see who's gaining on me.

So those are Ten Commandments for realizing our mission of building a mass market medium that is as central and valuable to people's lives as the television and telephone.

Together they represent a sort of compass we can use as we hurtle across unfamiliar terrain at speeds we have never before experienced.

I sometimes feel like I'm behind the wheel of a racecar. I need to keep my eyes on the horizon, but I also need to keep my attention on the rear-view mirror to see who's gaining on me. From the passenger seat, consumers are telling me where they want to be dropped off and when, and behind me my shareholders and business partners are engaged in loud backseat driving. One of the biggest challenges is that there are no road-signs to help navigate. And, in fact, every once in a while, a close call reminds me that no one has even yet determined which side of the road we're supposed to be driving on.

And the finish line is a long, long way away.

I look forward to accompanying all of you as we take many, many more exhilarating laps around the track.

1998

PART V

Inventors Turned Entrepreneurs

It's a natural process that many inventors evolve into entrepreneurs and then businessmen. They don't always succeed, however, which is why those included here are worth listening to—they made the transition successfully. Although it is apparent from their essays that their experiences and lessons are greatly varied, Henry Ford opens by touching on a universally crucial element to succeeding as both an inventor and an entrepreneur—understanding human nature. Whether it be Ford and the motor car, or Steven Jobs and the computer, or George Eastman and the camera, they all focused on satisfying a human need, which is to enhance our experience by giving us useful tools. For example, Jobs compares the computer with the bicycle, in that the bicycle expands our physical capabilities and the computer expands our mental. Ultimately, it's about serving the public and society. There are, however, other lessons to be learned from inventors, such as how the creative process works, which Polaroid founder Edwin Land discusses, or the need for curiosity, which frozen-food pioneer Clarence Birdseye gleefully indulges in. Birdseye's number one axiom: "Develop a questioning mind and don't be afraid to take a chance!"

Henry Ford believed too many people fear being called a fool for taking an original idea and going into business for themselves. His response: "The best of it is that such fools usually live long enough to prove that they were not fools—or the work they have begun lives long enough to prove they were not foolish." When Ford left his cozy job with the Edison Company in 1899 and spent all his money on car experiments, he was called foolish. When he doubled his workers' wages to $5 a day while reducing a shift from nine to eight hours in 1914, he wasn't just called foolish, but also blatantly immoral by *The Wall Street Journal*. For Ford, it meant good business; he got the best of the workers and his actions held union activity at bay. From the days of growing up on a farm and rebuilding watches as a kid, Ford thrived on being independent.

It wasn't until he was 40 years old, however, that he finally formed his own company—twice before investors had pulled out for lack of faith. Ford didn't enjoy those early false starts: "During my first experience I was not free—I could not give full play to my ideas. Everything had to be planned to make money; the last consideration was the work." In 1908, he introduced the durable and popular Model T, which buried any doubts he harbored. Over the next years, he slashed prices from $825 to $360, which was made possible by dramatic improvements in production efficiencies; specifically, his implementation of the first conveyor belt assembly line in 1913.

Ford also focused on service. "The most surprising feature of business as it was conducted was the large attention given to finance and the small attention to service," he said. "That seemed to me to be reversing the natural process . . ." For him, the completion of a sale was only the beginning of his relationship with the customer, not the end. He put himself in their shoes. In *How I Made a Success of My Business*, Ford explains the importance of viewing life from other people's perspectives and understanding human nature to figure out how best to serve the public's needs, and therefore, succeed as an entrepreneur.

How I Made a Success
of My Business
Henry Ford

T here is one principle which a man must follow if he wishes to succeed, and that is to understand human nature. I am convinced by my own experience, and by that of others, that if there is any secret of success it lies in the ability to get another person's point of view and see things from his angle as well as from your own.

It makes no difference if a man employs ten men or ten thousand, the success of his business will be in direct proportion to his understanding of human nature. I would even go so far as to say that this faculty is the business man's greatest asset.

It is easy enough to say: "Understand human nature," but it takes a lot of hard thinking and constant thinking really to get at the significance of that remark.

Why It Pays an Employer to "Take Thought" of His Employees

What do I mean by saying that success depends upon the ability to understand people? Well, in the first place, an employer must understand the people working for him. He must not make the mistake of thinking of them as units or wage earners or as being in any way different from himself. If he is going to get their best work and effort, their interest, and consequently the best results in his business, he has got to realize that he has human beings working for him who have the same ambitions and desires that he has.

Every one of us, no matter who or what we are, wants to succeed. Now when an employer begins to see his employees in this light he has gone a long way toward success in business, for what happens? He begins instinctively to understand that the success of his workmen and the success of his business are tied up together and he will begin to wonder how his men can best succeed in his business.

He will discover that one man can do one thing better than another, or one group of men, and they will be shifted to that particular kind of work. And just notice what is happening in that business organization: the employer is specializing, he is getting the right people in the right place where they can work to the best advantage not only to themselves but to the whole business. Don't ever forget that the welfare of any business and the welfare of the individual workers are just as closely related to one another as the law of cause and effect. This is the law of cause and effect of business success.

And, after all, this is simply common sense. There is no denying that a man who works with enthusiasm and interest is going to earn a lot more for his employer than the man who is indifferent and discouraged, if only the employer will give him a chance.

I wish I could say to every employer in the country: Remember that your workmen are human beings with ambition to succeed exactly like yourself. Give them a chance in your business to serve their own self-interest in serving yours. Make them valuable to you by giving them a chance to become valuable to themselves. There is no way under the sun to get valuable employees except by giving them a chance to get ahead for themselves.

Now you can't fool anyone along this line. A man may

have a lot of fine talk about having the interests of his workmen at heart, but if it is not there in fact and deed, his men
will know it and he will not get their support.

It is the easiest thing in the world to inspire this loyalty,
but it's not to be done by any trick. It's simply a matter of
honest and sincere understanding of the workman's interests, a recognition of his ambitions as a human being. If your
men feel that is your attitude toward them, they will do their
best work every hour of the day.

What Does "Serving the Public" Really Mean?

The trouble with a great many of us in the business world is
that we are thinking hardest of all about the dollars we want
to make. Now that is the wrong idea right at the start.

If people would go into business with the idea that they
are going to serve the public and their employees as well as
themselves, they would be assured of success from the very
start. Everything connected with such a business enterprise
would work toward its success and the money would come
in without any worry on the part of anyone.

Now this suggests another idea along the same line. The
business man who wants to succeed must, on the one hand,
understand his employees and so organize his business that
each man in doing the best he can for his employer is also
doing the best he can for himself; and, on the other hand, he
must apply exactly the same principle to the public.

He must make the public serve him in serving itself. By
that I mean he must render the public a genuine service in
selling it his products. The public is quick to get a sense of
confidence, but it is just as quick to lose it when there is
cause. Just let a man take advantage of the public for his
own selfish interest and see!

The great chance for success lies in finding out what the
public needs, and right here comes in the ability to under-

stand human nature. The next step after finding out something that is necessary to people's welfare is to make that article the very best you can and sell it as cheap as you can, no matter if it be shoes or automobiles. Make something that the people need and make it so good that they want to buy your particular product; actually render them a service by selling them that article.

I tell you the man who has this idea of service in his business will never need to worry about profits. The money is bound to come. This idea of service in business is the biggest guarantee of success that any man can have.

One of the first things that a man has to learn in business is how little he can do by himself. When he finds that out he begins to look around for people to do what he can't. He begins to study people, he begins to see that everyone has something good in him and he begins to cooperate with the good qualities in the people about him.

I believe in this idea of cooperation in business and I believe in big business organization. The bigger the business the bigger the chance to harness up a lot of people with special ability. And in this idea of specialization lies the chance of perfection, and perfection means success.

The more you think about anything, the more you understand it; you get special information about it, and the more special information you have the better you are equipped to meet competition. It's the man who is the ablest specialist in his line who wins the biggest success.

Everyone of us can do some one thing very well, but none can do a lot of things well at the same time. Perhaps he will do them as well as other people, but that idea of doing things as well as other people has no place in business. We have got to do things better than other people if we are going to win out.

I am sure that it would pay a firm to do one single thing, say make one particular size in boots. If one factory devoted its entire energy to making one size in boots, millions and millions of pairs exactly alike, think of the saving in time and energy! And what was saved in time and energy could be put into the perfecting of that particular boot, so that it could be made the best and the cheapest boot in the world.

The great trouble in business today is that most people are so busy doing a variety of things that they have not time to get a real grip on any one thing.

I can't say too often that it is thinking that counts in business. A man who wants to get ahead must be thinking about everything that comes his way: about the people he employs, the people he works with, the people to whom he sells.

Everything in this world is tied up in one way or another with everything else, and a man can get a million side lights on his own specialty if he is always awake to its relationship with the rest of the world. Everything in the successful business is evolved by thinking, everything starts with a thought; and this habit of analysis, this ability to get under the surface of things, to get at the vital essentials, gives a man a tremendous advantage over those of his competitors who do not do likewise.

There is not one single detail in business today but can be improved by thinking. We have not reached perfection in any line. Improvement means increased success, and improvement is the result of thinking. The great trouble in business today is that most people are so busy doing a variety of things that they have not time to get a real grip on any one thing.

Now weeds are a very good illustration of what I have been saying about business. For centuries people have thought that weeds were perfectly useless. Farmers have spent time and money pulling them up, burning them up, anything to get rid of them.

Do Business Men Think and Read
as Much as They Should?

But now comes along a man who has been thinking about weeds, analyzing and experimenting, and what does he find out? That weeds are the best fertilizer for the soil and that instead of spending money to enrich his fields, all the farmer has to do is to plow the weeds under!

Think of all the money that has been spent, the time wasted, in destroying weeds which contain the very chemicals the farmer has been buying in the form of fertilizers! And all because the farmer took it for granted that weeds were his enemy and never stopped to do some special thinking!

Now this principle of specialization applies to the small employer just as well as to the large. If a small manufacturer begins to do some special thinking he will get big ideas about his work and as he follows those up in practice his business will grow accordingly.

I started that way. I had an idea and I thought about it. I kept on thinking, and I'm still thinking.

Why, the first man I ever hired was a fellow I knew. He's still with me. Why did I hire that particular man? Because I knew him, I knew what he could do. I saw that he had something I needed. Cooperation, you see, but on a small scale.

The boy we hired to run errands and sweep out the shop is now our head chemist. I didn't hire him with any idea that he could ever be a chemist. He didn't know anything about chemistry when I hired him. But I got to know him while he was working around the shop. As business grew he had more to do. He naturally grew as he had more to do.

I found out there were certain things he could do better than others and I put him on those jobs. Then the time came when we needed someone to make steel tests. We found that the steel we were getting was not always up to the samples. So he was sent down to the mills to learn all about steel and how to analyze it and make the tests. He began to do some of this special thinking I have been talking about.

> My advice to every business man is to read a lot and think a lot and work a lot.

He still is. He has found out a lot of things we never knew about steel. Special thinking, that's what it has been from the start with us. Anyone else can do the same thing if he works the same way.

My advice to every business man is to read a lot and think a lot and work a lot. If he will think and think and keep on thinking, and follow up his thinking with work, he is certain to succeed.

But he must not fail to think about people as well as things. He must understand human nature, as I said at the start. And the best way to understand human nature is to be friendly toward people. Everyone has some good in him and the man that has that attitude toward people will find their good qualities, and it's those qualities he wants to use in his business.

Why Criticism Is Valuable to the Business Man

And one thing more. No business man ought ever to be afraid of criticism. Just as sure as he tries to do anything different, he will stir up a lot of criticism.

But criticism is exactly like those weeds I was talking about—full of valuable fertilization. Just plow it under and let it fertilize your thinking. Criticism is the best educator in the world. Everything I have learned has been through criticism and the thinking it induced in me.

1916

This college dropout, one time experimenter in psychedelic drugs and practitioner of meditation, enjoyed attending electronics lectures at nearby Hewlett-Packard, where he first met Wozniak, then an HP employee. In 1974, Jobs took a video game design position with Atari, but as soon as he saved enough money, he left for India in search of spiritual enlightenment. Upon return, he and Wozniak began planning their computer of the future. In 1975, Jobs sold his Volkswagen microbus and Wozniak his scientific calculator to raise $1,300 to start their company. They then assembled the computers in the Jobs' family garage, selling them for $666 to electronics buffs.

In 1980, sales of Apple II, the first popular personal computer, were almost $120 million and that same year the company went public. To bring professionalism to the management team, in 1983 Jobs hired John Sculley, who was president of Pepsi, as CEO. To capture Sculley's attention, Jobs threw down the challenge, "Do you want to spend the rest of your life selling sugared water or do you want a chance to change the world?" However, an internal power struggle soon developed and Jobs was forced out in 1985. Not one to lament, Jobs founded NeXT, a computer company that was to challenge Apple, but it floundered.

Jobs was next involved with Pixar, a company that uses computers to generate lifelike animated movies, creating such hits as *Toy Story.* Meanwhile, Apple was struggling, and he was asked to return as interim CEO in 1997. In a move Apple loyalists derided, Jobs convinced Microsoft to invest $150 million to give them some financial breathing room. It proved to be a masterful marketing move—Jobs ended up on the cover of *Time* magazine. Apple is everything to Jobs; as he once said, "It's more important than finding a girlfriend, it's more important . . . than cooking a meal, it's more important than whatever." In the following 1980 interview, he describes his vision for the twenty-first-century bicycle (which we can now assess 20 years later). Also, Jobs explains that he and Wozniak had no desire to start their own company, but when established firms rejected their vision, they had no choice.

When We Invented
the Personal Computer . . .
Steven P. Jobs

What Is a Personal Computer?

Let me answer with the analogy of the bicycle and the condor. A few years ago I read a study . . . I believe it was in *Scientific American* . . . about the efficiency of locomotion for
various species on the earth, including man. The study determined which species was the most efficient, in terms of getting from point A to point B with the least amount of energy
exerted. The condor won. Man made a rather unimpressive
showing about ⅓ of the way down the list.

But someone there had the insight to test man riding a
bicycle. Man was twice as efficient as the condor! This illustrated man's ability as a tool maker. When man created the
bicycle, he created a tool that amplified an inherent ability.
That's why I like to compare the personal computer to the
bicycle. The Apple personal computer is a 21st century bicycle if you will, because it's a tool that can amplify a certain
part of our inherent intelligence. There's a special relationship that develops between one person and one computer
that ultimately improves productivity on a personal level.

Today most people aren't even aware that the personal
computer exists. The challenge of our industry is not only to

help people learn about the personal computer, but to make the personal computer so easy to use that, by the end of this decade, it will be as common in our society as the bicycle.

That's one of the reasons I wanted to do this interview. I wanted to explain what a personal computer is, how it can help all of us make better decisions and how it will eventually impact all phases of society . . . from training dolphins to glaucoma research to growing a more nutritious crop of soybeans.

What Is the Difference between a Personal Computer and Other Computers?

The key difference is that one-on-one relationship between man and machine I was talking about, because the emphasis is on a personal interaction.

The whole concept is this: for the same capital equipment cost as a passenger train, you can now buy 1,000 Volkswagens. Think of the large computers (the mainframes and the minis) as the passenger train and the Apple personal computer as the Volkswagen. The Volkswagen isn't as fast or as comfortable as the passenger train. But the VW owners can go where they want, when they want and with whom they want. The VW owners have personal control of the machine.

In the 60s and early 70s, it wasn't economically feasible to have the interaction of one person with one computer. Computers were very costly and complicated; 50 people had to share one computer. Back then, you could have the passenger train but not the Volkswagen. But with the advent of microelectronics technology, parts got smaller and denser. Machines got faster. Power requirements went down. Finally, electronic intelligence was affordable. We finally had the chance to invent the personal computer, to invent the "intelligent bicycle."

Basically, Steve Wozniak and I invented the Apple

254

Steven P. Jobs

because we wanted a personal computer. Not only couldn't we afford the computers that were on the market, those computers were impractical for us to use. We needed a Volkswagen.

People like us were the initial market for the personal computer. After we launched the Apple in 1976, all our friends wanted one. By the time Apple II was on the market in mid-1977, the demand for the personal computer had already begun to skyrocket.

Today, we've sold over 150,000 Apple personal computer systems. That's because Apple recognized this passenger train/Volkswagen relationship about 2 or 3 years before anyone else. When we designed Apple II, we wanted to offer the benefit of a $15,000 computer or a $100,000 timesharing system with a computer that costs as little as $1,500. Obviously, one of the differences between a personal computer and other computers is price. Another difference is size.

I'd like to use another analogy here: the big motor and the fractional-horsepower motor. When the first motor was invented in the late 1800s, it was only possible to build a large and expensive motor, just like it was with the early computers. Those motors were used to power entire shops, with pulleys and belts running throughout the shops to drive the individual machines scattered within. Only with the advent of the fractional horsepower motor could horsepower be brought directly to where it was needed.

With the portable Apple, you could say we invented the first fractional-horsepower computer. The Apple is small enough to go where you need it. You can get the information you need on your desk, in your office, in the lab, the school or the home. In other words, Apple broke down the huge monolithic computer into small, easy to use parts. We made the computer friendly. So, like the fractional horsepower motor distributed horsepower to where it was needed, the personal computer can distribute intelligence to where it's needed. Ultimately, it will be this distribution of intelligence that will change the way we all make our decisions. . . .

255

What Are People Going to Use Apples for, Ten Years from Now?

The Apple isn't some futuristic dream, it's a creative tool people are relying on right now. The personal computer is changing lives today.

A personal computer isn't only a tool for people in business. There's a whole generation of kids growing up learning how to use the personal computer as a problem-solving tool — 97% of the students in Minnesota have the opportunity to solve problems with an Apple. But Apples aren't just being used to teach computer science courses. Students from Alaska to Mexico learn physics, mathematics, spelling and a slew of other subjects on their Apples. And kids who have problems learning how to read and write are actually overcoming their disabilities with the personal computer Apple's colorful graphics that make it fun to learn; so problems these kids have are being dealt with successfully in a very innovative way.

Silicon Valley is the finest example of the American entrepreneurial, risk-taking culture.

As all these students who are now using Apples grow older, they'll integrate the personal computer into their life as a friendly tool, just like their bicycle. And those kids are the ones who will create the applications we at Apple haven't even dreamt of.

By the end of the decade, the personal computer won't be a mystery to anybody. Society will realize that the opportunity for a man-machine partnership is well within everyone's reach. Let's put it all in perspective for you: five years ago, the personal computer didn't even exist. Yet, as of this interview, personal computing has statistically reached one in every 100 American households — and there are 72 million households in America! By the end of the 80s, that figure will be one in ten.

Like a lot of entrepreneurs, Woz and I didn't consciously set out to start a company.

The vast penetration of the personal computer into our society not only is inevitable, it's real. I feel privileged to be a part of it all, and to see the results in my lifetime.

How Is Apple Computer, Inc. Carrying on a Silicon Valley Tradition?

Silicon Valley is the finest example of the American entre-preneurial, risk-taking culture. You won't find this kind of culture anywhere else in the world. Hewlett-Packard started here. Intel invented the microprocessor just eight miles from where we're sitting now. The heart of the semiconductor industry is here. Woz (Steve Wozniak) and I grew up in this Valley. Bill Hewlett and Dave Packard literally were our heroes when we were growing up, so it just follows that Apple would carry on the tradition.

Like a lot of entrepreneurs, Woz and I didn't consciously set out to start a company. We tried very hard to convince two other established computer companies to fund us while we developed the personal computer. We spent a lot of time and got nowhere. Ultimately, we had no choice but to do it ourselves.

Today, that entrepreneurial spirit still exists throughout the company. That's one of the reasons Apple's been able to attract and retain some of the finest technological talent in the world. Our people want to work in an entrepreneurial environment—and they also want to help create a product that will affect the lives of millions of people. . . .

How Is Apple Going to Maintain Its Leadership in the Industry?

Our industry is still in its infancy. It's continually evolving. Rather than just a series of events happening in the industry—new products, new companies coming and going—there's an underlying process going on here, a process to which Apple is committed: the integration of computers into our society on a personal level. We think that process is going to take 10 to 15 years. Let me give you two examples of processes like the ones I'm talking about, which we've all witnessed in our lifetime.

When was the last time you saw a mimeograph machine or used a piece of carbon paper? You don't use either today because of the invention of the Xerox machine—a tool that has radically altered the way we all work. Yet the first Xerox machine was introduced only 20 years ago, in 1960.

Second example: HP introduced the first handheld scientific calculator, the HP-35, in the early 70s. In less than 10 years, the world's largest manufacturer of slide rules stopped making slide rules altogether. We believe the integration of personal computers into society will have an even greater effect than the calculator or the Xerox machine.

We also believe Apple's continuing success and leadership position will result from innovation, not duplication. Innovation in products and marketing as well as in distribution.

For example, we've learned that one of the factors in the growth of our marketplace is that it takes about 20 hours to get truly fluent with your Apple. We'd like to reduce that to under an hour. The way this will be accomplished is to spend a larger portion of the computer's computational power on what we call the "user interface." The user interface is the way the computer and user interact with each other. Future Apple systems will spend more of the computer's intelligence to translate or adapt information in a way people are already familiar with, instead of forcing people to adapt to the computer. Let me illustrate this:

Look at any desk in your office. You'll see stacks of paper, the telephone, a calculator and a typewriter. The people sitting at these desks must intuitively understand concurrency—several things occurring simultaneously. They understand priority—stacks of paper on a desk, with the one on top being most important. And they understand interruption—the phone rings, a memo gets put on top of a stack, etc.

But if you went up to any one of them and asked if he or she could define concurrency, priority and interruption—you would probably get a blank stare. Yet people intuitively understand things that they're not cognizant of; we all know more than we know we know.

Today, to use a personal computer, you must deal with these already-familiar concepts in a new way. Tomorrow, the computer will adapt itself to the way you're used to dealing with concurrency, priority and interruption—not vice versa.

But this leads to an interesting paradox: To make a computer easier to use requires a more sophisticated computer. And the more sophisticated the personal computer, the more expensive the personal computer. As this trend manifests itself—and it will—you should expect prices of useful personal computers not to decline over the next few years while we develop and perfect this new technology.

It's always been Apple's objective to build the least-expensive, useful personal computer—not necessarily the cheapest. We build tools, not toys. Ultimately, you will get more Apple power for the same dollar.

But that's just part of the Apple strategy for maintaining our leadership position in the 80s. Obviously, I've only been talking to you conceptually about what's going on at Apple. Ultimately, the Apple must adapt totally to the way people work. The Apple has to change, not the Apple owner. And that's exactly what Apple is planning through the next decade.

1981

GEORGE EASTMAN
1854–1932

George Eastman's father died when he was 7; his mother was an invalid; and he was forced to leave school and find employment at the age of 14, earning $3 a week as an office boy. Of this period in his life, he said, "I then conceived a terror of poverty. It haunted me by day and by night." It became his motivation. In 1874, he was hired by the Rochester Savings Bank, and once he saved a little money, he planned a vacation trip to Santo Domingo. The next logical step was to purchase a camera to bring on his journey, which he did. However, he found the whole process of taking and developing a picture awkward and cumbersome, so for the next three years he experimented in his mother's kitchen, searching for better methods. In addition, he paid a local photographer $5 for a detailed course in photography.

In 1880 he formed the Eastman Dry Plate and Film Company, and in 1888 he introduced his first camera for $25. Eastman realized his dream by inventing a compact camera that was sold with the film already loaded—no more bulky film plates and no more lengthy development process. To promote the ease of use, Eastman introduced the slogan, "You press the button, we do the rest." The 1888 camera produced 100 circular pictures that were two and one-half inches in diameter. The directions for use were: (1) point the camera, (2) press the button, (3) turn the key, and (4) pull the cord. Mass-production of the Kodak camera quickly transformed the field of photography into a popular hobby around the world. His ultimate goal was to make a camera as easy to use as a pen.

With all the success, Eastman was a pessimist at heart; his standard greeting when meeting a colleague, "Tell me the worst you know." It was part of his methodical approach to getting at problems. To solve an emulsion problem, he once ran 469 experiments. This methodical approach paralleled his straightforward management philosophy, which included *ideal curves,* a topic in *Make the Camera as Convenient as the Pencil.* Eastman also explains why he likes the letter *K,* as in Kodak.

Make the Camera as Convenient as the Pencil

George Eastman

A determination, after ten years of routine work, to get into something for myself that held a future is responsible for the idea that is expressed in the Kodak. For our company is built upon a single idea developed into an ideal that is contained in eight words, and whatever measure of success that has come to us has been in direct proportion to the nearness of our approach to that ideal. In the beginning, when we were far away from it, our business was small; as we drew nearer, the business increased.

If you draw a straight line across the top of a sheet of paper and call that our ideal and then, beginning at the lower left hand corner, plot a curve upward according to the development of our product, then that curve will also roughly represent the increase in the volume of our business. The curve will pass through making the first "dry" plate, then through the protection of those plates from quick deterioration, then on through the invention of the film and the cartridge film, to the making of a camera that would take a whole roll of films, and the beginning of the period of "You press the button and we do the rest."

It would go on past the daylight loading of the films, the simplification of development and printing for amateurs, the

261

autographing of the film at the time of exposure, and get into the complexities of motion pictures and cameras for aerial and other special uses. In each of these divisions would be many subdivisions and an accurate progress-of-product-chart would be very complex, but the big point is that the curve of sales would, excepting for such influences as the war and the growth of the motion picture, almost exactly correspond with the rise of the ideal curve toward the ideal.

What we have made and advertised and sold has always been the embodiment of an idea rather than a piece of photographic apparatus. We have, from time to time, put emphasis on some particular development that we especially wanted to tell the public about, but the ideal, not the product of the moment, has always ruled. The idea on which our institution is built is this: "Make the camera as convenient as the pencil . . ."

Our principle was to make photography ever easier; the dry plate was a step forward from the wet plate. The next logical step was to make the dry plate in some less bulky form. We had found that a coated paper treated with emulsion would take pictures. That was evidently the way toward simplicity, for, if the film could be placed on rollers, then not only would the objection of having to put in a fresh plate for each exposure be overcome, but also a photographer could carry in a small compass, a sufficient amount of film for a great number of photographs.

What we have made and advertised and sold has always been the embodiment of an idea rather than a piece of photographic apparatus.

William H. Walker, who had been in the dry-plate business and sold out, joined me in an effort to work out the film. He was the mechanic and I was the chemist—we divided roughly on those lines, but our work was nearly overlapping. We had to discover:

1. A substitute for the heavy glass plate.

2. An apparatus for coating the right flexible surface when we found it, for the methods used with plates would not work on a flexible surface.

3. A mechanism for the exposure in the camera of the substance we hit upon.

I invented what was known as the "American film," in which the negative image was received on paper and transferred to a gelatine sheet—it was not then as good as the best dry plate, but it was good enough for amateur purposes and the holder for the rolls could be attached to the back of the ordinary camera.

The idea on which our institution is built is this: "Make the camera as convenient as the pencil . . ."

That was the turning point of our business; from that time forward we were out of the rut and making a distinctive product. The public bought eagerly and, for the first time, we invaded Europe—the home of photography. Mr. Walker established our first European branch; today we are in every corner of the world.

The film did not function to the best advantage in the existing cameras, but we had an alternative—a camera of our own, especially designed to use films. We had made ourselves distinctive in the beginning by the quality of our dry plate. We continued the distinctiveness in being the first to make films. Now we had a camera—but it was not the ordinary camera. It was a distinctive camera and it needed a distinctive name instead of being just a particular make of camera. Hence the name "Kodak."

The Reasoning That Lies Back of the Name "Kodak"

I devised the name myself. A trademark should be short, vigorous, incapable of being mispelled to an extent that will destroy its identity and—in order to satisfy trade-mark laws—it must mean nothing. If the name has no dictionary definition, it must be associated only with your product and you will cease to be known as producing a "kind" of anything.

The letter "K" had been a favorite with me—it seems a strong, incisive sort of letter. Therefore, the word I wanted had to start with "K." Then it became a question of trying out a great number of combinations of letters that made words starting and ending with "K." The word "Kodak" is the result. Instead of merely making cameras and camera supplies, we made Kodaks and Kodak supplies. It became the distinctive word for our products. Hence the slogan: "If it isn't an Eastman, it isn't a Kodak."

A trademark should be short, vigorous, incapable of being mispelled to an extent that will destroy its identity and . . . it must mean nothing.

The first Kodak went on the market in July, 1888—10 years after we had started business. It was a square box and held a roll of 100 exposures, taking a round picture 2½ inches in diameter. It sold for $25.

We had in this the beginning of what we were after—a camera that would take pictures in the hands of a greenhorn. You only had to point it at an object and press the button. The user performed no photographic operation; we sold it loaded, and when the whole roll was exposed, the owner sent it back to us, or to the developers that sprang up all over the country and had the films developed and a new roll put in for $10. That camera was not perfect; the big roll of film meant that the camera user had to wait days and weeks to see the results of his work, for the ordinary amateur will not, after the first enthusiasm wears off, try to shoot everything in sight. He will wait. Therefore, 100 films in a roll was too much for him. But, in spite of this inconvenience, growing from the big roll of film, the new Kodak was a longer step toward simplicity than any that had previously been taken. Out of that situation arose the familiar advertising slogan "You press the button and we do the rest."

1920

EDWIN H. LAND
1909–1991

The inventor of the Polaroid camera holds 533 patents, second only to Thomas Edison. He developed everything from Polaroid sunglasses to guided missiles, but it was while on vacation in 1943 that he conceived his greatest moneymaker. This was all because his daughter asked innocently why she couldn't see right away the photographs they had just taken. The comment sent Land's mind reeling, and within an hour he had built the entire Polaroid camera in his mind. Not unexpected from a man who once said, "There is nothing more refreshing than thinking for a few minutes with your eyes closed." Five years later the camera that developed pictures in 60 seconds hit the market and was an instant hit.

Land first started working with light when he entered Harvard University in 1926, but he dropped out one semester short of a diploma to start the company he would lead until 1982. His first product was polaroid glass, which cuts down on sun glare. Considered a magician, Land explained that he was simply driven by an "urge to make a significant intellectual contribution that can be tangibly embodied in a product or process." His leadership style, according to a close associate, was "unconventional, indirect and elliptical. He seemed able to manipulate parts of his company without managing them." Land also created a company culture that encouraged pursuing art before meeting the payroll.

People who met with Land often felt as though their souls had been looked into and they found him aloof. He readily admitted that he liked to be alone, especially at work. "I think human beings in the mass are fun at square dances . . . At the same time . . . there is no such thing as *group* originality or *group* creativity or *group* perspicacity." He believed in the individual's capacity for greatness alone as the deciding factor when it came to civilization's progress. In the following selection, Land's expansive and sometimes wandering mind is on display as he discusses the need to create a working environment in which someone can simply sit and think for two years.

In the Creator's Mind
Edwin H. Land

As I review the nature of the creative drive in the inventive scientists who have been around me, as well as in myself, I find the first event is an urge to make a significant intellectual contribution that can be tangibly embodied in a product or process. The urge, as pure urge, precedes in a perfectly generalized way the specific contribution—so that the individual hunts for a *domain* in which to utilize the urge. This early stage need not be early in life, it can occur intermittently throughout life. The hunting process is fascinating to contemplate because during it there may be many abortive first approaches at the verbal level to fields that are then rejected as being either not significant enough or not feasible enough—and then, quite suddenly, a field will emerge conceptually so full blown in the creator's mind that the words can scarcely come from his mouth fast enough to describe the new field in its full implication and elaborateness.

This domain, which neither he nor the world had known until some magic moment, now is for him so vividly real and well populated with ideas and structures that he will lead you through it like a guide in a European city. Then it appears to him that all that is left to do is to parallel that intricate "reality" that came into being in his mind with a corresponding reality in the world outside his mind. Sometimes this process of creating the outside reality may take five years, sometimes five hours. For the creative person this process of establishing the correspondence between the outside reality and the one within his mind is a timeless undertaking, reminiscent of the relativistic trips through space in which people return to earth only a little older, while the rest of mankind has aged.

I recall a sunny vacation day in Santa Fe, New Mexico, when my little daughter asked why she could not see at once the picture I had just taken of her. As I walked around that charming town I undertook the task of solving the puzzle she had set me.

Whether the process is the five-hour process or the five-year process it always turns out to be true that many subsidiary and supporting inventions and insights are required to go from the thing in the mind to the thing in the world. These subsidiary inventions are born of accurate analysis, patient research, broad experience, and total devotion to the perfection of the final outer reality. For this sequence of rather tedious virtues there is available no new series of grand excitements. Basic emotional energy must continue to flow from the initial perception of the field and from that first excitement.

I take you through these details of the genesis of inventions because it must be clear that this kind of timeless life can be lived only in an appropriate environment, a different kind of environment from what we must establish for some of our important massive engineering undertakings, such as the moon probe, undertakings in which a date must be met at all costs, and in which individual profundity must be largely displaced by rapid-fire interaction between brilliant members of large groups. Since it is somewhat easier for the general public to understand and for the government to manage this latter type of intellectual activity, we must be extremely careful to nurture and protect the former type.

Now for examples. As for the generalized urge: Thirty-eight years later, I can still recall the full vividness of my own need at the age of seventeen to do something scientifically significant and tangibly demonstrable. At the age in which each week seems like a year, I picked field after field before I decided that the great opportunity was polarized light.

Jumping ahead seventeen years, I recall a sunny vacation day in Santa Fe, New Mexico, when my little daughter asked why she could not see at once the picture I had just taken of her. As I walked around that charming town I undertook the task of solving the puzzle she had set me. Within the hour, the camera, the film, and the physical chemistry became so clear to me that with a great sense of excitement I hurried over to the place where Donald Brown, our patent attorney (in Santa Fe by coincidence), was staying, to describe to him in great detail a dry camera that would give a picture immediately after exposure. In my mind it was so nearly complete and so real that I spent several hours describing it, after which it was perhaps more real to him than even the ultimate reality. Only three years later, three years of the timeless intensive work referred to above, we gave to the Optical Society of America the full demonstration of the working system. What is hard to convey, in anything short of a thick book, is the years of rich experience that were compressed into those three years. It was as if all that we had done in learning to make polarizers, the knowledge of plastics, and the properties of viscous liquids, the preparation of microscopic crystals smaller than the wavelength of light, the laminating of plastic sheets, living in the world of colloids in supersaturated solutions, had been a school and a preparation both for that first day in which I suddenly knew how to make a one-step dry photographic process and for the following three years in which we made the very vivid dream into a solid reality.

I find men around me in our laboratory . . . who now seem more alert, creative, and productive than when they were 30 years younger. That creativity is tied to some youthful age is a myth.

Once again we can see the significance of environment, of a corporate life whose managerial center was concerned with scientific ideas—a corporate life in which everyone participated in the mastery day by day of the new technological problems that arose in our search for better polarizers and new ways of using them. The transfer from the field of polarized light to the field of photography was for us all a miraculous experience, as if we had entered a new country with a different language and different customs, only to find that we could speak the language at once and master the customs. In short, the kind of training we had given ourselves in the field of polarized light had endowed us with a competence we had not sought and did not know we had; namely, a competence to transfer what must be a common denominator in all honestly pursued research from one field to an entirely different one. I am inclined to think that only in a corporation, however small or large, in which individuals are expected to make the center of their life the intellectual life of the laboratory can this kind of transferable talent be built. This process must continue for year upon year and decade upon decade. I find men around me in our laboratory who have lived this way and who now seem more alert, creative, and productive than when they were 30 years younger. That creativity is tied to some youthful age is a myth that comes about, I believe, because for one reason or another men stop living this way, perhaps because they are encouraged to

think that there is more dignity associated with tasks implying power over people than with tasks implying power over
nature.

> Frequently, the problems can be best solved,
> perhaps solved *only* if the work is done in a rel-
> atively short time. In most of the worthwhile
> problems, so many variables are involved that
> the human mind cannot keep them in order in
> the presence of interruptions.

We are searching these examples, not for the purpose of
intimate revelation, but to try to find out why more scientific
companies do not survive. Whatever the other reasons may
be, I think that a primary reason is that at just the time when
a man's talent might be maturing, he is drawn off into a variety of so-called managerial activities. It is impossible for the
long, long thoughts, the profound thoughts, the unconscious
accumulation of insights, to come into being after these serious digressions into management. I am not saying that other
good things do not come out of these diversions, but these
other good things are not our subject. Actually there is an
endless opportunity for use of managerial aptitude of every
research man, *within the intimate domain of his own investigation,*
and within that domain he may exercise his managerial aptitude without the stress and distractions he will necessarily
find outside of the domain of his own scientific investigation.

I think the important and nearly impossible projects such
as we set for our goal require prolonged periods of intensive
concentration. Frequently, the problems can be best solved,
perhaps solved *only* if the work is done in a relatively short
time. In most of the worthwhile problems, so many variables
are involved that the human mind cannot keep them in order
in the presence of interruptions. It is simultaneous mastery
of a hundred interacting variables that is the glory of the

kind of scientist we are talking about for our scientific companies.

When I started on the actual program of making the black-and-white film for our camera I set down the broad principles that would also apply to color. I invited Howard Rogers, who had worked with me for many years in the field of polarized light, to sit opposite me in the black-and-white laboratory and think about color. For several years he simply sat and, saying very little, assimilated the techniques we were using in black-and-white. Then one day he stood up and said, "I'm ready to start now." So we built the color laboratory next to the black-and-white laboratory and from then on until the time many years later when we released our color film, the program of matching the dream of the color process that was in our minds with the reality of the color process in the outside world never stopped. My point is that we created an environment in which a man was expected to sit and think for two years. May I suggest that there is a difference between that environment and the one that we tend to create when we think of national projects for massive engineering purposes.

We created an environment in which a man
was expected to sit and think for two years.

You will note that the qualities that I am concerned about in corporate life are not related to bigness or smallness as such. There are small companies and small businesses that are not oriented toward thoughtfulness and profundity, and there are a few large corporations in which they are encouraged. But our universities do not train for patient and extended thought, and those few areas in government that have provided thoughtful environments are in certain danger of being swamped by the great mass undertakings. The one *governmental* device for protecting the profound thinker is the patent system. During the period ahead of us, many of us will be working to invent methods whereby the government can catalyze the formation and growth of creative companies. We shall also be trying within the universities to generate men with competence for profound individuality. It would be most unfortunate if by the time we have succeeded with these undertakings the patent system is robbed of the power to perform its part of the new task.

1985

Nolan Bushnell was a pioneer in video games, founding Atari and introducing the world to Pong, the TV table tennis game. Back in the early 1970s, he was the king of high tech in Silicon Valley; at his peak, he owned two Lear jets, four mansions, a fleet of luxury cars, and a 67-foot yacht—aptly named *Pong.* Bushnell grew up in Utah, where his father was a cement contractor. In 1970, at age 27, he founded Atari with $500. Four years later, he hired Stephen Wozniak (future Apple cofounder) to help design another popular game, Breakout. "In the beginning," he said, "we were the gigafreaks, nerds, and dweebs. . . . We spawned the PC revolution, and we began it by meeting and selling products to each other. But we didn't get rich until we figured out how to sell the stuff to the 'others.' "

In 1976, Bushnell sold Atari to Warner Communications for an astounding $28 million and focused on his other start-up, the Chuck E. Cheese Pizza Time Restaurant chain, which was a combination pizza joint and video arcade. Before long, the chain grew to 300 restaurants and Bushnell's net worth ballooned to $100 million. In 1981, he founded Catalyst Technologies, a venture capital firm dedicated to funding cutting-edge ideas. "As with any genera," he said, "the game industry is not static; possibly more than any other genera, it contributes to and provides momentum for the technology of the future. We need to think of where this can take us in social interaction, entertainment, education, and in our work."

Unfortunately, in 1982 the video game industry took a dive (Warner's Atari lost $539 million in 1983) and brought Bushnell down with it, syphoning millions of his personal wealth. In 1984, Chuck E. Cheese had to file for Chapter 11 bankruptcy protection. His take: "I changed from being a hands-on manager to being a venture capitalist." The lesson was not lost on Bushnell, who's still an active entrepreneur, as he opens his essay, "To win the business game, the most important thing is to do what you know."

To Win the Business Game, Do What You Know
Nolan Bushnell

To win the business game, the most important thing is to do what you know. Sure, we'd all like to be renaissance men and women. But understanding one's strengths and weaknesses is absolutely essential to winning at business. I have stuck to an area of expertise I understand—the world's leisure mentality. I am probably the only trained engineer in the world who has also made a living running an amusement park, so I put those two things together. I did it at Atari with computer video games, and I'm doing it now at Pizza Time Theatre with fast food and Disneyland-type mechanical characters that provide entertainment. I worked at the amusement park in Salt Lake City summers during my college years, from 1962 to 1968, and I had lots of time to think about leisure time and how people like to spend it. For the first year and a half, I stood on the midway, cajoling people into playing my knock-the-milk-bottle-over-and-win-a-stuffed-animal game.

I saw a huge number of people and could observe them closely. So I made a game of trying to find out what was the one thing I could say that would hit the common denominator in all these people and make them listen to me. You might call my time on the midway an intensive behavioral training session—I could try different ideas on people every day. If one thing didn't work, I started my experiment over again with a new spiel and a different group of people.

For the next four years, I was manager of the park's games department. That involved managing people and choosing games and, for me, it also involved inventing games. I invented a baseball game and a variation of roll-down — that's carnival lingo for the game where you roll a ball down a slanted board and try to hit certain areas on the board.

We'd all like to be renaissance men and women. But understanding one's strengths and weaknesses is absolutely essential to winning at business.

During my time at the amusement park, I came to three conclusions about the leisure mentality. First, people want to be spontaneous in leisure. They want to have lots of options, yet the options must be kept simple. They want to react to stimuli, not think out or plan their actions. Second, the basics of leisure are having fun, eating and doing things as a family, yet being able to separate the kids from the parents for at least half the time. The parents love their children, but they also want time alone. The environment has to be non-threatening so the parents will feel relaxed enough to let their kids run off. Third, the decisions that need to be made should be clearly presented. There should be an easy structure — some rules, but not so many that people feel confined.

I'm using these conclusions successfully in Pizza Time Theatre. But first came Atari. The idea for Atari came to me while I was at college, playing math games on the University of Utah's huge general-purpose computer. If I could just put a coin slot on this machine, I thought, I'd have a business. There must be a million others out there, like me, who'd like to play computer games. But at $4 million apiece, the computers were too costly.

After I got my degree in electrical engineering, I went to work as a research engineer for Ampex Corp., a video equipment maker in Redwood City, California. The coin-slot computer idea was shelved.

But one day a new minicomputer price list crossed my desk at Ampex. The price was $40,000—still too high to be practical as the basis for a game, but the trend was too significant to miss. When I saw the price plummet another order of magnitude, to $4,000, in the next two years, I started to noodle out video-game ideas in my spare time.

The idea for Atari came to me while I was at college, playing math games on the University of Utah's huge general-purpose computer.

Suddenly, one day, I realized that a general-purpose machine, even a mini-computer that could do everything from billing to energy management, wasn't necessary. The computer I needed only had to do one thing—play a video game. If I could build the hardware and use microprocessor technology to shrink size and cost, while delivering reliability, I'd be home-free. That was my break through.

My first video game was an adaption of Space War, a game I used to play at college. I tried to simplify the game and aim it at the consumer instead of the college student. When I was ready with Computer Space, in 1971, I decided to leave Ampex. It was a little gutsy, but I thought I had a winning idea.

I was able to sell the game to wholesale distributors of coin-operated games, but it wasn't a fabulous success. I figured that it wasn't working because I'd been around engineers for the past few years and they had warped my impression of the layman. So I began to fool around with other ideas and came up with the game of Ping-Pong. It was a simple game to display and the name Pong really hit me, just as I hoped it would the public.

I incorporated under the name Atari in 1972. "Atari" comes from the oriental game of go. It is similar to the word "check" in chess. It sounded like a suitably aggressive name to me.

Pong made it big. The idea was so good that 28 competing companies marketed the same game under different names, like TV Tennis. Of 100,000 Ping-Pong video games that were produced, only 8,000 to 10,000 were made by Atari.

But we were the best because we beat all those competitors in the marketplace by coming up with a new game every nine months. It would take the imitators four months to copy the new game and five months or more to gear up to the level of distribution. By that time, we had moved on to another game. In all, we developed 35 games, including Space Race, Rebound, and Track 10. Not all of them were successful, but we stayed ahead of our competition, including the biggest of them all, Bally.

Atari worked financially for sound reasons. I figured it all out before we got started—I'm kind of a nut for statistics. From 1972 to 1974, with very limited initial capitalization, we reached consumers by continuing to sell to the coin-op market, for cash on delivery of the video game machine. These coin-op dealers distributed the games to places like Joe's Bar and Grill for us. That way, we could build for the market and turn our inventory over 12 to 15 times a year because of the constant demand. Our cash flow pulled us out of the hole very rapidly.

In 1974, we started to sell Pong direct to consumers in Sears, Roebuck stores. I knew that going after individual home consumers in really big numbers would turn us into a fourth-quarter, Christmas business with year-long overhead, one-time inventory turnover, and 60 to 90 days receivables—a totally different kind of business. To reach those huge consumer markets buying from stores, we'd need major infusions of capital. This would have diluted my personal share of the company: I estimate that we'd have had to do three times as well as before, just for me to stay even in personal net worth.

It made sense to sell it, and Warner Communications wanted to buy. They came to me in 1976, when Atari had sales of $40 million. It's now doing over $100 million a year for Warner. I sold Atari for $30 million and realized $15 million personally, since I owned a little over 50% of the company.

My new venture, Pizza Time Theatre, is something I thought of even before Atari. But the TV-game thing took off so fast that my fast-food theater got left behind. It was still in my mind; in fact, I launched it as part of Atari in 1976, just before I sold out to Warner. I ended up buying the activity back from Warner in 1978 for half a million dollars—not much money, but it wasn't in line with their goals.

Why get involved in another start-up? First, I was bored. I wasn't going to retire in my thirties, no matter how big the stake I'd secured. Second, there wasn't nearly enough challenge, or fun, in running someone else's company—even one I'd founded. Third, I guess I had to prove to myself that my big hit with Atari was more than just a fluke.

My idea behind Pizza Time Theatre was to bridge the gap between the fast-food experience and the amusement park experience. I wanted to have good food and a meal that a family could eat together. So I chose pizza instead of, say, ice cream. And I wanted people to spend the whole evening because they were having a good time. So I would have games on the premises.

My next question was, What do we do to bring them there? Entertainment was the answer, but live entertainment is expensive. That's when I hit on using the same idea as Walt Disney—technological mass entertainment. I developed a cast of life-size, three-dimensional stuffed animals and people called the Pizza Time Players, whose voices and movements are controlled by a computer. Their voices are taped human voices synchronized with their movements—blinking eyes, moving arms—and with a musical score.

Here's how it works at my original Pizza Time Theatre in San Jose. When Mom and Dad and their two kids walk in, they order a pizza and find a table. The large dining room has six framed stages up near the ceiling all around the room. There's one mechanical character filling each frame and the show has just begun. The M.C. is a cigar-smoking rat named Chuck E. Cheese. He introduces Jasper T. Jowls, a dumb dog who plays country and western music on the banjo. After a one-and-a-half-minute set, Jasper stops playing and closes his eyes. There's an eight-minute break and then Chuck E. introduces Pasquale, the mustachioed Italian pizza chef. He breaks into an operatic aria and Chuck E. tries to shut him up because nobody wants to hear opera. This goes on for a minute and a half. Then an eight-minute break. And so on.

"Atari" comes from the Oriental game of go. It is similar to the word "check" in chess. It sounded like a suitably aggressive name to me.

When the kids get tired of watching Jasper and Pasquale, they head for the game room, which has more than 100 pinball, arcade, and Atari video games. They can play them with tokens their parents received when they ordered the pizza. As soon as the kids run out of tokens, they come back to Mom and Dad to ask for quarters so they can keep playing.

After eating the pizza, the kids head back to the game room and Mom and Dad can get some more time to themselves by moving on to the piano bar. There, a piano-playing hippopotamus named Dolly Dimples stands behind the bar and does her own show.

The whole evening costs about $3 or $4 per person. I don't want it to be so expensive that no one will come back. But the average total spent per family visit is close to $10, at least 50% above the $6 or less tab at most pizza outlets. Typical revenues should run about $800,000 per restaurant.

What's particularly nice about this new venture is that I haven't had to market it. Because people already know about me from Atari, I don't have to go after them. They're coming to me.

We were the best because we beat all those competitors in the marketplace by coming up with a new game every nine months.

So far, since 1977, I've invested about $2.5 million in Pizza Time Theatre. There are now three restaurants on the West Coast, soon to be five. We've sold 50 franchises out here, and we just sold 285 to Topeka Inn Management, a Midwest developer. They will invest $200 million. This is probably the largest franchise deal ever signed in the United States.

Each one of the three Pizza Time Theatres is already profitable on a stand-alone basis, but the corporation itself isn't yet. Considering the development costs of the animated figures and computer software, initial capitalization and organization, getting the team together, plus the overhead of managing a business, I estimated that we will need six outlets to become profitable at the corporate level. We will have these six by the end of the summer 1979. By 1985, I expect that there will be over 1,000 Pizza Time Theatres. About 20% will be owned by the company, the other 80% franchised.

I think I've been successful because I've followed some of my own advice: Don't play in areas where you can't win; avoid that risk by knowing where your personal strengths and leverage lie. My strength lies in my first-hand knowledge of the leisure world. With Atari, as a manufacturer of video games, I was only giving people the tools to have fun. With Pizza Time Theatre, I've put another arrow in my quiver. Now, I can orchestrate the whole experience.

1979

There is much more to the man than the entertaining fable about an eccentric inventor who flew a kite in a lightning storm. He was not only one of the first great American entrepreneurs, but disciplined inventor, heroic diplomat, and founder of libraries, schools, and hospitals. It did not come easy. Franklin was a poor student who failed in math, and at the age of 12 was forced into an apprenticeship under his older brother, a printer. He was supposed to serve until he was 21, and according to the contract, only in the last year would he receive wages. By 17, Franklin had had enough, and left Boston for Philadelphia. He would see his parents just three more times in his life.

Once in Philadelphia, Franklin worked for another printer before he founded the *Pennsylvania Gazette* in 1728 and built a renowned print shop of his own—he published the first novel in the United States, Samuel Richardson's *Pamela*. Franklin also wrote and published the priceless *Poor Richard's Almanac* from 1733 to 1757. The preface for the 1757 Almanac was entitled *The Way to Wealth,* and is considered by many to be Franklin's highest literary and philosophical achievement. In the essay are such golden nuggets as ". . . he that riseth late, must trot all day, and shall scarce overtake his business at night."

Franklin carefully cultivated his image as a businessman. He later wrote, "I took care not only to be in reality industrious and frugal but to avoid all appearances to the contrary. I dressed plainly; I was seen at no places of idle diversion. I never went out a-fishing or shooting; a book, indeed, sometimes debauched me from my work, but that was seldom, snug, and gave no scandal . . ." That attentiveness paid off as he built a media empire that included gazettes in Rhode Island and South Carolina, as well as being chosen the "public" printer for Pennsylvania, Delaware, Maryland, and New Jersey. In *Advice to a Young Tradesman,* a letter to a fellow interested in starting his own business, Franklin shares some real jewels, such as "The good paymaster is lord of another man's purse."

Advice to a Young Tradesman
Benjamin Franklin

To my friend, A.B.:

As you have desired it of me, I write the following hints, which have been of service to me, and may, if observed, be so to you.

Remember that *time* is money. He that can earn ten shillings a day by his labor, and goes abroad, or sits idle, one half of that day, though he spends but sixpence during his diversion or idleness, ought not to reckon *that* the only expense; he has really spent, or rather thrown away, five shillings besides.

Money is of the prolific, generating nature. Money can beget money, and its offspring can beget more, and so on.

Remember that *credit* is money. If a man lets his money lie in my hands after it is due, he gives me the interest, or so much as I can make of it during that time. This amounts to a considerable sum where a man has good and large credit, and makes good use of it.

Remember that money is of the prolific, generating nature. Money can beget money, and its offspring can beget more, and so on. Five shillings turned is six, turned again it is seven and three-pence, and so on till it becomes an hundred pounds. The more there is of it, the more it produces every turning, so that the profits rise quicker and quicker. He that kills a breeding sow destroys all her offspring to the thousandth generation. He that murders a crown destroys all that it might have produced, even scores of pounds.

Remember that *credit* is money. If a man lets his money lie in my hands after it is due, he gives me the interest.

Remember that six pounds a year is but a groat a day. For this little sum (which may be daily wasted either in time or expense unperceived) a man of credit may, on his own security, have the constant possession and use of an hundred pounds. So much in stock, briskly turned by an industrious man, produces great advantage.

Remember this saying: *The good paymaster is lord of another man's purse.* He that is known to pay punctually and exactly to the time he promises, may at any time, and on any occasion, raise all the money his friends can spare. This is sometimes of great use. After industry and frugality, nothing contributes more to the raising of a young man in the world than punctuality and justice in all his dealings; therefore, never keep borrowed money an hour beyond the time you promised, lest a disappointment shut up your friend's purse for ever.

The most trifling actions that affect a man's credit are to be regarded. The sound of your hammer at five in the morning, or nine at night, heard by a creditor, makes him easy six months longer; but if he sees you at a billiard-table or hears your voice at a tavern when you should be at work, he sends for his money the next day; demands it, before he can receive it, in a lump.

It shows, besides, that you are mindful of what you owe; it makes you appear a careful as well as an honest man, and that still increases your credit.

Beware of thinking all your own that you possess, and of living accordingly. It is a mistake that many people who have credit fall into. To prevent this, keep an exact account for some time, both of your expenses and your income. If you take the pains at first to mention particulars, it will have this good effect: you will discover how wonderfully small, trifling expenses mount up to large sums, and will discern what might have been and may for the future be saved, without occasioning any great inconvenience.

The most trifling actions that affect a man's credit are to be regarded. The sound of your hammer at five in the morning, or nine at night, heard by a creditor, makes him easy six months longer.

In short, the way to wealth, if you desire it, is as plain as the way to market. It depends chiefly on two words, *industry* and *frugality*—that is, waste neither *time* nor *money*, but make the best use of both. Without industry and frugality nothing will do, and with them every thing. He that gets all he can honestly, and saves all he gets (necessary expenses excepted), will certainly become *rich*, if that Being who governs the world, to whom all should look for a blessing on their honest endeavours, doth not, in his wise providence, otherwise determine.

1748

CLARENCE BIRDSEYE
1886–1956

If you've ever bought frozen vegetables, you've most likely encountered the Birds Eye brand. It's namesake, Clarence Birdseye, was a prolific inventor who stumbled upon a process for freezing foods without losing their freshness while fur trapping in Canada, a long way from where he grew up in Brooklyn. One of eight children, he managed to attend Amherst College for a short while, focusing his study on such scientific subjects as entomology, ornithology, and mammology. After Amherst, he worked as a naturalist for the federal government and wrote books on wildflowers, western birds, and mammals. Then he met the lady of his dreams, only he was too poor to marry her, so he went to Canada as a fur trapper for the Hudson Bay Trading Company, in hopes of earning enough money to win his lady's hand. Three years later, in 1915, he did just that, bringing her back to the snowy north.

In 1922, he opened a wholesale fish distributorship in Manhattan, but was frustrated by the inability to ship without spoilage. It was then that he recalled his days in the north where in the winter quickly frozen fish kept a fresh taste. So he invested $7 in some brine, ice, and an electric fan and started experimenting. The key was reducing the temperature to −45°F and freezing the tissue and fiber fast enough so that the formation of ice crystals didn't burst cell walls. In 1925, his company, the General Foods Company, began selling frozen haddock fillets. In 1929, Birdseye sold his patents, process, and plants for $22 million, and five years later General Foods had 80 percent of the quick-frozen food market in the United States.

Birdseye continued to invent and peddle his wares, including a reflecting lightbulb, an electric fishing reel, and a recoiless harpoon for whale hunting. Was he a mechanical genius or a scientist? Neither, but he was curious and he held more than 250 U.S. and foreign patents. In *If I Were Twenty-One*, Birdseye lists curiosity along with chance taking as his two prerequisites for succeeding on your own. As he says, "Only through curiosity can we discover opportunities, and only by gambling can we take advantage of them."

If I Were Twenty-One
Clarence Birdseye

Ayoung college graduate asked me recently what I would do if I were his age. "Would you follow the same occupation," he said, "that you did in the past?"

"Which occupation?" I asked him.

The boy thought I was joking, but I was serious. I am a jack-of-all-trades without any one job or profession. The public customarily thinks of me as an inventor, because among a number of other ideas which I developed, or helped to develop, was the quick-freezing process that was named for me.

But inventing is only one of my lines. I am also a bank director, a president of companies, a fisherman, an author, an engineer, a cook, a naturalist, a stockholder, a consultant, and a dock-walloper. Whenever anyone asks me what I am I become rather confused, because I don't know which one of these occupations to give.

"To be perfectly honest," I told my young friend, "I am best described as just a guy with a very large bump of curiosity and a gambling instinct. If I were your age I would do the same kind of thing I have been doing all my life. I would go around asking a lot of damn-fool questions and taking chances."

I meant what I said. I do not consider myself a remarkable person. I did not make exceptionally high grades when I went to school. I never finished college. I am not the world's best salesman. But I am intensely curious about the things which I see around me, and this curiosity, combined with a willingness to assume risks, has been responsible for such success and satisfaction as I have achieved in life.

I am best described as just a guy with a very large bump of curiosity and a gambling instinct.

These two qualities—curiosity and the chance-taking spirit—are inherent in all of us, and I strongly recommend them to every ambitious youth who is starting out today. He should develop them through constant exercise, just as an athlete develops his muscles. Otherwise, his chances of doing big things will be small. Only through curiosity can we discover opportunities, and only by gambling can we take advantage of them.

There are some people, of course, who say opportunity went out with the horse and buggy. That is rubbish. Change is the very essence of American life, and change brings with it an ever-increasing complexity of human wants. New instruments, devices, and machinery of all kinds have brought in demands for new things and new services which formerly were not even dreamed of. There are at least 20 times as many opportunities as there were when I was a young man of 21.

I do not mean to say there is a bag of gold in sight for every youth who asks questions and takes risks. Enthusiasm and hard work are also indispensable ingredients of achievement. So is stick-to-itiveness. Worthwhile success is impossible on a 40-hour week. It is true, moreover, that the dice fall against the risk-taker more often than not, but his chances of ultimate success are far greater than those of the man who seeks merely security. And, whether he wins or not, he will find life much more interesting than if he always plays safe.

There are some people, of course, who say opportunity went out with the horse and buggy. That is rubbish.

In my own case, life has been an exciting adventure since my earliest remembrance, and today, at 64, I am having just as much fun as I ever did. I am never bored, because I am always prying into something or other which fascinates me.

If I see a man skinning a fish, for example, a host of questions pop into my mind: Why is he skinning the fish? Why is he doing it by hand? Is the skin good for anything? If I am in a restaurant and get biscuits which I like, I ask the chef how he made them: What did he put in the dough? How did he mix it? How long did the biscuits bake? At what temperature? When I visit a strange city, I go through the local industrial plants to see how they make things. I don't care what the product is. I am just as much interested in the manufacture of chewing gum as of steel.

Not long ago, while visiting a plant where lard is rendered, I observed a process which suggested to me a new way of "digesting" wood chips in pulp mills. Why shouldn't it be tried? My curiosity aroused, I gambled some time and money on research, and today, in collaboration with a group of other interested persons, am perfecting a process which I believe will simplify and speed up the manufacture of paper.

That is just one of the current ventures into which my curiosity has led me. More recently, while wintering on the Gulf of Mexico, a friend and I became inquisitive about the methods used by commercial fishermen in catching red snappers and other deep-sea fish. We found they put their fishing lines down many fathoms to coral outcroppings on the ocean floor where the snappers lurked. Then, when they got a bite, they hauled the fish in hand over hand—mighty slow, hard work.

Worthwhile success is impossible on a 40-hour week.

"Isn't there an easier way of doing that?" we asked.

The fishermen shook their heads. That was the way snappers had always been caught in the Gulf by them and their fathers and grandfathers. Consequently, they figured that was the only way to catch them.

We didn't agree. Just because something has always been done in a certain way is never a sufficient reason for continuing to do it that way. Quite the contrary. My associates and I felt sure there must be a better way of harvesting deep-sea fish. As a result, we have developed an automatic electric reel for catching fish. The idea was not brand-new—few ideas are—but no one had ever worked it out on what we considered a practical basis. The reel which we have developed is not yet perfected, but it looks very promising. As a matter of fact, it is almost human. Fastened to the side of a fishing boat, it lets down a thin steel line to depths of 100 fathoms or more. Then, when a fish takes the hook, it plays him, quickly pulls him to the surface, and lands him on deck.

The gadget does everything, in fact, except mix a mint julep for the fisherman. Because it can catch as many fish in a day as three men using hand lines and may be used to exploit deeper banks than are customarily fished, we are hopeful that it will revolutionize some kinds of commercial fishing, make more sea food available, and increase fishermen's earnings.

There is always a better way of doing almost everything. Today anything which is 20 years old is, or should be, apt to be obsolete. But to discover better ways of doing things one

290

must question existent methods and practices and be courageous enough to gamble on something new or something different.

Some pious people say gambling is sinful, but actually it has always been and still is responsible for all progress, both spiritual and material. The Twelve Apostles would never have spread the Christian faith if they had not taken fearful risks. Such men as Galileo and Pasteur, Edison and Ford could not have made their great contributions to society if, as young men, they had gone in for the concept of economic security.

Just because something has always been done in a certain way is never a sufficient reason for continuing to do it that way.

Few of us can hope to achieve as much as these great men of the past but, no matter how ordinary our endowments, we can at least emulate them by being daring. Any youth who makes security his main goal shackles himself at the very start of life's race. He will go much farther, in all probability, if he steps out for himself, asks questions, and takes chances.

My own question-asking and chance-taking propensities manifested themselves at an early age. Born in Brooklyn, one of 8 children, I never cared a great deal for formal games and sports, but I was very fond of the outdoors. Our family spent the summers on a large farm on Long Island and I liked nothing better than to tramp alone through the fields or along the seashore studying the birds and other wildlife which I encountered. I noticed there were a lot of muskrats near the farm and I investigated their habits.

One day, when I was about 10 years old, I was casting around for ways to raise money to buy a shotgun, and I thought of the muskrats. So I wrote a letter to Dr. William T.

Hornaday, then director of the Bronx Park Zoo in New York, and asked him if the zoo was in the market for live muskrats.

There is always a better way of doing almost everything. Today anything which is 20 years old is, or should be, apt to be obsolete.

Dr. Hornaday replied that the zoo didn't need any muskrats, but he gave me the name of an English lord who would pay $1 apiece for 12 live "rats" with which to stock his estate. That was a real opportunity. I trapped 12 fine specimens and shipped them to his lordship. Three of the rats died en route but the others survived and I collected $9 with which I bought a fine single-barreled shotgun. My curiosity about muskrats had paid off. I was embarked on the path of free enterprise.

By the time I reached college age our family fortunes had declined to such an extent that it was obvious I would have to work for any higher education I might receive. I held various jobs during high-school vacations, including one as a $3-a-week Wall Street office boy and another as an inspector of the New York City street cleaning department, but when I entered Amherst College, where my father and older brothers had been educated, I decided to go into business for myself instead of tending furnaces, washing dishes, or waiting on tables.

My first venture was an attempt to sell mail-order courses in taxidermy, a skill I had picked up from reading books on the subject and hanging around taxidermists' shops. This didn't prove very profitable, so I scouted around for something else. I was just about flat broke one day when I was walking through some frozen fields near Amherst with my shotgun over my arm. Suddenly I came upon an open spring-hole where thousands of small frogs were congregated—layers and layers of them come to hibernate for the winter.

"What are those frogs good for?" I asked myself. "They must be good for something."

Any youth who makes security his main goal shackles himself at the very start of life's race.

My knowledge of natural history gave me the answer. "They are good for snakes," I said. "There are a lot of hungry snakes somewhere that would love to have those frogs for dinner. It is just a question of locating them."

Again I wrote to the Bronx Zoo for information and, to my delight, found that the zoo itself would pay a good price for live frogs for the denizens of its snake house. I collected the frogs, shipped them in wet burlap bags, and netted $115—more money than I could have earned washing dishes for months.

Later, my curiosity led me to another small gold mine. I happened to see a black rat scurry out of a stone shed back of an Amherst butcher shop. Knowing that black rats were almost extinct in this country, I investigated the shed to see if there were any more there. Old bones from the butcher shop were stored in the place and it was alive with black rats. I earned another $135 selling them to a geneticist at Columbia University.

I kept very quiet, though, about my enterprises as a frog entrepreneur and rat merchant, for I was afraid of being kidded by my fellow students. I did not realize at that time, as I have discovered since, that anyone who attempts anything original in this world must expect a bit of ridicule. I have long since learned to take it in my stride.

At the end of my second year at Amherst, I was offered a job as assistant naturalist by the Biological Survey of the United States Department of Agriculture, and spent an adventurous summer with a scientific party which was studying birds and mammals in New Mexico and Arizona. While on the trip I made the acquaintance of several Indian traders who were paying 25 cents apiece for the skins of bobcats and coyotes.

My first venture was an attempt to sell mail-order courses in taxidermy, a skill I had picked up from reading books on the subject and hanging around taxidermists' shops. This didn't prove very profitable.

That seemed a ridiculously low price to me, and when I got back to New York I prowled around the fur district and found that furriers would pay as much as $1 for such skins. I promptly wrote to the Indian traders and offered 50 cents for every bobcat and coyote pelt they would send me. Furs poured in and I resold the skins at a profit of $600. Once more curiosity had paid off.

By the time I was 26 I had become a full-fledged naturalist and had a good job with the Federal Government which would have given me lifetime security. My friends really thought I had lost my mind when I chucked it overnight to make a 6-week trip up the Labrador coast on a hospital ship commanded by Sir Wilfred Grenfell, the world-famous medical missionary.

But the risk I took was a calculated one. I had decided that I was not cut out for a career of pure science and wanted to get into some field where I could apply scientific knowledge to an economic opportunity. I had learned quite a lot about fur-bearing animals and believed that live silver foxes could be collected in Labrador and exported to the United States as breeding stock. Perhaps there would be an opportunity for me there.

As it turned out, there was. I got acquainted with fur

traders all up and down the Labrador coast and, when the Grenfell expedition was over, stayed on and traveled to collect what promised to be a fortune in live foxes.

But my little business was knocked into a cocked hat when, in 1914, the Newfoundland government, which owned Labrador, passed a law prohibiting the export of live foxes; and I was broke, after two years and some 5,000 miles of dog-team travel.

Anyone who attempts anything original in this world must expect a bit of ridicule. I have long since learned to take it in my stride.

Prior to 1914, few American women wore fine furs and the greatest fur markets of the world were London and Leipsic. When the war closed these markets, fur prices crashed and it looked as though all fur traders in the North would be ruined. I had a strong conviction, however, that with the new prosperity which the war was bringing to the United States it wouldn't be long before American women started buying furs in large quantities.

I communicated this belief to a fur house in New York, and the concern agreed to gamble $8,000 cash on my hunch if I would gamble my time. Consequently, I traveled more thousands of miles over Labrador by dogsled buying up furs with the cash. At the end of a year my share of the profit was some $6,000.

That was a tidy sum in those days—equivalent to about $25,000 today—and more money than I could have saved in years if I had continued to work for the Government. I made a quick trip to Washington, D.C., married the girl I was in love with, and took her back to Labrador with me. She was just as willing to take a chance as I was, so we moved into a three-room shack which was 250 miles from the nearest doctor, and I resumed my fur trading.

It was shortly after my bride and I had settled down in the wilds that my inquisitive nature led me to make certain observations which were later to play an important part in the development of my quick-freezing process.

In the winter, I frequently went fishing through holes chopped in the ice. The fish which I caught would freeze almost instantly in the very low temperatures that prevailed—of 30, 40, and often 50 below zero—and we would keep them outdoors until we were ready to use them. We would then thaw them out in a tub of water. I observed that caribou, wild geese, partridges, fish, and other flesh foods frozen almost instantly in the sub-zero blasts of midwinter were juicier and more flavorful than similar foods frozen in relatively mild spring and fall weather. "Why?" I wondered.

I cut paper-thin slices from the frozen foods and discovered that the quick-frozen flesh was firm, smooth, and marblelike, whereas the slower-frozen foods were of a grainy texture because of large ice crystals in the flesh. The slow-frozen foods leaked juice when these crystals thawed and were drier and less tasty when cooked than were quick-frozen foods.

My curiosity was aroused to such an extent that I made experiments with vegetables, too. We had had a large quantity of cabbage shipped to us from Newfoundland before the winter closed in. We kept this cabbage indoors, but when the weather got very cold I placed an empty barrel outside and into it put an inch of sea water, then a layer of cabbage. When this froze solid, I put in another inch of water, another layer of cabbage—and so on until the barrel was full. Later, when we wanted cabbage, we simply cut out a chunk with an ax. When cooked, the quick-frozen stuff was as delicious as fresh cabbage.

I tucked this knowledge away in my subconscious mind, but its commercial possibilities did not dawn on me at that time. My occupation was fur trading, and I concentrated on it until America's entrance into the war in 1917 brought me back to the States for good.

For two years I had a job with the Housing Corporation in Washington, then went into the wholesale fish business. Americans would eat more fish, I felt, if it could be kept fresh during shipment. How could it be kept really fresh? I invented an inexpensive container for shipping chilled fish, but it didn't solve the problem. What was the answer?

The subconscious mind, I often think, is similar to an electronic calculating machine. If you feed the right information into it, it will quietly go to work in mysterious ways of its own and, by-and-by, produce the answer to your problem.

That happened when I was stumped by what to do about keeping fish fresh during shipment. Then my subconscious suddenly told me that perishable foods could be kept perfectly preserved in the same way I had kept them in Labrador—by quick-freezing!

The subconscious mind . . . is similar to an electronic calculating machine. If you feed the right information into it, it will quietly go to work in mysterious ways.

I borrowed a corner of an ice-cream plant in New Jersey and started experiments in mechanical freezing. In 1923 I organized a company and the next year put quick-frozen fish on the market. But many difficulties confronted me. American housewives had deep-seated prejudices against "cold storage" foods of all kinds. Money was needed, a lot of money, to set up a large organization for producing, distributing, promoting and advertising the new product. I soon exhausted my savings and went broke.

My wife and I did not let that keep us from taking another chance. We had four small children coming along at the time, but we hocked our insurance and used the money to design an automatic freezer and form a new company.

Eventually, I got the backing of several wealthy men who saw my vision and were not afraid to gamble on something new. In 1929 we sold out for $22,000,000.

That was about the largest sum, I believe, ever paid for a patent in this country, but I am not being overly modest when I say there was nothing very remarkable about what I had done. I did not discover quick-freezing. The Eskimos had used it for centuries before I came along, and there were scientists in Europe who had made experiments along the same lines that I had. What I accomplished, with the direction and cooperation of many other men and a lot of other folks' money, was merely to make packaged quick-frozen foods available to the general public.

I was in my forties when this transaction made me financially independent for the first time in my life. A good many of my friends advised me to retire and take it easy. I had no more intention of doing so than I have today. Following one's curiosity is much more fun than taking things easy and I continued to ask questions and take chances. . . .

I have pointed out only a few of the opportunities which exist in just one area of American enterprise—the food industry. Practically every other field is just as inviting. This country holds far greater opportunities for youth today than it did when the first settlers trekked over the mountains and took up land in the West.

What is needed to grasp them? I've already expressed my opinion over and over again: Develop a questioning mind and don't be afraid to take a chance!

1951

PART VI

Branding, Image, and Selling

Whether working quietly behind the scenes or acting as a showman in front of the public, it is important for entrepreneurs to quickly establish an image to reflect their product and a sales strategy to establish their position in the market. The authors in Part VI tackle the marketing and sales issues associated with winning market share. Howard Schultz, CEO of Starbucks, provides a unique lesson on how to create an exciting brand in a mature industry. It isn't flashy advertising; instead, it involves investing in "employees who were zealous about good coffee" and who educate the customer. Colonel Sanders, founder of Kentucky Fried Chicken, took a different tack: He created a powerful personal image for himself and he alone promoted his product. P. T. Barnum relied on gimmicks, and John H. Johnson, founder of *Ebony* magazine, relied on sheer perseverance to attract customers. As for selling, Michael Dell offers lessons as a pioneer in direct distribution, a unique strategy that includes what he calls mass customization. Dell is careful not to push on the customer what they don't need as each customer designs their own computer. Admittedly, the mass customization approach cannot be applied to every industry. Although the authors here have their own unique methods for marketing their product, the key is to identify what methods best suit your product and your market.

As founder of Il Giornale, a small Seattle chain of coffee and espresso bars, and then as CEO of Starbucks, Howard Schultz knows a few things about reinventing a product and creating a brand. However, it was a long road from his birthplace of Brooklyn, where Schultz's blue-collar family relied on government-subsidized housing, and barely made ends meet. Fortunately, he won a football scholarship to Northern Michigan University. After earning a business degree in 1975, he joined Xerox as a sales representative, becoming a star employee. Schultz reflected, "Fear of failure drove me at first, but as I tackled each challenge, my anxiety was replaced by a growing sense of optimism. Once you overcome seemingly insurmountable obstacles, other hurdles become less daunting."

After three years at Xerox, he joined Perstorp, a Swedish company, which is where he first came in contact with Starbucks, then just a small Seattle-based roaster and wholesaler of coffee beans. Bitten by the coffee bug, Schultz asked them for a job in 1982. The next year, while visiting Italy, he had what he calls an epiphany. "The Italians understood the personal relationship that people could have to coffee, its social aspect," he wrote. He returned wanting to open a chain of coffee bars, but the principles at Starbucks didn't share his enthusiasm, so Schultz left in 1986 to pursue his dream, calling the chain Il Giornale.

In 1987, he heard Starbucks was for sale and bought the company for $3.8 million, and later took it public in 1992. As of 1997, they had more than 1,300 stores around the world. For each, he wants to emulate what he witnessed in Italy: "We try to create, in our stores, an oasis, a little neighborhood spot where you can take a break, listen to some jazz, and ponder universal or personal or even whimsical questions over a cup of coffee." The first priority, however, is always the product. "The number-one factor in creating a great, enduring brand is having an appealing product. There's no substitute," he wrote. In the following selection, he explains how to build a brand by educating the customers one at a time.

The Best Way to Build a Brand
Howard M. Schultz

W e never set out to build a brand. Our goal was to build a great company, one that stood for something, one that valued the authenticity of its product and the passion of its people. In the early days, we were so busy selling coffee, one cup at a time, opening stores and educating people about dark-roasted coffee that we never thought much about "brand strategy."

We never set out to build a brand. Our goal
was to build a great company, one that stood
for something, one that valued the authenticity of its product and the passion of its people.

Then one day I started getting calls. "Can you come and tell us how you built a national brand in only five years?" It was unusual, people told me, for a brand to burst onto the national consciousness as quickly as Starbucks had. In some cities, it seemed to catch on overnight. When I looked back,

I realized we had fashioned a brand in a way no business-school textbook could ever have prescribed.

We built the Starbucks brand first with our people, not with consumers—the opposite approach from that of the crackers-and-cereal companies. Because we believed the best way to meet and exceed the expectations of customers was to hire and train great people, we invested in employees who were zealous about good coffee. Their passion and commitment made our retail partners our best ambassadors for the coffee and for the brand. Their knowledge and fervor created a buzz among customers and inspired them to come back. That's the secret of the power of the Starbucks brand: the personal attachment our partners feel and the connection they make with our customers.

I've learned a lot about great brands from Jamie Shennan, the Starbucks board member who had devised marketing strategies for Procter & Gamble, Anheuser-Busch, Pepsi, and General Foods. He invested in the company in 1990 because he believed Starbucks was already becoming a powerful brand. Great brands, he says, have a distinctive, memorable identity, a product that makes people look or feel better, and a strong but comfortable delivery channel, which in Starbucks' case was the store. To succeed, you need to be in a category large enough to be robust and vibrant and to have a clear and original vision. All of these factors are essential, he says, but they fuse only if the management team can execute well. Jamie thinks Starbucks can eventually become as widely known as Coke around the world.

We had fashioned a brand in a way no business-school textbook could ever have prescribed.

Most national brands in America are marketing-driven. Although my background is in marketing, that hasn't been the engine that drives Starbucks—at least not in the traditional sense. In the ten years after 1987, we spent less than $10 million on advertising, not because we didn't believe in it but because we couldn't afford it. Instead, we've been product-driven, people-driven, values-driven.

If you look for wisdom on brand marketing, most of what you'll find is based on the Procter & Gamble model. That is, you go after mass markets with mass distribution and mass advertising, and then focus on grabbing market share from your competitors. That's the basic way of life for mature products in established markets. If Pepsi gains a point or two, Coke loses. The same is true of cars and cigarette brands. The big packaged-goods companies spend many millions of dollars and design highly innovative ad campaigns with the goal of gaining a few percentage points of market share.

> Great brands . . . have a distinctive, memorable identity, a product that makes people look or feel better, and a strong but comfortable delivery channel, which in Starbucks' case was the store.

At Starbucks, we have a different approach. We're creating something new. We're expanding and defining the market. We didn't set out to steal customers away from Folgers or Maxwell House or Hills Brothers. We didn't go for the widest possible distribution. We set out, rather, to educate our customers about the romance of coffee drinking. We wanted to introduce them to fine coffees the way wine stewards bring forward fine wines. Just as they might discuss the characteristics of a wine grown in a specific region or district of France, we want our baristas to be able to intelligently explain the flavors of Kenya and Costa Rica and Sulawesi.

Starbucks built up brand loyalty one customer at a time, communicated through our people, in the setting of company-owned retail stores. Today, even managers of big consumer brands are starting to realize that if you can control your own distribution, you will not find yourself at the mercy of a retailer who may or may not understand your product. It's an enormously effective way to build an authentic brand, but it's certainly not the easiest way.

About 80 percent of the coffee sold in the United States is purchased on supermarket aisles. But from the beginning, we left these traditional channels to others and concentrated our efforts instead on our own retail stores in highly visible, high-traffic downtown sites and residential neighborhoods. We located in lobbies and on the going-to-work side of the street. We attracted people and got them to try our whole-bean coffee by first romancing them with espresso drinks.

Our competitive advantage over the big coffee brands turned out to be our people. Supermarket sales are non-verbal and impersonal, with no personal interaction. But in a Starbucks store, you encounter real people who are informed and excited about the coffee, and enthusiastic about the brand. Which brand name are you most likely to remember?

Today, there's a lot of marketing rhetoric about adding value to products. At Starbucks, the value was there from the beginning, in the coffee itself. When your average sale is only $3.50, you have to make sure customers come back. And ours do—on average eighteen times a month.

Starbucks certainly wasn't the first company to build a reputation through retail stores. Hundreds of local specialty retailers in cities everywhere do the same thing. Your local pizza shop may take pride in its unique spicy sauce. Or you may know a Chinese restaurant that has authentic *dim sum,* with a great chef from Hong Kong. Or you may frequent a local bookstore because the owner will special order obscure books for you. The point is, you know from experience, or from word of mouth, that they're the best in town.

Traditionally, local retailers have always thrived by differentiating themselves from the competition and by winning loyal customers with products or services or quality unobtainable nearby. What's extraordinary about Starbucks is that we used that model to become a national company and then leveraged our brand reputation beyond our stores, to wholesale and food-service channels as well as to new products sold through grocery stores and other outlets.

> By word of mouth, with patience and discipline, over a period of years, you can elevate a good local brand to a great national brand.

Starbucks' success proves that a multimillion-dollar advertising program isn't a prerequisite for building a national brand—nor are the deep pockets of a big corporation. You can do it one customer at a time, one store at a time, one market at a time. In fact, that may be the best way to inspire loyalty and trust in customers. By word of mouth, with patience and discipline, over a period of years, you can elevate a good local brand to a great national brand—one that remains relevant to individual customers and communities for years.

Authenticity Makes Brands Last

In this ever-changing society, the most powerful and enduring brands are built from the heart. They are real and sustainable. Their foundations are stronger because they are built with the strength of the human spirit, not an ad campaign. The companies that are lasting are those that are authentic.

Take Nike as an example. Few people remember that Phil Knight disdained advertising for years, preferring event promotions and athlete endorsements. He built Nike's reputation on the basis of authenticity, focusing on how its shoes improved athletic performance. Long after running shoes became a fashion statement and street wear, Nike continued to highlight technical superiority. Long after Nike became known for its megamillion-dollar award-winning TV ad campaigns, the company still embraced its legacy as the shoe of choice of the best athletes.

By contrast, take Gloria Jean's, a coffee company started near Chicago, which began franchising nationwide in 1986. By late 1991, it was ahead of Starbucks, with 120 stores, compared to our 110. But Gloria Jean's never developed the loyalty Starbucks did, and ownership ended up changing hands several times. One reason is that the company franchised the concept in more than 100 cities across the country, and each isolated franchise failed to create strong loyalty among customers. More fundamentally, though, the company never established a word-of-mouth reputation for authenticity and quality.

Mass advertising can help build brands, but authenticity is what makes them last. If people believe they share values with a company, they will stay loyal to a brand.

The Starbucks Brand Is More Than Coffee

The number-one factor in creating a great, enduring brand is having an appealing product. There's no substitute.

In Starbucks' case, our product is a lot more than coffee. Customers choose to come to us for three reasons: our coffee, our people, and the experience in our stores.

Romancing the Bean
Nothing matters more in our business than the taste of the coffee. We are fanatical about buying the highest-quality arabica coffees in the world and roasting them to the desired fla-

vor characteristics for each variety. It's become a benchmark for us; everything else we do has to be as good as our coffee.

We make much of the romance of coffee buying, telling the story of how Dave Olsen and Mary Williams travel to origin countries and talk to growers. But ultimately, the point is not the mystique but the performance in the cup.

Mass advertising can help build brands, but authenticity is what makes them last. If people believe they share values with a company, they will stay loyal to a brand.

Coffee is easily ruined. Even if you buy the right beans, they can go stale on the shelf, be under- or over-roasted, brewed improperly, or served lukewarm. We are fastidious about making sure nothing goes wrong any step of the way.

Behind the scenes, our retail partners go to great lengths to ensure our coffee stays fresh and flavorful. We keep the beans in vacuum-sealed bags or dark drawers to minimize the harmful effects of air, light, and moisture. We grind them to a precise level of coarseness or fineness depending on how they'll be brewed. Then we measure the proportions of coffee and water according to exacting standards. If a barista-in-training takes less than eighteen or more than twenty-three seconds to pull a shot of espresso, we ask him or her to keep trying until the timing is right.

Because 98 percent of coffee is water, bad water can ruin the taste of even the best coffee beans. So, behind the counter in every store, where most customers can't even see it, we even have a special water filtration system. Each of these careful steps adds to our cost of operation, but they make a difference customers can taste and guarantee a standard of flavor and quality that is consistent from store to store and region to region.

1997

COLONEL HARLAND SANDERS
1890–1980

The Colonel's image, the white suit and goatee, has left an indelible mark on America—the founder of Kentucky Fried Chicken is Americana. His drive to succeed was formed by an event in his youth. When Sanders, who was born in Indiana, was 10 years old, his widowed mother hired him out to a local farmer for $2 a month plus board. However, the lad didn't exactly enjoy breaking a sweat, so the farmer let him go and his mother was bitterly disappointed. He wrote in his autobiography, "I never felt so remorseful to think I let my mom down like I did. I made a resolve right then and there: If I ever get a job again, nothing will ever keep me from finishin' what I'm called on to do." However, it took a while for Sanders to keep that promise.

His mother eventually remarried, but Sanders didn't get along with his stepfather, so he left home at age 12. He worked for a farmer for a couple of years, then a kindly uncle found him a job as a streetcar conductor. Over the years, Sanders went on to work as a locomotive fireman, an insurance salesman, a gas station operator, among others, before becoming a motel operator and restaurateur. But when a new highway bypassed the town where he had his hotel and restaurant, he found himself, at age 65, with nothing but social security to live on. He reflected, "But as I took stock of what I had left to work with it somehow seemed to me that the recipe I had developed for my Kentucky Fried Chicken might be something I could work with." Sanders had perfected the recipe (all 11 herbs and spices) back in the 1930s.

Colonel Sanders started peddling his recipe to other restaurants, and by 1960, two hundred were selling his fried chicken. While he was on the road his wife, working out of their home, would mix the herbs and spices and ship out the packages. "The business I developed was a personal one," he wrote. "I knew most all the franchises by their first names, and many of them had slept in my beds and eat breakfast at my table. We was just one big family." His image was a very personal one, too, and in the following selection he describes how he created it. Not only did he build the company upon it, but even today, his image remains central to KFC's advertising campaign.

The Making of a Colonel
Colonel Harland Sanders

The Kentucky Colonel, of course, is an honorary title. Maybe the reason I hadn't thought too much about the title before this was the story I heard about a Kentucky Colonel on the witness stand. The attorney who was questioning him wasn't getting the kind of answers from the colonel that he wanted. Knowin' the old man had never had a command in the army, he thought he would try a little sarcasm on him.

"Colonel, were you colonel of a regiment in the army? "No, suh."

"Well, what kind of a colonel are you?"

"That title 'colonel' before my name is like the 'honorable' before your name, Mr. Attorney. It don't mean a daggone thing."

There are thousands of Kentucky Colonels, of course, and we have what is known as the Honorable Order of Kentucky Colonels. Every year on the Friday night before the Kentucky Derby, which is always held the first Saturday in May, we have a big banquet. The governor of Kentucky presides, because he is commander-in-chief of the colonels. During the year we contribute money to a charity fund we have created. Each colonel gives whatever contribution he wants to the Colonels' Fund for Charity. Last year we gave away better than a quarter of a million dollars to worthy organizations. I nominated a Salvation Army boys' camp and they received $27,000. So that way we kind of justify our existence as colonels.

Of course, the wife of a colonel is referred to as "the colonel's lady," and that happens to be the name my wife has on her restaurant in the back of our place in Shelbyville, "The Colonel's Lady Dinner House."

So when we decided to use "Colonel Sanders" with the Kentucky Fried Chicken I thought that I should look like a colonel. I grew my little goatee, wore my mustache, and carried a cane.

My hair was white already. But I had dark auburn hair mixed in my chin whiskers and my mustache. I tried to bleach them out. But beauty parlors that was makin' blondes out of gray-headed women couldn't help me. Then I told my barber about my problem.

"The next time you come in for a shave, colonel, I'll bleach them out for you. I'll guarantee it," he said.

The next day when I went in for a shave he had a customer in his chair gettin' his hair cut. I got a shoeshine while that was going on.

"I'll be ready for you soon's I get through here," he said.

Then he thought to himself, *I better test this bleach out to see how long it will take to bleach the colonel's mustache.*

So he picked up a bunch of black hair off the floor and put them in a cup where he had the material he was gonna use on my chin. After three or four minutes he looked to see how it was doin'.

"I'll be dadblamed," he said. "There ain't no hair there at all. The bleach done eat it all up."

So I had to wait for my mustache to turn white to look more like an authentic colonel. The white suit was to come at another time.

During the next couple of years inquiries regarding Kentucky Fried Chicken increased to the point where I just couldn't get around to handle all of them. And besides, that was an expensive way to do it. So, I got to invitin' the prospects to come and see me. If they became a franchisee, I'd pay their way.

By this time we had moved to a big old country house in Shelbyville, which is thirty miles from Louisville. It had five bedrooms. So we would usually have anywhere from one to four rooms filled with prospective franchisees. We'd have dinner and talk about chicken. Maybe we'd go someplace to one of the franchisees in the neighborhood.

I wasn't fryin' chicken then at our place because we didn't have the restaurant yet. But I'd always have some place close to take them to, so they could see what success another man was having. The next morning I fed them country ham and eggs. So we'd cook up a big platter of country ham, red-eye gravy, and hot biscuits.

We have a large dining room in the home there. And sometimes we'd have eight or ten people around, all of them eatin' breakfast. We just had a lot of good fellowship. And it had a wholesome effect on the business. Those men would become part of the family right there, and they'd leave maybe the next day and take their franchise contract with them. It wasn't much—more or less a handshake proposition. It done more for them than it did for me.

Some people want to know why I call it Kentucky Fried Chicken.

Well, every greasy-spoon restaurant in the country has fried chicken on its menu and most of them call it Southern fried chicken. It's fried in the same French fryer as they fry fish, onions, shrimp, and everything else. Well, I didn't want my chicken to be in that category. So I called mine Kentucky Fried Chicken, way back from its very inception when I first started fryin' chicken in the state of Kentucky. Never thought about franchising then—not until the guinea pig franchise with Pete Harman in Salt Lake City and later Darrel Gillam in Kokomo, Indiana.

Soon after I also thought up the slogan "America's Hospitality Dish." When I went into Canada, I naturally changed that to "North America's Hospitality Dish."

In the Southeast, we usually season our food more highly

than the people in the Midwest or the West. Also, folks in the big cities usually like their food cooked in one way, while people in the country another way. But it didn't seem to make no difference where people came from, they liked my Kentucky Fried Chicken just the way it was.

When I started out on the road selling Kentucky Fried Chicken franchises, I didn't have no money for advertising or promotion. So I had to do the best I could.

Since then we have seen this fact demonstrated in many parts of the world where Kentucky Fried franchises have been opened—thirty-three countries in all.

I told you before how the name *colonel* became important in developing the franchise business. The white suit idea came along about this time, but the idea of using white goes back to my railroad days. As a fireman, I always wore white overalls and white cotton gloves when I was workin' for the Southern Railroad. I just like the looks of being clean.

In later years I wore white Palm Beach suits in summer. But then Palm Beach stopped making white suits, and if it hadn't been for a couple of experiences I had along about that time I might have stopped wearin' white.

The first came when I had gone north in late fall or early winter still wearin' my white suit. We had a sudden cold spell, and the temperature dropped to ten degrees below zero. Well, here I was walking through the airport in Cleveland in a white suit with my overcoat over my arm. Then I became aware that folks was turnin' and lookin'.

"Who's that? Where's he from?" I could hear them askin'.

Then somebody in the crowd remembered that I was the chicken man they'd heard of. And so Kentucky Fried Chicken got some publicity, don'tcha see?

312

The second time came when I was introduced to TV cameras—a promotion for Garth's Drive-In in Colorado Springs. When I come out of the studio folks told me how the white suit stood out from the rest.

"You have no idea, colonel, how that white suit attracted attention," they said.

I soon discovered the unusual uniform also gave me the opportunity of getting more TV appearances. You got to remember that when I started out on the road selling Kentucky Fried Chicken franchises, I didn't have no money for advertising or promotion. So I had to do the best I could.

Well, the white suit as a part of the Kentucky Colonel outfit worked out fine.

1974

AKIO MORITA
1921–

The cofounder of Sony was born into a family that had run a sake-brewing company for 14 generations, and as first son, Akio Morita was expected to someday lead the family operation. From age 10 he sat beside his father during "long and boring board meetings." From his father, he also learned to appreciate music and technological advances as his father always bought the best phonograph for fear of hurting his children's ears. The fancy machine hit a nerve: "I began to buy books about electronics, and I subscribed to Japanese and foreign magazines that contained all the latest information about sound reproduction and radio. . . . In fact, I became so engrossed in my electronic tinkering that I almost flunked out of school," Morita wrote in his autobiography.

Morita studied physics at Osaka Imperial University, and after graduation, he served with the navy during World War II as a researcher. After the war, although the family business beckoned, Morita chose to start a new company with a friend. Their mission: to be "an innovator, a clever company that would make new high-technology products in ingenious ways" and help rebuild Japan's economy. Their first innovative product was a tape recorder, but no one in postwar Japan was interested in spending valuable money on a toy. Morita realized, "Having a unique technology and being able to make unique products are not enough to keep a business going. You have to sell the products, and to do that you have to show the potential buyer the real value of what you are selling."

The man of science had to become a merchandiser. Morita took his tape recorder to the Japanese court system, which was overwhelmed with postwar problems and stenographers were scarce—the tape recorder became an invaluable replacement. The innovations continued with the first transistorized television set in 1959 and later the fabulously popular Walkman. Many of their innovations first met with resistance, which is why in *Moving Up in Marketing by Getting Down to Basics,* Morita explains the dangers of relying on market research—he prefers to make the market.

Moving Up in Marketing by Getting Down to Basics
Akio Morita

Good marketing, I believe, requires some degree of courage, and so I shall try to draw on mine in discussing frankly my marketing concepts. These come from my experience and not from theory. I was a physicist by education and have had no formal training in the field of marketing. I shall, therefore, lean on my past experience rather than try to theorize.

In 1946 our present chairman, Mr. Masaru Ibuka, and I established our company with a little over 20 persons and less than $600 of capital. We started making communication equipment for the reconstruction of Japan. We dealt with various government agencies.

Good marketing, I believe, requires some degree of courage.

It required a great deal of effort to get the purchasing officers in these large organizations to understand that we were a company that could be relied on for its unique technology and sincerity. We were finally able to gain their trust and get a continuous flow of orders from them. However, one day a horrible thing happened. The person in charge of purchase, whose trust I had won after long effort, was transferred to another position. An entirely new person now sat in the purchaser's seat. This meant that I had to start all over again to convince him of our capabilities.

After a few repetitions of this experience, I began to think about the problem. I realized that it is not good business if our efforts do not accumulate and continue to bring results. From the standpoint of efficiency, our efforts should accumulate and remain as an asset of the business. When we deal with a large organization it is true that a large, one-time sale may be achieved if the purchasing agent of the organization has been convinced of our company's ability. However, such large sales are influenced by a small handful of individuals in charge of the purchase. Once these individuals disappear, all the effort of the past is lost. I began to wonder whether this manner of doing business was a wise policy or not.

I discussed this matter with Mr. Ibuka, and we arrived at the conclusion to go into the consumer market. In other words, we decided to do business with unspecified millions of individuals instead of with a specific few. On this basis we started to produce the first tape recorder and tapes in Japan.

We had dreams of making a great fortune, and we devoted huge amounts of money and personnel, in comparison with the size of the company, to the development of the product. But this dream disappeared when we started to market this first tape recorder, for we visited many prospective customers, demonstrating the new tape recorder ourselves, and they would only say that the device was very interesting but too expensive for a toy. Facing this fact, we spent many days trying to find out how we could sell the product.

One weekend I took a stroll in my neighborhood and stopped in front of an antique shop. I am not interested in antiques, but I gazed at the various articles displayed in the show window. Out of curiosity I walked into the shop where a customer was asking the salesman various questions. And then the customer paid an amazingly high price for an antique that would not have attracted me in the least, and he walked out happily with it. I thought that our tape recorder was much more valuable, but he had gladly paid an even higher price for an antique.

I was surprised and intrigued by this behavior. It taught me a basic principle of sales. This principle is that no sale can be achieved unless the buyer appreciates the value of the merchandise. I would not have paid such a price to buy the antique piece, because I am not interested in such things. But the other person, who understood the value of antiques, was willing to pay the price.

The tape recorder was a tremendous technical achievement in the eyes of those of us who had struggled to create it. For us it had a very high value, and we thought that the price we had put on it was even less than its true value. But the general public looked on it only as an interesting toy. This meant that unless the customer understood that the tape recorder was a valuable device with a wide variety of uses, he would not pay the price. The principle was this simple, but we realized that we were ignorant of even this basic principle. We therefore embarked on the task of teaching people how useful the tape recorder was in practical life.

> No sale can be achieved unless the buyer appreciates the value of the merchandise.

This experience taught us a basic lesson in the marketing of our product, which has guided our policy ever since. A company such as ours, which is constantly developing new products, must always have the capability of educating prospective customers. Otherwise, new markets for new products will never be created. However, it is impossible for us, who are limited in time and number, to educate large numbers of customers. We realize that marketing means increasing the number of persons who can communicate to

317

customers the usefulness and value of our new products in the same way as we would ourselves.

Firstly, therefore, I had to educate our marketing group in this purpose, and then they would transfer my concepts to the next stage of marketing. In this process an accurate message had to be communicated fully from myself to our marketing group, and from them to distributor salesmen in each region, and then from the distributor salesmen to the dealer salesmen. This meant that our marketing task was a communication task.

Marketing as Communication

In the technology of electronic communication, the more relay stages there are in the channel, the greater is the possibility for distortion to accumulate. It is important, therefore, to keep the number of relay stages to a minimum. Yet in earlier days in our industry Japan had a very complex sales distribution system. So it took a very long time to build up our own sales organization to enable our sales personnel to deliver the message directly to the dealers.

Now the concept that marketing is communication has become very firmly established. Moreover, this concept is not limited to the sales network alone. It is very important inside our own company whenever we develop a new product. It involves transmitting the intent of top management in the development of a product through all stages, from the production department to the floor salesman of the dealer and to the customer. Moreover, the communication is not just one-way. Customers' views must be fed back accurately through the marketing network to the factory. Only when this two-way communication is adequate can it be said that the marketing mechanism works out well.

People nowadays pay great attention to market research. The belief has grown that by learning promptly what things the consumers want and by producing those things, good sales will be achieved. However, in our type of society, where new technology is constantly being developed, I think it is risky to rely too heavily on market research. The customer in general has some knowledge about the products he presently owns, but he is not usually an expert who knows the technology involved. Therefore, if we are too strongly influenced by his demands in our development efforts, we may end up working on a product which other manufacturers may already have introduced on the market by the time we are able to put ours on sale. This would mean that we could not be competitive.

Utilizing our technological capacity, we must create products having new features that customers have not expected nor have had any knowledge about. These products and features, when they are created, must then be communicated to the customer so that he can understand what benefits he can obtain. In this way a market is created. This is the concept that our company has about marketing.

In our type of society, where new technology is constantly being developed, I think it is risky to rely too heavily on market research.

Developing an International Market

In referring to the need to reduce the number of relay steps in order to improve communication, I also indicated that each relay step should be manned by those having the same concepts and interests as we have. When we began to produce the world's first small transistor radio, we decided that our products should be sold all around the world, and these ideas of relay steps in communication were also applied to the system of exporting our products.

At that time Japanese manufacturers found it very difficult to sell their products abroad. They felt that the only way to sell their products outside Japan was to rely on various trading companies. However, we felt that we could not communicate our new knowledge adequately through trading firms that had different interests from ours. We therefore decided to export our products ourselves.

I took the small radio myself to the United States to sell it. I spent a great deal of time learning how best to conduct sales in the United States. My knowledge of the country was nil. I was amazed at the huge market; I was amazed at the huge size of the country; and I was amazed at the strength of the competition. But I became confident that our marketing concept need not change and that the basic principles need not be different.

However, we ran into a very big obstacle. That was the name of our company, Tokyo Tsushin Kogyo. I found that no American could pronounce it. We realized that we needed a trademark that could be easily recognized by Americans. The establishment of a reputation for reliability among the public is of prime importance in consumer marketing, but this could not be achieved unless the name of the company could be easily remembered. It would be impossible to ask the public to trust a company whose name they could not even pronounce.

Realizing, therefore, that the company should be identified easily and clearly, we concluded that the name of our company was not appropriate for international business. We started a search for a name that would be the best. We set up three conditions to be met. One was that it must be an internationally acceptable name. Another was that it must be short, and thirdly, it would have to be pronounced in the same way wherever it was seen.

Thinking of various possibilities, we came across the Latin word *sonus*, meaning "sound." We also thought of the English word "sonny," or "sonny boy," and we combined it with the Latin word to form SONY. At that time we were a group of young people handling sound equipment, in other words, "sonny boys" dealing in "sonus." And so the name SONY was coined, and on that first tiny radio, therefore, we put the letters S-O-N-Y as a trademark. Also, we changed our company name to this, so that the advertising cost would not have to be split in two to advertise two names. In this way, all of our advertising funds could be spent on communicating information about our products.

It was quite a decision to change our company name Tokyo Tsushin Kogyo, a name that sounded good in Japanese, to a new name like SONY. When we did this, some Japanese thought that the Japanese company called Tokyo Tsushin Kogyo had been taken over by a foreign company called Sony Corporation. Today, however, we believe that the bold step we took was a good one. Marketing is something that I believe must be continued over many years in communicating the company philosophy and concepts. Customers will then become fully confident that any new products we would offer under our name can also be bought with a sense of reliability.

However, I believe that marketing requires investments for the future. Just as the manufacturer invests in the future by expending research funds for new products, and, in some cases, for basic science, so must investments be made in the sales area for future marketing. My experience tells me that this is often forgotten in the Western system. To understand this point, it may be helpful to consider the difference between the attitude of employees toward their companies in the United States and Japan.

Investing in the Future

In Japan nearly all the employees of a company stay in the firm for many long years. In our company, our managers and other key staff members have been with the firm for many years and will continue to cast their lot with the company for another 10, 20 or 30 years. For these employees it is not only important that the company business be good at present but also necessary that the company be healthy in the decades ahead. Therefore young, middle-level employees can clearly understand the need to make investments at present, even with some degree of sacrifice, to build for the future. It is, therefore, possible to establish long-range plans and invest to create future markets.

In contrast, those working in an American company are rated on the results they show every year. It is difficult for them to think of sacrificing today's profits for the sake of the company's well-being one or two decades from now. It is much more likely that they will want to cash in on all of the company's current possessions for the sake of profits today. However, very logical management principles have been derived from this kind of approach in the United States, and I have learned much from this American management method. Still, I cannot avoid the impression that the great attention given to making profits today causes a lack of willingness to sacrifice some of today's profits for developing markets in the future.

While many companies are willing to spend research funds for future technology, very often they forget to spend money for marketing in the distant future.

This is illustrated by the fact that, with the exception of a small number of companies, most firms in the United States are not export-minded. The development of export markets requires a great deal of investment, so that business can be conducted successfully in other countries having different customs and attitudes. This type of investment appears only as a negative figure in the business at the early stages. And this causes many American companies to regard exports as a nonprofitable business.

In order to gain trust in the United States we had to devote great efforts and invest money over a very long time. Even today we station many of our Japanese engineers in countries all around the world to study design preferences among customers, the attitude of such customers towards technology, and the many different regulations of those nations, so that our own designers and planners can be adequately aware of them. These efforts require a great deal of expense. But we believe that this expense provides us with the ability to produce products which will be appropriate for those nations five and ten years from now.

There are some companies in the United States that are like this. They are the truly multinational corporations that have accumulated a wealth of experience abroad. All such firms have invested considerably in the future. But while many companies are willing to spend research funds for future technology, very often they forget to spend money for marketing in the distant future.

A new product resulting from such studies may not at first be understood by even those inside the company. But the first step in marketing is to exert efforts to get these inside personnel to understand the new product. And I believe that the real marketing experts are those who approach the new product with a will to understand it and go out and sell it. This creating of markets involves efforts to increase further the trust of customers in the company and at the same time to communicate to the customer the benefits derived from new technology in new products. In this way the strength of the company is fostered every day.

For, marketing is not just marketing for today. An enterprise is not well off by being well off only today. To continue to be successful, there must be an adequate understanding of the need to invest today's profits for the future, not only in research and development but also in marketing.

1974

Long before Nike and Reebok battled for superstars to endorse their sneakers, Marquis Converse had the savvy to hire a well-known basketball coach to assist in his marketing effort of his renowned Converse All Star basketball shoe. In 1924, he said, "I believe that advertising is directly productive in proportion to the extent to which it is different." He also applied that attitude to his products. For example, the Converse All Star, introduced in 1917 and one of the world's first basketball shoes, was designed with the signature leather ankle patch to protect the ankle bone and to differentiate their product.

Before founding his shoe company, he lived a varied life. Converse, who grew up on a New Hampshire farm, was directly descended from Puritans who settled in Massachusetts in 1630, and he claimed he could trace his roots to Edward III of England, who ruled from 1327 to 1377. Looking to escape the sometimes dreary farm life, in 1880 he found a clerk's position with a department store in Boston, eventually rising to the post of general manager. In 1886, he returned to New Hampshire to buy his own general store. Not long afterward, Converse returned to Boston to start a rubber boot company, but quickly moved on to work for the Beacon Falls Rubber Shoe Company. Finally, he launched the Converse Rubber Company in 1908 with $350,000 in capital, $100,000 of which was his own.

Within a few years, Converse had 350 employees and was making 4,000 pairs of boots and rubbers daily. It wasn't until 1915 that he started selling canvas tennis shoes—his legacy. Sales that year were $1.5 million and $2.5 the next. Unfortunately, Converse decided to enter the rubber tire market, which ultimately became his undoing as it drained profits, and he was forced to give up his business in 1929 (he died a year later). In a classic entrepreneurial mistake, he ventured outside of his realm of expertise, shoes, and therein lies one lesson. Converse begins his essay by describing another lesson, from his days at the department store when he learned the importance of breaking from the crowd and "doing things differently." Building upon that, he also offers his marketing philosophy.

My Test of Good Management
Marquis M. Converse

When I was a young man of 19, my employer gave me, under rather striking circumstances, a precept which has had a strong influence upon me ever since; in fact, it has been one of my chief guiding principles in 35 years of business.

The circumstances were these. After working a year as a clerk in the department store of Houghton and Dutton in Boston, I was promoted to the position of buyer. Now, while clerks' hours were from 8 to 6, buyers came in at 8:30 and went home at 5:30. I started to do likewise. About a week after this I received a message from Mr. Houghton, who had taken me into the store, that thereafter I was to come in at 11:00 and leave at 2:00. Somewhat mystified, but unquestioning, I followed instructions. Life soon began to pall, however; so after a few days I went to Mr. Houghton and said I was going to quit, explaining that I wanted a job where I could work.

Mr. Houghton fixed me with a severe look. "Young man," he said sternly, "if you are ready again to do a full day's work, sit down: I'd like to talk with you." Then he explained that his instructions were only a method of impressing a lesson: and it was then he laid down the precept which I took so much to heart. He said:

"If you want to be what most others are, do what most others do; if you want to be different, do things differently and better."

I have been using that precept ever since: applying it has been a great help in building up a business which last year totaled $6,000,000. It has been especially helpful in the matter of meeting competition.

The extent to which one concern follows another's methods is indeed surprising. If the leading concern does one thing, then others feel they must do the same thing. They must sell the same goods, at the same price, or perhaps lower, and in the same way. Our policy always is to look for a different and better way. Because a competitor is selling a certain type of shoe at $1.30, we don't necessarily feel we must sell a similar shoe at $1.30. We would rather work out a better shoe and sell it at $1.50, putting enough extra quality in it to warrant the increase in price. Then we have something to talk about, something to sell that the other fellow hasn't. This plan has worked out exceedingly well.

Our leading line of rubbers retails at 10 to 25 cents higher than the usual price. When we set out to develop a leader, we deliberately made it higher priced—but we put extra mileage into it. The result has been that the leader, thus planned, enjoys a very large sale. Curiously enough, we have found that one of the very best territories for this higher priced rubber is on the East Side of New York. The reason is that the class of trade there studies carefully what it gets for its money and hence is more likely to take notice of the comparative wear it gets from different grades of rubbers.

When I started in the manufacturing business 15 years ago, I was up against the big fellows—the "trusts" they were called in those days. If I had started out to compete with them on their own basis, it would have been hard sledding. If I had tried to compete with them on the basis of price, that would have been a game in which I would easily have been beaten.

Rubbers were pretty much the same everywhere. I had observed that they wore out from the inside as well as the outside, from friction of the heel nails. One of the first things I did, therefore, in attempting to find a different and better way, was to put a piece of leather inside the heel, getting a patent on the idea. That served to differentiate our rubber and gave us a talking point that competitors did not have.

When we started making basketball and athletic shoes, we looked around to see what we could do to make our merchandise different. The ankles, we found, were vulnerable points. So we started putting a leather patch on the ankles. That has since become a standard method of construction, but it was a new and different idea when we started out. It was simply the result of trying deliberately to think of a way to make it different. It helped us to break into a market where there was more than ordinary selling resistance. When others adopted the patch, we put on an extension heel and sole, called "stub-guard."

Then we adopted a different method of selling them. We hired a well-known basketball coach who had used our shoes and become enthusiastic about them. As a result our basketball shoes have become very well known and are extensively used among basketball teams in the United States.

When we started making basketball and athletic shoes, we looked around to see what we could do to make our merchandise different.

We followed the same plan when we went into the tire business. In experimenting to learn how we could make the product different and better we worked out the compression tread principle; when the tire is inflated the rubber in the tread is compressed instead of stretched, which gives it greater resistance to wear. We have always leaned toward making the better grades of products; so in tires we set out to make the best quality we could learn to turn out. We concentrated on cord tires exclusively with the exception of one size. Then we set out to sell them on the basis of their worth.

Our present marketing plan of selling rubber shoes direct to the retailer on an agency basis was also the result of similar methods of thinking. Rubber goods were mostly sold through jobbers when we started in business. Instead of taking this method for granted as the proper marketing plan, I commenced to study the situation. A jobber's function primarily is to collect goods from many sources and sell to the retailer a single large order instead of requiring that the same quantity of goods should be broken up into many small, direct-to-manufacturer orders. I concluded, with this thought as a basis, that while the jobber performed a real service in many lines of merchandise, the unit of sale with our merchandise was large enough to make it more economical to sell direct. That was the plan, therefore, that we adopted. Again, the nearer the source of consumption a manufacturer gets, the greater possibility he has of controlling and directing his business. The direct retailer plan has worked out very advantageously for us.

Applying "Something Different" to Advertising

The policy of finding a different and better way applies to our advertising as well as to manufacturing. I believe that advertising is directly productive in proportion to the extent to which it is different. Recently we decided upon a newspaper campaign in the East for our tires. Layouts and plans were submitted to me. They were very good looking advertisements, but it seemed to me there was nothing about them that was different from or better than scores of similar advertisements.

Accordingly, we set to work to see if we could find any plan which would make them different and better. The result was a plan by which we offered a tube free with every tire. Dealers were supplied with coupons which they distributed to customers and prospects: these coupons being redeemed at full value by us when used. List prices remained as before; we stood the extra cost in the expectation that increased volume would make up for it. This gave the plan a hook, made it different, attracted attention, and got results.

I would rather have people criticize an advertisement, no matter how severely, than to have them make no comment at all.

Similarly, we were getting up a folder reproducing some testimonials. The natural title that suggested itself was, "What Users Say." Thinking along the lines of finding the different and better way, we worked out the title, "How's the Roast Beef?" with an illustration showing a diner asking that question of the waiter, who, of course, replies, "fine!" The moral is that a manufacturer naturally speaks well of his merchandise, but the true test is what those who have used it say.

I would rather have people criticize an advertisement, no matter how severely, than to have them make no comment at all. We want our advertising to be different enough to make an impression of some kind.

This precept which I got from Mr. Houghton 35 years ago is, I feel, still as good as it ever was. It applies to any department of our business, or to any business, for that matter. Whenever we get out a new product, or work out a new marketing plan, our first thought is to set out consciously and deliberately to try and find a different and better way. The precept has percolated through to our executives so that it has become more or less of a habit not alone in connection with major events, but in connection with the everyday happenings of the business.

1924

JOHN H. JOHNSON
1918–

John Johnson, founder of *Negro Digest, Ebony,* and Fashion Fair Cosmetics, among other ventures, has long been considered the most powerful African-American businessman in the United States. Although his father was killed when he was a child and he lived in poverty, Johnson claimed he was lucky because in his neighborhood Blacks looked out for Blacks. In high school, he made a habit of reading Dale Carnegie's *How to Win Friends and Influence People,* which came into play later when he wanted to start his own magazine. After high school, Johnson took a job with an African-American life insurance company, and received some scholarship money to study at the University of Chicago.

Over the next few years he built a network of friends and business associates, and in 1942 he seized his destiny by founding the *Negro Digest,* a magazine to keep African Americans informed about current events. When he launched *Negro Digest,* he needed $500 worth of stamps for his direct-mail effort to win subscribers, so he went looking for a loan. As the first banker explained, "Boy, we don't make any loans to colored people." The banker did refer him to a bank that would, but he had to put up his mother's furniture as collateral. Johnson then wrote a pitch letter to 20,000 Black people in 1942. Three thousand responded, spending a total of $6,000, and his business was launched.

Three years later he started *Ebony,* which would become the cornerstone of his empire. To succeed in publishing, he knew he had to reverse the prejudice against advertising in African-American magazines; White businesspeople were blind to the African-American consumer and their purchasing power. Johnson emphatically argued "that Blacks were brand-conscious consumers who wanted to be treated like everyone else—not better, not worse." Persistence helped, too. "I refused to give up. I refused to take no for an answer, and I refused to let others take no for an answer," he wrote. In *Breaking Through the Ad Barrier,* Johnson depicts that persistence as he explores the mysterious world of White advertisers and battles to convince them that they should advertise in his magazine.

Breaking Through the Ad Barrier
John H. Johnson

B y creative financing and PMA* and JRT—Johnson Reinforcement Techniques—I bought enough time to identify and formulate the three elements necessary for a strategy of success.

The first element is identification of the problem. This is the most important point in developing a success strategy, and it's the one most frequently overlooked by business people from the mail room to the boardroom who leap into the saddle and ride off in all directions before they identify the objective and the obstacles.

That's the wrong approach. The first problem of any problem is to decide exactly what the problem is. . . .

I didn't have a big staff and I didn't have a big bank account. The thing that saved me and Johnson Publishing Company is that I made the right diagnosis. I did what every businessman in a tight corner should do. I sat down and wrote a declarative sentence that defined the problem.

My problem was not the editorial content of the magazine—the readers were yelling for more. My problem was not circulation—I couldn't print enough copies. My problem was advertising or, to come right out with it, the lack of advertising.

*Positive mental attitude.

331

How did I intend to deal with the problem?

I intended to deal with the problem by persuading corporations and advertising executives to give *Ebony* the *same* consideration they gave *Life* and *Look*.

To do that I had to convince corporations and advertising executives that there was an untapped, underdeveloped Black consumer market larger and more affluent than some of the major White foreign markets.

The first problem of any problem is to decide exactly what the problem is.

This was a revolutionary approach—revolutionary from a racial, marketing, and advertising standpoint—and I couldn't sell it to lower-level functionaries. I had to go to the top and sell the Black consumer market the same way you sell a foreign market.

The plan of action was implicit in the definition of the problem.

I needed, first of all, a team of advertising specialists who understood the new concept and believed in it with the passion of true believers.

The team didn't exist.

I had to invent it.

I started, as usual, small. A small step gives you the confidence to make a big step. And a big step gives you courage to run.

I started small, hiring a White advertising manager, a man named Irwin J. Stein, one of the most honorable men I've known. There were no Blacks who knew the mysteries of the White advertising world, and I hired Stein with the understanding that he would train a Black to take his place.

Stein wasn't a salesman; he was a manager. He helped design the rate cards and worked with me in determining rates. He also trained Isaac Payne, who succeeded him as advertising production manager and remained with the company until his death.

Since we didn't have a staff of salesmen, we asked a Black-owned firm of publishers' representatives to sell ads and look out for our interests on Madison Avenue. When our self-imposed advertising moratorium ended in May 1946, two of the first four ads in *Ebony* (Chesterfield, Kotex) were sold by this firm. I sold the other ads, Murray's Hair Pomade and Supreme Liberty Life Insurance Company.

The Chesterfield, Kotex, and Murray's ads were full-page color ads, and the Supreme ad was a full-page black-and-white. Murray's used a Black woman model. Chesterfield, which ran several ads in 1946 and 1947, used a White male model, and Kotex used a White couple.

When, after a few months, the Black firm did not seem to be making substantial progress, I turned reluctantly to a White firm. I was told that Whites could get in to see White advertising managers more easily and could socialize with them and promote the magazine better.

It didn't turn out that way. White salesmen were no more effective than Black salesmen, and they created other problems. The turning point came on the day I got a call from an angry man in an advertising agency.

"John Johnson," he said, "I don't know whether I'm ever going to advertise with you, but I want to give you some free advice. You sent a White man to sell me an ad for a magazine about Black people. This White man doesn't know any more about Blacks than I do. If you've got all those intelligent, affluent Blacks reading the magazine, why don't you send one to sell me an ad?"

It was a good question, and I decided, after thinking about it for a while, to send myself. What did I have to lose? I had tried everything, or almost everything, and I was floundering in a rough sea and going down for the third time.

From that day in 1946 until we turned the corner a year later, I spent almost every waking hour selling advertising.

Ebony readers helped. They jumped the gun and started asking manufacturers why they weren't advertising in *Ebony.* Some went further and told backsliders that they were only going to spend their money with companies that showed them the elementary respect of asking for their business.

An avalanche of postcards and handwritten petitions prepared the ground, and I planted seeds with letters and phone calls to corporate chiefs and agency heads. It was hard getting through, but I was fighting for my life and I placed as many as four hundred telephone calls to the same CEO.

There's an art in talking to secretaries, and it should be taught at MBA schools. I taught myself, and soon became a master of the art of leaping over secretarial shields. I was so persistent, and so patient, that some secretaries either put me through or gave me helpful hints.

The secretary to Fairfax M. Cone of Foote, Cone & Belding advertising agency told me that she couldn't make an appointment for anyone.

"But," she said, "I'll give you a tip. He doesn't like to fly. He goes to New York every Sunday afternoon on the *Twentieth Century Limited.* He has a couple of drinks in the bar, eats dinner, and goes to bed. If I were you, I would just happen to be on that train, and I would wander into the club car and strike up a conversation with him."

I was fighting for my life and I placed as many as four hundred telephone calls to the same CEO.

I caught the train and wandered into the club car. And I was surprised and delighted to find Fairfax Cone there. I talked to him on that Sunday and the next Sunday and the Sunday after that. I became a regular on the *Twentieth Century Limited,* and Fairfax Cone and I became good friends. He arranged for me to talk to executives at his agency, and I sold some accounts. Cone himself later made a movie for us on the importance of the Black consumer market.

I used another approach to break the barrier at Tatham and Laird, headed by Kenneth Laird. Ken and I were active in the Roundtable of Christians and Jews. We served together on a number of committees and were virtually inseparable during Brotherhood Week. But the brotherhood slogans never led to anything concrete. We didn't get any business from Ken's agency, and when one of our standard accounts moved to his agency, we lost it. I pointed this out to him one day at a committee meeting on brotherhood, and he bristled with indignation.

"We don't believe in anything like that around here," he said. "I'll check it out and let you talk to our key people."

I talked to his executives and discovered what I already knew. They weren't the real stumbling block.

I went back to Ken and said, "Ken, I've finally found the person in your agency who's keeping us from getting business."

"Who?" he said. "Tell me who it is, and I'll fire him."

"Ken," I said, "it's you."

He denied it. But he was forced to reexamine his own attitudes and to come to grips with the fact that a corporation or agency necessarily reflects the attitudes of the chief executive. Before long, we started getting business from Tatham and Laird.

In this instance, as in others, I anticipated the insights of a book called *Selling Dangerously*, by Elmer Wheeler. When all of the traditional selling strategies have failed, Wheeler said, and when you've gotten a final and definite no despite all your efforts, anything you do—shouting, cursing, standing on the table, denouncing racism—is right. What Wheeler neglected to say is that all selling, if it's effective selling, is dangerous selling. And that it takes a master salesman or an artist to identify the right psychological moment for turning insult into gold.

1989

MICHAEL S. DELL
1965–

Michael Dell is anything but a flamboyant marketer or a renegade entrepreneur; on the other hand, he has quietly changed the way computer companies do business. Dell grew up in an upper-middle-class Houston suburb, where his dad was an orthodontist and his mother a stockbroker. They wanted him to be a doctor, so he enrolled at the University of Texas as a premed student. His first love, however, was computers, so in his first semester in 1983, operating out of his dorm room, Dell started buying old computers and upgrading them for resale. That summer he sold $180,000 worth of upgraded PCs and never went back to school. As a next step, he realized he could buy the components and build new computers himself, which he did.

Dell has become a legend for his well-executed just-in-time manufacturing. His company builds everything to order for their customers and doesn't force anything down their throats. "We introduce technology that meets the needs of our customers," he wrote, "rather than introducing technology for its own sake, which is still a very common strategy in our industry today." There's no shipping to stores. There's no excess inventory. Dell calls it "mass customization" and a "direct distribution system" that includes their "Stealth Warehouse" (virtual warehouse). The time elapsed from phone call to delivery: about 36 hours.

Dell Computers went public in 1988, and at one point, his company's stock was up more than 30,000 percent in the 1990s. The one major road bump was in 1993 when the company posted a $36 million loss. Growth had come too fast. "One of the things that is confusing and almost intoxicating when you are growing a business is that you really have little way of determining what the problems are," he said. Rapid growth has killed many an entrepreneur. Fortunately, Dell realized quickly that he couldn't run the company without top-notch, experienced help, so he hired seasoned executives away from Motorola and Apple Computer. Dell's own maturation as an industry pioneer is on display in *Service Sells* as he explains why the ideas of pleasing and satisfying customers are the "chromosomes" of the company.

Service Sells
Michael S. Dell

Our company started in 1983, when the PC business blossomed. I was in high school at the time and became interested in computers. I realized then that the industry's distribution and sales systems were poor. When I would go to a computer store, I would pay a 25 percent retail mark-up for a computer and be served by a person who knew little about computers.

I thought that there must be a better way to sell computers. The better way, I thought, would be to provide custom products directly to end users with much better service and support and to take the day-to-day feedback from customers and turn that into better products and services.

That's what our company set out to do. It must be working because last year we had revenues of over $2 billion, and this year we will have revenues of $3 billion. That's still a very small share of the $70 billion PC market. Three or four companies control about 25 percent of the market. Remember that the PC is the ultimate consumer product because you will likely buy three PCs every 10 years. Whatever you buy today will be obsolete in four years. And so this product continually replaces itself, which makes for an interesting market.

Focus on Total Value

We recognize that service is very important in this market, along with efficiency and effectiveness in delivery. We started the business with a consumer point of view and with a strategy of mass customization to enable us to tailor our products and services to specific customers. Our company has become a consumer advocate—as opposed to a technology advocate or an advocate of a particular product, strategy, or direction. We interpret the needs of the market and deliver those to customers.

We focus not on the price of the computers we sell but on the total value—as defined by the product integrity, quality, service, support, brand name, ease of purchase, and all of the feelings and attitudes that come with buying the product and dealing with the company. We do not introduce technology for its own sake; we introduce technology that meets the needs of customers.

We maintain a direct relationship with our customers. We speak with them every day. We target and segment our customers in an increasingly specialized fashion. Our product strategy is driven by customer input. We've made the customer the most important person in the business; the ideas of satisfying and pleasing customers are the chromosomes of our company. Every part of our company is crafted around serving the customer and being accountable to the customer. This focus enables us to customize hardware, software, peripherals, and services. Every area of our business—manufacturing, finance, services, product development, management, sales—receives feedback from customers daily and turns that into changes that improve our products and processes.

This strategy has been met enthusiastically. We have grown rapidly, expanding throughout Western Europe, Central Europe, Mexico, and Japan. Japan has been our fastest-growing new subsidiary. The Japanese quickly accepted our direct marketing approach because the distribution systems in Japan are incredibly inefficient. Our computers sell for about half the price of any Japanese PC, and yet our gross margins are highest in Japan. Japanese customers are quality and brand conscious, and so establishing a brand and a service attitude within a Japanese operation is critical. But U.S. companies have a huge opportunity to introduce new approaches that play to the weaknesses of Japanese systems. In the next five years, our Japanese operation may become our second largest.

Database Marketing Model

Because of the efficiency and economy of scale of our database marketing model, we believe the customer satisfaction strategies that we bring to the market will yield a strong long-term business. In the first quarter alone, our company mailed about 15 million catalogs in the United States. In every market we enter, we hire a local business person who can execute our model effectively and ask that person to implement the model with the nuances of a given culture.

We do not introduce technology for its own sake; we introduce technology that meets the needs of customers.

By acquiring customers through various distribution channels and then segmenting them by customer type and by application type, we're able to target and focus our marketing in a very specialized way. Of course, we are best known for our direct distribution system. One of our executives once said: "If you wake up every morning at 4 a.m. and do 300 push-ups, you're likely to get a strong upper body." In our business, if you take 25,000 phone calls every day and respond to the customer, your business is likely to change in many ways. Our business listens and responds to those phone calls. Being close to the customer fosters a partnership with our customers. We install many tools to ensure that we maintain a high level of responsiveness. Having this contact with customers allows us to provide follow-on selling opportunities and to contact them at exactly the right point with new offerings.

The best way to segment a business is by customer type. As our business grows, we become increasingly segmented. The ultimate segmentation is a personal phone number for the customer. If you're a large Dell account, you can call us toll free using your own special phone number, type in your company name, and speak directly to the Dell Account Team assigned to serve you 24 hours a day. Such specialization makes us very attractive to large corporations. We're organized to serve the needs of each customer.

While we have been very active in the direct distribution approach, we don't believe that buying directly from Dell is a religious experience, nor do we believe that our channels of distribution are sacred. We believe that we should provide our products and services in the best possible way as defined by the customer. For example, we've signed agreements with super stores and mass merchant companies like the Price Club and Sam's and Wal-Mart to provide products to the growing consumer PC business. While we don't sell that product directly to the customer, we provide them with the services directly, and we have many follow-on selling opportunities to that customer. All customers flow into a huge database; and the more customers we have, the more specialized our marketing gets.

In addition to the 25,000 phone calls a day, we also conduct focus groups, one-on-one interviews, mail-in surveys, advisory groups, and meetings with key customers. In focus groups, we will often expose customers who represent a trend in leading new demand to new product concepts. For example, we will show them Concept A, Concept B, and

Concept C, and then get their reaction to the new products. We can't always take the approach of "Well, they haven't asked for it, therefore, they don't want it," because our business technology evolves at such a rate that customers are unaware of what we are likely to have in a year in terms of the art of the possible. So we often have to construct logical alternatives and present those to customers and then receive input and feedback. Our process is validated when we introduce the product and it does well in the market.

This whole customer passion has become so strong that it's like a highway where cars speed along at 120 miles per hour. I you get on the highway at a slower speed, you get run over: Our culture is so strong that if you come into the company and you're not up to speed, it just chews you up and spits you out fast. It doesn't accept a non-customer responsive attitude. In our orientation, we expose new employees to our business strategies, and we reinforce this training after the indoctrination. The incentives, the profit sharing, and the bonus plans are clearly tied to customer responsiveness. All of our communications and all of the company communication efforts are customer centered. We tell stories about service heroes and give risk-taking awards to people who go the extra mile to take care of a customer. Those things become part of the culture of the company, and the culture rewards taking care of the customer.

In addition to the 25,000 phone calls a day, we also conduct focus groups, one-on-one interviews, mail-in surveys, advisory groups, and meetings with key customers.

Even when we sell computers through Wal-Mart, we keep close to the customer by being completely responsible for all the after-sales support to those customers. We also do post-sale surveys; in fact, feedback from customers is more important two years after the initial purchase because current satisfaction levels reflect what they will buy as a replacement PC.

Efficient Distribution

We have, in effect, built a large electronic super store. In some cases, we provide products and services through a virtual (Stealth) warehouse. We sell several products that never sit on our shelves, but are delivered to customers within the next business day by various distribution partners who are more capable at packaging and providing software, peripheral, and accessory products to customers in a rapid deployment fashion. We intend to be the easiest PC company to do business with, easiest to buy from, and we believe we have many advantages in our logistics and distribution system. Our inventory turns are twice that of our major competitors, and our asset utilization is much higher.

We believe more in a vertically connected enterprise than in a vertically integrated enterprise. So we have close relationships with suppliers and partners who are more capable and more specialized in specific areas. Our strategy is to supply customers with products they want to buy — not just with new technology that they find interesting or exciting. Our focus is on taking customer feedback and driving that into the right products and strategies. We focus on value engineering because cost and reliability are very important to our customers.

Service and Support

Service and support have become part of our brand in the sense that customers believe that when they buy a Dell product, the Dell Company takes care of them. Service is the ultimate competitive weapon. Customers delight over the responsiveness and the quality of our replies to their queries. We don't have any particular rules in terms of how many times you can or can't call us or what questions we do or don't answer. We simply say that when you buy one of our products, we take care of you.

Our customer focus has grown with the company from the beginning. As the company grew, the executive team had to make decisions as to how we would treat our customers, and those decisions created an understanding among employees as to how we would collectively deal with our customers. It's been a very positive experience for us because the management team walks its talk about being customer-focused. We have been intent on making sure our customers are satisfied and that our employees are empowered to make changes and do special things for customers. We believe that having a group of passionate employees who care about the customer is a huge competitive advantage.

Many businesses get caught in the trap of having a mission which is confusing to their associates. For example, if in a company meeting, I stand up and say, "The goal of this company is to make a lot of money and run away," few people would be inspired by that vision or mission. They might say to themselves, "I need this job, but if the mission is to make a lot of money and run away, is this the right thing for me to be doing! Are we doing right by our customers?"

> We believe that having a group of passionate
> employees who care about the customer is
> a huge competitive advantage.

Now, if I get up in a meeting and say, "Our job is to take care of our customers and to make them happy," I think that many people will naturally identify with the goal and become passionate about carrying it out. If you can identify with people's core concerns, and put in place a reward system that focuses on those, you will cultivate a very positive cultural element within the business.

Every Friday at 7:30 a.m., we hold a Customer Advocate Meeting. A group of about 175 people throughout the business get together in Austin, and for 90 minutes we review as a team the key statistics around customer responsiveness. We talk about our abandonment rates, about the time it takes for us to process orders, about how our process works in satisfying the needs of our customers. We then call a customer who has had a difficult problem during the past week and ask that customer to profile for us what went wrong with our process. Every area of the company is represented in this meeting. And we all talk with these customers to understand their concerns and understand what we need to do as a company to improve our processes. On occasion, we call our own phone lines and pretend to be a customer. We time our responsiveness, and track the quality of the telephone call to see how well we are satisfying customer needs.

It's fairly easy for those people on the front lines to be sensitive to customer needs because they talk to customers every day, but it's harder for someone in manufacturing or product development to understand customer needs. Tools like the Customer Advocate Meeting involves everyone in the company in the process of satisfying customers.

Adapt and Grow

We continue to make adjustments based on what we understand from customers and based on the evolution of the business and—technology. We approach service as a product, and we focus on continuously improving it. In our company, the things that are average are considered messed up or in need of great improvement by our employees—and that's why we enjoy great success. To instill that continuous improvement culture within the business, we have made the customer the most important person in our business and made our obsession and essential goal to satisfy our customers.

We take the approach that one size does not fit all and that one size fits one. Our mass customization system allows us to build computers one at a time and to segment our marketing finely and to approach customers in ways that are targeted to their specific needs.

We assign our business leaders the role and responsibility of both strategy development and implementation. As an executive team, we meet for two days about every three months to talk about the key success factors of our business. We talk about what we believe the key strategic elements of our company need to be in five years and in ten years. We then assemble cross-functional teams to drive major projects throughout the company.

We want to be the best place to buy computer products and services. Our company is well positioned because we are a pure play on delivering the right products and services to customers. We also have the technology capability to adapt those products. We have a huge opportunity to be the leading supplier of computers by the year 2000.

I don't think our company has any silver bullets, myself included, that are the answer to all the issues. What we have is a unique culture and way of doing business. We don't sprinkle pixy dust on our employees to make them customer oriented. We don't give them customer responsiveness injections. This is just the way the company operates.

Companies like IBM, Sears, and General Motors have found that it's tough to turn around the culture of a well established company to cope with the challenge of an aggressive fast player. To stay fast and aggressive, we are committed to change. There are signs hanging up in our offices that say, "We're Changing Everything." We change everything all the time. We like to change things. Change is good, and everybody knows that. At least, everybody at our company knows that change is good.

1993

AL NEUHARTH
1924–

The founder of *USA Today* and former Gannett chairman, who merrily calls himself a Son of a Bitch, is another marketer in the spirit of P. T. Barnum. His roots, however, are a bit more humble. When Neuharth was only 22 months old, his dad died, and when his impoverished mother considered remarrying later on, he threw a fit: "That tantrum was probably my debut as a self-centered S.O.B.," he wrote in his autobiography, *Confessions of an S.O.B.* At age 10, Neuharth took a newspaper delivery job for about 12 cents a week. As a senior in high school, he was editor of the school newspaper and had his first taste of power, which he relished.

It was during World War II, however, that he witnessed real power in his first hero. "I met my first S.O.B. role model at a crossroads near Heidelberg, Germany, in the final weeks of World War II. He threatened to lock me up behind barbed wire," Neuharth wrote. It was General George S. Patton. In 1946, he enrolled at the University of South Dakota and junior year became editor of the school paper. After college, with $50,000 start-up money, Neuharth and a friend founded *SoDak Sports*, a newspaper dedicated to sports, serving South Dakota. In less than two years it folded, but Neuharth used the failure to spur himself on. He wrote, "I always like to keep reminders of failures around. That's why my memos are still on peach paper—the same color we used to print *SoDak Sports*."

After stints at the *Miami Herald* and the *Detroit Free Press*, Neuharth was offered a job managing 2 of the Gannett's 16 newspapers. At first hesitant because it involved less prestigious markets, he took the job for a change of pace. He later reflected, "All my life boredom has pushed me to new adventures. I'm bored easily. . . . I can only cure it by moving around or moving on. A new job. A new venture. A new setting." He subsequently built Gannett into a formidable chain and in 1982 he launched *USA Today*. One of the keys to its success was the free publicity Neuharth drummed up, which he describes in *Showmanship and Salesmanship*. He also warns, "Some hucksters think there's no such thing as too much hype."

Showmanship and Salesmanship
Al Neuharth

W e stood on a platform
under a tent with the U.S. Capitol behind us and the Washington Monument in front. We were:

- The President of the United States, Ronald Reagan,
  and First Lady Nancy.
- The Speaker of the House of Representatives, Tip
  O'Neill of Massachusetts.
- The Majority Leader of the U.S. Senate, Howard
  Baker of Tennessee.
- The founder of *USA TODAY,* Al Neuharth, country boy
  from South Dakota.

The three most powerful men in the USA and our First
Lady had joined me at the microphone to celebrate the
launch of *USA TODAY,* September 15, 1982.

Under the huge tent around us were hundreds of members of the House and Senate, Cabinet members, ambassadors, media executives from across the country, and
working journalists.

The President had come to salute the launch of the
nation's first general-interest national daily newspaper.

USA TODAY "is a testimony to the kind of dream free

men and women can dream and turn into reality here in America," Reagan said.

The President of the United States, huckstering for my new newspaper for free!

Tip O'Neill's House of Representatives was in session late that day. But he recessed it for an hour so he and others could join the tent party at 6:30 P.M. O'Neill, a Democrat, noted that he and the President and Senate Majority Leader Baker, both Republicans, didn't often appear on the same platform together.

Indeed, they didn't. And especially not to plug a commercial product.

"How did you get the President and the others to do that?" I was asked over and over that night and in the weeks that followed.

"I invited them," I quipped.

Actually there was a message in that. It's like "Ask and ye shall receive" from John 16:24 in the Bible.

Far too often we fail to get what we want, especially in dealing with VIPs, simply because we are afraid to ask or don't ask the right people.

Of course, in the case of the President, it took more than just an invitation. For months I had used contacts and charm to get the President's people to put the *USA TODAY* launch party on his schedule.

Far too often we fail to get what we want, especially in dealing with VIPs, simply because we are afraid to ask or don't ask the right people.

It was a classy party. Red, white, and blue banners and balloons greeted the guests. Like our newspaper, the food and drink had an "across the USA" theme.

King crab from Alaska and crab cakes from Maryland,

clams and oysters from New York, walleyed pike from Minnesota, pheasant from my home state of South Dakota, barbecued beef from Texas, poi from Hawaii.

All washed down with wines from California.

Getting Ten Times Your Money's Worth

The price tag: less than $100,000.

Not even our bean counters objected to that. They knew, as we all did, that we got more than a million dollars worth of free publicity.

A lot of promotions miss because they don't reflect the product. That can easily happen when outsiders . . . call the shots on a company or a product they don't fully understand.

Pictures of the President, the Speaker, the Majority Leader, and me, displaying the first issue of *USA TODAY,* were on the tube and in print across the country. The party got as much attention from the columnists and commentators as did the newspaper itself.

And it set the pattern for similar launch affairs as we rolled out the newspaper market by market across the USA over the next eight months.

The huckstering and hype that went into *USA TODAY* was an important part of its success. But the most important aspect of it was that the promotion reflected the product.

USA TODAY was designed to be different. Breezy. Bright. Colorful. Attention-getting. Sometimes irreverent. Always upbeat. Most of all, fun. All of our promotions combined some or all of those features.

A lot of promotions miss because they don't reflect the product. That can easily happen when outsiders—even at the best of creative ad agencies — call the shots on a company or a product they don't fully understand.

That's why the CEO must be involved. No one has as good a feel for a product as its creator or founder or boss.

A CEO must make sure that the hype isn't overdone. Too much promotion is as bad as too little. Some hucksters think there's no such thing as too much hype. A CEO must watch them as closely as he does the bean counters.

The entry of *USA TODAY* into local markets wasn't always a welcomed event — certainly not by some local newspapers.

The local launch parties were important to show the community that other parts of the establishment were glad to welcome *USA TODAY.* It became the in thing for political leaders or sports and entertainment celebrities to join us and plug the paper.

Governors and mayors actually made their appearances at some peril, because local newspapers sometimes boycotted the events.

Sometimes we were criticized by the local press for the way we moved our blue-and-white vending machines onto their street corners. New York was an example.

A CEO must make sure that the hype isn't overdone. Too much promotion is as bad as too little. Some hucksters think there's no such thing as too much hype. A CEO must watch them as closely as he does the bean counters.

The weekend before our launch in the Big Apple, circulation chief Frank Vega's troops stormed the city and bolted three thousand vending machines to the sidewalks of New York.

At a press conference that Monday morning, reporters from *The New York Times,* the *Daily News,* and the *Post* goaded

Mayor Koch into criticizing the *USA TODAY* machines as "unsightly." He said he would have his legal department look into whether he could force us to remove them.

But that night Koch showed up as scheduled at our big bash at Radio City Music Hall. He followed a spectacular All-American performance we had arranged by the Rockettes.

Chutzpah à la Ed Koch

With his usual chutzpah, Koch welcomed us to New York and wished us well. "I don't know too much about Gannett. But any outfit that can bolt down three thousand vending machines on the sidewalks of New York overnight can't be all bad," he wisecracked before the audience of several hundred of the Big Apple's big names.

The vending machines became a huge part of our nationwide hype. Ultimately we put over 135,000 of them in place. Not only do they serve as sales outlets, but they are mini-billboards that millions of people see daily.

We had carefully researched and been convinced that local politicians or competing media could not prevent their installation or force us to remove the boxes. They are a vehicle for distributing news and the First Amendment protects them. That argument prevailed at several locations where a legal challenge against them was launched.

Even the controversy over the vending machines generated a lot of free publicity. "I'm giving you a hundred thousand dollars of P.R.," Mayor Koch joked.

Some local newspapers were so bitter they carefully cut out or brushed out our newsboxes in pictures of street accidents or other such scenes. Or published them only in scenes depicting slums.

But television stations loved showing the boxes on their TV news bites. Movie producers soon panned street corners across the USA showing this new blue-and-white landmark.

CBS's Charles Kuralt said, "Meandering across the land seeking out 'On the Road' stories, I have plunked quarters into *USA TODAY* vending machines outside the Holiday Inn in Klamath Falls, Oregon; the 7-Eleven stores in Great Bridge, Virginia; at the last bus stop as the road runs out at Homestead Valley, California; chained to the light pole at Eighth Avenue and Fourteenth Street in New York City; in Lincoln, Missouri, right under the only stoplight in town.

"I have reason to think Al Neuharth has made a bright and inventive addition to the newsstands and light poles of America."

The vending machines probably were and are the biggest single ongoing free promotion any company ever was able to design for a new commercial product. But they didn't just happen.

From the beginning I knew we had to design a *USA TODAY* newsrack that would be different, one that would really catch the eyes of passersby, as well as dispense newspapers.

Newspaper vending machines had looked the same for decades. Studying how to modernize them was Frank Vega's job. I wanted something that looked like a TV set on street corners, with newspapers displayed so that people would stop and look at them the way they do at TV screens.

Vega traveled across the USA looking at different newsracks and brought dozens back to Washington.

Defying the Laws of Gravity

The traditional, most commonly used racks all had a coin box at the very top. The front page of the newspapers was displayed well below the coin box so that people couldn't read it without bending down at the knees.

When I told Vega I wanted to promote the paper, not the coin box, he didn't get it right away. He said if we were going to display the front page the way I wanted it displayed, we would have to build racks with electric motors in them.

"And Al," Vega said, in his usual smartass way, "there aren't electrical outlets on every street corner of the country."

Because of the laws of gravity, Vega explained, we would have to keep the coin mechanism on top.

"Mr. Vega," I said, with an edge in my voice, drumming my fingers on top of a rack as he and a half dozen associates listened, "I understand the fucking laws of gravity. But I want that coin mechanism out of the way of the newspaper display!"

Besides rattling a few coins, I had rattled Vega's composure. He returned to the drawing board with a renewed sense of imagination and determination.

Again I had had to resort to a little drama to make a point.

Vega took my concept to Fred Gore, a Texas product designer. Vega told Gore that we wanted a rack with a Space Age look, one that would appeal to a television generation.

Gore came up with a winner: Our new rack was on a pedestal, and the display window was tilted back at a slight angle. The front page was presented to the reader in an inviting way—it said, "Read me, buy me."

And Gore found a way to move the coin mechanism.

We had our unique vending machines, and Gore gave Kaspar Wire Works and the city of Shiner, Texas, a new industry employing 450 to manufacture them exclusively for us.

Our main strategy during the early years of *USA TODAY* was to get as much free publicity as possible. Dozens of launch parties, hundreds of TV, radio, newspaper, and magazine mentions, thousands of vending machines, all free or low-cost ways to attract readers. And they worked.

1989

P. T. Barnum
1810–1891

More than 100 years later, P. T. Barnum's legacy as the greatest showman on earth lives on in today's Ringling Brothers and Barnum & Bailey Circus and the Barnum Museum in Bridgeport, Connecticut. While growing up on a farm in Connecticut, he realized early on that handwork was not to his liking; he much preferred "laying plans for moneymaking." As a boy he found work with the local merchants and learned the art of trading goods. Eventually, he became the proprietor of his own shop in New York City, and it was there he realized his first opportunity as a showman.

Barnum heard of Joice Heth, a black slave reputed to be 161 years old and to have been George Washington's nurse, who was on display in Philadelphia. He was convinced she would be a hit in New York, so he bought her for $1,000 in 1835. Indeed, she was a hit, and before long Barnum found himself touring the country with a circus full of human curiosities. However, after one eight-month stretch on the road in 1840–1841, he was ready to return to his family in New York and settle down. Therefore, in 1841, he bought the American Museum, which housed a collection of oddities from around the world. For all his flamboyance, Barnum was proud that women and children could visit his museum without being offended—grossed out by shrunken heads and a mummified mermaid maybe, but not offended.

Barnum went to extremes to please his clientele and attract attention: ". . . I often engaged some exhibition, knowing that it would directly bring no extra dollars to the treasury, but hoping that it would incite a newspaper paragraph which would float through the columns of the American press. . . ." Although he was often derided for his antics and exploitation of deformed people, Barnum just wanted to entertain an America he thought worked too hard and laughed too little. Of course, he worked plenty hard himself, believing, "Fortune always favors the brave, and never helps a man who does not help himself." In *The American Museum*, Barnum provides a glimpse of how hard he worked at marketing, including some hilarious examples.

The American Museum
P. T. Barnum

At the very outset, I was determined to deserve success. My plan of economy included the intention to support my family in New York on $600 a year, and my treasure of a wife not only gladly assented, but was willing to reduce the sum to $400, if necessary. Some six months after I had bought the Museum, Mr. Olmsted happened in at my ticket-office at noon and found me eating a frugal dinner of cold corned beef and bread, which I had brought from home.

"Is this the way you eat your dinner?" he asked.

"I have not eaten a warm dinner, except on Sundays," I replied, "since I bought the Museum, and I never intend to, on a week day, till I am out of debt."

"Ah!" said he, clapping me on the shoulder, "you are safe, and will pay for the Museum before the year is out."

And he was right, for within twelve months I was in full possession of the property as my own and it was entirely paid for from the profits of the business.

In 1865, the space occupied for my Museum purposes was more than double what it was in 1842. The Lecture Room, originally narrow, ill-contrived and inconvenient, was so enlarged and improved that it became one of the most commodious and beautiful amusement halls in the City of

New York. At first, my attractions and inducements were merely the collection of curiosities by day, and an evening entertainment, consisting of such variety performances as were current in ordinary shows. Then Saturday afternoons, and, soon afterwards, Wednesday afternoons were devoted to entertainments and the popularity of the Museum grew so rapidly that I presently found it expedient and profitable to open the great Lecture Room every afternoon, as well as every evening, on every week-day in the year. The first experiments in this direction, more than justified my expectations, for the day exhibitions were always more thronged than those of the evening. Of course I made the most of the holidays, advertising extensively and presenting extra inducements; nor did attractions elsewhere seem to keep the crowd from coming to the Museum. On great holidays, I gave as many as twelve performances to as many different audiences.

By degrees the character of the stage performances was changed. The transient attractions of the Museum were constantly diversified, and educated dogs, industrious fleas, automatons, jugglers, ventriloquists, living statuary, tableaux, gipsies, Albinoes, fat boys, giants, dwarfs, rope-dancers, live "Yankees," pantomime, instrumental music, singing and dancing in great variety, dioramas, panoramas, models of Niagara, Dublin, Paris, and Jerusalem; Hannington's dioramas of the Creation, the Deluge, Fairy Grotto, Storm at Sea; the first English Punch and Judy in this country, Italian Fantoccini, mechanical figures, fancy glass-blowing, knitting machines and other triumphs in the mechanical arts; dissolving views, American Indians, who enacted their warlike and religious ceremonies on the stage—these, among others, were all exceedingly successful.

I thoroughly understood the art of advertising, not merely by means of printer's ink, which I have always used freely, and to which I confess myself so much indebted for my success, but by turning every possible circumstance to my account. It was my monomania to make the Museum the town wonder and town talk. I often seized upon an opportunity by instinct, even before I had a very definite conception as to how it should be used, and it seemed, somehow, to mature itself and serve my purpose. As an illustration, one morning a stout, hearty-looking man, came into my ticket-office and begged some money. I asked him why he did not work and earn his living? He replied that he could get nothing to do and that he would be glad of any job at a dollar a day. I handed him a quarter of a dollar, told him to go and get his breakfast and return, and I would employ him at light labor at a dollar and a half a day. When he returned I gave him five common bricks.

"Now," said I, "go and lay a brick on the sidewalk at the corner of Broadway and Ann Street; another close by the Museum; a third diagonally across the way at the corner of Broadway and Vesey Street, by the Astor House; put down the fourth on the sidewalk in front of St. Paul's Church, opposite; then, with the fifth brick in hand, take up a rapid march from one point to the other, making the circuit, exchanging your brick at every point, and say nothing to any one."

> I thoroughly understood the art of advertising, not merely by means of printer's ink, which I have always used freely, . . . but by turning every possible circumstance to my account.

"What is the object of this?" inquired the man.

"No matter," I replied; "all you need to know is that it brings you fifteen cents wages per hour. It is a bit of my fun, and to assist me properly you must seem to be as deaf as a post; wear a serious countenance; answer no questions; pay no attention to any one; but attend faithfully to the work and at the end of every hour by St. Paul's clock show this ticket at the Museum door; enter, walking solemnly through every hall in the building; pass out, and resume your work."

With the remark that it was "all one to him, so long as he could earn his living," the man placed his bricks and began his round. Half an hour afterwards, at least five hundred people were watching his mysterious movements. He had assumed a military step and bearing, and looking as sober as a judge, he made no response whatever to the constant inquiries as to the object of his singular conduct. At the end of the first hour, the sidewalks in the vicinity were packed with people all anxious to solve the mystery. The man, as directed, then went into the Museum, devoting fifteen minutes to a solemn survey of the halls, and afterwards returning to his round. This was repeated every hour till sundown and whenever the man went into the Museum a dozen or more persons would buy tickets and follow him, hoping to gratify their curiosity in regard to the purpose of his movements. This was continued for several days—the curious people who followed the man into the Museum considerably more than paying his wages—till finally the policeman, to whom I had imparted my object, complained that the obstruction of the sidewalk by crowds had become so serious that I must call in my "brick man." This trivial incident excited considerable talk and amusement; it advertised me; and it materially advanced my purpose of making a lively corner near the Museum. . . .

From the first, it was my study to give my patrons a superfluity of novelties, and for this I make no special claim to generosity, for it was strictly a business transaction. To send away my visitors more than doubly satisfied, was to induce them to come again and to bring their friends. I meant to make people talk about my Museum; to exclaim over its wonders; to have men and women all over the country say: "There is not another place in the United States where so much can be seen for twenty-five cents as in Barnum's American Museum." It was the best advertisement I could possibly have, and one for which I could afford to pay. I knew, too, that it was an honorable advertisement, because it was as deserved as it was spontaneous. And so, in addition to the permanent collection and the ordinary attractions of the stage, I labored to keep the Museum well supplied with transient novelties; I exhibited such living curiosities as a rhinoceros, giraffes, grizzly bears, ourang-outangs, great serpents, and whatever else of the kind money would buy or enterprise secure.

Knowing that a visit to my varied attractions and genuine curiosities was well worth to any one three times the amount asked as an entrance fee, I confess that I was not so scrupulous, as possibly I should have been, about the methods used to call public attention to my establishment. The one end aimed at was to make men and women think and talk and wonder, and, as a practical result, go to the Museum. This was my constant study and occupation.

It was the world's way then, as it is now, to excite the community with flaming posters, promising almost everything for next to nothing. I confess that I took no pains to set my enterprising fellow-citizens a better example. I fell in with the world's way; and if my "puffing" was more persistent, my advertising more audacious, my posters more glaring, my pictures more exaggerated, my flags more patriotic and my transparencies more brilliant than they would have been under the management of my neighbors, it was not because I had less scruple than they, but more energy, far more ingenuity, and a better foundation for such promises. In all this, if I cannot be justified, I at least find palliation in the fact that I presented a wilderness of wonderful, instructive and amusing realities of such evident and marked merit that I have yet to learn of a single instance where a visitor went away from the Museum complaining that he had been defrauded of his money. Surely this is an offset to any eccentricities to which I may have resorted to make my establishment widely known. . . .

A curiosity, which in an extraordinary degree served my ever-present object of extending the notoriety of the Museum was the so-called "Fejee Mermaid." It has been supposed that this mermaid was manufactured by my order, but such is not the fact. I was known as a successful showman, and strange things of every sort were brought to me from all quarters for sale or exhibition. In the summer of 1842, Mr. Moses Kimball, of the Boston Museum, came to New York and showed me what purported to be a mermaid. He had bought it from a sailor whose father, a sea captain, had purchased it in Calcutta, in 1822, from some Japanese sailors. I may mention here that this identical preserved specimen was exhibited in London in 1822, as I fully verified in my visit to that city in 1858, for I found an advertisement of it in an old file of the London *Times*, and a friend gave me a copy of the *Mirror*, published by J. Limbird, 335 Strand, November 9, 1822, containing a cut of this same creature and two pages of letter-press describing it, together with an account of other mermaids said to have been captured in different parts of the world. The *Mirror* stated that this specimen was "the great source of attraction in the British metropolis, and three to four hundred people every day pay their shilling to see it."

It was my study to give my patrons a superfluity of novelties. . . . To send away my visitors
more than doubly satisfied, was to induce
them to come again and to bring their friends.

This was the curiosity which had fallen into Mr. Kimball's hands. I requested my naturalist's opinion of the genuineness of the animal and he said he could not conceive how it could have been manufactured, for he never saw a monkey with such peculiar teeth, arms, hands, etc., and he never saw a fish with such peculiar fins; but he did not believe in mermaids. Nevertheless, I concluded to hire this curiosity and to modify the general incredulity as to the possibility of the existence of mermaids, and to awaken curiosity to see and examine the specimen, I invoked the potent power of printer's ink.

Since Japan has been opened to the outer world it has been discovered that certain "artists" in that country manufacture a great variety of fabulous animals, with an ingenuity and mechanical perfection well calculated to deceive. No doubt my mermaid was a specimen of this curious manufacture. I used it mainly to advertise the regular business of the Museum, and this effective indirect advertising is the only feature I can commend, in a special show of which, I confess, I am not proud. I might have published columns in the newspapers, presenting and praising the great collection of genuine specimens of natural history in my exhibition, and they would not have attracted nearly so much attention as did a few paragraphs about the mermaid which was only a small part of my show. Newspapers throughout the country copied the mermaid notices, for they were novel and caught the attention of readers. Thus was the fame of the Museum, as well as the mermaid, wafted from one end of the land to the other. I was careful to keep up the excitement, for I knew that every dollar sown in advertising would return in tens, and perhaps hundreds, in a future harvest, and after obtaining all the notoriety possible by advertising and by exhibiting the mermaid at the Museum, I sent the curiosity throughout the country, directing my agent to everywhere advertise it as "From Barnum's Great American Museum, New York." The effect was immediately felt; money flowed in rapidly and was readily expended in more advertising.

When people expect to get "something for nothing" they are sure to be cheated, and generally deserve to be.

While I expended money liberally for attractions for the inside of my Museum, and bought or hired everything curious or rare which was offered or could be found, I was prodigal in my outlays to arrest or arouse public attention.

When I became proprietor of the establishment, there were only the words: "American Museum," to indicate the character of the concern; there was no bustle or activity about the place; no posters to announce what was to be seen;—the whole exterior was as dead as the skeletons and stuffed skins within. My experiences had taught me the advantages of advertising. I printed whole columns in the papers, setting forth the wonders of my establishment. Old "fogies" opened their eyes in amazement at a man who could expend hundreds of dollars in announcing a show of "stuffed monkey skins"; but these same old fogies paid their quarters, nevertheless, and when they saw the curiosities and novelties in the Museum halls, they, like all other visitors, were astonished as well as pleased, and went home and told their families and neighbors and thus assisted in advertising my business.

For other and not less effective advertising,—flags and banners, began to adorn the exterior of the building. I kept a band of music on the front balcony and announced "Free Music for the Million." People said, "Well, that Barnum is a liberal fellow to give us music for nothing," and they flocked down to hear my outdoor free concerts. But I took pains to select and maintain the poorest band I could find—one whose discordant notes would drive the crowd into the Museum, out of earshot of my outside orchestra. Of course, the music was poor. When people expect to get "something for nothing" they are sure to be cheated, and generally deserve to be, and so, no doubt, some of my out-door patrons were sorely disappointed; but when they came inside and paid to be amused and instructed, I took care to see that they not only received the full worth of their money, but were more than satisfied.

1869

PART VII

Entrepreneurial Management

Success for the entrepreneur often proves to be a double-edged sword: growth brings headaches. One of the toughest periods an entrepreneur faces is making the transition to businessperson and manager of a thriving company. As Alfred Fuller, founder of the Fuller Brush Company, admits, he was overwhelmed by the daily details of running a burgeoning firm. Through trial and error he learned how to institute procedures and controls. Anita Roddick, founder of The Body Shop, and Ross Perot provide concrete advice on how to be a good manager and leader of people. For example, Roddick reminds the entrepreneur that their employees are no different than they are in that they "are in search of something more than a nine-to-five death." Other management factors entrepreneurs must consider include hiring and firing employees, establishing a management team, the willingness to delegate (no easy task for the gunslinger type), and training programs, among others. Developing good people, IBM founder Thomas Watson says, made his success and it's a great feeling when you can take a breather from the office knowing it's in good hands. The authors in Part VII provide a powerful reminder that entrepreneurs must be prepared to make that leap to business manager and leader — not just for their companies' health, but for their own sakes, too.

ALFRED C. FULLER
1885–1973

The founder of the Fuller Brush Company, which in turn spawned an army of salesman that became part of American lore, was a decedent of Edward Fuller, a Mayflower passenger. Alfred Fuller's branch of the family migrated to Nova Scotia, where he was born and raised on a modest farm, the 11th of 12 children. In the summers, he earned a penny for every quart of strawberries he picked. "The only way I learned to earn money was by giving a definite measure of production for it," he reflected. Fuller would later apply that same notion of piece-work to his brush company, only paying sales reps commissions.

Before starting his company, Fuller found himself fired as a streetcar conductor, fired as a gardener and groom, and fired (by his own brother) as a delivery boy—and all before the age of 20. He admitted, "The brutal truth is that at age twenty I was a country bumpkin, overgrown and awkward, unsophisticated and virtually unschooled." Next he worked as a brush salesman and found he excelled because he took a sincere interest in other people. Along the way he made note of his clients' cleaning needs and started making his own brushes to meet them. In 1906, Fuller struck out on his own, manufacturing brushes in his sister's basement by night and taking orders by day.

The company officially organized in 1913 and by 1918 there were more than 100 branch offices. Fuller readily admitted that he had no vision for his business, no idea of how to "think big," no particular plan for success. Events just seemed to happen, because he was desperate to eat. "You might say quite truthfully that our $100,000,000-a-year company is the product of mediocrity, since almost everyone who grew up with it in the early days was, like myself, a failure who took his job with me in desperation, often in despair, and had to make it go or starve." For Fuller, it was "learn as you go," an experience that many entrepreneurs face, which he honestly presents in *The Need for Controls*. He admits that as the business mushroomed, he was quite bewildered, often finding himself carrying about paper sacks of money and unable to estimate his profits.

The Need for Controls
Alfred C. Fuller

Some persons date important milestones in their lives by momentous events that occur: graduation from high school or college, the first job, marriage, or the birth of an heir. For me, a significant period was 1910, which might be called the year in which I learned the value of human relationships. To that time I had been, except for the influences of a devoted family, almost alone in the world. From that time on, I placed my trust in persons who were willing to put their skills in my hands for our mutual benefit.

Within a frantic period of three months, I became the employer, so to speak, of two hundred men, most of whom I had never met. As a result, my life and work were revolutionized. Unequipped to master this upheaval, I could only do as the Bible directed. I practiced the Golden Rule, sure that if I did so I would receive a like response from others.

The early mimeographed messages which I sent to the sales force were not so much concerned with merchandising as with the character of the dealers. To be sure, I gave the men many hints. One of these was to wear during wet weather a pair of rubbers a size too large, for any awkwardness at the door is disastrous. As I look back over these early communications, I find that I concentrated on the ethics of door-to-door salesmanship, and the necessity to maintain impeccable deportment. Already evolving was one of the major contributions of the Fuller Brush Company to the industry. This was that the local dealer is not an employee of a faraway, hard-driving corporation, but a trustworthy independent small businessman in his town, with a franchise to sell the finest line of household products in the world.

These communications were of necessity composed late at night. During the day I was overwhelmed by details which often made me remember the doubts, expressed by both my father and my brother Robert, that I had shown little ability to manage either a business or a staff. Often I was dizzy, not from excitement but from bewilderment. Clearly, a bookkeeping and accounting system must be set up. Orderly channels must be created to maintain a constant flow of raw materials, which also involved establishing short-term credit. My own direct selling ended.

The haphazardness seems incredible today. I had expected my new dealers to drop away after a few weeks, as had most of the men I had hired personally. I was sure that the frenzy would blow over and that I would soon be back in a one-man undertaking.

The flow increased, rather than abated. Unbelievable orders came in. I was conditioned to think in terms of my own one-day sales. Some dealers, particularly those in Cincinnati and Cleveland, Ohio, and in Sacramento, California, consistently sent in orders totaling seventy-five to eighty dollars per week. They worked all day Saturday while their wives made deliveries and collections. For men who had been working as office clerks or store employees at seven to ten dollars a week, this was big money. Those who gave up—about half the recruits—abandoned the effort within three months. This seemed to be the critical period. I was not worried over this statistic, which today is vital to us, because new magazine want ads continued to bring inquiries. For the moment we had no difficulty in maintaining several hundred dealers. Not many of them were in the seventy-five-dollar-a-week class. The old sales book shows that each earned more than he was capable of producing in his former occupation. About one in four averaged from twenty to forty dollars weekly for himself. The majority ranged from ten to fifteen dollars. Keep in mind that in 1910 a day laborer toiled twelve hours for one dollar, whereas my dealers were rarely out more than eight hours.

> Perhaps it is just as well that I was innocent of complicated business procedures. Meeting my problems from day to day, I avoided big and costly mistakes.

One has only to look at the old sales figures to realize what happened to me, and with what frenzy I was required to call upon unknown resources merely to keep from being destroyed by success. The retail sales figure in 1910 leaped to $30,000. By 1916 it stood at $86,649. We crossed the $250,000 mark in 1917, the $700,000 gross in 1918, the $1,000,000 magnet in 1919. (By 1960 our pace was $2,000,000 a week.) When the inundation of 1910 struck, I met all at once three imperatives of modern business: mass production, mass sales techniques, and cost accounting. In all of them I was unschooled. Horrified of borrowing, I utilized the unorthodox practice of selling only for cash.

Perhaps it is just as well that I was innocent of complicated business procedures. Meeting my problems from day to day, I avoided big and costly mistakes. Even with sales volume so turbulent that I sometimes carried a thousand dollars to the bank in a paper sack, I could not estimate the profits. As fast as receipts gushed in, they rushed out again for payroll, raw materials and office expenses. I moved once again to larger quarters, and sought for someone to set up an orderly bookkeeping system and act as a bookkeeper on a part-time basis.

I had met a young man named George Marsh who worked for one of Hartford's large manufacturing companies. He was a high school graduate—a fact I emphasize, since it underscores my preferences at that time. I distrusted experts, perhaps fearful that they might take the business away from me. But I could trust men who, like myself, had learned their skills by work rather than from theoretical education. Marsh had studied general accounting, but his practical knowledge had been gained from his employer. Working for me in the evenings, Marsh brought fiscal order out of the chaos of notebooks, bits of paper on spikes, and reminders chalked on a blackboard. (To this day we have a vestigial tail of this old system in one department, where a chalkboard, headed "Broken Promises," reminds us of urgencies which should have been met yesterday.) Marsh was amazed that we carried on our business with such a lack of controls.

"How much does it cost you to make a clothes brush?" he asked late one night when we were studying the books, wondering where four thousand dollars in receipts that week had gone. Our bank balance, $202.15 at the end of the previous week, now stood at $199.97. "You've sold more than a hundred clothes brushes this week at forty-eight cents each. How do you know they didn't cost you forty-nine cents to produce and ship, figuring five percent for general overhead?"

"We've always made money," I said.

"Are you sure?" he persisted. "You never before had any general overhead. Maybe your profit came from your personal sales at retail. Now your living, and my fee, and this big postage bill must all come from the sales of others. Such items show up as overhead."

This had not occurred to me. Right there I learned a lesson in management which saved me from ruin. When a man knows more than I do about his work, I pay him well and trust his judgment. When I know nothing about his department, I pay him even better and leave him alone, keeping an eye on him from an empirical level. Many men have chosen careers since then with the Fuller Brush Company because I encouraged them to solve their own problems, then backed up their decisions.

No man has ever worked for me. He cooperates with me. We are in the enterprise together, and respect the contribution each is capable of making. This may lead to trouble. Occasionally a man mistakes the authority he has been granted for management weakness. He may then be tempted to forget his team role and try to dictate. When that occurs there is only one solution: find someone else of equal talent but balanced perspective. My experience would indicate that any employee who has his own department makes a greater contribution to the organization, is happier in his work and at home, and is more adjusted to all of life, than someone who is constantly told what to do. Every worker, man or woman, must preserve self-respect. This is contrary to the concept of automation-oriented management which too often seeks to demote the individual to robot status. The executive then wonders why his workers take no initiative. It is because they have had no chance, and if given it, would soon be overruled and thus degraded.

I learned a lesson in management which saved me from ruin. When a man knows more than I do about his work, I pay him well and trust his judgment. When I know nothing about his department, I pay him even better and leave him alone.

The new shop solved many of my production problems. It was a spacious third floor with room for several banks of electric-powered machinery. The beginnings of a real assembly line were evident. My thrift did not permit me to order special shipping cases. Instead, I arranged to buy used cartons from a local shoe store.

My new quarters had an office of sorts, in which George Marsh kept his books, and in which I had a desk. But often I worked on the production line, still wearing my old overalls with the right leg cut off. When I employed my first secretarial help, I had to set up an office in my home. The only room available was the spare bedroom. Mornings I lifted a folding bed to a wall slot, and two girls from a nearby business college came in for a few hours to transcribe my dictation from Dictaphone cylinders. My letters were somewhat ungrammatical, but were received for the most part by salesmen who were not too critical.

No man has ever worked for me. He cooperates with me. We are in the enterprise together, and respect the contribution each is capable of making.

I felt like a person suddenly forced to make the leap from age ten to twenty-five overnight, unequipped to assume the responsibilities of adult life. It was not easy. Emotionally I was immature, and there were collisions between my native stubbornness and my wife's implacable resolution. She knew more than I about some procedures, and insisted on her opinion. This was difficult for both of us.

At last the disruption to Evelyn's home, which now was merely an adjunct to the shop, forced me to hire a secretary. In my frugality, I also fancied she might function as bookkeeper and office manager. Evelyn was sick to death of the business, a symptom of a deeper emotion which I should have diagnosed but did not: acute loneliness. She still had few friends, and, with her house a shambles, had no incentive to make any. She was homesick for Boston and Nova Scotia. When her relatives visited her, they returned home, Evelyn once said, "Feeling that they have been living in a factory." Our mealtime conversation principally concerned the business. I no longer relaxed over my supper, following the genial Nova Scotia custom, but bolted my food and rushed back to work. Finally Evelyn asked me to employ a full-time secretary.

A business college sent over three girls. I preferred a gangly, blue-eyed young woman with the milky skin and honest countenance of a country girl. Her name was Ruby Perkins, and she had been reared on a Connecticut farm. But she professed no bookkeeping experience, so I chose another. Two days later I was aware that my new employee had only rudimentary skills in typing and Dictaphone transcription, and none in bookkeeping. Since she had misrepresented herself to me, I let her go and summoned Ruby Perkins; I could understand country girls. But I had no place for her to work except in the bedroom. Since I could not be alone with a secretary in such surroundings, Evelyn remained at home if I was in the house, and Ruby's work day often extended until nine or ten P.M.

Ruby Perkins was a wonder. She corrected my awkward phraseology, making my correspondence succinct and neat. Obviously she knew more about letter writing than I. So I abandoned the Dictaphone. Instead, I riffled through a pile of routine correspondence with Ruby, and in one sentence suggested a reply which she drafted. This saved me hours of work. Ruby's mimeographing was legible and quick, and she posted the books accurately. In half an hour, from eight A.M., I could chart Ruby's entire day, later approving her stencils and signing my mail when I returned to supper. I knew at once that Ruby was honest. She handled the receipts, cashed money orders at the post office, and deposited our funds. On Saturday she brought the payroll from the bank in cash. This primitive system continued for some years, and there were a few days when Ruby walked unaccompanied to the bank with as much as sixteen thousand dollars in an imitation-leather bag.

As Ruby assumed more responsibility, Evelyn receded into the background of the business. She placed herself on the perimeter. She remained my sounding board, however, until the office was moved from the bedroom.

About this time, through coincidence or miracle, I acquired another invaluable colleague who was destined to make a fifty-year career of his work. His name was Philip Colturi, a native born Italian from the Lake Comi district whose lighthearted and puckish nature I could not understand. He knew much that I did not about hand skills, was a natural leader among artisans, and had a genius for improvisation. He was often a thorn that dug deeply into me, because of his practical jokes. One day he put a nasal irritant on my trimming machine, so that the dust flew into my face and eyes, and brought on an attack of sneezing. To Colturi this was great sport. From him I learned a great deal about patience.

I did not hire Colturi. For that reason he claimed for half a century until his retirement in 1960 that he could not be fired. One day, having been absent during the morning, I entered the shop and saw a strange figure flailing away with remarkable adeptness at my job of brush-twisting. Finished products bulged the mail receptacle, testimony to the teamwork between this unknown person and Harry Linden.

I said, "How did you get in here?" He grinned as though I was playing a joke on him.

"Why," he replied, "didn't Mr. Herbert telephone you?"

"I have no telephone," I said rather coldly. The only Mr. Herbert I had heard of was scarcely a recommendation; he was a bartender in a saloon down the street.

All this time Colturi went on working, which pleased me. He said that he had held six jobs in three months, from road repair to grave digging, and he wanted to settle down. Mr. Herbert had informed him that the Capitol Brush Company needed help, and had promised to telephone the proprietor. Colturi had arrived at seven o'clock that morning, telling Linden he had come to help. Linden accepted this statement at face value, assuming I had hired the fellow.

"Suppose you stay on a while then," I said. "If business justifies, I'll hire you." Nothing was said about money. I was

372

tremendously relieved during the next hour to proceed with other matters while hearing the brisk spins of the trimmer. After the noon meal, I set to work packing mail cartons, which were shipped that afternoon instead of the next morning, gaining a day in the delivery schedule.

On Saturday I rewarded Colturi with seven silver dollars. He poured the clinking metal into his hand, looked up and said, "Are you kidding?"

"What's the trouble?" I asked. Linden worked for eight dollars, and had more responsibility, so I thought I was fair.

"You ought to know better than that," Colturi answered impudently. "Seven dollars for what I've done this week? I can earn that digging graves, and resting half the time. Here I stand and cut, cut all day long. This kind of work is push-push all the time. It's worth more."

"If this business prospers, you'll prosper with it," I replied, not realizing that the day would come when Colturi, a divisional superintendent and member of a country club, would have cause to remember the prophecy.

He shrugged.

"Promises," he said, "make thin spaghetti sauce." But he resumed his work.

For the remainder of that year, Colturi, Linden and I made a mass-production team, the first in the history of brush manufacture. A rhythm developed among us, somewhat akin to that of circus roustabouts who sledge down a stake in timed rotation. When finally I decided that our prosperity was permanent, and added three more men to form another production line, Linden supervised one of them, Colturi supervised the other.

This transition was awkward in one respect. Colturi, who had volunteered to hire the new employees, came to me while rolling down his sleeves for the night.

"Look, Boss," he said. "These Italians I'm going to get for you never saw machine work like this—push-push all the time. They may not like it. Works them too hard. But if you paid them so much for each brush, so much for each mop, by the piece instead of wages, they want to work hard and get more money. See?"

To a Nova Scotian who had harvested cranberries, this made sense. I said so.

"So what you pay them?"

I named a figure which seemed about right. Colturi did a bit of headwork and his eyes gleamed.

"No trouble finding the boys, Boss," he said. "They be here tomorrow."

I had done no cost accounting to figure out how many items each team might produce. I had made a guess, and it was bad. The first week, much to the delight of Linden and Colturi, and to the astonishment of the others, my six factory hands earned about eighteen dollars each.

Just because I owned the business, I was no better than anyone else. We were all in this together, and would rise or fall with it.

That evening George Marsh, who had known nothing about this development, concluded that we should cut the piecework payment in half. The workers accepted this, happy over their one-week windfall. But on Saturday I still owed each of them eighteen dollars. They had doubled their production.

The experiences with George Marsh, Ruby Perkins and Philip Colturi convinced me, by the spring of 1911, that the time had come to evolve a definite philosophy as an employer. As usual in moments when I needed infallible advice on matters beyond my comprehension, I studied my Bible for enlightenment. Finally I came on this passage in Luke: "When thou art bidden of any man to a marriage feast, sit not down in the chief seat, lest haply a more honorable man than thou be bidden. And he that bade thee shall come and say to thee, Give this man place; and then thou shalt with shame take the lower place. But when thou art bidden, go and sit down in the lowest place, that when he that hath bidden thee cometh, he may say to thee, Friend, go up higher."

All three of my workers deserved higher places than I in their own skills. I saw, however faintly, that building a business was essentially a matter of manpower possessed of facilities which I lacked. How then to reward them, and what should my attitude be toward them? The Book of Matthew gave me a suggestion. "He that was sown upon the good ground, this is he that heareth the word, and understandeth it; who verily beareth fruit, and bringeth forth, some a hundred-fold, some sixty, some thirty."

From these passages I concluded that personal elevation at the expense of my associates was unsound. I must remain as I was, and find from among those about me the stock that would bear good fruit, and reward each man according to his contribution. The husbandman, nurturing his orchard, provides the food and cultivation, then expects the trees to bear the apples. Just because I owned the business, I was no better than anyone else. We were all in this together, and would rise or fall with it. If I remembered this, I knew that I also would grow in stature and in the ability to contribute.

So I placed my trust in others for the skills which I lacked.

When confronted with a technical problem, I did not ask myself, "What can I do about it," but rather, "Who can do it for me?" Delegation of authority is never easy. Many men never learn to trust others implicitly. They insist on making the petty decisions, burdening their minds with inconsequentials and distorting their empirical view. I never fell into this trap.

1960

DEBBI FIELDS

It takes great business instincts and a good recipe to create a global cookie store franchise, but Debbi Fields did just that and has been recognized by a number of organizations as a top entrepreneur. She grew up, along with her four sisters, in a working-class neighborhood of East Oakland, California, where her father was a welder who refused promotions because he didn't want to boss his buddies. Consequently, they experienced little luxury. Fields reflected, "I would—the fantasy went—somehow find the money to shower them with all those possessions they'd never had." Her dreams found little outlet at school; she attended a parochial school where conformity ruled.

At the age of 13, Fields took a job as the Oakland As' foul-line ball girl and discovered work, not school, made her feel good. She started working in a department store at age 15. "I became almost religiously dedicated to customer service," she said, "to making sure that the customer had what he or she wanted." After high school, she took a few part-time jobs and blew her savings on ski trips. Fortunately, there was some good news—she met her future husband, an economist, in the Denver airport. Once married, she started baking chocolate chip cookies. However, it was not until after one of her husband's colleagues mocked her for doing nothing with her life, that Fields decided it was time to contribute to the world. Despite everyone telling her it was a bad idea, she plunged into the cookie business and opened her first store at age 20.

As Fields opened more stores, design became critical. "First and foremost, there had to be no barriers of any kind. The customers had to be able to flow effortlessly to the counter, to drift over and check out what was going on, without any difficulty whatsoever," she wrote. Growth was a problem for her because she didn't want to delegate. "Eventually, I was forced, kicking and screaming, to delegate authority because that was the only way the business could grow." After finally delegating, one of the major problems she encountered was unwittingly setting people up for failure by getting them in over their heads. She addresses that issue and how to deal with failures in the following selection.

My Style
Debbi Fields

Because Mrs. Fields Cookies has gained some prominence as a company, I am sometimes asked to make public appearances. And because I'm often asked the same questions, I've begun to have a feel for what people particularly want to know from me. It may sound presumptuous to say that I've got a business philosophy, but I know what I've always believed about myself and others, and I know what I've learned by experience. Let's just call it my "style." And this is how it works in almost every aspect of my business and my personal life.

Management

I learned my management style instinctively in my first store, and I've never really changed it. I believed in having fun then, and I believe in it now. At our corporate headquarters in Park City, we combine intense work with spontaneous wackiness that keeps everybody loose and relaxed in the middle of tension. Dress styles are informal most of the time. Occasionally, when we have important visitors coming, Randy* will announce over the intercom, "Senior prom

---

*Debbi Fields's husband.

tomorrow!" and everybody appears the next day in proper business attire.

Michael Murphy, who doesn't speak a word of Japanese, was once left alone in our Ginza store in Tokyo. A series of demands on other employees had them all out somewhere, and he had to cope on his own. In honor of that memorable day, he made a tabletop model of Godzilla, with a sign referring to the Fields company conquering the world. He is likely, in times of corporate extremity, to bring Godzilla out and march around the office with him.

We combine intense work with spontaneous wackiness that keeps everybody loose and relaxed in the middle of tension.

I like corporate employees to work in the stores, so they get to know what's happening there and what it all means. I travel a great deal and I love to call employees on the spur of the moment and ask them if they'd maybe like to go to Boston the following morning. I've hardly ever been turned down. It's exciting to get out of the office and take off on one of these safaris. *Anybody* in the Fields organization may be asked to change jobs. We don't feel that narrow specialization is healthy. Okay, you're an accountant, but maybe you'd like to work with our construction people, or fly down to Florida for a day or two and bake some cookies.

Because Randy and I work in the same office every day we try to keep things light. We enjoy practical jokes, odd songs sung over the intercom, just any goofy thing at all to perk up the atmosphere. The way we both see it, a sense of humor is invaluable in business—a good, crazy sense of humor that can blunt the edges of all the little (and not so little) disasters that the world serves up every day. We may have certain failings as bosses, but we love to laugh and the people who work for us know this and appreciate it.

There is great flow and commotion within our offices. In fact, we recently had a suggestion that passing lanes be provided so that informal groups and gatherings in hallways could be circumnavigated by people in a hurry to get someplace in the office. Meetings are often informal, and people always seem to enjoy strolling around to talk face-to-face, rather than using the interoffice phones. Other folks happen by, and soon it feels like a party—but serious work is being done.

Anybody in the Fields organization may be asked to change jobs. We don't feel that narrow specialization is healthy.

But there is no need to *look* serious, or to act in a serious way. As long as the work gets done, we feel everybody should have a good time doing it.

There are, of course, difficult moments. Because we want people to stretch to the limits of their capabilities, we have sometimes unwittingly set them up for failure—given them challenges that they could not meet. Watching this happen is terribly painful for me, but when you take management risks, there is no guarantee that they will work out all the time. Still, it's worth it, especially in those cases—and they are in the majority—where people grow and stretch and meet the challenges of new responsibility. That pleasure makes up for the pain caused by the experiments that don't work out.

Failure

I've had my share of failures, and it doesn't look as if it's going to stop anytime soon. Beyond the usual lost boyfriends and social snubs of my high school years, beyond the rejections of bankers in my early years with Randy, are the worst failures of all: instances in which, unknowingly, I've caused other people to fail. This was all too often the case when we were expanding the company. We'd take a man or a woman who'd been very successful as a store manager and, with our policy of promotion from within, make that individual a district manager with, say, five stores to manage. We didn't have the time to train them—we were ourselves constantly feeling our way into this business—and such promotions were the equivalent of throwing someone into a pool to see if they'd learn to swim.

Failure only can work for you if it teaches you to be a survivor, and if you're a survivor you won't let anything stop you from chasing whatever dream is in front of you.

Some did, and some didn't. We watched people work eighty-hour weeks as they tried to cope with their new responsibilities. They'd baked great cookies, now they had to teach other people to do it. Not everyone has a natural flair for the kind of communication and tactics required to succeed in management, and we watched with dismay as some people failed and had to leave the company. These episodes were, in several senses, our fault, and our failure. Just this year we're establishing a cookie college—a place in Park City where people can come to learn this business. But it comes too late for a number of individuals, and for that I apologize.

What's worked best for me as a counterbalance to failure is the belief that there is always a lesson to be learned. I say to myself that this was meant to be, I'm meant to learn from this, I'm meant to make something better. Failure only can work for you if it teaches you to be a survivor, and if you're a survivor you won't let anything stop you from chasing whatever dream is in front of you. People are meant to chase dreams—I think it's an important part of our human nature—and actually quitting, abandoning hope, has very sad consequences. Not just for you, for everybody. When you stop trying, then you *really* fail, it becomes official. As long as you're still chugging along, failures are only hurdles that hurt your shins.

That's not to say that there won't be times when you have to admit to failure. I've had stores that had to be closed, products that didn't work, and I've failed with people, too. Those, to me, are by far the worst. But the odd thing is that when you look back at old failures, you can often see that they weren't really failures at all, that they were only signs of your destiny correcting itself. Failure can truly be a blessing in disguise. And if old failures can lead you in a new and better direction, old successes can sometimes be diversions, because they let you think you had everything solved when that turns out not to be true later on. The best thing I can say is don't take any of it too seriously, because the scoreboard is always changing. And, it's worth remembering, failure happens to *everybody*.

No matter what happens, good or bad, it's happening to other people and they are dealing with it. So can you.

When you feel singled out by failure—sure that you're the only person in the world to feel so rotten—then you're courting *real* trouble. I've known people who gave up, gave up completely, and what they had in common was the feeling that they were unique, that no one could understand how terrible things were, that what happened to them was worse than what happened to anybody else. Don't kid yourself. No matter what happens, good or bad, it's happening to other people and they are dealing with it. So can you.

1987

H. ROSS PEROT
1930–

Most entrepreneurs would be happy with one start-up that made them millions, but Ross Perot just completed his second huge success by taking Perot Systems public in February of 1999. To retain control, he owns about 38 percent of the company; also, more than 90 percent of his employees have a stake. All this after founding Electronic Data Systems (EDS) in 1962, taking it public in 1968, and selling it to General Motors for $2.5 billion in 1984. Perot believes wholeheartedly in the American dream; as he once said, "In 1936, I didn't think I could own a car. In 1986, I was the largest shareholder in General Motors. That's the kind of thing that can happen in America."

Back when he was a kid, Perot held a variety of jobs, from breaking horses to roofing barns, and merely dreamed of an indoor job. He then won himself an appointment to the U.S. Naval Academy by writing letter after letter to his congressman. Perot has always been known for his persistence. After a stint with the Navy, he became a top salesman for IBM, but detested the company's bureaucracy, which is why he left to start EDS with $1,000. First, he acted as a consultant, then quickly branched out, offering mainframe computer access and programming services. In 1964, he had 15 employees and generated $500,000 in revenue.

At EDS, Perot's primary commandment to his management team was simple: "All people who manage in an authoritarian way will be fired." The feisty Texan wanted results-oriented leaders who encouraged fresh ideas; he feared his company becoming another stodgy IBM. After selling EDS, he founded Perot Systems in 1988. In more recent years, the wily Texan is best known for his runs at the White House in 1992 and 1996 as a third-party candidate. He loves to buck the system. In a speech, he once admitted, "As a young man I wanted to be a pearl. Unfortunately my lot in life is to be the grain of sand that irritates the oyster." In *Change Is Fun,* Perot provides insight into how he cares for his current pearl, advising on a spectrum of topics, from cafeteria food, to playing with the family, to how to build a team.

Change Is Fun
H. Ross Perot

Change is constant. And in business, the pace of change is accelerating. Everything is dynamic. Today's products will soon be obsolete. And that's part of the challenge. That keeps the adrenaline going, if you look at it that way. Or you can say, "Oh gee, we just built this thing; now we've got to build another one."

You ought to be excited about building another one, excited to lead the pack and to be the first to change. Success breeds arrogance and complacency; adversity breeds strength. You will never be better than during the tough times. And while tough times don't last, tough people do.

Success breeds arrogance and complacency; adversity breeds strength. You will never be better than during the tough times. And while tough times don't last, tough people do.

You're most fragile and most likely to fail when everything is going so well that you think you can stop changing and innovating. You start thinking that you don't have to fight for your company's future everyday. And so you're like

383

the heavyweight champion who reads his headlines, gets his millions, and then gets knocked out by a nobody because he stops doing the things that make a champion. So work your mind just as hard as you work your body. Keep doing great things as long as you can.

Don't Tolerate Abuse of Privilege

One basic rule in every successful company is this: do not abuse people, particularly people who report to you, because if you are authoritarian and abusive, they become intimidated. And the odds that they're going to be creative when they're intimidated are zip. It's bad business.

We make it very clear in employment interviews, training programs, and daily work that we don't want anybody to look up to anybody else. And if anybody looks down on anybody else, they're probably going to be fired if they can't cure that problem fast. I want everybody to look at everybody else as full partners. We are all equal, and we have one goal—to build the greatest company in the world, and to have fun doing it.

One basic rule in every successful company is this: do not abuse people, particularly people who report to you, because if you are authoritarian and abusive, they become intimidated.

People will not trust you and respect you unless you are honest and call it the way it is, do what has to be done, and do not flinch. As the leader, your job is to build a united team. In many companies, you've got management, white-collar workers, blue-collar workers; everybody's all divided up into segments. They spend half their time fighting with one another. People go out on strike because they feel that they're not being properly treated. I've been around companies where the people at the top literally hated the people who did the work. That's a team that's going to fail.

Dealing with Difficult Employees

You have to deal with people who have an attitude problem. Discuss it candidly with them. Give them specific examples of how they are impacting their own careers and the morale of the team. Coach and counsel them. I've seen remarkable progress and results from that. But some people won't listen. Every now and then, you find that you have people who are square pegs in round holes where they are. Maybe you can move them to another place where they can be more successful. In many cases, though, they just need a good tutor.

People will not trust you and respect you unless you are honest and call it the way it is, do what has to be done, and do not flinch. As the leader, your job is to build a united team.

Promote honesty and integrity. When we interview people for positions, we make it clear what happens if anybody lies, cheats, steals, or takes advantage of another person by being a corporate politician who tries to move ahead at the expense of others or who takes credit for another person's work. We think that's rotten stuff. First we make sure that it is true, that they did it, and then no matter where they are in the world, they come to my office and I personally terminate them as a signal to everybody in the company that we don't do that. We then help that person get on with his life.

When people don't live up to your expectations, you've got to tell them very candidly: "Here's the problem." If you've got an Olympic team, you're going to have some people who can't perform at the Olympic level. But they may be a roaring success somewhere else. So help them get relocated and make a smooth transition, so they never miss a payday. Let them find a job; let them announce they're leaving; be graceful. Turn a problem into a victory for that person.

If your team, department, division, or company is just not cutting it, bring the key players together, drop the cards on the table (cards they already know exist) and say, "We have a problem that is going to result in failure to this company. Let's sit down here today and brainstorm about what we need to do to correct it." And then listen. Let them take the floor. Stop being defensive about why the problem exists.

In more than one case, I've had the team that created the problem totally unable to unhook from their responsibility of creating a problem. I would bring in a new young team, and I'd say, "All right, we have this problem.

"Everybody knows we have this problem. What do you think we should do about it?" And since they didn't create it, incredible creative ideas would flow. In some cases, I have put the young team in charge of solving the problem. They need a lot of support and coaching, but they come in filled with enthusiasm and go fix the situation.

Abraham Maslow said, "You don't have to be sick to get better." Companies today are working very hard at excellence and quality. I ask, "If they're really good, how do they get a lot better?"

In *Running Scared*, Satchel Page said, "Never look back. Somebody may be gaining." I would add: "No matter how fast you're running, you know somebody's gaining." So don't be complacent. It's fun to change. Just grinding out the same old stuff day after day gets boring. But if you get up every day to change the world and go where no person's ever been, walk the tightwire across the Grand Canyon, and so on, that gets the adrenaline going. That's exciting. If you say, "Let's just go turn out the product," you're dying.

I love the song "Tomorrow" in the musical *Annie*, which depicts the Depression. "When you're stuck with a day that's gray and dreary, just stick out your chin and grin and say, 'Tomorrow, tomorrow, I love you tomorrow. You're only a day away.' "

Don't be complacent. It's fun to change. Just grinding out the same old stuff day after day gets boring.

Our society was built around the notion that you are responsible for yourself. Nobody is gonna take care of you; you take care of yourself. Each individual takes full responsibility for his or her own actions. But, when you see people who are down on their luck, help them. "Help the man who is down today. Give him a lift in his sorrow. Life has a very strange way. No one knows what will happen tomorrow."

Once you're lucky, and once you have been fortunate, you have an enormous responsibility to help the man who's down today. And there will always be people like that.

Leadership can be taught. The earlier you start teaching it, the better. Only teach the principles. The basic principles never change because human nature never changes.

People who set goals for themselves are far more demanding than we would ever dare ask them to be. If your goal is to do better than anyone else, to be the best in your industry, the financial success will come as a by-product. Things don't bring happiness. Happiness is a state of mind. If you make all the money in the world and your children are a mess, you will consider yourself a failure.

So go home at night, have dinner with them, help them with their lessons, play games with them on the weekend.

Self-directed work teams. Finally corporate America is listening to the workers. And that's where the best ideas are.

To get all of the people to move in the same direction

toward the same goal, first set a goal. But then, in everything you do, you live it. For example, the building in which they work should be spotlessly clean. It doesn't have to be fancy, but it should be spotlessly clean.

Our society was built around the notion that you are responsible for yourself. Nobody is gonna take care of you; you take care of yourself. Each individual takes full responsibility for his or her own actions.

If you have a cafeteria, the food should be great. If everything they see is world class, then everything they do will tend to be world class. And they will know the company has high expectations, which is not nearly as important as all the people who are there having high expectations and thriving on competing to be better than the other teams within the industry. And then you build this very positive spirit.

As you walk around your company, do you see people smiling? At the General Motors factories, I learned to follow the manager around. I've been in factories where employees wouldn't even look up at the manager. I've been in factories where they look up, nod, and look back down. My favorite thing is to have them look up and say, "Hey Charlie, how are you?" Now you see the spirit in that factory, and there is a direct correlation between the smiles, the grins, and the quality of the cars.

The fun part of building a company from scratch is, if you have a defined culture, you tend to attract good people. If you're building a company from scratch, make it very clear what your standards are. And people will either be so excited about your company that they can't stand not to join, or they'll say, "I don't want to be a part of that. It's too tough." Then go out and look for the best people. Don't just run ads in the paper. I always had recruiters. And they asked, "Who are you looking for, needles in the haystack?" And I said, "No, needles in the haystack with a red dot—very special people. I want people who are smart, tough, self-reliant—people who have a history of success, people who love to win. I don't care who they are. I don't care where they come from. I don't care where they went to school. I don't even care if they went to school. I care about what they can do and what they've done lately."

I want people who are smart, tough, self-reliant—people who have a history of success, people who love to win.

One more thing, and please, as you build your company, keep this figure in mind: 80 percent of the customers of my company said "No" once. And to us, that meant "later." And we got 80 percent of them later. So 80 percent of our customer base came from people who said "No" the first time. And our people just couldn't recognize they'd failed, kept on trying, and got the business later. And learned from the failure, learned about why people said "No," changed what we were presenting, and got a "Yes."

1996

PHILIP KNIGHT
1938–

The Nike "swoosh" logo and accompanying slogan, "Just Do It," are recognized around the world. In fact, as recently as 1994, one in three sneakers and 60 percent of all basketball shoes sold were Nikes. Shoes, according to Nike founder Philip Knight, symbolize coolness. "In my era, kids grew up knowing their cars. The kids nowadays grow up knowing their shoes," he said. He has a "swoosh" tattoo and is known for wearing a suit and sneakers to high-powered meetings. While growing up in Oregon, Knight, who was nicknamed Buck, was never considered high-powered, but was a decent runner on his high school track team.

Knight attended the University of Oregon, where he majored in accounting and was again on the track team. His college coach was always trying to make shoes lighter and to customize them to his athletes, but it wasn't until Knight was in the MBA program at Stanford University that he seriously considered going into shoe manufacturing himself. There, he wrote a term paper on how low-cost, high-quality shoes could be made in Asia. "I had determined when I wrote that paper that what I wanted to do with my life was to be the best track and field shoe distributor in the United States," he said.

After receiving an MBA in 1964, Knight visited Japan and found a company making quality, yet inexpensive shoes; subsequently, he and his former college track coach started importing shoes from Japan and selling them at track meets. In 1972, with sales at $3 million, Knight decided it was time to manufacture their own. One employee literally dreamed the name Nike, the Greek goddess of victory. The swoosh logo was designed by a Portland State University art student, who was paid $35. The rest is history with the company going public in 1980. All has not been glamourous as Nike has come under attack for its manufacturing practices in developing countries such as Vietnam and Singapore. For any entrepreneur considering the manufacture or the purchase of their product in or from developing countries, the following speech is a must-read as Knight describes what it is like to be referred to as Satan.

Global Manufacturing: The Nike Story Is Just Good Business
Philip Knight

T he thing that I'm going to focus on today is the cloud that has been over Nike's head over the last couple years, and it has to do with our global manufacturing processes. A recent story I think is interesting from Nike's perspective. Mark Thomashow, a long-time Nike employee, has had a ten-year correspondence with Garry Trudeau, the cartoonist who has been bashing Nike lately. The correspondence went like this: "Hey, Garry, would you like to see some facts on this issue," to which Garry Trudeau answered, "No, I'm not interested in facts. I'm not a journalist; I'm a social satirist."

Forgive us out in the Pacific Northwest — sometimes it's a little hard for us to tell the difference.

But in recent times, Philip Knight has been described in print as a corporate crook, the perfect corporate villain for these times. In addition, it's been said that Nike has single-handedly lowered the human rights standards for the sole purpose of maximizing profits. And Nike products have become synonymous with slave wages, forced overtime, and arbitrary abuse. One columnist said, "Nike represents not only everything that's wrong with sports, but everything that is wrong with the world."

So I figured that I'd just come out and let you journalists

have a look at the "Great Satan" up close and personal. But as long as I was going to do that, I thought that I might as well bring along some of the "Satanettes" who are sitting out among you—six of the owners and managers of Nike foreign factories as well as four of the owners or managers of U.S. apparel manufacturers. I don't know whether the U.S. apparel guys are "Satanettes" or the "good guys," but I will say this: Without the foreign manufacturing processes, we wouldn't have the orders going to the U.S. manufacturers that we do, and U.S. manufacturers supply about 40% of Nike's apparel sold in the United States.

In recent times, Philip Knight has been described in print as a corporate crook, the perfect corporate villain for these times. . . . So I figured that I'd just come out and let you journalists have a look at the "Great Satan" up close and personal.

If I accomplish my objectives today, it is not to change the dynamics of the debate, but rather for those who are truly interested, those who want to look beyond the sound bite, to give you a base of facts for context on an issue that I believe will be with us for the better part of the next decade. We have some significant announcements today, but first I want to put them in perspective.

The company that became Nike began life in 1964 as an importer and distributor of Japanese track shoes made by Onitsuka Company, Ltd., of Kobe, Japan. Starting out, everything was done either on a commission basis or a relative. We had no money, no sales force, no employees, and no clout. Our first year sales were $8,000, and we made a $254 profit. The outgoing freight company was the trunk of my 1963 Plymouth Valiant. And as an asterisk to all that, factory workers at Onitsuka made about $4.00 a day.

After eight years, our annual sales were up to $2 million, which was 10% of the total sales of Onitsuka Company, Ltd. And they decided if that little company in Oregon could do all that, what could we do with big-time distributors? So they pulled their distribution rights. But we thought our 45 employers had been instrumental in the success we had, so we started to do it again, this time in our way and under our own name. The brand we picked was Nike. Whenever I'm asked about how we became the biggest sports and fitness company in the world, I'm reminded of John Kennedy's answer on how he became a war hero. "It was easy," he said. "They sank my boat."

The company that became Nike began life in 1964 as an importer and distributor of Japanese track shoes . . . The outgoing freight company was the trunk of my 1963 Plymouth Valiant.

When we started Nike, we had two other manufacturers in Japan make our shoes for us. One was in Hiroshima, Japan and the other was Kurume, just outside of Fukuoka. In neither case were we 10% of their volume. We actually considered ourselves fortunate that they would make shoes to our design. It never occurred to us that we should dictate what their factory should look like, which really didn't matter since we had no idea what a shoe factory should look like anyway. But some 26 years later, I can tell you one of the few absolutes of this business. Whatever you may think of Nike shoe factories today, they are far, far better than those factories in Japan some 26 years ago.

When the Nixon administration cut the yen dollar loose from its exchange rate that had existed since the end of World War II, in just a few short months it went from 360 yen to the dollar to 180. And within the last couple of years it went all the way down to 80, although it's back to 130 today. In that process, basically all shoemakers quit making shoes in Japan. Even our old friends at Onitsuka now get approximately 90% of their product outside of Japan.

We began making shoes in Taiwan and Korea, and in a bold experiment in 1977 we made up to 15% of our shoe products in two owned facilities in Maine and New Hampshire. With lots of ups and downs and the emotional charge of being kicked out of the two banks from a state that only had two banks, using innovative design which spelled waffle sole, and then later patented air midsoles, we grew to be number one in the U.S. And in 1980, just eight years after starting the Nike brand, we had a public offering.

There are a couple of things about those days. The early success we had in making shoes in the United States happened during a severe recession. As New England came out of that recession, we began to lose workers to other industries until in 1984, the two factories became so uneconomical we closed them. The write-off was about $10 million in a year when our total profit was $15 million.

Since that time, the U.S. economy has become by far the most robust in the world, and shoemaking has moved again to Southeast Asia. A lot of people say, "Why don't you bring shoemaking back to the United States?" Our studies show that using the same production techniques, the average retail cost of a pair of Nike shoes if we did that would go up $100. The average retail price for a pair of Nike shoes is between $70 and $75, so therefore it would go up to $170 or $175. The price of a pair of Air Jordans, which today sell for about $150, would increase to $250.

There are only two ways to bring back shoe production to the United States. Either by creating new advances in automation, which we believe are a few years away, or by establishing tariffs and quotas that dictate that shoes have to be made in the United States.

But just as in Japan, the factories in Taiwan and Korea that we established back in those early days were far better in terms of their quality of work conditions than the factories we had in Taiwan and Korea, and frankly the factories that we had in the United States in the '70s and early '80s.

One of the great experiments and successes of that time was taking Taiwan shoe managers and moving them into China in the early 1990s.

The early 1990s brought another shift—sending shoe production to Southeast Asia. But we did it a different way. Instead of the way we did it before, which was to move production, this time we said we don't want to lose the management skill and the partnerships that we have built up with our Asian manufacturers. So when we went into the Southeast Asian countries, we took the managers and owners from Taiwan and Korea with us. It was essentially a new type of manufacturing. It is not a legal partnership; it is an emotional partnership between our factories and us. And it does involve the way we think about the business, including the responsibility that we believe we have for the men and women who manufacture our products—we see them as our employees and our responsibility.

One of the great experiments and successes of that time was taking Taiwan shoe managers and moving them into China in the early 1990s. One of the great heroes of that time is here today, C. H. Wong, who, according to local people, has done more than any single outside foreign investor to uplift the province of Fujian.

In addition, as we went into these new factories in Southeast Asia, we got to build them from scratch. And now Nike, having had quite a lot of experience, was able to have quite a bit of input into what these factories look like. And we believe they are the most advanced and best physical facilities in the world.

From our experiences in the 1990s, we had experiences that caused us to really believe in the benefits of international trade. The uplifting of impoverished people, the better values for consumers in industrialized nations, and most of all, the increased understandings between peoples of different cultures. As a Nike vice president recently said, "When you go to check out a Nike shoe factory, you now fly across the Pacific River."

So when we saw the need for advanced production going to Southeast Asia, one of the most adventurous things we did was to decide to make shoes in Vietnam, an area that has had a lot of observation and criticism over these last couple of years. It is a grand and bold adventure, and there are a lot of aspects of it that I believe you have not heard.

There was a lot that was attractive about making shoes in that country, not the least of which was to have commerce flow where a dreadful war had once been. But there was one serious problem. There was no existing shoe industry. So we realized that if we were going to make it work, we would once again have to take our Taiwan and Korean managers with us.

There were two problems with that. First of all, foreign owned factories by law in Vietnam must pay a minimum wage 50% higher than Vietnamese owned factories. So if we were successful, we would then in turn create a shoe industry in which our competitors would be able to come in and start their businesses with Vietnamese owned factories and have a competitive advantage.

The second thing, of course, is very simplistic, but it's true. There was historical hatred between the two ethnic groups, but we did it anyway. A couple months ago I had dinner with my friend, the author David Halberstam, who's had quite an experience out in Vietnam as well. When we told him that we were using Korean and Taiwanese managers in Vietnam, his comment was simple: "How could you have been so stupid?"

But the flip side is equally simple: No Koreans and Taiwanese — no Vietnamese shoe industry. And for all you have read, Nike shoes make up 5% of the total export of the whole nation of Vietnam. So we contribute on two counts: we provide jobs and we generate a significant amount of foreign currency.

We have about 530,000 workers working on Nike shoes and clothes on a given day. There are going to be incidents.

But there are, with all of that, lots of problems. The management of the Vietnamese work force by foreign managers has complicated the whole process, and it has come under a great spotlight, which has given our critics lots of anecdotes to talk about. Essentially, those critics will hang around restaurants, outside factories and in pubs to get those anecdotes, to illustrate how dreadful this whole globalization process is in general and how evil Nike is in specific.

We have about 530,000 workers working on Nike shoes and clothes on a given day. There are going to be incidents. There have been some in the past, and there certainly will be more in the future. There are too many workers, too many interactions daily; and in Vietnam, too much tension based on nationality to avoid any incidents. That there have been as few as you have read about I think in many ways is remarkable.

Back in 1992, before anybody else in the athletic footwear industry — and I believe that only Levi-Strauss had one — Nike instituted a code of conduct for use in factories throughout Asia. In 1994, we became the first in any industry to have that code of conduct audited by the international accounting firm of Ernst & Young. We've been criticized for using a firm that we are paying for this review, and I think this is really pretty funny. The only reason that a CPA firm has for its very existence is its independence. And if in fact it was not independent, we have a much bigger problem than Nike foreign factory relations. The whole New York Stock Exchange would be built on a fraud.

There is another incident, which I think is somewhat instructive of Nike's activities in Asia. Kushid Soofi is not able to be here today because his father took ill. He is from Sialkot, Pakistan. . . .

In 1994, Jack Becraft of our Singapore office flew into Sialkot, Pakistan to check out the first ever Nike soccer ball holder. What he found were unacceptable conditions. What he found were conditions that did not meet Nike's Code of Conduct. For 50 years, the Pakistan soccer ball industry had been made up of a process in which the ball uppers were sent out into a cottage industry with very little control on who the uppers were sewn by. They were sewed by children, old people, and blind people, under all kinds of bad conditions. Seeing this, he said, "This is not acceptable under the way we do business." And he and Mr. Soofi got together in Beaverton, Oregon three months later to plan out a very different way of making soccer balls in Pakistan.

It's been two years now since we set up the first controlled soccer ball stitching centers under which we have a minimum age of 16. They are well lit, and the balls are made under our control. Nine months after we began that process, Reebok started a similar process in their soccer ball factories in Pakistan as well. But the European athletic firms who make by far the greatest number of soccer balls in Pakistan—as much as 70% of the total export of soccer balls— have not changed the way they do business at all. And I point this out to show that the often-used phrasing of Nike critics, that they pick on Nike because as an industry leader, if Nike changes their manufacturing process, the others will follow, is simply not true.

A couple of other things about some of our people doing business in Southeast Asia. Narong Chatnahat who is here today, 30 years ago faced a career decision. He was to either become a Buddhist monk or go into the family business. His choice was to go into the family business. But I'll say this: The very thought that he went into the family business to abuse Thai workers is absolutely absurd. Hundreds of Nike people have worked with him over the last 15 years, and not a single one of them has ever heard Narong tell a lie.

David Tsai who is here today began as a worker in a shoe factory in Taiwan 30 years ago. He made $15 per week. Today he is a major shareholder of the largest manufacturer of athletic shoes in the world. And his associate Wong Li, who started at $2.00 a day in Taiwan and is not here, today makes $1,500 a month working in a shoe factory in Taiwan. And it is a story told thousands of times throughout this whole process.

Recently we have come across an interesting incident in China. Young women come from farms clear across China to go to work in a shoe factory to make their lives better. These women—average age, 18 to 22 years old—have never had a TV, have never had a VCR, have never had a DVD, have never had a camera, and usually [do] not even own a radio. But what we have found in a couple of instances over the last couple of months is that hundreds of them will pool their money and buy a personal computer. And after hours, they are entertaining themselves by going on the Internet.

The thing that we have learned more than anything else in this process is that when Nike has gone into a country with its manufacturing operations, wages have increased and poverty has decreased. Nike of course is not solely responsible for that, but we have been a part of that process, and we are proud of it and not ashamed of it.

With this as a background, we have on this day six new initiatives to announce.

1. The first one has to do with health conditions within the factories. I believe it is true that every Olympic marathon champion in this century but one has run the 26 miles, 286 yards in shoes made with potentially harmful chemicals,

including the much-publicized toluene. It is just the way rubber soled athletic shoes have always been made. And the one marathon exception, of course, was Abebe Bikila, who won the 1960 Olympic marathon in Tokyo running barefoot. Today, marathoners and most other athletes for the first time have a choice. After four years of extensive research and hard work with our partners in Asia, we have developed and put into practice water-based cements, which allow shoes to be cemented without the use of the most potentially harmful solvents, including toluene. Today we use water-based cement in 80 to 90 percent of all our shoe production. We still haven't figured out a way to bond the plastic soled cleated shoes, the baseball, football, and soccer cleats, but they represent less than 15% of our production. So what we say is that with that major breakthrough in footwear manufacturing, that by the end of this calendar year all Nike shoe factories will meet OSHA standards in indoor air quality.

2. We have raised the minimum age of all footwear factories to 18. And at all apparel and equipment factories, the minimum age is 16—the same as it is in the United States. And I really do have to add this: There has never been a time in Nike's history where child labor has been a problem. And I also say that it really hasn't been a problem in the shoe industry as a whole.

3. We've publicly recognized the need for expanded monitoring to include NGOs and the need for a summary statement about this monitoring. We are not ready to announce how that will be done, but our current guess is it will include a CPA firm as well as health and social auditing by an NGO. The specifics of this will come some time down the road, but we are working hard to put this into effect.

4. We are expanding our education program in our footwear factories. It began this year in Vietnam and it includes middle and high school equivalency course availability for all workers in Nike footwear factories.

5. We are increasing our support of our current microenterprise loan program to a thousand families each in the

countries of Vietnam, Indonesia, Pakistan, and Thailand. These micro-enterprise loans are used for small businesses such as pig farming and the making of rice paper. The limited amount of experience we've had in doing that in Vietnam is showing that they've been extremely well received and also extremely successful.

6. We will fund university research and open forums to explore issues related to global manufacturing and responsible business practices such as independent monitoring and health issues. We will begin by funding four programs in United States universities in the 1998–99 academic year, and we'll have our first public forum in October of this year in Hong Kong.

Having lived through this business for 35 years and the current debate for the last couple, I know that these announcements will not end the debate. In fact, perhaps just the opposite. It will create many more targets to shoot at. Opponents will certainly be able to find incidents and anecdotes of exception. "Aha! Got you there!" But for those that are truly interested, the North Carolinas and Dartmouths of this world will set the standard for our industry and related industries to follow. We believe that these are processes that the conscientious, good companies will follow in the twenty-first century. These moves do more than just set industry standards. They reflect who we are as a company. I don't necessarily expect you to believe that, but I will tell you this: It makes us feel better about ourselves.

1998

The founder of The Body Shop, a cosmetics retailer, is renowned for her activism; in fact, Anita Roddick's true interests lie in three areas: human rights, environmental protection, and management of the environment. Even at age 12 she was an activist; the BBC filmed Roddick, whose parents had immigrated to Britain from Italy, campaigning for an ice skating rink. While a retailer of beauty products, Roddick dislikes society's obsession with beauty. She said, "We've never been part of the business's obsession with youth and phoney conditions like cellulite. It's amazing that 30 years after the women's movement so little has changed." Her activism invites criticism, but her response is in the entrepreneurial spirit: "Of course you are knocked down. But you just groan and pick yourself up."

After attending college for three years and then traveling the world, Roddick married in 1971 and bought a hotel/restaurant with her husband. It was a grind and they sold it after only a few years. At that time, her husband also decided to pursue a lifelong dream: to ride a horse from Buenos Aires to New York City. Faced with having to support her two children, Roddick decided to open a health and beauty store, dedicated to offering affordable products that were made from natural ingredients packaged in environmentally friendly containers. Although morticians didn't particularly like the name she chose, business boomed, ultimately growing to over 1,000 stores in over 40 countries. Not knowing the many obstacles she would face has helped her. "A great advantage I had when I started The Body Shop, was that I had never been to business school," she said.

The rapid growth has had its drawbacks as the company became mired down in bureaucracy. She admitted, "We've gone through a period of squashing one hell of a lot of the entrepreneurial spirit." To keep the human spirit incubating, she has introduced a number of initiatives such as hanging sheets on the bathroom walls for employees to write feedback on. In *Four-Letter Words!*, Roddick lists some other employee programs and explains why there's a sign over her office that reads "Department of the Future."

Four-Letter Words!
Anita Roddick

I have long been associated with certain four-letter words: love, give, care, feel, hope, fair, soul and true all to be found in work, my all-time favorite four-letter word.

I believe that you can bring your heart to work. Most of us spend most of our time at work. It is the place where we have our greatest daily contact with others, where we expend creative energy, and where we form relationships. For me, the workplace is an incubator for the human spirit. The workplace is where the compulsive search for connection, common purpose, and a sense of friendship and neighborhood can find a special place. It is where a continuous sense of spiritual education can take place, and where self-esteem gives us the ability to express ourselves and to contribute selflessly to a greater good.

Management from the Heart

If leaders will learn to manage from the heart, great things will happen.

The people I work with are mostly young and mostly females whose ethics are about "care." They are in search of something more than a nine-to-five death. They want to find deep meaning in what they do. In them, I look for that secret ingredient called "enthusiasm." Enthusiasm created from the heart guides your whole system so that everything seems possible. It increases self-esteem in the workplace of its own free will. But enthusiasm cannot be managed; it cannot be taught. It's habit forming and contagious and is caught from the people you work with.

Real communication is about heart-to-heart, open dialogue. I don't wait for people to come and see me. I go and talk to staff, without appointments. It's more insightful taking them by surprise and talking about their work. Also, when I see an interesting gathering of people, I will often crash their meeting. The communication is spontaneous, and in this way I find out more about what is happening in the company, and how people are reacting, than babysitting in my office with the door closed. It works both ways: staff abandon the telephone or the e-mail and come over to see me for a face-to-face chat (and a hug!).

Enthusiasm cannot be managed; it cannot be taught. It's habit forming and contagious and is caught from the people you work with.

But as the company grows, it's becoming harder to see everyone and share news in an informal way. My solution to this is to have my own newsletter in which I talk personally to staff across the world. I share stories of my travels, let staff know what's getting my creative juices flowing, tell them where I see us going, and this is the important bit—I ask them for their feedback, their ideas, and their hopes.

Developing Tactics for Empowerment

In one edition, we inserted a fax sheet for staff to return to me with their thoughts and feelings. Boy, did we ever get a huge response!

Giving staff the opportunity to tell the CEO what they are feeling about the company is empowering and is a big boost to self-esteem. Empowerment means that each staff member is responsible for creating the company's culture. Empowerment, however, doesn't appear overnight. It takes time to gain and develop trust and respect.

If leaders will learn to manage from the heart, great things will happen.

It also comes in many guises: from writing on sheets hung on the walls of lavatories, to talking about values in two-hour meetings with a board of directors and a cross-section of staff, to conducting a full social audit of all stakeholders.

The directors may not want to hear everything that's being said, but knowing that they listen encourages staff to be true to themselves. Whatever the tactic employed, it is vital that everyone, no matter what their position, is given the opportunity to talk straight to the person at the top of the company and have their views heard and responded to in some way. Being heard is often a reward in itself.

Strategies for Self-Development

I have a board above my office door that reads "Department of the Future." In the future, I don't see how business can operate in isolation of the community. One important job I have is to develop more opportunities for our staff to spend company time in the service of the local community, to measure their greatness by those experiences, and to find the heroes in themselves by caring for others.

All staff at The Body Shop are allowed paid time off, half a day per month, to take part in a community project of their choice. Whether caring for disadvantaged people, cleaning up the local environment or working with sick animals, staff can feel connected and uplifted.

Politics of Consciousness

For too long, business has been teaching that politics and commerce are two different arenas. I disagree. Political awareness and activism must be incorporated into business. In a global world, there are no value-free or politically disentangled actions. Few motivating forces are more potent than giving your staff an opportunity to exercise and express their idealism to influence change locally, nationally, and globally.

> Empowerment means that each staff member is responsible for creating the company's culture. Empowerment, however, doesn't appear overnight. It takes time to gain and develop trust and respect.

Campaigning is not only about changing the world, but changing how individuals work together. Giving people a sense of their own power is as much a part of the goal as resolving the issues. It provides a new forum for staff education. They can get into issues and into areas where they might not normally venture. Campaigns are a fabulous way of integrating the behavior of staff at work with the values they hold dear as individual citizens. Business leaders need to realize that this is the way forward in the workplace: the personal becomes the political, which becomes the global.

There are no rules or formulas for success. You just have to live it and do it. Knowing this gives us enormous freedom to experiment toward what we want. Believe me, it's a crazy, complicated journey. It's trial and error. It's opportunism. It's quite literally, "Let's try lots of this stuff and see how it works." I'm proud to look at my company and see that we're at least on the right track.

1998

Anita Brattina founded Direct Response Marketing, Inc., in 1984, and just over 10 years later won the 1995 Business Marketing Association's Direct Marketer of the Year award. Also, she is the author of the well-received 1995 book, *Diary of a Small Business Owner,* inspired by a 1993 article she wrote for *Inc.* magazine that vividly portrays the everyday life of an entrepreneur. From early on, Brattina expected to eventually be an entrepreneur. Her parents immigrated from Istanbul, Turkey, and she, being the oldest of four children and the most proficient in English, was always helping the family negotiate life in America. She relished the autonomy and being in charge. After earning a degree in journalism in 1976, she worked in a variety of corporate marketing positions. Then, a new boss and some unsavory corporate politics prompted her to leave.

Brattina started her company, which develops direct mail and telemarketing programs for major corporations, in the second bedroom of her apartment with $8,000 from a pension fund distribution and no customers. In the first few months, she made a lot of cold calls. In her *Diary,* she wrote, "I've tried to send at least five marketing letters per day. If I read the newspaper and see a company that I think can use my service, I send a letter to them too." After four months, she had generated less than $1,000. In year two, business revenue grew to $100,000 with one other employee. Year ten revenue hit $750,000 with 35 employees.

As growth accelerated, one of the problems she personally faced was being a nanomanager. "A lack of confidence makes you want to check and recheck and explain things," she said. The result of her constant checking was high employee turnover. To break out, she learned to focus on guiding the company, rather than the operational details. "It's vision that gets you out of the prison of nanomanagement. You need to have a clear picture of what the company will look like so many years from now. . . . This makes it easier to delegate." In the following essay, Brattina draws the reader in as she contemplates growth and struggles with such issues as actually listening to her board members and her employees.

The Diary of a
Small Business Owner
Anita F. Brattina

I'm changing, and my company is changing with me. The employees want to see regular client-feedback sessions, get more recognition, and have a customer newsletter that they help with; they have definite and good ideas about how to market the company. I feel proud to be a part of this.

It doesn't seem like just me alone anymore.

JULY 2, 1992 Tonight I pull out the business plan I wrote last October. It is already outdated. I still don't know what I want out of this business. I need to sit quietly and think about it. Since I've been working 60 to 70 hours a week lately, when exactly do I do that? My husband, Bill, is going away in September for four days. Decide to take four days off at the same time, go up to our cottage at the lake with the dogs, and write a new business plan.

JULY 6, 1992 Take Sarah K. to lunch. She announced at our April board meeting that she is leaving Pittsburgh and her job as a quality-control manager. This is the last time we will see each other. I ask her what she thinks of our company and the board experience. I still hold my breath after those kinds of questions.

She is straightforward. I need to be more clear about what I want from the board. She is right. I haven't really thought through how to best use their talents. And because some of them have never sat on a board before, they wait for me to lead, to tell them what it is I need from them. Then, when they do give suggestions, they expect me to drop what I am doing and act immediately. Adding the board to my life is on the verge of being overwhelming. [Note: Again, the feeling that running this business is like being the juggler on "The Ed Sullivan Show" who balanced spinning dinner plates on the ends of tall sticks, with more plates being added by the minute.]

JULY 8, 1992 Have lunch with Cathy R., CEO of a manufacturing company that was on the Inc. 500 last year. I've been polling people who have advisory boards to see how open they are with them. "I tell them everything," Cathy says. "Why should I hold back? I want them to know everything so they can help me."

Running this business is like being the juggler on "The Ed Sullivan Show" who balanced spinning dinner plates on the ends of tall sticks, with more plates being added by the minute.

I am uncomfortable with that still. After keeping everything to myself for eight years, after never telling anyone the full scope of my deepest fears . . . not even my husband knows about all the nights I lay in bed chewing on a problem. This idea of verbalizing everything is new and difficult, though I can't put my finger on why.

JULY 10, 1992 Ilana D. from PowerLink calls in response to my memo. [Note: I'd done a six-month evaluation of my relationship with the board for my own review and had sent a copy to her.] We talk on the phone for almost 45 minutes. Why did I need to be told what kind of questions to ask the board? she asks. Isn't that obvious?

I remind her that the reason I asked for a board in the first place is that I feel I need help to get "unstuck."

I tell her I am still reluctant to present full financial statements at the board meetings. She is amazed. She insists that financials are the only scorecard that makes sense. That my primary focus and the board's should be how to maximize profitability with the financial statement as the tool to determine that. I counter that my goal is to get help in planning a well-run company in terms of marketing, operations, and management. And that I will worry about profitability. She insists I am missing the whole point and that therein may be the key to my problem of being stuck. "If you are not looking at how to maximize profitability, you'd better have a damn good other reason," she says.

Think about the call all afternoon. I respect her opinion and realize what I have been doing up to now has not been good enough. I am willing to shift my focus at least for the remainder of the year. I call her back. Will she agree to be the substitute board member in place of Sarah K.? Ilana agrees. She also recommends I add Larry R., her boss at Price Waterhouse, to the board. I agree.

AUGUST 10, 1992 Business has been building steadily. We have rehired all the people laid off in April. Also set up a more careful analysis of DRM's performance and job profitability. And devised a weird mathematical formula that has been evening out our cash needs. Payroll for two weeks must be at 80% of one week's billings or we will be in trouble a few weeks down the road.

Diane N. is becoming more comfortable in her new job as operations manager. She gives me a list of 50 goals she'd like to achieve by year-end. We agree not to initiate a formal marketing program until her three-month trial period as operations manager is over and until her department is ready to handle it.

I had sent a meeting agenda and packet of information to each board member (and to my accountant, attorney, banker, financial consultant, insurance agent, and marketing consultant). My accountant calls me today. Will I need financials for the September board meeting? He has never asked me that before. I guess the board makes him feel accountable, too. I accept.

AUGUST 24, 1992 Mike P., a board member and CEO of a multimillion-dollar metals-brokering firm, calls. Says his telemarketing friend has a contract that may require our services. It is teleselling, he says happily. That's the idea he suggested at the very first board meeting, in February—selling products directly over the phone. I call. The proposal will exceed $80,000. We'll know in October.

AUGUST 25, 1992 Lunch with Dwight F., a longtime client, handpicked by me to be on the board. He has referred a substantial amount of business to me over the years. He says I don't need to be so worried about the health of the company. Even after looking behind the curtain, he says he knows I am a good businessperson and that I am responsible to my clients and creative in my work, and he has no doubts that I will meet any objective I set for myself.

I can't tell him how much I appreciate his words. I rarely get that kind of unadulterated praise from an insider. It feels wonderful. I vow to keep his advice and counsel near me for my next depth-of-despair day. [Note: One of those awful days when I'd like to walk away from the whole business and join Wal-Mart as a cashier.]

SEPTEMBER 1, 1992 Third board meeting. Only two board members attend. The rest cancel at the last minute. I am used to this. My regular contacts with the board between meetings are so valuable that I do not begrudge the ones who cancel. I will have my own board next year, though, selected by me. And will pay a small stipend, $50 or $75 per meeting attended.

We go ahead with the meeting anyway because I have a problem I want help with. A woman—Molly P.—has approached me about taking our languishing direct-mail operation and building it into a much more profitable division over the next five years, for a piece of the action. She feels she can do $200,000 in the first year and $100,000 more a year for each of the next four years. Am I interested? I asked her to put it in writing for the board meeting.

The two board members think her proposal is thin and

that we have not hammered out enough financial details to initiate anything serious.

I admit to them that when I wrote my business plan last fall, I had decided that telemarketing had less competition and better profit margins, and that I enjoyed selling it more. Then, Ilana D. says that should give you your answer. Don't do it. Mike P., having been through a rough experience himself, cautions against taking on a partner without getting to know her better. (He suggests knowing a potential partner for at least 10 years.) I don't have 10 years, but I agree to put Molly off for two weeks and to draft a new business plan and a new agreement.

The final board agenda item arrives. We review the financials, and I wait for comments. I get surprisingly few. It is not the reaction I expect.

SEPTEMBER 4, 1992 We will have our best quarter in the history of the company.

SEPTEMBER 8, 1992 I leave for the lake, determined to finish my list of personal business goals while Bill is golfing in Myrtle Beach.

SEPTEMBER 9, 1992 I sit with pen and journal, writing around the goals, and then start a list. I tear it up and start over. The goals keep sounding like a business plan for the bank or my staff or the board. Hard to write goals for myself. In some ways I feel the business is bigger than I am. Suppose I decide that my real goal is to live at the lake on Bill's income and read all the Great Books? Suppose I decide that I want to become a rock star? Who cares? I have employees who count on me for their livelihood, I have clients who rely on us. I come in every day, work hard until the day is over, and start again the next day.

SEPTEMBER 10, 1992 I put my personal business goals aside. So that the time here is not a total waste, I write a statement of philosophy about the company. It is the first time I have put a lot of these ideas into words. At least I feel I have accomplished something. I also rewrite the agreement with Molly P. We will do a 12-month trial to see how it works out. If we are both happy, we will spin off the division and she will have to buy in.

SEPTEMBER 22, 1992 I review minutes from the last board meeting. There are two main things I need to do. First, Mike P. insisted I need to get our accounting computerized and offered to find a local consultant to help us.

Second, the minutes state that "Mike and Ilana were concerned about whether expanding the existing direct-mail service fits into DRM's vision for the future." [Note: My new business plan is only halfway done. I've found it easier to write at our cottage by the lake, so I've moved a computer up there. I will take a stab at finishing it the last weekend in September.] But here's the catch: Molly P. started with us September 17. I know that sounds like the preboard Anita, charging ahead, not doing the necessary planning. Yet I feel much more comfortable with the compromise.

SEPTEMBER 25, 1992 Mike P. has invited me to attend a meeting of company CEOs who meet monthly at one of the most exclusive clubs in the city.

When I walk into the room, I see Barb M., the cofounder of PowerLink and the friend who recommended I apply for the board. She is there as a guest. We sit together and introduce ourselves to the mostly male crowd. Mike also attends. The meeting is a presentation by four authors of business publications. The author getting the most questions is Robert Kelley, who wrote *The Power of Followership.* He asks how many people in the room consider themselves good followers. I am surprised that most of the people raise their hands. I struggle to think of a personal example.

Actually, I sit on someone else's board as a "follower." One of 10, I was invited to the position by the owner of a private club where I am a member. With a fresh kind of clarity I can see this owner sitting at the club's board meetings, talking with authority for so long without interruption that finally no one bothers to interrupt. Instead, we sit quietly, looking at our watches. Our independent ideas are not really needed.

That sets me to wondering, How many times have I asked for opinions and then raced ahead without listening to the answers of my board? Of my employees? How many times have I withheld information that I didn't think they were ready to hear or that I didn't want to bother explaining?

As I sit looking around the table at these men, I wonder how many of them have built their companies by having all the answers. Or how many have let other people come up with ideas that they have listened to with great interest and enthusiasm and then followed. How hard is it, really, to let go of your own company? I order Kelley's book.

How many times have I asked for opinions and then raced ahead without listening to the answers of my board? Of my employees?

SEPTEMBER 29, 1992 Meet with Diane N. and Mary Z., my two top people. It is all I can do to keep my mouth shut and listen. These two women have worked so hard for the company and their employees all week, and they are bringing me up to date on their progress. Am I letting them run the company and keeping out of their way? It is very, very hard. I find myself scheduling time outside the office lately. It is easier not to make decisions if I am not forced to confront them. I go on sales calls, and take work home to my home office. I read over the reports and think of ways to ask questions without second-guessing decisions.

OCTOBER 19, 1992 I meet with Mike P.'s friend who asked us for the telemarketing quote. We did not get the job. Our price was competitive and our references were excellent, but his client had gone directly to a vendor without his knowledge.

Over lunch he tells me how he grew his business. (It has become a standard question I ask anyone who owns a business.) It is a fascinating story about a great success and a few setbacks. I do not know him well enough to ask him if he ever sat down and wrote out his personal business goals.

OCTOBER 22, 1992 We are expanding the telemarketing department, and I offer to clean out the area it will move into. In jeans and a sweater, I sit on the floor, sifting through boxes of files taken out of the old sales office. This is where nine salespeople have come and gone over the last eight years.

Business is going well. Yet my work load seems to be more and more overwhelming. . . . I feel I am delegating more than ever before, and yet, I have never felt busier. Can't figure it out.

It's a little like looking at the history of the company compressed into "general correspondence." Letters to companies no longer in our market, proposals long forgotten because they were filed by someone who is no longer here. I wonder how a huge company prevents this from happening. Who sits on the floor weeding out sales-proposal files at Westinghouse or Apple? Who makes sure all those prospective customers are treated well, not lost in the shuffle during employee turnover?

OCTOBER 26, 1992 Business is going well. Yet my work load seems to be more and more overwhelming. I bring all my paperwork home tonight in a big box. We have more employees than ever, I feel I am delegating more than ever before, and yet, I have never felt busier. Can't figure it out.

OCTOBER 29, 1992 In the last week I have received inquiries for our business-to-business telemarketing that put my lack of long-term objectives to the test. If 50% of the inquiries from this month alone turn into jobs, we could expand from 25 employees to 50 employees by the end of the year.

I share my problem with him. He admits that planning for growth sounds good but is not always so easy. Even at a company the size of his, he and his partners work on it constantly. [Note: My board has helped me to open up and share insights like never before. I see that the companies doing $5 million, $10 million, $20 million look and act like mine. The owners are not geniuses or unique by some entrepreneurial definition that could not apply to me. They admit that grave mistakes mark their histories. But they also share great ideas.]

In James's case, he and his cofounders began working in partnership with one of the largest computer manufacturers in the world six months after they formed the company. They have been asking for help from that manufacturer — also a client of ours — and getting it for 12 years.

NOVEMBER 10, 1992 Lunch with my banker, Jim S. He is the one who championed my line of credit and equipment loan last fall. He calls me periodically to see "if the patient is healthy." Mostly I tell him about proposals we are working on and new contracts. We are meeting our loan payments easily these days. That feels very good to me. Jim does not mention it. He had suggested we hire business students from the University of Pittsburgh to help us with daytime projects. We had done that and found a great employee. I thank him for the idea. [Note: We are in the sixth month of a major newspaper strike, so it is not easy to find people to keep up with our growth. Our turnover rate is less than 25%, excellent for telemarketing. Hiring full-time people and paying benefits seem to be paying off.]

I tell Jim we may want to extend our line of credit next spring, based on increased receivables — but that I'd like to see if we can meet payroll without it. The idea of borrowing money still goes against the grain with me. I still don't know how to do a cash-flow analysis.

NOVEMBER 13, 1992 Mary Z. buys pizza, and I buy champagne. Everyone wears jeans. Lunch is in the conference room, and we stop work at one o'clock to celebrate the past month. Bills are all paid, receivables are at their highest point in the year, and we have two new contracts that could mean more than $250,000 of work next year if the initial tests go well. Molly P. has brought in three small contracts from existing clients for direct mail and has more than $250,000 in pending proposals.

NOVEMBER 15, 1992 Finish Joline Godfrey's book, *Our Wildest Dreams*. She touched on a subject that has been disturbing me ever since I started working with the board. I keep wanting to talk about running a good company, and they keep talking about money. I keep talking about empowering employees, and they keep talking about profits. It is a little as if they are speaking Italian and I know only a few words and have to use hand signals. Joline's research among other women in business tells me I am not alone. That is a comfort.

NOVEMBER 17, 1992 Mike P. has invited me to my second CEO Club meeting at the Duquesne Club. The guest speaker talks about negotiating skills. I am sitting next to Cathy R., the Inc. 500 business owner I had lunch with this summer. She joined the CEO Club last year and urges me to join. The dues are $1,700, and I have to think about it. I have new chairs, desks, and phones on order. I want to computerize my accounting, which may take up to $2,000 in consulting expenses.

The four negotiating styles the speaker talks about are familiar to me. I wonder if men negotiate differently with women than they do with other men, but in this room of mostly gray suits, I do not bring it up.

One of the business owners asks me to sit at his table for lunch. He may need our services and wants to talk further. Perhaps I can squeeze the $1,700 out of the bank before year-end after all.

NOVEMBER 19, 1992 Received a note of apology from Steve M., board member and marketing manager for a local cultural organization. He had been immersed in a tough work schedule but wanted to get caught up on the board. We agreed to meet this morning at his office. In reviewing the past four months, I find myself telling him about the lack of focus I have been accused of by the board. It is something I have been wrestling with on paper. If nothing else, I have come to one conclusion in my personal business plan.

To me, the most important thing is to create a growth company that is exhilarating to work for. Growth means I can afford to pay employees better, I can be more generous with benefits, I can provide a career track. I feel that if I can recruit great employees and keep them, we can do absolutely anything! I feel we have that kind of culture now. And I am furiously working on my goal of getting the turnover below 10%. [Note: I have continually seen the effects of turnover: systems abandoned when an employee leaves, clients having to be reintroduced, projects having to be relearned, mistakes repeated by a new person.]

Steve listens. I can see he finds this interesting, and he agrees with me on one major point—the board doesn't need to be told the entire rationale for my wanting to grow. All they need to know about and help with is the growth itself. I can do the rest within the company.

To me, the most important thing is to create a growth company that is exhilarating to work for. Growth means I can afford to pay employees better, I can be more generous with benefits, I can provide a career track.

NOVEMBER 28, 1992 It is two days after Thanksgiving, and Bill and I are visiting my family in Philadelphia. Of the four kids, three of us own our own businesses. We've never really talked about why that happened, but we often use the time together to compare notes. Tonight my brother Ed and I went to visit a family friend who started his consulting firm in 1985, a year after I founded Direct Response Marketing.

Tom S.'s progress interests me, but I do not want to pry. So instead I find myself talking about my own company. We sit talking far into the night about how hard it can be to make decisions about so many things when you are alone. Tom and Ed ask me about the board. It is still difficult for me to explain this arrangement. No, I don't do everything they tell me. Actually, if I were keeping score (which I'm not), I would say I have followed their advice less than half the time. But what I have overcome is the urge to keep absolutely everything to myself. I no longer consider it a sign of weakness to ask for help.

DECEMBER 15, 1992 At three o'clock today the heart of our computer network goes down. The technician I had hired full-time only a month ago tells me he has called in our equipment supplier but that it doesn't look good.

DECEMBER 16, 1992 I find out that the hard drive on our file server is defective and that we don't have adequate backup to replace the data. Our part-time technician had been assigned to do backup the previous four weekends, I am told, but never got around to it. Another Wal-Mart moment. One of those times when I feel for a split second like walking out the door and applying for a cashier's job.

We are sitting in the conference room. The full-time tech, John D.; our operations director, Diane N., and her assistant, Mary Z.; our computer supplier, Bill G.; and me.

"So what are our options?" I ask. Bill says there is a company in California that can probably retrieve 99% of the data. The hard drive is under warranty and can be replaced. He apologizes for not reminding us to do backups daily after receiving a memo I had sent him a month before on that very subject. John apologizes for not taking the backup more seriously. He knew it had not been done the previous weekend and had just been too busy to do anything about it. Diane and Mary are quiet. They know that they too are responsible.

I realize that no matter how many tasks I delegate, the most important ones have to be clearly tagged by me with fluorescent markers—THIS IS IMPORTANT! Backups? Well, I just didn't say it loud enough. [Note: That computer "lesson" cost $4,100 that we didn't really have, and we lost three and half weeks of working time on the system.]

DECEMBER 28, 1992 We spend all day downtown at a training facility. It is the Monday after Christmas, and I close the office and let voice mail handle the calls while the entire staff meets with me to set our 1993 goals.

By the end of the day we have more than 25 sheets of flip-chart paper taped to the walls and filled with ideas. We narrow those down to 70 ideas, and each person takes two goals to work on. It takes a lot of effort not to jump in and volunteer to do half the goals, but I decide not to take any myself. Instead, I write down major issues that seem to crop up that will go on my list. Employees want to see regular client-feedback sessions that can be monitored by them; they want more employee recognition; they want more of our policies in writing; they want notice of job openings before we go outside the company; they want to see us send out a newsletter that they help with. They have definite and good ideas about how to market the company.

I feel so proud to be a part of this. It doesn't feel like just me alone anymore.

JANUARY 5, 1993 Tonight is my last meeting with the PowerLink board. Eight people squeeze around the conference table in the room we used to use for meetings. [Note: Last week we installed six more workstations in that room. We also officially rented space across the hall. By the end of February we will be able to handle 84,000 calls a week from our offices. Last January we were at 25,000 a week.]

I finally feel comfortable with these people. I have spent hours and hours in phone calls, meetings, lunches, and more meetings with each of them. We sit tonight with the financials. Our preliminary numbers show that we will hit $484,046 in sales for the year. Up from $367,422 in 1991. Although we have grown by 32%, we have not hit my goal of $750,000 yet, but I am not disappointed. We spent the year doing important work—improving operations, training new management, establishing procedures and quality controls.

Most of the meeting is devoted to marketing. I want to reach a million in sales by year-end. What do I need to do to get there?

We end up talking mostly about the very topic that started the year—focus. I watch eight heads nod. Going from $500,000 to $1 million is a no-brainer, according to Mike P. and Steve M. "Just keep working with the customers you have now and find similar companies in similar markets."

"Did you do a market analysis yet?" Larry R. asks. I'm not sure what that is. "You write down how much business you expect to get from each customer for the year, which determines your budget. Then analyze the source markets and look for like business in those markets." It sounds simple, but I have never done it. Steve offers to help me construct one.

Again, I realize that getting where we are has not taken marketing brilliance on my part. We are in a needed industry. We do our work well. People find us. But that does not make for a great marketing strategy.

The last board member leaves at close to 9 p.m., and I return to my office. I am kind of jarred by their comments, as usual. I had listed eight ideas to hit the million-dollar mark. Eight different services we could offer in addition to what we already do. They nixed almost all of them. Most of the board members work for major companies, and they look at my tiny firm and wonder why I need help with this issue of growth.

For a moment I see these last eight years and nine months very clearly: I love variety. I love challenge. I am good at executing ideas. So there I am with a bunch of sticks and some saucers back in 1984. I toss a saucer up in the air, catch it on the end of a stick, and start rotating. It is tricky at first, but I catch on. Sometimes it slips and I catch it. Sometimes I drop the saucer and it breaks. Doggedly, perhaps, I keep throwing saucers up there until I have the hang of it. Then I put up a second stick and throw up a . . . dinner plate!

I realize that getting where we are has not taken marketing brilliance on my part. We are in a needed industry. We do our work well. People find us. But that does not make for a great marketing strategy.

No . . . no . . . no . . . the board is telling me. Not a dinner plate—throw another saucer in the air. In fact, toss up 10 saucers and hire a saucer manager to watch the sticks for you. And find a volume-discount supplier who can sell you more saucers. And set up inventory control of those saucers and get really, really good at spinning hundreds of saucers. THEN YOU CAN SWITCH TO DINNER PLATES.

Boring. Too easy. I can feel myself resisting. But slowly and with great effort I am willing to fight this resistance. Someday I want us to have thousands of employees, each part of a team working on telemarketing and direct-mail projects for customers all over the world. So for this year, if they think it is that important, I will do what does not come so easily. I will work on saucers.

1993

423

THOMAS J. WATSON
1874–1956

If not for the potato famine in Ireland, the great IBM corporation may never have existed—its founder's family migrated to the United States to escape the tragedy. Although Thomas Watson grew up on the family farm in the state of New York, his father wanted him to become a lawyer. Instead, he tried his hand at teaching, but couldn't take the kids all day, so he quit. Next, in 1892, he took some courses in accounting and business and landed a $6-a-week job as a bookkeeper. He quickly decided, however, he didn't want to keep books all his life, so he started selling pianos, organs, and sewing machines off the back of a wagon. The more he traveled, he said, the more he saw well-to-do businessmen, which led to an ever greater desire to succeed.

Watson then landed a job with the National Cash Register Company, becoming a devout student of John Henry Patterson, who is considered the father of modern salesmanship. However, Watson, a selling genius in his own right, was eventually forced out by the egotistical Patterson. He was recruited to become president of the Computing-Tabulating-Recording Company in 1914, which at the time specialized in punch card machines, recording census data, and handling payrolls, among other tasks. In the early 1920s, he gained control of the company, and changed the name to International Business Machines, envisioning the day it would be a global operation. Not until 1952 did he hand over the reins to his son, Thomas, Jr.

The success of IBM relied more on Watson's ability to forge and lead a well-trained, devoted sales force than it did on technological leadership. The enduring loyalty of his salesmen sprung from Watson's own dedication to them; for example, he refused to lay off anyone during the Great Depression. He brought both a family and an entrepreneurial spirit to the company. To further enthusiasm, employees were *requested* to memorize such slogans as "Ever Onward," "Beat Your Best," and the simple but famous "Think," which was hung throughout the offices. In the following selection, he depicts his five key points for growing a business through people management: hiring, training, supervising, promoting, and discharging.

To Make a Business Grow —
Begin Growing Men
Thomas J. Watson

W hen I became the head of this company in 1914, it was suggested that I dispense with a number of men connected with the executive staff. That is one thing I did not do; that is the one thing no thinking person in the same position should do. And yet it is the course of least resistance which some executives coming into a business under similar circumstances have followed — while the stockholders paid the bill.

Those men that it would have been mine to discharge knew more about the details of this business than I did. They had specific knowledge that I lacked. My problem was to bring it out of them, to revamp them and to develop them. It does not take executive ability to discharge a man, but it does take it to develop men.

This business — from experiences in which I must necessarily write — is a large one; but it is the large business as well as the small one that needs definite consideration of the basic business fundamentals in connection with the growing of men.

The success of every major executive depends on the men under him. Their success depends on the men under them. Really successful men are pushed up, not pulled up. Whether he be president or foreman, manager or chief clerk, that man who gets ahead in this or any other business is the one who has learned that next to himself he is absolutely dependent for the progress he makes on the men he controls.

It does not take executive ability to discharge a man, but it does take it to develop men.

Today several of the men I was advised to replace when I came to International are the mainstays of this business. One in particular—then a chief clerk in one of our divisions—whose antagonism to me and my policies was apparent on all sides from the start, is today a vice-president. It was a long, up-hill fight to his confidence, but I won it.

How much easier to have discharged that man, but how much more satisfying to have won him over and to have helped him develop those things in him in which this company had an investment, and which today, plus the loyalty of associate and friend, are paying extra dividends on a share of confidence.

Sometimes I think we overemphasize the mechanics of this age. Often we lay too much stress on the machinery of production. When we start thinking of men as automatons, clicking their respective ways through the processes of life with mechanical exactness, that day we lose our own identity and become automatons ourselves. When we cease to realize the interdependence of men we are on the brink of failure.

When a man comes into this business, no matter what his capacity, the job of being president is as accessible to him as the next one above him. And that man in this business who is not looking for and does not recognize outstanding ability on the part of a man under him, and who fails to give that ability an opportunity to express itself in greater responsibility and better work, is of no further use to us.

Our men know that. They are constantly looking for men. They know that it is human ability above all else that will help this company succeed; and they are vitally interested in its progress. Our general manager of manufacturing started at an assembly bench. Our vice-president in charge of sales began with a sample case. The secretary of this company came here as a clerk. Men? We do not have to go outside our own company to get topnotchers. We develop them.

There are five points to consider in regard to men. First, the hiring, which must be carefully done; second, the training, which must be thorough; third, the supervising, which must be fair; fourth, the promoting, which must be just; and, fifth, the discharging, which should be the last resort. If we will give more attention to the first four of these points, we will have less occasion for the fifth. If we hire and train, supervise and promote to the best of our ability, we will profit the more, because one of the heaviest expenditures in business is the expenditure for labor turnover.

Developing and keeping men is one of the biggest jobs the heads of American business have. Our modern organizations are so complex and our establishments so departmentalized that it is easy to lose contact with the very essence of business—the men who operate and maintain it. An age of specialists in great measure, we stick to our specialty.

Take my own experience as an example: I started as a salesman when I was 19. Later I became sales manager of The National Cash Register Company and for years felt the influence of one of the greatest salesmen the world has ever known—the late John H. Patterson. Small wonder that I should have developed a sales complex.

That was a problem. It behooved me to school myself to the fact that business is more than sales—that the successful business operator has three "concerns"—manufacturing, recording, and selling.

The "school"—so called, and rightly—is a great thing for any business. We held schools from the beginning, our executives "teaching" the people under them that they might be more valuable, first to themselves and then to the company.

One day we began to wonder whose job it was to "teach the teachers"—how we who bore the responsibility of imparting knowledge were to obtain a greater knowledge for ourselves. It was with this idea in mind that we held our first executives' school, just prior to America's entry into the World War.

We, as executives, had been teaching others. Here was an opportunity for us to enlighten ourselves. We were all taking part in a "clearing house of ideas"—exchanging our own on the successful conduct of our business for the proved ideas of our associates.

It was at one of these schools that we awakened to the fact that our foremen were executives, and that, as teachers of the men under them, they belonged in our executives' school—as executives themselves.

There was the way to the men on the firing line, through their "platoon and squad leaders."

We started the work of our school by having each man make suggestions for the adoption of better methods of operation. We asked the foremen to tell the field representatives where they could be of greater help to the factory, and the field men to make suggestions in connection with manufacture. We declared the objective of the meeting the manufacturing of better goods for less money, that we might be able to sell more goods at a lower cost. We imbued every man in charge of men with an idea of the importance of those men to his own and the company's progress and success.

There is no mystery about running a business. It is simply a matter of sound policies and the exercising of common sense in carrying them out. Our business policies are formulated by the men who must put them into effect. Many of these policies have originated in the field or in the factory. Those that have not are first submitted to the field and factory for approval or suggestion. In theory? No, in fact.

And with what result? Take for instance the savings brought about through standardization of product, a direct outcome of our executives' school, where it took the manufacturing department to call the sales department's attention to the fact that we were losing money by building so many "specials," where salesmen had taken the course of least resistance and acceded to the customer's whims rather than exercising a little salesmanship in behalf of the standard product they had to sell.

There is no mystery about running a business. It is simply a matter of sound policies and the exercising of common sense in carrying them out.

The attitude of our foremen is typified by the expression of one of our foremen in charge of our finishing department at Dayton. He said:

"I want to say that the enthusiasm I received from the last meeting stayed with me throughout the year. I received a larger vision of the great work this company is doing than I ever expected to receive. And I know that as the executives of this company try to help the foremen and supervisors to grow in their work, just so much in proportion will the company's business grow and, of course, the more money we will all make.

"I think that every one holding a supervisory position does realize, or he should realize, that we do have to make a profit if we stay in the business, and the quicker we realize that it is the small things that cost us the money, the quicker will we be able to get on our feet and go forward.

"As far as the special equipment is concerned, I think we always have to give the customer special equipment, but I would say that the customer is always willing to pay the difference in price. We all realize that service is one of the big things—service to the customer, service to the men working for us straight down the line.

"When I take over a new department, the first thing I do is to find out how the people there feel and then I increase the morale of that department. I tell them that I have come in there to help them, not to boss them, to help them to do better work and more of it, at the same time not using up any more of their energy.

"One of the smallest departments I have is the tinning department. The first thing we did was to get the things we needed most, and then we went along, and by cleaning up the different things we have increased the production 50%, with the same number of men. We have actually done that. How? By rearranging the department and lining things up, we have done away with 30% of the walking.

"Some time ago we got the idea of reclaiming the tin from the sweepings on the floor. It didn't seem like much. It looked like just a little pile of dirt there. We put sawdust on the floor in the morning and about 10 days ago I put a man on the job at fifty cents an hour—$4.50 a day. He is showing a big profit on the company's investment in him through the tin he reclaims.

"I think that when we get down to looking after the small things, that is where the real saving comes in."

Does it pay to make our foremen policy executives? Does it pay to get across the idea that the success of every man in the organization depends on the performance of the men under him? One does not have to go beyond the sincere expression of that head of our finishing department at Dayton to be convinced that it does—and that it pays well.

Take another instance where the cooperation between departments—a cooperation inspired by our schools—netted a saving of $15,000 annually in one operation. That incident was recited at our recent school, at a session attended by the production, recording, and sales personnel. It made such an impression that one of the sales heads mentioned it when the sales department met.

But beyond that, our executives' school started the men at our Endicott division thinking, and an IBM club was the result. Starting with 11 members who desired to obtain a closer understanding of each other's work, the club today has 118 active and 12 honorary members, embracing engineers, foremen, heads of departments, and members of the organization at Endicott who show promise of developing and who express a desire to improve themselves and their jobs.

The president of the club last year was the chief factory clerk, the vice-president a foreman in the assembly room, the secretary and the treasurer clerks in the time-study department. The men in that club will go a long way. They will progress because they want to progress, and because the men under them and the men around them want them to progress. The club is their club, organized by them with but one aim — to afford an opportunity of development. I was a guest at their closing meeting for the 1925–1926 season, as were others of our officers and directors. It gave us a new faith in the future of our business because it justified our faith in our men.

The success of our executives' school was responsible for a similar school for branch managers. Here again are our contacts with the men on the firing line. Here again are the men who are this company in so far as the majority of our salesmen are concerned. And here again the individual success depends on the men that individual supervises, in greater measure perhaps than in the factory because the branches are so far removed from the personal observation of our operating heads that their personnel must be judged by net results.

Our branch managers are charged with the responsibility of representing our company to our customers. They are responsible for the development of the men they employ. They must be quick to catch the necessity of changes in policy, in design of product, in range of price. And at the same time, they must serve the manufacturing department faithfully and profitably.

Industry's field representatives carry a burden beyond the casual mind's appreciation. Theirs must be the courage to accept responsibility and to carry out orders with due thought for the unusual situation. Our men in the field as well as our men in the office or factory are given every opportunity to work out their own individual salvation. If they make a mistake and admit it, forgiveness is automatic.

But the same mistake must not be made a second time. Too, whether he be foreman or manager, the man in this business who has responsibility also has actual support from his superiors. And yet he knows that any man in his direct employ has every privilege of appealing to the man higher up if he thinks he has a grievance.

Here again we endeavor to prove our faith in our men, to demonstrate the dependence of this business on the men who run it and their dependence upon the men who help them carry out their respective operations.

No one has to be a genius to succeed in business. One does not have to lie awake nights worrying about his job. All we ask our men to do is to look their work squarely in the face and say, "This is the right thing to do." If they do what common sense tells them to do, 9 times out of 10 it will be the right thing.

Those of us at the head of America's businesses face the necessity and the opportunity of taking more of our men into our confidence and showing them the way, realizing that their knowledge will produce dollars in profits where insignificant but appreciated nickels were available before.

But regardless of the monetary value, think of the personal satisfaction in realizing that from your first vice-president to the machinist's helper, every one in the organization is working with a vision of the prime objective of the business, and a realization that his contribution to the obtaining of that objective will be rewarded with promotion as he merits it.

When I go away on a trip it is with the full assurance that the interests of the company are in capable, knowing, and loyal hands from the vice-president-in-charge to the executive foremen, and from the vice-president in charge of sales to the sales supervisor in the field.

There is no need of detailed instructions, no necessity for "pep" talks or caution lectures. When I leave 50 Broad Street all I have to say is, "Good-by."

1926

PART VIII

Personal Stories

Some entrepreneurs are determined from day one to strike out on their own, others fall into their own businesses through necessity, or unforeseen circumstances. The authors in Part VIII each have their own unique story that offers insights into what can be a very grueling and trying experience. For example, Herman Lay (the Lay in Frito-Lay snack food) was almost done in several times by both his own carelessness and unexpected events like the rats who ate his inventory. He likens running your own business to a boxing match, only you're fighting a three-fisted competitor. Ben and Jerry, the ice cream magnates, are an example of two people sitting down together and deciding to start a business. Why ice cream? Because they liked to eat and they couldn't afford the equipment to make bagels. Joseph C. Wilson, who created Xerox as we know it, became an entrepreneur out of necessity. His photographic paper company was in competition with powerful Kodak, and he was desperate for a new product and a new direction. Samuel Goldwyn, a gloves salesman before becoming a Hollywood producer, best summarizes one basic element that drives entrepreneurs—"You can always do better." As a young man he climbed a greased pole to win $10, and it was then he learned how hard it is to stay at the top—unless you always improve upon yourself. These sometimes wandering, but always dramatic and poignant, narratives provide a final rallying cry.

Herman Lay was the king of snack food; his company, Frito-Lay, is currently owned by Pepsi. The North Carolina native targeted the year 1920 as the time he first became an entrepreneur: "Our house was across the street from the old Sally League ball park and I started my first business venture on the front lawn, a piano box set up as a soft drink stand." His price for drinks was a nickel, half the rate of those inside the park. When the team moved, he followed, only now becoming a hawker of peanuts inside the stadium. Upon reflection, he said, "It wasn't *what* you sold at the park but *how* you sold it. . . . [I] was a real screecher, and I expect that some people bought from me just to get me to move on."

In his sophomore year at college, Lay dropped out and bought an ice cream concession in a Houston hotel for the Democratic National Convention. The parade route was to pass right by, only at the last minute they changed the route. "This was my first lesson in failure. I had acted too fast. The old-timers in the ice-cream business had set up their stands nearer the convention hall, where changes couldn't hurt them," he said. For the next two years he was a farm laborer. Lay also took some correspondence courses in business to make up for dropping out of college, a mistake he regretted. "The management of business, large or small, calls for the most solid preparation, both from formal education and experience; and a man simply cannot know too much as he undertakes to judge buying habits, select processing methods, and make use of the engineering and technological advances of our time," he said.

In 1930, Lay became a salesman and distributor of potato chips and then an independent food distributor from 1932 to 1939. He finally founded H. W. Lay & Company in 1939, eventually merging with Frito in 1961. He depicts a powerful personal story in *Your Own Business,* from his battles with rats to the fulfillment of paying his stockholder dividends. He also warns, "The head of a company who is always searching for angles and gimmicks to enrich himself does not always gain permanently what he may seem to profit at the moment."

Your Own Business
Herman W. Lay

M̲ost young people, I
suppose, at some time in their lives think about starting a
business of their own. Now and then, you meet a young man
who knows from the beginning what he is going to do: be a
lawyer, be a doctor; but I expect that most of them shop
around, and sooner or later they probably consider business.
Probably, too, a good many of them think about a business of
their own. I am not suggesting it or advising it, because each
man has to make up his own mind about his career; but I
would like to talk to those who want to go into business, and
seriously want a business of their own.

In the beginning, let's establish that I will have little to
say about the theories of business. I want to talk some about
my own business, because, of course, I know the *details* of it
better than any other; but I believe that a man who knows
his own business has a pretty good idea of all business and all
business practice. Also, I will be calling on the advice given
me through the years by older, more-experienced men.
Maybe, I can partly pay the debt I owe them by passing on
to you some of the things they taught me.

I remember an old ball player I knew when I was a boy.
He wasn't the best ball player and he hadn't made any
records, but he had worked his way up through the minors

and had played a little big-league ball—even stayed on Con-
nie Mack's team for three years. We kids would get around
and ask him about baseball, and he would start telling us
about the old Athletics with Home-run Baker on third,
telling about Ty Cobb and his whirlwind slide and you better get out of his way. Sooner or later, he would get around
to himself, what he had done, the time he made a winning
hit, the time he struck out. We didn't think he was bragging,
that was just the best way he knew to tell us his story of baseball. The best way I know to tell you about starting a business of your own is to tell you how I started mine.

I don't want to be dramatic or set the stage for a
punch line, but the simple truth is that I started
in business thirty years ago with a potato.

But before I do that, I want to impress you with one fact—
and impress it so hard that you will never forget it, hoping that
you will set your sights on it now, while you are young, and
will start living by it. What I did in my business, starting out
with just about nothing, has been done in America over and
over again. And the most important fact is this: *it is being done
today.* You hear men moan about taxes and government controls; you hear them bemoan foreign competition and wonder
what the unions are going to demand next. Sure, this can be
worrisome. Sure, it can be a burden; but it is all a part of this
remarkable, magnificent Capitalist system that we live in,
operate our business in, and most of us prosper in. You young
men standing back a little, wondering about business, and
particularly about a business of your own—you can come on
in, carry the taxes, face the controls, meet foreign competition,
and go just as far as your own brains and your imagination
and your energy can carry you. Unless you are greedy and
want all the money in the world, you can make enough, and
more than enough, to live on and be satisfied with.

Now, let's get back to this business of mine. I don't want
to be dramatic or set the stage for a punch line, but the simple truth is that I started in business thirty years ago with a
potato. That was it—a potato! During 1961, our business
totaled about $50,000,000 and still chiefly out of potatoes. I
was a country boy from South Carolina. I didn't finish college. Don't tell me what can't be done in this country! Don't
you listen to these "can't" people, when they grumble and
say it's not like the good old days. For my part, I can't imagine any better day than right now—unless it's tomorrow.

So let's go back to 1932, when I was getting started. And
something else: when I am talking about *my* getting started,
about *my* business, I'm talking about young fellows in Texas
and Topeka, in Spokane or wherever in this country they
may open a shop or a store or a plant or start selling whatever their products may be. All of us are the same; all are
Americans getting started, getting going.

I was a country boy from South Carolina. I
didn't finish college. Don't tell me what can't
be done in this country!

Well, I was twenty-two years old in 1932, and I had a
Model-A Ford that was four years old. I had a few dollars in
my pocket and I was ready, like most young fellows my age,
to take on the world. But the world, I found out, wasn't
ready for me. We were in the midst of the worst depression
in our history and I kept looking for a job, but I got nothing.
I advertised and I wrote letters. I wrote two hundred letters,
and the only answer I got was "Sorry." When you are
twenty-two and ambitious, you want to get going, get climbing. Finding out that nobody wants you, nobody needs you,
can turn the world into a frightening place. Even now, I
remember that feeling.

I wasn't afraid in the same way that the Depression made

so many afraid; those in the long, dismal bread lines, the Salvation Army soup kitchens, the ragged, defeated men that moved in waves with each passing freight train, looking for any job in exchange for a meal at the back door. I had a place to stay and I could have found *some* kind of job, but that didn't satisfy me. I wanted a particular kind: I wanted to sell.

My love of selling came to me early, from the best salesman I ever knew. You might call him a drummer, but a drummer in the grand fashion. He was my dad, and he sold in a time when a salesman knew his territory better than he knew his home town. He knew every hotel desk clerk by his first name and usually had a favorite room in each hotel. Often, he carried the news ahead of the newspaper, and he was as welcome a sight as the mailman. I can still see him sitting on the front porch of a South Carolina farmhouse on one of those hot, dusty afternoons, in his galluses with his shirtsleeves rolled up and his tie loose, drinking lemonade, and gradually, always gradually, working around to his favorite topic, the advantage of horsepower over horses. He sold heavy farm machinery in a time when the horse was still holding its own, and he did it with finesse and ease; he did it softly and with care; and it was a pleasure to watch him sell, because most of all he did it well.

He was selling something else, too; he was selling the farmers of the South the idea that they had to pull the crown off King Cotton's head and plant other crops, to diversify their crops and save their land. He was one of the first to preach this gospel, and he preached it wherever he went: the South had to rid itself of its cross of cotton. I suppose there is something of the preacher in every salesman, his fervor and his enthusiasm, and one reason my father was such a salesman was that he was the most enthusiastic person I ever knew, and what he was selling was always the best.

I learned three things about salesmanship from watching my dad sell: The salesman must know his product well. He must have faith in it. He must have a kind of self-confidence, unobtrusive but sincere, that makes other people feel his faith. It is forty years since my father was drumming through South Carolina, spreading the gospel of mechanization and diversification, but selling has not changed much since then. It still takes brains; it takes looking ahead, energy, a real love of selling, and, most of all, it takes enthusiasm. A lot of young men have energy and a good many have brains, but I can thank my father for the enthusiasm he instilled in me to sell. I guess that was why, during the Depression, when any job was worth having, I kept on looking for a selling job.

Yet, late in the summer of 1932, when I finally got my break, I almost missed it. I had heard that The Barrett Potato Chip Company of Atlanta was looking for a route salesman and I went in and talked with them. But I couldn't see any future in potato chips and food snacks, and I walked out. I wanted to be a salesman, all right, but the idea of driving a truck from store to store selling potato chips wasn't my idea of a job. It just wasn't "good enough" for me.

After a week, and I hadn't found anything to do, I went back to see the Barrett Company again. The job was gone, of course, but they said that they would take me on as an extra salesman, a kind of helper. So I worked at it, and I worked at it hard, selling and making deliveries, and I liked it. I found out that you can like just about any job, if you work at it. It's when you loaf and slouch that you begin beefing about the job being no darn good.

The Barrett Company had a small branch office in Nashville, Tennessee, and things weren't going so well there. They needed a man who had an automobile, and, hearing about my Model-A, they called me in and offered me the distributorship in Nashville. I would get a weekly allotment of potato chips and a weekly cash allowance. There was no salary, just the advance against whatever commissions I earned on sales. The territory would be in northern Tennessee and southern Kentucky, including the city of Nashville, and I jumped at the independence it offered, the chance to get started on my own.

In Nashville, I lived with my aunt, where my sister had

lived since our mother's death. My income was $100 a month—$23.08 a week—which wasn't much, even during a depression, particularly since out of it I had to pay my automobile and travel expenses. Living with my aunt and giving her just a little enabled me to get by.

Inexperienced, confident, paying little attention to details and seldom stopping to find out where I stood, I thought I was doing fine—and this is part of what I mean about having so much to learn in business. You take things for granted when you first start out and you live day by day. You don't think to look into the corners or behind things and see what is really going on. For instance, I didn't look around in our warehouse.

I found out that you can like just about any job, if you work at it. It's when you loaf and slouch that you begin beefing about the job being no darn good.

The warehouse where we stored the potato chips—for which I was responsible—was on a street in Nashville called Produce Row, where the farmers brought fresh vegetables and fruit. The warehouse, old and poorly lighted, was across the street from the city dump, where there were rats by the thousands. Whenever they wanted a tidbit, they sauntered over and went to work on my potato chips. I knew they were doing it, because sometimes I would glimpse them, gray shadows disappearing, and I could hear the ripping of the paper bags and the chips snapping. But it didn't bother me too much. Rats! They couldn't eat a lot. Then one day the company told me to take an inventory. And I found out! I learned just what my loss had been to those rats.

At the same time, I discovered that the company had made an honest error in billing me, a small error, but on my income nearly disastrous. I can still remember the night I sat down and painfully prepared a report to the company on the shortages, both from the rats and the error. The next morning, discouraged and miserable, I set out on my hundred-and-fifty-mile swing, doubting if I could ever land enough business to offset my losses.

My customers were roadstands, grocery stores, filling stations, soda shops, and anywhere else that sold potato chips—or might sell them—even schools and hospitals. It was common to work on until late at night, sometimes making the last call well past midnight. Usually, I worked the retail grocers during the day, then caught the drug stores in the early evening, and finished up at roadstands and restaurants after everything else had closed.

To make the swing of one hundred and fifty miles usually took a day and a half or two days, and in December, in northern Tennessee and in Kentucky, it could be cold. Car heaters weren't what they are today and I would drape a blanket over my legs as I drove. The roads snaked around hills, the double-s curves following each other, and the last fifty miles from Clarksville to Nashville always seemed the longest. On cold nights, the closer I got to home the heavier my foot got, and frequently I took those curves at high speed in the gray hours before dawn.

So it was that I was ripping up the highway from Clarksville well past midnight one cold December night. There had been a drizzle earlier in the evening, but now the stars were out and I hunched over the wheel. At one curve, the road cut through an old-fashioned covered bridge. I had been through there many times before and I started into the curve; then I touched my brakes, but they didn't hold. The road was covered with ice. I roared into that bridge and tore out two-by-fours for half its length, until the car hit a steel beam and spun around.

When I came to, I was staring out over the hood at a cold, black night. I could hear the river swishing quietly past the bridge pilings down below. The car was balanced on the edge of the bridge, its rear wheels out in space. I crawled out as carefully as I could and sat down on the bridge, my head roaring. How long I sat there, shivering against the wind, I don't know. Finally, though, a man came along and took me into town. The next morning I got a wrecker and we went out and towed my car back to Clarksville.

Many a person has been in an automobile wreck and there would be no point in my telling about this one except for what I learned from it about business. Taking care of a business when everything is running smoothly is nothing to be proud of. It's when trouble comes that you find out whether you're a businessman or not. In business you have got to be ready for *anything*. It's as if you were boxing a man and doing all right, when suddenly, and from nowhere you ever expected or even heard of, here comes a *third* fist to knock you out. That's the way it is in business, and if you can't take care of the unexpected, if you don't have some reserve and quick adaptability, you can get knocked flat.

What kind of thing am I talking about? I don't know. It might be anything. A fire. A flood. A mechanical failure. The death of a partner. An error in addition. An incorrect estimate. A lawsuit. It can be your fault, as it was my short-sightedness about the inventory, or it can be one of those things that just happen. But whatever it is, it can put you out of business in a hurry if you aren't prepared to meet it and keep going.

In business you have got to be ready for *any-thing*. It's as if you were boxing a man and doing all right, when suddenly, and from nowhere you ever expected or even heard of, here comes a *third* fist to knock you out.

Mine? Rats and a slick road. Two days later, I was back in Nashville with the threat of bankruptcy facing me. The damage to the car and the loss to the rats totaled $165. With my income and my thin margin of profit, it might as well have been a million. It meant the difference between my being in business or being bankrupt and out of a job.

> I had to watch out, too, for every penny I spent, for a meal, for anything. I learned that a man can live on next to nothing if he has to.

I told the Barrett Company that I was getting the territory started, and I told them of my losses and my problems. If they turned me out, they would have to close the territory and lose everything or start a new man and lose money until he learned our customers and the route. I asked them to lend me enough to take care of me and my losses. They saw that I had learned something, was a better businessman for it, and they let me have the money to cover my inventory and the damages to the car. I was to pay it back at $4 a week.

So I started out again, this time with a weekly allowance of $19.08. I was making less money, but I was traveling with what I had learned. My carelessness about the inventory, about the slick road had taught me something. From now on, I was watching out for a third fist. I had to watch out, too, for every penny I spent, for a meal, for anything. I learned that a man can live on next to nothing if he has to.

For the next six months it was get out and go, meet my customers, talk, sell, hand over the merchandise, and go again. I was in debt, and in some ways I was in trouble—the left door of my automobile had been so smashed in the wreck that it wouldn't fit and I had to throw it away and drive with a chain across the opening—but I had a job and a territory of my own. I kept telling myself that it was *my* territory and *my* business. This sense of independence kept me working. Out in the morning and on the road, all day, half the night, sleep where I was, and go again.

That was the way it was, and the way it kept on being

until, at the end of the year, my territory had expanded and my profits were climbing. Nothing big, but they were going up. Then, one day I realized that I was doing all the business I could by myself, but there was still more business to be had in the territory. Slowly, almost frightening me, came the idea that I needed a helper. However, I had learned some lessons and I checked into everything, finding out and testing every fact until I finally decided that I really did need a man, a salesman. It wasn't so very long before I needed still another man, this one a warehouseman who doubled as a book-keeper.

Things were breaking for me and my luck was good. There is always a bit of what we call "luck" in any business venture, I suppose. Sometimes there can be a stroke of such blind luck that a man is suddenly made rich or suddenly boosted far along toward success. But let me suggest something to you, and suggest it as strong as I can: don't you put a penny's faith in luck. It will trick you. You may have a bar-relful of luck tomorrow. If so—fine. But don't expect it, and, most of all, don't sit around waiting for it.

Actually, when it comes down to the long record and the hard facts, *you* are your own luck. What we ordinarily call luck may really be a bit of chance, all right, really something unprepared for and unexpected, but usually there is more to it than that. I think that it is partly *intuition*, which is a kind of thinking that goes on when we aren't aware of it, when we aren't consciously working at our thinking. I believe, too, that it is a sense of *timeliness* that you develop and that tells you *when* to make your move. A person may say that the man who opened a new territory last year, established a market for his product, and caught the crest of the sales was "lucky." The man who waited a year and had to take what was left was "unlucky." I don't believe a word of that.

A man makes his success by the decisions that he himself makes and by when he makes them. I was fortunate in going to work for Barrett; but before I did, I had to decide to go back there and ask them for a job, then decide to take the one they gave me. It was a break for me that they offered me the distributor's job in Nashville, but I had to decide to take it. It was another break that they lent me the money when I was in trouble, but don't forget that I had to decide how to present my case to them and convince them. There is always "luck," if you want to call it that, and always a lot of "if's"; but in the end, whether or not you succeed and get where you want to go will depend on the decisions that *you* make. There will be many little decisions and there will be big ones, and it is your average on how you decide, right or wrong, that will determine whether you go up or down. In the long run, in the final judgment of you and your business, this factor of chance will have mighty little to do with it. You can bet your last nickel that there is no "lucky" way, no short, slick, fast-buck way to *permanent* success in business. . . .

You may have a barrelful of luck tomorrow. If so—fine. But don't expect it, and, most of all, don't sit around waiting for it.

The business prospered, even in the Depression, and I hired my first two men. Before long, I added others until, by 1935, there were seven of us.

I also added new products. One was prepackaged popcorn, which we introduced into the South. A short time later, we went into the peanut-butter sandwich business. The snack industry was building up, and buying habits were changing fast. Packaged food snacks were on the counters, close at hand and easy to pick up, at many food stores, drug counters, filling stations, and lunchstands, and, what's more, people were buying them.

Our chief line, though, continued to be potato chips, and I thought we were doing fine until, in 1938, I went to a food distribution convention in Cleveland. There I saw new plants where potato chips were being manufactured in a new way, and there I learned another lesson, or rather had an old lesson confirmed, one that no one can ever learn too well or be told too often — in business, if you aren't on the alert all the time, somebody will come along and get ahead of you. He will make a better product, make it cheaper, cut a fraction off selling cost, develop a fraction faster distribution, figure a fraction onto profits. In business, it is constant and endless competition all the way, the toughest kind, and if you aren't on the lookout and quick to advance, your competition will pass you and leave you back there somewhere, wondering what happened to you and your business and how long you can hold on.

When the potato chip was first produced, it was a fairly uncomplicated item. Today, it is very complicated in its method of production.

The story of the potato chip is said to have begun with an Indian chief at the Moon Lake House in the resort town of Saratoga Springs, New York, in 1853. His name was Chief George Crum, and history is a little fuzzy about whether he was a real chief or just boasting a bit. At any rate, he was the chef at the hotel, and one evening he was having a hard time quieting one of the leading guests. This gentleman had just returned from Paris, where his palate had been titillated with Parisian dishes, and he was sending back plate after plate of French fries on the grounds that they were soggy and unfit to eat.

Finally, Chief Crum, angry and fed up with this paleface and his snooty palate, sliced a potato into paper-thin slices, threw them into a kettle of boiling fat, sprinkled them with salt, and served them to an absolutely delighted guest. So the potato chip was born! Before the summer was out, "Saratoga Chips" were a regular part of the menu at Moon Lake House, and were being widely introduced elsewhere.

Basically, this method of preparing potato chips continued from its beginning, in 1853, until well into this century. Then, in 1938, in Cleveland, I saw a method that made me know that the old way was done for. A company could no longer succeed if it followed the original way of cooking up a large batch of chips in vegetable oil, packaging them, and cooking up another batch. With the new machinery, the chips were produced in a continuous production line. It was either get into the business in this way or be forced out.

A decision had to be made and my associates and I made it quickly; we would install this new method of manufacturing. We were figuring on how to do it, how to get it started, when I received an offer that was totally unexpected. Sometime before this I had left the Barrett Company, and I was completely surprised when a representative of that firm came to see me and offered me the opportunity to buy the Atlanta and Memphis plants of the company.

"How much cash will it take?" I asked.

"Sixty to a hundred thousand dollars . . ."

"I'll give you my answer tomorrow."

It might as well have been sixty million, but I was being offered my "luck." I made my decision and hurried to the bank, hardly expecting anyone really to listen to me, but I told one of the officers of my opportunity.

"Let them know you are interested," he said.

The bank, however, told me that we must have additional equity capital. I had long before decided never to ask anyone to put money into my company, and I didn't then, and I never have; but the key employees in the company set out to raise what funds they could. Some of my friends and business associates also wanted to participate. The officer of the bank I had talked to became an investor. So did my life-insurance broker, my casualty-insurance broker, the operator of the filling station across the street.

In a month, we raised what we had set out to raise: $5,000 for working capital. The bank lent us $30,000. The Barretts took the remainder in preferred stock. October 2, 1939, the old sign came down and the new one went up: H. W. Lay & Company.

Now I would lie awake at night wondering about the decisions I had made that day, some of them fast, some with

447

a lot of money riding on them. Were they right? Almost immediately we needed additional capital to build a new plant for the continuous-manufacturing process. We made the decision and old and new friends came in, investing in the company; and we built the plant. What next? Where did we stop? Where did we slow down? In business, do you ever stop? Ever slow down?

A man remembers his family and he should remember his health. He takes into account his civic, charitable, and church obligations. But always in his mind is his business, with its endless responsibilities. In his planning and decision-making, his responsibilities extend to the people who work in the plant, to his stockholders, and to his executive associates who helped him start the company and helped him build it. Lying awake is no figure of speech, and that is what you will do if you start a company of your own and make it grow. But be sure and understand this: it isn't all lying awake, wondering a lot and worrying some. There is satisfaction in seeing your company grow and knowing that you are a part of its growth; in seeing the men who have trusted you get the job advancement and the salary increase that they want and have earned. There is a great satisfaction, too, in seeing your stockholders receive the dividends they deserve. It isn't all work and worry in business, not by a long shot; there is pleasure and often there is a great and enduring sense of fulfillment.

Let me give you one touch of advice: put your faith in your company. Give it everything you've got: your thought, your time, your work. And don't be trying to get too much out of it, or even bits out of it, for yourself. The head of a company who is always searching for angles and gimmicks to enrich himself does not always gain permanently what he may seem to profit at the moment. Build your company, and its growth will pay you back. But, you say, you see a way of making ten thousand this year on a quick private deal for yourself. Forget it! Five years from now it may make a million for your company. The company comes before you do, even if you own every share of stock and have total control. Make the welfare of your business your objective, and it will take care of you.

In our company, after we were well started, we kept on with our planning and our figuring. Year after year we kept asking: what next? During the 1950's, we had continued to join with other companies, either through acquisition or merger, in order to increase our operating area and our product line. Then, early in 1961, we began to see what seemed to be next; a merger was concluded with Red Dot Foods, Inc., a Midwestern snack food business. Simultaneously, the business of the Rold Gold Pretzel Company of St. Louis and Los Angeles was purchased. Overnight, our business was almost fifty per cent larger and our area of operations was materially increased. We were growing fast, but we were mindful of advice given us by our elders a long time ago: "It is not how big or how fast you grow but how soundly." It turned out, I am glad to say, that our expansion programs were soundly conceived in the best interests of our customers, our employees, and our stockholders.

Lying awake is no figure of speech, and that is what you will do if you start a company of your own and make it grow.

Then, finally, late in 1961, we began discussing a merger with another company, the Frito Company of Dallas, Texas. Such a merger would open up vast new areas for our potato chips, and we began talking about a time—we can already envision it—when our potato chips and corn chips will be sold anywhere in the world where there are people to buy them.

This talk of the world, of the whole earth, sounds ambitious—and it is. But the earth is no more impossible now than were Middle Tennessee and Southern Kentucky back in the days when a young fellow could stake his future on a slice of potato or a sack of popcorn or a jar of peanut butter, and any of these could open the door of a new world to him.

Since there were benefits for both companies, the decision for the merger was made. Twenty-five years after H. W. Lay & Company was formed, we joined, in 1961, with the Frito Company (which, incidentally, was founded some thirty years ago on $100 borrowed capital), and we are now Frito-Lay, Inc.

This merger was a big decision for us to make, but every company is continually faced with such decisions, some of them so important that they shape the whole future of the company. Of the innumerable decisions we have had to make, some five or six have been turning points. One was the decision to purchase the Barrett plants in Atlanta and Memphis. A second was the decision to build our own plant, and manufacture chips with the continuous process. A third was to buy another plant in Jacksonville, Florida, paying the creditors 50¢ on a dollar on a nearly bankrupt business, then to come back later, when there was no legal claim on us, and pay the full amount.

Another decision was the renting of an old barn in Greensboro, North Carolina, shortly after World War II, and opening up the whole territory of the Carolinas to our chips. Still another resulted in the building of our present plant in Atlanta. We had been scattered over the city in seven plants, and we needed a great, modern, central plant. How could we build it? How could we finance it? Well, we did finance it, and we went on from there to build our business beyond the dreams that even we, young men and hopeful, would have dared to dream ten years before.

Luck? Call it luck, if you like; but any time you are looking around for your luck in business, be sure also to think and plan and work—and make your decisions with all your intuition and all your care, and make them at the right time.

So what lies ahead for us? For you? For me? It is my most honest belief that there is more ahead for us, for anybody in American business, than at any time in our history. I say this, knowing about the days when they built the railroads across the continent and sent airplanes into the sky. Well, today we are shuttling the oceans as if we were crossing the street, and we are having a closer and closer look at the moon.

Size is nothing but time. Any business is likely to be small in the beginning. Whether it grows with the years depends on how much *you* grow.

This, today, is the earth where we live, and this is the space into which we are moving. Where do you want to build your business? Go ahead. Help yourself.

We are all looking ahead and planning, these days. My old company is now a part of a new company, and I am planning a new business, learning to work with new friends, and beginning to live a new business life. I am the chief executive officer of Frito-Lay, Inc., made up of the two old companies, and their combined income for the 1962 fiscal year was in excess of $145,000,000. This is a tremendous responsibility, but there is a tremendous future for the new company, and for me.

There is a future, too, equally as important for you, in whatever company you may be starting, even if its plant is in one room, and its income is the few hundred dollars you borrow to get going. Don't let this make any difference to you. Size is nothing but time. Any business is likely to be small in the beginning. Whether it grows with the years depends on how much *you* grow. Don't be impatient. Just work like blazes today, keep looking at tomorrow, and figuring on next week.

1963

More than 20 years after its founding, Ben & Jerry's is still going strong. As recently as 1992, a new ice cream flavor, Chocolate Chip Cookie Dough, was named one of *Fortune* magazine's "Products of the Year." It's been a long and strange trip for two Long Island kids who met in gym class and became fast friends when they realized they shared a joy for eating, not athletics. In 1969, they went their separate ways to college. Ben became a potter and Jerry tried to get into medical school, but failed.

Finally, in 1977, they reunited with a plan to start their own business—and that's when the trip started for the self-described hippies. It took a turn toward the strange when they discovered that Häagen-Dazs was trying to get distributors to not carry Ben & Jerry's. Therefore, in 1984, the duo began an antitrust campaign against Häagen-Dazs and its parent company Pillsbury. The slogan for their fight, "What's the Doughboy afraid of?" was named after the lovable Pillsbury Doughboy. In another adventure, Ben & Jerry were cowinners of the 1988 National Small Business Person of the Year award, presented to them by President Ronald Reagan himself. Ironically, the company was about to introduce their Peace Pops, part of their campaign against Reagan's military arms buildup. From early on, both Ben and Jerry wanted their company to be a "values-led business."

As they wrote in their book, *Double-Dip,* "When we started making ice cream in 1978 we had simple goals. We wanted to have fun, we wanted to earn a living, and we wanted to give something back to the community." That giving back became incorporated into their management style. Take their marketing philosophy: "Values-led marketing . . . promotes products and brands by integrating social benefits into many different aspects of a business enterprise." Thus, Peace Pops, among other products, tied to environmentally conscious programs. Their style has proved profitable, often generating tons of free publicity. In the following selection, they walk through their decision process in deciding to enter the ice cream business and what it takes to start from scratch, namely, eating a lot of saltine crackers and canned sardines.

Bagels, Ice Cream, or . . . Pizza?
Ben Cohen and Jerry Greenfield

Since the day we met in seventh-grade gym class at Merrick Avenue Junior High, we knew ours was a friendship made in Husky Heaven. We were the two slowest, fattest kids in the class. On the day we met we were lagging far behind the pack of runners on the school track. The coach yelled, "If you can't do the mile in under seven minutes, you're gonna have to do it again." Ben said, "But, Coach, if we can't do the mile in under seven minutes the first time, how are we gonna do it in under seven minutes the second time?"

All through junior high and high school we hung out — eating lunch together, sharing those one-calorie candies Jerry's mom used to stuff into his lunch box. (Attempting to lose weight by subsisting on those candies alone, Jerry keeled over at school one day.) During the summer we drove around in our parents' cars and worked for Ben's father, sorting direct mail by zip code. In our senior year Ben made what turned out to be a seminal career decision: he got a job driving an ice cream vending truck. The pitter-patter of little feet chasing the truck down the street, the happiness that lit up the children's faces when they took their first lick of an ice cream bar made a deep and lasting impression.

Like a lot of middle-class eighteen-year-old guys of our

generation, we assumed we'd go to college—partly because it was the best way to avoid the military draft, and also to get out on our own. It was the sixties, a time when an unusually large number of young people were exploring and trying to find themselves. Jerry applied to several schools but was accepted only by Oberlin. Ben applied to just one college, Colgate University, because the brochure said it had fireplaces in the dorms. Surprisingly, Colgate accepted him. In the fall of 1969 we said our farewells, promised to stay in touch, and went our separate ways.

After several failed attempts at various universities to impersonate a serious student, Ben decided to devote himself to becoming a potter. He dropped out of college in 1972, moved to the East Village, in Manhattan, and soon proved himself unredeemably unemployable. He'd taken a series of "McJobs" to support his pottery apprenticeship—as a baker's helper, a short-order cook, a Yellow Pages deliveryperson, a garbageman, a hospital admissions clerk, and a night mopper, among other short-lived vocations. To qualify for one job Ben had to take a Minnesota Multiphasic Personality Inventory test, which labelled him as having "unresolved conflicts with authority." This came as no surprise to those who knew and loved him.

In 1974, in search of greener pastures, Ben found the one meaningful job he'd ever had (and kept): as a crafts teacher at a residential school for troubled teenagers, in the Adirondacks. The school's director, staff, and philosophy were as nontraditional and unstructured as Ben himself, and Ben was a big hit with the students and teachers. But then, in 1976, the school was shut down. Ben tried to make a living as a potter, failed, and was unemployed once again. Fully aware of his limitations as an employee, Ben started thinking about opening a business. He called Jerry and asked him to come back, to upstate New York and think about it with him.

The timing couldn't have been better. Having been rejected by every medical school he'd applied to for the second year in a row, Jerry had just given up on his plan to become a doctor. After graduating from Oberlin, Jerry had moved to Manhattan, where he worked as a lab technician. There he and Ben made a happy home with their dog, Malcolm. Two years later Jerry left for Chapel Hill, North Carolina, to live with his girlfriend (and future wife), Elizabeth. He got a job as a lab assistant at UNC Hospital, where he was assigned the task of chopping off rats' heads. The job was a bit unappealing, so when Elizabeth broke up with him Jerry found himself fresh out of reasons to stay in North Carolina. He packed his belongings and headed to New York to see what Ben had in mind.

What Ben had in mind was finding a way for us to work together without having to work for someone else. A way for us to have a good time. And we shared a fantasy about earning $20,000 a year, which in those days seemed like a lot of money to us.

Bagels, Ice Cream, or . . . Pizza?

One day in 1977 we found ourselves sitting on the front steps of Jerry's parents' house in Merrick, Long Island, talking about what kind of business to go into. Since eating was our greatest passion, it seemed logical to start a restaurant. Some people in that industry had told us that most restaurants fail, even more often than most small businesses, but the ones that are most likely to succeed are those with limited menus. So we were sitting there talking about fondue. Talking about crepes. Talking about kebobs. And then somehow we got focused on bagels or ice cream.

We wanted to pick a product that was becoming popular in big cities and move it to a rural college town, because we wanted to live in that kind of environment. We wanted to have a lot of interaction with our customers and enjoy ourselves. And, of course, we wanted a product that we liked to eat.

First we thought about bagels. We had this idea: UBS—United Bagel Service. We were going to deliver bagels, lox, cream cheese, and the *New York Times* to people's doors in the morning.

Since eating was our greatest passion, it seemed logical to start a restaurant.

We stopped in at G&G Equipment, a used-restaurant-supply joint in Albany, New York, and priced used bagel-making equipment. We were talking to the owner, Lou G&G (as he came to be known). He drove a big Cadillac and smoked a big cigar. Lou kept saying, "You gotta have this. You gotta have this. If you're gonna make a real New York bagel, you gotta have that." The equipment came to $40,000.

That was more money than we thought we could ever get. We figured ice cream had to be cheaper. What do you need to make ice cream? An oversized homemade-ice-cream machine—how could that cost $40,000? We found an ad for a $5 ice-cream-making correspondence course offered through Penn State. Due to extreme poverty, we decided to split one course between us, sent in our five bucks, read the material they sent back, and passed the open-book tests with flying colors. That settled it. We were going into the ice cream business.

Ben: I used to have regrets because the ingredients in our products are so expensive. I mean, bagels! Flour and water, that's it.

Jerry: But bagels go stale really fast. Think about it, Ben. Ice cream—you freeze it and it lasts forever.

Ben: Pizza. That's gotta be a good one. Did you ever see a pizza place go out of business?

Jerry: I'm convinced we would have made a great bagel.

We would have made a great pizza. It might not
have turned into what Ben & Jerry's has turned
into, but it would have been great, because we put
our hearts and souls into it.

Ben: We'd have a lot more room for social-action messages on a pizza box than we have on pint containers. Think about *that*, Jer. We could print the
whole Bill of Rights on the side of a pizza box.

Jerry: I think we're doing okay for now with ice cream,
Ben.

Once we'd decided on an ice cream parlor, the next step
was deciding where to put it. We knew college students eat a
lot of ice cream; we knew they eat more of it in warm weather.
Determined to make an informed decision (but lacking in
technological and financial resources), we developed our
own low-budget "manual cross-correlation analysis." Ben sat
at the kitchen table, leafing through a U.S. almanac to
research towns that had the highest average temperatures.
Jerry sat on the floor, reading a guide to American colleges,
searching for the rural towns that had the most college kids.
Then we merged our lists. When we investigated the towns
that came up we discovered that apparently someone had
already done this work ahead of us. All the warm towns that
had a decent number of college kids already had homemade-
ice-cream parlors. So we threw out the temperature criterion
and ended up in Burlington, Vermont. Burlington had a
young population, a significant college population, and virtually no competition. Later we realized the *reason* there was no
competition: it's so cold in Burlington for so much of the year,
and the summer season is so short, it was obvious (to everyone except us) that there was no way an ice cream parlor
could succeed there. Or so it seemed.

We found an abandoned gas station in downtown
Burlington. It was only a block from Church Street, the
main shopping street, right across from a park. Plus, there
was some parking where the gas pumps used to be.

We had a few other potential locations, so before we made our final decision we bought a couple of little clicker-counters. We went from one location to the next, clicking and counting as people walked by. After we'd checked out all our other options, we stood outside the gas station for a couple of hours. "Seems like a lot of foot traffic to me, Ben." "Seems like a lot of foot traffic to me, Jerry." We headed off to rent the place.

Starting Up Is Hard to Do

So there we were in the winter of '77, fixing up this broken-down gas station, trying out all these recipes for ice cream and crepes, renting somebody's summer house on Lake Champlain. . . .

Talk about living hand-to-mouth. We were eating saltine crackers and sardines from Woolworth's—three boxes for a dollar, three cans for a dollar, respectively. There was no heat in the gas station, so it was just as cold at work as it was at home. When we took the place over, there was a three-inch sheet of ice on the floor because the roof had failed. While we were working—and we were pretty much always working—we'd take breaks at the bus station down the street to go to the bathroom and warm up.

After months of frantic renovating, just before the grand opening, we gave the gas station its final touch: a fresh coat of orange paint on the walls and ceiling. Ben picked the color. The job took several people all day and night to finish. It came out looking like Grossman's Lumber. Gross. Garish. Not the warm peach color Ben had in mind.

Jerry: As soon as we finished painting, Ben stepped back and said we had to paint it again, a different color.

Ben: The gas station had very high ceilings, which were very difficult to paint.

Jerry: This was before we'd even opened, and already he'd changed his mind. That's one thing about Ben that drives people crazy: he's often said he needs to make a mistake first in order to make the right decision.

Ben: It was a bad decision to paint it that color orange the first time. But it was a good decision to change it.

Jerry: So it goes.

During those first few months there were really fun times, really bad times, really exciting times—not many relaxing times. Occasionally we made inedible batches of ice cream. We could afford to hire waitpersons only for the busiest times, so our customers had to stand in long lines at the counter. Even when there were waitpeople working, there were really long lines. Actually, we had no idea what we were doing. We had to fire people, the job we both detested most, for scooping too slowly or scooping overly large portions. We were paying ourselves $150 a week and working our tails off. Every piece of machinery we owned was breaking down, one after the other. Our checkbook was always empty, and our bills were piling up.

Still, we were having a great time. We were totally engaged in what we were doing. It was clear people loved our ice cream, and that felt really good. We weren't thinking about the future; we were just getting from one day to the next.

Of course, it helped that we shared this big delusion. We had thought there were maybe twenty things we didn't know how to do. Obviously, as soon as we figured out how to do them, we'd get out from under all these problems. Then things would run smoothly. The business would run itself. After about three years, however, we realized we'd been kidding ourselves—the business was never going to run itself. It was quite a disheartening revelation.

Good Vibes, Good Business

During our first summer we were averaging about $650 a day in sales. We were still making all our ice cream in the four-and-a-half-gallon freezer; when we ran out we'd hang our international No Ice Cream sign (an ice cream cone inside a red circle with a slash through it) in the window. But even when we were sold out of ice cream, people still came into the shop. They drank the fresh-squeezed lemonade. They listened to Don Rose, a guy who would pound out his own ragtime tunes on our old piano in exchange for fresh-squeezed orange juice. Or they came in just to hang out.

Right from the beginning, even though the business wasn't making any money and we weren't making any money, we were always thinking up new excuses to give away ice cream. When we opened the gas station we had our Grand Opening Special: buy one, get one free. Then we started giving away cones at random to people waiting on the ice cream line. Then we had free cones for all mothers on Mother's Day. Visibly expectant mothers got two. To promote winter sales, we held the Penny Off per Celsius Degree Below Zero Winter Extravaganza (affectionately known as POPCDBZWE), thereby turning a liability (being located in a very cold winter town) into an asset.

After about three years, however, we realized we'd been kidding ourselves—the business was never going to run itself. It was quite a disheartening revelation.

At the end of the summer we threw a Fall Down Festival for the people of Burlington. There, Jerry finally got to make use of his college education. He had actually gotten a credit at Oberlin for taking a course entitled "Carnival Technique" from Bill Irwin, one of the foremost new vaudeville performers. Jerry would appear on the stage in his pith helmet while his partner—who assumed for the occasion his alter identity, that of noted mystic Habeeni Ben Coheeni—was carried out sitting on a platform, clothed only in a bedsheet, chanting himself into a metabolic trance. At the proper moment Coheeni, rigid as a board, would fall backward into a supine position. His dedicated followers would suspend him by his head and feet upon two properly spaced chairs. Then, with great dramatic flair, Jerry would place a real cinder block on Coheeni's bare stomach, raise a real sledgehammer high above his head, and bring it crashing down, smashing the cinder block into many real pieces. His incoherent chanting interrupted only by his periodic trance states, Coheeni would arise from amidst the rubble, tossing flower petals into the delighted, cheering crowd.

We'd always promised ourselves that if the business made it through its first year, we'd celebrate by giving away ice cream. So on our first anniversary, May 5, 1979, we started a ritual that's still with us today: Free Cone Day. On Free Cone Day every year, all Ben & Jerry's franchisees give away ice cream at their shops all day. All the scoopers come in; everybody works together. The line goes really fast because there's no money being exchanged. Last year on Free Cone Day the scoop shops gave away 358,850 cones. (You can get on line as many times as you want.)

That's one of the beauties of ice cream. We're not giving away cars. It's a comparatively inexpensive thing. There are disadvantages to ice cream, too: it doesn't have a very high ticket price. Our average sale is rather low. So why not take advantage of the good aspects? Who wants to have an ice cream parlor if you can't give away free ice cream every now and then? As we said on the flyer telling people about the first Free Cone Day:

"If it's not fun, why do it?" (Jerry).

And, "Business has a responsibility to give back to the community from which it draws its support" (Ben).

In the gas station, people used to come to the counter to order ice cream cones and we'd say, "How can we serve you better?" We really wanted to know.

In the early days our major "marketing campaign" consisted of putting stacks of Ben & Jerry's bumper stickers on the counters in the store. Much to our surprise, a large percentage of people in Burlington started putting these bumper stickers on their cars. There wasn't any contest. There wasn't anything to gain. People didn't get any prizes for driving around with our bumper sticker. People were responding to a great product, genuine customer service, and genuine caring. . . .

Ice Cream for the People

We learned a lot, most of it the hard way. Being a small business, we had no human resources department and no human resources expertise, so we did a thoroughly amateur job of hiring and firing—perfecting our dysfunctional behaviors which persist to this day. . . . And then there was our famous pricing epiphany. We were working our hearts out for the first two or three years, and every year we just barely broke even. The first year we were thrilled to break even. We'd made our overhead; we could see the light at the end of the tunnel.

Then the next year came and we'd just broken even again, even though our sales had grown by $50,000. This went on for three years. Each year we would break even and say we needed only to do a little more business to make a profit. Then the next year we'd do a lot more business and still only break even. One day we were talking to Ben's dad, who was an accountant. He said, "Since you're gonna make such a high-quality product instead of pumping it full of air, why don't you raise your prices?"

At the time we were charging fifty-two cents a cone. Coming out of the sixties, our reason for going into business was that ours was going to be "ice cream for the people." It was going to be great quality products for everybody—not some elitist treat. We aren't just *selling* to people. We *are* the people! Ice cream for the people!

We learned a lot, most of it the hard way. Being a small business, we had no human resources department and no human resources expertise, so we did a thoroughly amateur job of hiring and firing.

Ben said, "But, Dad, the reason we're not making money is because we're not doing the job right. We're overscooping. We're wasting ice cream. Our labor costs are too high—we're not doing a good job of scheduling our employees. We're not running our business efficiently. Why should the customer have to pay for our mistakes? That's why everything costs twice as much as it should."

And Mr. Cohen said, "You guys have to understand—that's human. That's as good as people do. You can't price for doing everything exactly right. Raise your prices."

Eventually we said, either we're going to raise our prices or we're going to go out of business. And then where will the people's ice cream be? They'll have to get their ice cream from somebody else. So we raised the prices. And we stayed in business.

1997

Joseph Wilson was one of those extraordinary visionaries who joined a relatively small family company and built it into an industrial giant—the name, Xerox. He was an intellect who enjoyed classic literature as well as high technology. His favorite poem was Robert Frost's "The Road not Taken," and he could quote Montaigne, the great essayist; in particular, Wilson was fond of "Fortis imaginato generat casum" ("A strong imagination begets the event"). After attending the University of Rochester and Harvard for an MBA, he was convinced by his father to join the family company, Haloid, a photographic paper manufacturer, which he did in 1945. That same year he became president.

Wilson realized that for the company to survive, they would need to diversify into new products, so he ordered his research chief to keep abreast of any interesting inventions or patents. In 1945, he did indeed run across something unique—electrophotography, or xerography, an invention by an attorney, Chester Carlson, who figured out how to adhere ink to paper using electrical charges. In 1947, they acquired the necessary patent, but it would be years and some $15 million on research and development before a practical machine hit the market. Although even in the late 1950s prototypes were still reducing the paper to ashes, Wilson never lost his vision, and even loaned some of his personal funds to the company to keep it going. Finally, in 1960, the Xerox 914 arrived and made Wilson rich. To show people how easy it was to use (unlike the prior models that involved several steps and came with a fire extinguisher), the marketers had a chimpanzee trained to make it go.

The name of the company was changed from Haloid to Xerox, giving them a strong quirky name in the spirit of Kodak, their competitor in photographic paper. Wilson reflected, "I would have to be psychoanalyzed to see if I would take the same risk again. It's when you're very young and naïve that you have the courage to make the right decisions." He tells his dramatic story in *The Product Nobody Wanted,* including how he defied every management rule by not dropping the whole idea of xerography.

The Product Nobody Wanted
Joseph C. Wilson

In 1946, Xerox was a small firm known as The Haloid Co., located in Rochester, NY. There was little about Haloid to set it apart from hundreds of other small businesses at the end of World War II. It had a solid reputation in a narrow field, production of photocopy equipment and machines.

Haloid had increased its production during the war but was beginning to experience a profit squeeze. While sales rose from $1.4 million in 1936 to just under $7 million in 1946, profits did not keep pace. They hit a high of $300,000 in 1939, but drifted down to $150,000 in 1946.

Along with me, a few young men in the company saw very clearly that Haloid would have to change direction.

I am not at all sure that we knew precisely what avenues we wanted to explore. We thought ideally of finding some entirely new process or product that would revitalize our 40-year-old company.

The people responsible for the search that ultimately propelled us to the forefront of the graphic communications industry were not seeking simply a new product. All who were involved 20 years ago when The Haloid Co. made its big decision—men like Dr. John J. Dessauer, John B. Hartnett, the late Harold Kuhns, and the late Homer A. Piper—

shared a feeling that we must direct our energies toward a valuable activity—one that was worthwhile for people, not just for making money.

Today this sort of thinking remains an integral part of our business life. We seek not only to be an effective commercial enterprise, but also to establish an institution that is socially responsible and constructive.

Discovery of an Invention

It was during our search for new directions that John Dessauer ran across a potentially interesting invention. John was then and until recently our director of research. He is now vice chairman of our board, and we still seek his wise counsel. He noticed an abstract referring to an article in the July, 1944 issue of *Radio News* describing a new invention, "electrophotography."

The inventor of that process, the late Chester F. Carlson, had struggled for years despite extreme hardships. Finally he produced the first "electrophotographic" image-making plate on Oct. 22, 1938, in Astoria, Queens. Carlson coated a two-inch by three-inch zinc plate with sulfur, then charged the plate electrostatically by rubbing it with a handkerchief, and exposed it for about 10 seconds to a glass slide on which the words "10-22-38 Astoria" were written.

A dusting of lycopodium powder made the latent image visible, and by pressing a piece of wax paper against the powdered image, Carlson completed the first successful demonstration that his process could make a copy. The experiment, although rudimentary, established the feasibility of completely dry copying. It was later renamed xerography, from the Greek words xeros meaning "dry" and graphein, "to write."

Chet Carlson, with all his laboratory work, had also managed to become a patent lawyer by going to school nights. He prepared and filed his own patent application and later, with additional patent applications that were granted, refined the process somewhat. His persistent efforts to kindle a commercial interest in his invention, however, were disheartening. More than 20 major corporations could see nothing in it worth developing.

Finally in 1944, eight years after his discovery, Chet had a chance meeting with Dr. Russell Dayton of Battelle Memorial Institute in Columbus, Ohio, and the Battelle staff subsequently invited Carlson to discuss his process with them. This led to an agreement under which Battelle would develop the process in exchange for 75 per cent of any royalties from commercial sale or licensing.

Happily for Chet, as it turned out, the agreement allowed him to invest his own money in the research. Battelle ran through the initial budget for the project, and Chet was able to raise enough to continue the research, thereby increasing his royalty interest to 40 per cent.

Shortly after John Dessauer read of Chet's invention, he called my attention to the article. The more we thought about the process, the more it appealed to us. So John and I visited Battelle in 1946. We negotiated a limited agreement with the Institute that went into effect Jan. 1, 1947.

The 22 months that followed before we and Battelle unveiled the process on its tenth anniversary—Oct. 22, 1948, at the annual meeting of the Optical Society of America in Detroit—were hectic at best. Battelle conducted further research, and we at Haloid made a concerted, often frantic, effort to prepare for our own development of the process based on that research. We also made an intensive effort to raise additional money—John Dessauer even mortgaged his house.

By 1948 we recognized it would take a considerable amount of money to bring Carlson's process to market. In the six years following our first visit to Columbus, indeed, Haloid was to raise more than $3.5 million for development and exploitation of xerography, a sizable sum for us then.

We also realized our agreement with Battelle was too limiting in light of our projected investment. A young Rochester lawyer I knew, Sol M. Linowitz, agreed to renegotiate the contract for us. He was later to become our general counsel, negotiate our overseas arrangement with the Rank Organization, and become chairman of the board before leaving to become U.S. Ambassador to the Organization of American States in 1967.

The new agreement gave us an exclusive license on all xerographic developments in return for a substantial royalty arrangement.

An Unusual Pricing Scheme

In 1949 we introduced the first Xerox non-automatic copier—a similar model is still in use for special purposes—and made the critical decision to offer xerographic products for lease, giving the customer decreasing costs per copy as the number of reproductions increased. It was an unusual pricing scheme and demonstrates the beginning of our innovative sales approach.

Between 1949 and 1956, the company's sales tripled. These were years of technical growth, of developing products and market, of single-minded commitment. We had staked so much on the new process that we had to emphasize commercial success. But I am sure none of us who were caught up in the exciting development of xerography ever forgot our desire to render truly valuable service to mankind.

In 1955 we concluded a new agreement with Battelle: the old licenses and royalties were eliminated and actual title to the basic Carlson patents was transferred to Haloid. In return, Battelle received until 1965 modest cash royalties, a portion of royalties we acquired from sublicensing, and additional royalties in stock, depending on our annual revenues from xerography. Since payment in stock satisfied much of Haloid's continuing obligation to the Institute, we could use our cash and borrowing power to develop the process we believed so promising.

The company made its final payment to the Institute in 1965 (except for a modest research commitment of $25,000 a year), and by then, the total Xerox stock paid to Battelle under the agreement had a market value of more than $355 million. We have never regretted these arrangements, nor, I should guess, has Battelle.

By 1955, a number of office copiers based on technologies other than xerography had been introduced. Our respected neighbor, Eastman Kodak Co., and Minnesota Mining and Manufacturing Co., for instance, were marketing copiers.

That year Dr. Dessauer formed a committee, including Chester Carlson, to study the feasibility of building an automatic copier using our technology. The committee concluded that the machine would have to be as large as a four-drawer filing cabinet and would weigh a thousand pounds. Outside consultants hired by us predicted that those specifications — hardly anything to alarm the existing manufacturers of copiers — would sharply limit the market. But our commitment seemed too great to turn back.

The Dessauer report presented two alternatives: go ahead or go broke.

Our own people were enthusiastic. Between 1955 and 1957, when management recommended to shareholders that our name be changed to Haloid-Xerox, Inc., we had but one goal — accelerated development of this machine. It was not an easy time.

For every technical problem we solved, we encountered another for which we had no answer.

Considering our excitement about the potential of the Xerox 914 during the years preceding the introduction of it, I wonder in retrospect how we managed to keep it a secret as long as we did. From the very beginning, the major goal of our research program was the development of an automatic office copier based on Chester Carlson's process.

For reasons now lost to history, we had assigned it the code designation E 100.

In 1957 we presented our board of directors a "breadboard" version of the E 100.

Nobody Wanted It

They were interested enough to retain a well-known organization to study market feasibility. Another company that we had approached with the product ordered a similar study. And, again, the consulting firms arrived at substantially the same conclusion—the market for a machine like the E 100 was relatively limited. Another Haloid consultant was slightly more optimistic: there was promise for such a large copier within a systems application, but not as an independently functioning unit for general document copying.

It looked as if we were entering the home stretch with a product nobody wanted.

I suppose by every logical rule of management we should have abandoned the whole idea right there.

Fortunately, some unusually perceptive young men on our staff saw a major flaw in the case against the E 100 made by the consultants. The consultants had applied established criteria to evaluate an entirely new product. Our people identified a much larger market for such a machine because they did not follow conventional guidelines.

In today's complex society, of course, you cannot make much progress by following conventional guidelines. No enterprise is unchanging nor are markets. The results of change depend on the purpose and management of it. If change is successful, in retrospect we call it growth.

At the beginning, it wasn't easy to manage the growth of the E 100. We introduced it to the public in 1959 as the

Xerox 914 (it could make copies on ordinary paper up to 9"
by 14"). The first production line machine was delivered in
March, 1960. The story of what happened to it from then on
is, in a way, the opening chapter of a story that I do not
expect to see completed in my lifetime.

The copier's immediate success not only refuted most of
the market experts, it also astonished the most optimistic of
us. The product that nobody wanted, it seems, had become a
product that *everybody* wanted.

By the end of 1960, we were producing machines at a
rate 50 per cent greater than we had anticipated—and were
working against a huge backlog. Orders taken during the
first nine months of the 914's commercial life far exceeded
our total projections for it. Even more significant (because of
our per-copy charge), users of the machines were making
more copies than we expected.

The copier's immediate success not only
refuted most of the market experts, it also
astonished the most optimistic of us. The
product that nobody wanted, it seems, had
become a product that *everybody* wanted.

A New Name

We recognized almost immediately that more than three
quarters of our revenue during the coming decade would
come from xerographic products. So we recommended to
our shareholders at the 1960 annual meeting that the name
of Haloid Xerox undergo one more change—this time to
Xerox Corp.

Our annual reports for the first two full years of 914 production tell the story of the machine's success. People began

developing whole new office systems around it. Customers discovered uses we hadn't imagined. A Food and Drug Administration office used it to copy labels without taking them off the bottles; police officers recorded the contents of a suspect's pockets with one pass of the machine.

In 1961, our total revenues were 60 per cent greater than the previous year, while net income jumped 109 per cent. The following year, net income rose 151 per cent on a sales gain of 70 per cent.

Our annual reports for the first two full years of 914 production tell the story of the machine's success. People began developing whole new office systems around it. Customers discovered uses we hadn't imagined.

The success of the 914 provided abundant evidence that our approach to the copying market was a sound one. We hastened the design and production of machines that covered the entire spectrum of copying and medium-range duplicating. By late 1965, we had introduced a "family of products" meeting diverse needs of the copying market. We are still adding to that family and starting on "second generation" machines.

The field of copying continues to grow, but like all markets it will have a saturation point. To avoid stagnation once we reach that point, we carefully selected new ventures related to our basic field — graphic communications, or more broadly, the dissemination of knowledge.

As early as 1956, we recognized that overseas markets could furnish added growth. That year Haloid agreed to form a jointly owned company with The Rank Organisation of London, then best known in the motion picture field. The product of our union, Rank Xerox Limited, now markets xerographic products throughout the Eastern Hemisphere.

In recent years it has grown faster than Xerox itself in revenues and earnings.

At Xerox we believe it is essential to *retain* the concept of change to keep the innovative spirit alive in our organization.

In 1962 we began—with University Microfilms the first of our acquisitions in this area—to move from our by-then traditional base in copying to the education field. We now have made a full commitment to serve this field by publishing textbooks, by marketing library services, and by developing supplementary teaching materials and, indeed, whole courses for industrial and public classrooms.

Another goal was to participate in the exciting research taking place for the federal government, and that led us to acquire Electro-Optical Systems, Inc., a company chiefly engaged in military research, aerospace and other advanced technology. At Xerox we believe it is essential to *retain* the concept of change to keep the innovative spirit alive in our organization.

I think an essential quality in a manager, even on a relatively low level, is the ability to know when to depart from the normal, when to take risks. On the other hand, the manager who always upsets the applecart can be a disruptive influence. The art, I think, is to provide an atmosphere in which professional managers can retain the sensitivity so essential to the successful operation of a small business—the entrepreneurial spirit, as it were.

1969

KENNETH H. OLSEN
1926–

Back in 1986, *Fortune* magazine named Ken Olsen "America's Most Successful Entrepreneur." Since then, the founder of the Digital Equipment Corporation has been on a roller-coaster ride, with Compaq eventually buying his company in 1998. He was born to invent and create; his father was a machine tool designer, who held several patents, and young Olsen spent hours in the family basement fiddling with tools, fixing radios, and building gadgets. After a stint in the Navy, where he participated in their electronics technician training, Olsen enrolled at MIT. He earned a masters in electrical engineering in 1952, and there he remained, working in MIT's Lincoln Laboratory. One of his first projects was Whirlwind, a Navy computer project that was to help simulate cockpit flight.

Life was easy at MIT, but Olsen felt his research wasn't appreciated, so in 1957, at age 31, he and a fellow engineer decided to enter the computer business; their vision, to build something more efficient and less costly than the huge mainframes that then dominated. "We had a vision of computing that we knew the world needed," Olsen stated simply. For start-up money, they approached Georges Doriot, a Harvard Business School professor, who also happened to head a venture capital firm, American Research and Development. When making their proposal, they were advised not to even use the word "computer" because RCA and General Electric were losing money with them. In 1959, they presented their prototype—a minimainframe that was the size of a refrigerator, not the size of a garage. Thirty years later, it was an $11 billion company.

Unfortunately, Olsen's vision never included personal computers, which he pooh-poohed. In 1992, the company had a net loss of $2 billion and Olsen quit. Always an entrepreneur, within a year Olsen was involved in a new start-up, Advanced Modular Solutions, which allows a company's employees to download only the software they need from a network of servers to their desktop computer. In the following selection, Olsen divulges what it takes to get off the ground, which includes telling your potential investors what they want to hear, not what you know.

Digital Equipment Corporation:
The First Twenty-Five Years
Kenneth H. Olsen

B ack when I was at MIT, I was perfectly happy—I had all the things I had ever dreamed of, and I thought I could talk them into any project—thought I could get all the money I wanted for research, not for pay, and this is where it developed.

A couple of things happened along the way. When I was a young man, I was asked to be Sunday School superintendent at Park Street Church in Boston. It was a very imposing job for a thirty year old because everybody at the church looked ancient. But I accepted the job and immediately went off to Lexington library and took out all the books on management. It was my first taste of management. I can tell you all the things I learned then, but I can't tell you much I've learned since.

Another important thing happened while I was doing research at MIT. I discovered there was one thing missing in research. Nobody cared. That really set the idea that we had to show people at MIT how to make transistor computers, but nobody paid any attention to us. So, we decided to go into business.

In 1957, we went to American Research and Development Corporation, a risk capital company in Boston. General Georges F. Doriot was president, Dorothy Rowe was senior vice president and treasurer. They were a conservative organization because the recession of 1957 was under-way, and they were worried about us because we had no business background. I'd asked Harlan Anderson to join me, and we worked together on the business proposal. American Research was fascinated. Andy (Harlan Anderson) and I went to the Lexington library again, took out a lot of books, and wrote a proposal. We went through *Moody's* and studied all the companies that we felt were reputable and made out our pro forma financial statement. Then we made the pro-posal to American Research Development.

> While I was doing research at MIT. . . we had to show people at MIT how to make transistor computers, but nobody paid any attention to us. So, we decided to go into business.

Their reaction was concern. Some of the more senior vice presidents were very worried. But they said "We'll let you go to the board of directors," and they gave us three bits of advice. First was, don't use the word computer because *FORTUNE* magazine said no one had made any money in computers, and no one was about to. So we took that out. We said we'd make modules which were the pieces we had to make first anyway. Second, they suggested that five percent profit wasn't enough. You see, when we looked through *Moody's* it seemed that all the good companies made five percent. I think Dorothy Rowe said, "If you're going to risk somebody's money you've got to promise more return than RCA." So we promised ten percent. And, of course, the lesson is obvious. If we aimed for five percent, that's all we would have made. So we aimed for ten percent. Lastly, they suggested, promise fast results because most of the board is over eighty. So we promised to make a profit in a year, which we did.

Our first profit was so small the accounting could have made a difference between profit and loss. Andy and I went down to see the General. We were so proud after twelve months, and we laid our financial statements down. The General looked at them and looked up and scowled. He was rather imposing then; still is. And he paused and said, "I'm sorry to see this." He said, "No one has ever succeeded this soon and ever survived." So with that challenge we still survive.

American Research gave us $70,000 to start the company. The nice thing about seventy thousand dollars—there are so few of them you can watch every one. We found space in the old woolen mill in Maynard, Massachusetts, on the second floor, with a narrow stairway and no elevator. A discount store had just moved out. We paid twenty-five cents a square foot per year with watchman service and heat. And the next lease was fifty cents a square foot, so it was extravagant. There were nine thousand square feet. It seemed tremendously large when there were just three of us—my brother, Stan, joined us just as we started. So the three of us moved in.

American Research suggested that we get a downtown lawyer, downtown bank and a downtown accounting firm. The first thing we did was call in our downtown accounting firm. This was Lybrand Ross Bros. and Montgomery. When we invited them in we said we wanted big company accounting. In our rather humble offices, with Andy's lawn furniture and a leftover rolltop desk, it took a little bit of convincing to let them know that we really wanted big company accounting. When they set up this system we discovered it cost us more to do the accounting than it did to do the manufacturing.

We learned a lot in those early days. We did everything ourselves, from building the offices to moving the equipment. We did the photography in my basement, and printed our circuits with real silk on wooden frames and etched them in aquarium tanks we bought from the five and ten. We frequently spilled the etch solution onto the furniture store below—I think we bought the same set of furniture several times. We had the opportunity to learn accounting, and all the steps in manufacturing. Things which, in time, became very valuable because we became sensitive to people in many different jobs.

American Research gave us $70,000 to start the company. The nice thing about seventy thousand dollars—there are so few of them you can watch every one.

We initially thought we were going to use circuits we had developed at MIT, but just as we started, we had to make a difficult business decision because a new transistor had just come out. We decided to go with the new transistor, design all new circuitry, start from scratch. It was a much better one, but a terrible gamble. They cost $12.50 each and we bought a thousand of them. So out of $70,000, twelve and a half thousand went into one little box, that you could hold in your hand. Before we used any of them, the price went down to around eight dollars . . . we had a four thousand dollar inventory loss before we did anything.

By planning everything and doing it carefully, we were able to design and build modules that sold well. For a while we had a monopoly. Not much of a market, but a monopoly.

Financial Responsibility

We had a number of ideas that were quite unique at the time but are rather normal now. First of all, in those days there was a belief that making a profit was bad. That sounds strange now but at the time it really was true. Companies would hire an engineer and say, "We're hiring you for the good of science; we're going to hire you to develop yourself professionally." Secretly, they hoped he'd help them make a profit but they wouldn't say that to the engineer. We had a very straightforward relationship. We'd borrowed $70,000 of someone else's money, with an understanding that we would try to give a return. With that simple relationship, most of the people in Digital understood that our obligation was to make a profit. That basic premise was a very definite advantage and it's paid off quite consistently.

We had another idea that appeared strange at the time. At that time most people who came from research environments looked down on manufacturing. They were researchers, and they would contract out for manufacturing. We immediately engraved our letterhead with the statement that we were designers and manufacturers. It's obvious today but at that time it was unusual.

The other idea we had was that we didn't want to take military contracts. We weren't pacifists; in fact, we came from a military part of MIT, but we felt it limited our efforts to become a civilian company. At that time, some of the research money just seemed too easy to come by.

Trying to explain our ideas to financial analysts was impossible. We tried to explain to them why we wouldn't take free money from the government, and they didn't understand. We also told them that we didn't think growth was a goal. At that time all you had to do was grow and sell your company. Explaining to Wall Street why growth wasn't a goal was impossible. We gave up and just mouthed the words because they wouldn't understand.

We also brought some organizational ideas from MIT. There was an attitude and environment at MIT that we wanted to duplicate. It's hard to describe but MIT was and, I think to a large degree is, a very generous, a very trusting, and a very challenging environment. That environment was one of the things we wanted to capture and bring to our own company. We had so much confidence in MIT that we even followed the MIT operations manual. We took the same hours, we took the same vacations, we paid the same holidays. The state came by and said you can't pay on those days, it's illegal. We said MIT does, the state said we can't control MIT, but we can control you.

Interactive Computers

We also had some very unusual computer ideas. The computer developed at MIT by Jay Forrester and Bob Everett was quite unique, partly because it was very simple. Most computers at that time were designed by professors who had an obligation to make things complicated so they would have something over their students. Jay and the crew were not professors and had a vested interest in making it simple—they hired retired television repairmen to do the work. The other idea was that computers had to be very fast. So all the complexity given up to make the machine simple was put into making it fast. This was also the opportunity to make an interactive computer—one that would interact directly with its user through a video or keyboard terminal. Out of that idea came the computers that we've been selling for twenty-five years.

The idea of an interactive computer, where both machinery or people can interact, was one of the key concepts at MIT and was really the basis upon which we built Digital.

Throughout our career, some of the most important decisions we made were negative ones—things we decided not to pursue as a company.

The advantages of an interactive computer were never more apparent than at MIT itself, when we gave them one of our very first computers. It was in a room on the second floor above an IBM machine. The contrast was quite interesting. On the floor where the IBM machine was installed, there were two layers of glass in front of this very imposing machine. People entered their problem on a batch of IBM cards. The next day they got their answer back, and it usually said you made a mistake. On the floor above the students could use the interactive machines any hour of the day or night, for any reason, and they could sign up for it months ahead. The reaction was quite different. If you walked in there at three o'clock in the morning, the kids were doing what they do today with personal computers. They were all involved. These computers were so captivating that a number of times the administration thought of getting rid of them because people stopped washing, stopped eating, stopped their social life and, of course, stopped studying. But out of that group of bright students came so many of the things which we take for granted today, including timesharing and even video games. Many of the key people in the industry today came out of that group, and many of the things that we know about computers were formulated during that period.

Decision Making

Throughout our career, some of the most important decisions we made were negative ones—things we decided not to pursue as a company. For example, at one time we pretty much owned the cathode ray tube market in the computer business. We decided we just couldn't dominate that market, no one company could, so we decided to offer a range of products but not to try to dominate the market.

Sometimes we are ridiculed for not exploiting all the opportunities we have. Jay Forrester once said you're either going to have too many managers or too few managers, you're never going to hit it exactly right, so plan to have more managers than you can use and let some of the others go to the rest of the industry. It seems obvious that you never hit it right on. Having more qualified managers has always been our goal. The corollary says you're never going to be as good as people think you are, so our goal is always to be better than people think we are. We always want to have more products than we can use and sell because the only other

481

alternative is to have too few. Sometimes it looks like we have more products than we've exploited, but it is just so much safer to have more.

We're also financially conservative. I believe that if we are to grow this fast, we have to be very safe financially. In general, we raise our money before we expand. Over the years we've been criticized for not understanding what the word leverage means. We may be researchers, but we do know what leverage means, and having a few million dollars cash in the bank is much nicer than being heavily leveraged.

Responsibility

There was a major change in the company back when we were just a fourteen million dollar company. Coming from a research environment we ran the company like a research project. Everybody got together and we made decisions. But it stopped working well. We had twenty people on the Works Committee then, and they all had ideas, for example, on how to spend money. I was the only one to say no. People started to think I was a little dictator; some even complained to the directors. It got to the point where one day I said, "We're a new company. You all now have responsibility." We broke the company into product lines and service groups to the product lines. The product line managers made the budgets and everybody else budgeted to serve them. Miracles started to happen. We gave them responsibilities, told them to establish a budget, and said they would be reviewed once a month against their budgets. When the managers asked how many people they could hire, I told them they couldn't hire anybody, because that was the only simple rule. I admit it was unfair, but they doubled the profit of the company in the first year. When they were telling others what to do things didn't work out well at all, but when they suddenly had the responsibility, it's amazing how smart they were.

When they had the responsibility, things became very clear. The company was doing well financially before then but suddenly there was a sharp increase in growth and in profit when we assigned responsibility. That's been the basis upon which we've been running the company.

> We've been criticized for not understanding
> what the word leverage means. . . . We do
> know what leverage means, and having a few
> million dollars cash in the bank is much nicer
> than being heavily leveraged.

We've had particularly good results in a number of plants we built even though when we built them it appeared to be quite risky. For example, we built a plant in Springfield, Massachusetts, in the old Armory that George Washington built. It was in a depressed area where there were a few problems. Good people, but a depressed area. Our approach was not to say, "We're do gooders from Boston going to help you poor people." We said, "We're going to hire you if you're good and fire you if you're bad." We gave them responsibility, and the results were just beautiful. We also did it without any publicity.

We had the same experience with our plant in Puerto Rico. Originally we only expected to assemble parts there, but as our employees got better they made complete computers and they're very good. They're good because we trusted them to learn and take responsibility.

We also built in Ireland. Again, in a somewhat rural area in Galway where we had showed confidence in the people, gave them the chance to do what they wanted to do, the results are magnificent.

When we don't do well with people is when we don't give people clear responsibilities or when one person doesn't share responsibility.

Today, many of our leaders come from our manufacturing, field service and sales organizations—not areas of a company where you typically expect to find good managers. Managers normally came from marketing and engineering, but we choose the other disciplines because they break out responsibility, delegate it, measure it regularly. They learn to take responsibility and measure it and grow with it. Those creative areas, where it's more inspiration and art, are often harder to measure exactly.

Success

The past five or six years have been boom times for Digital. I said publicly, "We're big enough now, we don't need recessions to straighten us out," but it's not true. I don't think human beings are made to survive one good year after another, with all the flattery and success that goes with it—at least we're not. If we go many years with too many orders and too much appreciation we become weak individually and as a company. This recession [1981–1982], even though it's a strain and a worry, has made us strong. We've developed more products recently, and we have strengthened our organizational structure at the same time.

Henry LeMaire, one of our vice presidents, died a few years ago, and it had a significant effect on our managers. When the company was doing well, many of our senior managers really thought they were good. They were driving to get ahead. After Henry died, it started to sink in. Henry was never a driver, never pushed others, never proud, never cocky, never confident. He was well-educated but quiet, thoughtful of others and hard working. When people realized the effect he had on others and how he grew in his responsibility within the company by these human characteristics, it had a very serious, sobering effect on all of us.

There's a story I tell sometimes which has an effect on me and I'd like to pass it on to you. Someone wrote that the Puritans were successful because they had some unusual ideas about God. They believed that God proved their position with Him by their economic success so they worked very hard for economic success. I was a little suspicious of this so I did some research. A book called *The Puritans* said that the Puritans had two characteristics. First of all, they believed that mankind was fallen. This did not make them cynical; but they believed that you should never be disappointed with mankind. If you believe this, it has a very important meaning to your relationship with others in business and how you approach business. For example, our marketers will say engineering is always six months late. Now, if you know that to start with, you should never be disappointed because you know what to expect, and that won't change. Therefore, you should always have a positive point of view, and never be disappointed.

The other thing the Puritans believed was that every night they should systematically review what they learned that day about their fellow man, their relationship with their God and themselves. Now that's a very unusual idea, particularly in business. So often, we blame the government, those "other" people, or the boss, or anything. For example, one of our people made a proposal which we turned down. It was a terrible proposal. He was misleading, and he made a poor proposal. He slammed his briefcase, walked out and quit, and went to work for another company. A thoughtful person would have assumed that maybe he hadn't done his homework and tried again.

1982

SAMUEL GOLDWYN
1879–1974

Samuel Goldwyn was a pioneer in movies and his production company was among the first to settle in Hollywood. California was a long way from where he was raised—Warsaw, Poland. His father, who ran a struggling secondhand goods store, unexpectedly died at age 43, and one by one, the six small Gelbfisz children went to work. Young Schmuel Gelbfisz, as he was then called, had dreams: "When I was a kid . . . the only place I wanted to go was to America. . . . Even then America, actually only the name of a faraway country, was a vision of paradise." In 1895, he began his journey: a three-hundred-mile walk to Germany; a boat ride from Hamburg to London; a 120-mile walk to Birmingham to find his aunt; a stint of selling sponges and then stealing the money to get to the United States, arriving in 1899.

Goldwyn found work at a glove factory in upstate New York and eventually became a top salesman. Bitten by the showbiz bug in 1913, Goldwyn hounded his brother-in-law, Jesse Lasky, who had some theatrical experience, to start a motion picture company. As a third partner, they recruited Cecil B. deMille, then a playwright. They started their company with $15,000 in capital. For their first movie, they adapted the hit play, *The Squaw Man,* and filmed it in southern California. The budget soon escalated and Goldwyn raised funds by promising theater owners rights to show his films—12 films, he said, for the next year. Little did they realize they were funding the first.

The Squaw Man grossed about $250,000, and needless to say the entire industry blossomed. While making 80 movies, he signed such stars as Marlin Brando, Gary Cooper, Laurence Olivier, Will Rogers, and Barbara Stanwyck. Like many pioneers, he remained largely a lone wolf. He once admitted, "They called me the lone wolf, and I have been called some other things, too. I had partners but I discovered I was spending more time trying to explain to them what I was doing than in making pictures." In *You Can Always Do Better,* Goldwyn tells his rags-to-riches story with plenty of poignant anecdotes such as what he learned at a greased-pole-climbing contest.

You Can Always Do Better
Samuel Goldwyn

When I was a young man
I read many inspiring articles by business leaders and states-
men in *The American Magazine.* It never occurred to me that I
might some day be asked to contribute an article of my own.
Yet the fact that a penniless immigrant boy from Poland
grew up to tell this story of what America has meant to
him — that, in itself, is a proof of the boundless opportunity
which makes our country great.

I recall that the articles I read often contained precepts
on which the writers had based their lives. I don't intend to
add to this list, because I am convinced that every individual
must make his own rules and follow his own road of achievement. The important thing is that no lucky accidents of birth,
wealth, or superior education are necessary to travel that
road. In a country such as ours it is open to everyone. From
personal experience I've learned that whoever you are or
whatever you have accomplished, in America you can
always do better. You have a chance to make today brighter
than yesterday, and tomorrow brighter than today.

During a recent visit to New York I was interviewed by
a young reporter who said to me, "Mr. Goldwyn, you have
reached the peak as a motion-picture producer. Can you
explain how you did it?"

"Just a minute," I protested. "If that were true, there would be only one thing left for me to do: I would have to go out of business and retire. I don't intend to do that, so please do not say I have reached the peak."

Every individual must make his own rules and follow his own road of achievement. The important thing is that no lucky accidents of birth, wealth, or superior education are necessary to travel that road.

I remembered how I felt when one of my pictures, *The Best Years of Our Lives*, received the Academy Award and the Thalberg Trophy. I knew that this should be the happiest day of my life, yet something worried me. "Today people are saying that you have produced a great picture," an inner voice seemed to whisper. "But what about tomorrow? The audience won't remember these prizes while they're watching your next one."

In other words, I am not interested in past successes, but only in future opportunities. To me, every picture is the first one—because I know that unless I give it the best effort of which I am capable, it may be the last. Therefore, the soundest advice to anyone who has ever won an award in any business is simply this: Forget it.

I believe that in any occupation it is harder to stay on top than to get there. In fact, it's rather like trying to climb a greased pole—a sport that I discovered as a boy at a county fair near Gloversville, N.Y., many years ago. Although recently an immigrant from Europe, I understood immediately when it was announced that whoever got to the top would win $10. The sum, to me, was a vast fortune. I wrapped my arms around the pole and snaked up with what seemed a superhuman effort. Probably I made it because I was a skinny youngster who didn't have much weight to carry.

At any rate, I won the $10. In addition, I learned a very important lesson — namely, that while I could climb the pole, it was more difficult to stay on it once I had reached the top. The moment I stopped climbing, I skidded down to the bottom. I have found that life is much like that, and I am sorry for anyone who really feels that he has reached the top in his profession.

I am not interested in past successes, but only in future opportunities. . . . Therefore, the soundest advice to anyone who has ever won an award in any business is simply this: Forget it.

In motion pictures, for example, the producer who tries to repeat the success of his last picture by making another one like it is in a position similar to the boy trying to stay on the greased pole. He is almost sure to skid down. You've got to make the next one better, and keep on climbing.

If this seems like an impossible ideal, think how far motion pictures, and the entire entertainment industry, have advanced in a generation. Since I became interested in the production of pictures 37 years ago, a whole city has grown up around the industry, employing some 30,000 artists and craftsmen who make 400 or more films every year. Actors, writers, producers, and directors who once had only the stage to work on have seen their opportunities multiplied a hundred times over in pictures, radio, and the challenging new field of television.

I remember that pessimists once predicted that movies would kill the stage. Then, a few years later, they announced that radio would hurt motion pictures. Today, they speak of television as though it were a threat to all other forms of entertainment. Yet I'm certain that in the future, as in the past, all these new developments will only bring more enjoyment to the public and more jobs for youngsters growing up today.

My own search for opportunity began at the age of 11, when I realized that there was little future or freedom behind the walls of the ghetto in Warsaw. I decided to go to America. My plan was to cross Germany and stop in England for a while. I had an aunt living in Birmingham who would put me up on the way, I knew.

It was not an easy journey. In order to escape from Poland I had to pay a smuggler to row me across a river into Germany, past the Russian and German police who guarded the border. This took most of the little money in my pocket, and then I tumbled into the water, got a good soaking, and lost the rest.

I managed to reach the port of Hamburg, Germany, but there I stood on the dock, penniless, and watched the boats departing for England. I wandered aimlessly through the streets, until I saw a store front with a name similar to that of a family I knew in Warsaw. I stormed into the shop with my ragged clothes and dirty, tearstained face, and told the proprietor my story. "I can't go back," I cried. "I am on my way to America and I won't go back."

I must have been something of a salesman even at that age, because my story impressed the man. He took up a collection for me and put me on a boat to England. Finally I reached Birmingham, after living for two days on a single loaf of bread.

I found that my aunt was too poor to give me much help, and I went to work in a blacksmith shop, where my job was to pump the bellows with my feet. This did not last long, however, because I lacked the strength to keep up a good fire. Another collection was taken up by friends and neighbors to send me on my way, and I arrived at last in the United States, where I had heard that a man could work with his brains instead of with his feet.

On landing in America, I was told of a place called Gloversville, N.Y., where Polish immigrants were already working, and where I could learn a trade. Soon I was cutting out gloves for a few dollars a week. To me and my fellow workers this was a dream come true. We were in a free land; we could go where we liked; by improving our skill and cutting more skins we could increase our wages.

The factory where I worked would probably be called a "sweatshop" today. Yet it was a revelation to me to find a place where work was rewarded, and where the more a man worked, the more he was paid. I used to arrive before the morning whistle blew at 10 minutes to 7. I ate a hasty lunch, and worked late.

Before two years had passed I was making as much as $20 a week, and the owner of the factory had become so curious about me that he invited me home for dinner. He asked me what made a youngster work so hard and what I was after in life. I was surprised that anyone would think of such a question. "How can you get ahead, except by working harder than everyone else?" I demanded.

Today, children do not work in factories as I did, because we know that their proper place is in school. This, to me, is a part of America's greatness—that we can constantly better the conditions under which we live. Radicals and revolutionaries, on the other hand, look only for grievances, and would destroy our way of life rather than improve it.

Some of my friends in Gloversville were so well satisfied that they thought they had already reached the top. They had arrived in America; they had steady jobs; they could bring up their children in freedom. What more could a man ask?

They were, of course, right, but there were also others who looked beyond the factory walls. I listened to them, and I noticed that those who lived best were not the makers but the sellers of gloves. I saw well-dressed salesmen in the lobby of the best hotel, sitting in comfortable chairs, and decided that there was no reason why I, too, could not become a salesman. Since I had reached the peak as a glove cutter, this was the way to keep on climbing.

First of all, I knew that if I was going to sell, I would have to learn better English than I heard in the factory. I enrolled in night school and began to study as hard as I could. Since I had little time for education, I tried to make the most of it. To learn penmanship, we wrote out sentences from a copybook, and I saw that most of the students wrote the exercises without paying any attention to what the sentences meant. To me, however, it was a revelation of wisdom to copy down such proverbs as "Haste makes waste," "Work overcomes all," and "Early to bed and early to rise . . ." They still make sense. Nothing can be accomplished without spending time and effort.

At the age of 16 I decided that I was ready to become a salesman. Convincing my boss was not so easy, and I had to use the best selling arguments I could think of to persuade him to give me a chance. At last I begged him to assign me to a territory where no one had been able to sell our gloves before.

"All right," he said; "I'll give you Pittsfield, Mass., to start. The leading store there has never carried our goods. If you can sell them, you can sell anyone, and I'll make you a regular salesman."

At Pittsfield I found out what he meant. When I arrived at the store I was told that the buyer was out. The next day he was too busy to see me. I waited outside his office one day—two days—three days. Finally he stopped as he walked by and said, "Look here, son, we've done business with another firm for years. You're wasting your time."

"Maybe I am," I said, "but I intend to sit here until you look at my gloves. You don't have to buy them, but you shouldn't turn me down without seeing what I've got to sell. You may be missing a bargain."

The buyer smiled, but he let me into his office. I was able to prove to him at once that I knew gloves, because I had made them. I explained every detail of construction, and how they could be advertised to bring customers into the store. My first order was for $300.

My boss kept his word, and I became a regular salesman. Eventually, I was given the choice territory of New York City. Today, as a motion-picture producer, salesmanship is just as important to me as it was in the glove business. Not only must I make good pictures, but I must also tell the public why they're good. The old saying that if you build a better mousetrap, the world will beat a path to your door, is not the whole story. Today, you also must tell people about your mousetrap and let them know where to find you, before they can make a path through the modern woods.

By 1913 I had become sales manager for a glove manufacturer in New York. My office was on Fifth Avenue at 19th Street, and every day I walked to my home on 61st Street. On my way uptown I used to pass a nickelodeon, where moving pictures were shown. They ran for about 5 minutes, and showed cops and robbers, barroom slapstick, and characters like "Bronco Billy" chasing a train. I went in one day to see what it was all about, after making sure first that no one was around who might recognize me.

The old saying that if you build a better mousetrap, the world will beat a path to your door, is not the whole story. Today, you also must tell people about your mousetrap and let them know where to find you.

Going into a nickelodeon wasn't considered in entire good taste, but the experience gave me an idea. A few days later I had a talk with Jesse Lasky, a young vaudeville producer. "I am going to quit my job," I told him, "and go into the motion-picture business. How would you like to join me?" I also suggested that we ask Cecil deMille, a friend of ours who had done a little acting and writing, to come in with us.

Lasky looked at me as if he thought I was crazy. "That

will be some business," he said. "Cecil and I have never seen a moving picture in our lives, and you've seen one. It will be a very unusual company."

We argued for days. At that time films were used in some vaudeville theaters to get people out of the house after each show, and were called "chasers."

"I don't want to chase people out of the theater," Jesse said. "I want to get them in." He told me that he had a better idea, since I wanted to change jobs. He had heard the Mexican-style tamales were a favorite dish in California, and was sure that if we tied up the tamale concession in New York we could make a fortune.

"You can have the tamales," I said. "I'll bet on the pictures." Then I used a trick I had learned as a salesman — which is to show the other fellow how your idea will be to his advantage. "We could call the company 'The Jesse Lasky Feature Play Company,'" I suggested. "That sounds better than 'Lasky's Hot Tamales,' doesn't it?"

Jesse was convinced, and our company was formed, with deMille as the director. Cecil went out to California, where he could work in year-round sunshine, and rented a barn for $75 a month in a place called Hollywood, which we had never heard of.

I recall that some time later the publisher of the *Los Angeles Times* asked me if we would include the words, "Made in Hollywood," with the screen credits, to give the community a boost. He predicted that some day there would be a million people in Los Angeles. Today, Los Angeles is the fifth largest city in the United States, and I doubt if there's anyone in the world who does not know that pictures are made in Hollywood.

All this was far in the future, however, when we went to work on our first picture, based on a Broadway play, called *The Squaw Man.* Our main problem was one which is familiar to everyone who ever started a business — namely, how to raise money. We had about $15,000 between us, and needed $50,000 to make the film.

Someone suggested, at this point, that it might be possible to sell the distribution rights to a picture before it was actually made. I went to a film distributor in California and told him about *The Squaw Man*. I described it as a prospective epic of the screen for which theaters would be able to charge as much as 25 cents—a top admission price in those days! "The films you have seen so far are only rehearsals for what we're going to do," I said. "The time is coming when the best plays and the best actors will be in pictures. This is going to be the greatest entertainment medium in the world."

My enthusiastic speech evidently convinced the California theater man, for he proceeded to pay me $4,000, in advance, for the right to show our picture. I then went on to other states making similar contracts, and finally raised the $50,000.

When *The Squaw Man* was completed, it was one of the first full-length motion pictures made in America. Along with the early films of D. W. Griffith and Adolph Zukor, it demonstrated that serious adult drama could be shown on the screen. The nickelodeon days were over.

Today, the old-fashioned comedy "chasers" have grown into one of the world's great art forms, all as a result of the American belief that whatever we have done can be improved. Of course, people still want to be entertained when they go to see a picture. But today they want their comedies, as well as their dramas, tragedies, and love stories, to be true to life. They want to recognize themselves and their neighbors in the stories they see on the screen.

Occasionally, in the past, I used to hear film makers in Hollywood say of a motion-picture script: "This is great, but people won't understand it." Or, "This story is true, but the public doesn't want the truth." Today, many of the individuals who thought in such terms are no longer in business.

Screen plays cannot be turned out like doughnuts from a machine. Once people have paid their money to see a picture, no matter how wonderful it is, they want to see something different the next time they go to a theater. In fact, if I were asked to define showmanship in a single sentence, I would say: "Whatever everyone is doing—do something else."

This rule is necessary because an increasingly well-educated public is constantly demanding different and better motion pictures. Hollywood has had to improve continually the quality of its films in order to satisfy these millions of ever-more-exacting theatergoers.

Whatever everyone is doing—do something else.

Not so long ago a successful young dramatist and screen writer named Philip Yordan, who had worked with me on several pictures, came into my office and said, "Mr. Goldwyn, I haven't been really happy since I left your studio. I miss the discipline."

I told him I had heard that he was doing very well.

"Yes, I'm not doing badly," Yordan said. "But, working with you, I learned never to be satisfied with my own work. While other producers tell me that my writing is pretty good, I had to work very hard to get a 'well done' from you. You're the only man who has constantly reminded me I could do better, no matter how well I thought I had done. I want you to know that has helped me."

This fine writer recently finished working on my latest picture, which we have called, *Edge of Doom*. I think it's a fine picture; in many ways, perhaps, the best we have ever made. But only the audiences, in theaters all over the world, can decide that. Whatever their verdict may be, I will *still* not be satisfied. I know that we must make the next one better, because, to me, that is the philosophy of America.

1950

Acknowledgments

For Diana and Mark
Hey, there's nothing like space.

For me, there's nothing more enjoyable than digging through some old magazines or books at the public library and discovering a gem of an essay by the likes of P. T. Barnum or Samuel Goldwyn or J. C. Penney, among other business legends. The opportunity to continue researching these great characters that make up the Wisdom Series has been provided by Ruth Mills, my champion and fantastic editor at John Wiley & Sons. I will be forever grateful and I give the same heartfelt thanks to Ed Knappman, the agent who took me on out of the clear blue sky.

The primary characters in my life (i.e., my family) who offer much needed support include: Diana, who does a superlative job as ghost editor and masseuse; Pierson, who challenges me to a mean game of basketball to reinvigorate me; Alex, who is a wiz at puzzles and shows me how all the pieces fit together; and Julia, who throws a great tea party and keeps me nourished. It's an understatement to say that having a family to share with makes this work all the more enjoyable.

Thanks also to Mark LoGiurato, who gives me much needed space and a sanctuary of sorts, and to Kathy Leeds and the other Wilton Librarians, who help in so many ways.

Notes

Wally Amos:

Amos, Wally, with Leroy Robinson. *The Famous Amos Story.* Garden City, NY: Doubleday & Company, 1983.

Applegate, Jane. "Former Famous Amos Cooks Up New Name for Himself." *Lexington Herald-Leader,* 1997.

Warren Avis:

Avis, Warren. *Take a Chance to Be First.* New York: MacMillan Publishing, 1986.

Bray, Hiawatha. "Avis Founder to Launch Sporting Goods Marketing Network in October." *Knight-Ridder/Tribune Business News,* May 3, 1994.

Flint, Jerry. "Every Day, in Every Way." *Forbes,* November 4, 1985.

P. T. Barnum:

Barnum, P. T. *Struggles and Triumphs: or, Forty Years' Recollections of P. T. Barnum.* New York: Penguin Books, 1981.

Harris, Neil. *Hum Bug: The Art of P. T. Barnum.* Boston: Little, Brown and Company, 1973.

Clarence Birdseye:

Groner, Alex, and the editors of *American Heritage* and *Business Week. American Business and Industry.* New York: American Heritage Publishing, 1972.

Hallott, Anthony, and Diane Hallett. *Encyclopedia of Entrepreneurs.* New York: John Wiley & Sons, 1997.

Michael Bloomberg:

Auletta, Ken. "The Bloomberg Threat." *The New Yorker,* March 10, 1997.

Bloomberg, Michael, with invaluable help from Mathew Winkler. *Bloomberg on Bloomberg.* New York: John Wiley & Sons, 1997.

Richard Branson:

"Behind Branson." *The Economist,* February 21, 1998.

Branson, Richard. *Losing My Virginity.* New York: Times Business, 1998.

Flynn, Julia, with Wendy Zellner, Larry Light, and Joseph Weber. "Then Came Branson." *Business Week,* October 26, 1998.

Anita F. Brattina:

Brattina, Anita F. *Diary of a Small Business Owner.* New York: AMACOM, 1996.

Fortnichelli, Linda. "Letting Go of the Details." *Nation's Business,* November 1997.

Norm Brodsky:
Brodsky, Norm. "Caveat Emptor." *Inc.*, August 1998.
Brodsky, Norm. "Where the Money Is." *Inc.*, October 1998.
"How to Attract Investors." *Inc. Online*, August 12, 1997.

Nolan Bushnell:
Bushnell, Nolan. "Relationships Between Funa and the Computer Business." *Communications of the ACM*, August 1996.
Bushnell, Nolan. "The Artichoke Theory." *Byte*, September 1992.
Button, Kate. "Outrageous Fortune." *Computer Weekly*, December 16, 1993.
Martin, Richard. "Comebacks: Cooking Up Second Chances for Glory." *Nation's Restaurant News*, September 23, 1996.

Andrew Carnegie:
Carnegie, Andrew. "The Road to Business Success." A speech at Curry Commercial College, June 23, 1885.
Wall, Joseph Frazier. *Andrew Carnegie*. New York: Oxford University Press, 1970.

Steve Case:
McHugh, Josh. "Web Warrior." *Forbes*, January 1, 1999.
Ramo, Joshua Cooper, John Greenwald, and Michael Krantz. "How AOL Lost the Battles but Won the War." *Time*, September 22, 1997.

Ben Cohen and Jerry Greenfield:
Cohen, Ben, and Jerry Greenfield. *Ben & Jerry's Double-Dip*. New York: Simon & Schuster, 1997.
Lager, Fred "Chico." *Ben & Jerry's: The Inside Scoop*. New York: Crown Publishers, 1994.

Marquis Converse:
Fucini, Joseph J., and Suzy Fucini. *Entrepreneurs: The Men and Women behind Famous Brand Names and How They Made It*. Boston: G. K. Hall, 1985.
Hallett, Anthony, and Diane Hallett. *Entrepreneur Magazine: Encyclopedia of Entrepreneurs*. New York: John Wiley & Sons, 1997.

Michael S. Dell:
Dell, Michael S. "Making the Right Choices for the New Consumer." *Planning Review*, September/October 1993.
Jacob, Rahul. "The Resurrection of Michael Dell." *Fortune*, September 18, 1995.
"Money Machine." *New York*, August 3, 1998.
Serwer, Andrew E. "Michael Dell Turns the PC World Inside Out." *Fortune*, September 8, 1997.

Barry Diller:
Auletta, Ken. *The Highwaymen*. New York: Random House, 1997.
Goodell, Jeff. "Barry Diller Interview." *Rolling Stone*, August 25, 1994.
LaFranco, Robert. "Against the Odds." *Forbes*, March 10, 1997.
Machan, Dyan. "Barry Diller's Next Course." *Forbes*, March 9, 1998.

Doris Drucker:
Drucker, Doris. "Invent Radium or I'll Pull Your Hair." *The Atlantic Monthly*, August 1998.
Drucker, Peter F. *Adventures of a Bystander*. New York: Harper & Row, 1978.

Notes

George Eastman:
Brayer, Elizabeth. *George Eastman: A Biography*. Baltimore, MD: Johns Hopkins University Press, 1996.
Eastman, George. "Why I Turned 1/3 of My Stock Over to Employees." *System: the Magazine of Business*, June 1927.

Debbi Fields:
Fields, Debbi, and Alan Furst. *One Smart Cookie*. New York: Simon & Schuster, 1987.

Harvey Firestone:
Firestone, Harvey S., with Samuel Crowther. *Men and Rubber: The Story of Business*. Garden City, NY: Doubleday, Page & Company, 1926.

Henry Ford:
Ford, Henry, with Samuel Crowther. *My Life and Work*. Garden City, NY: Doubleday, Page & Company, 1922.
Gelderman, Carol. *Henry Ford: The Wayward Capitalist*. New York: The Dial Press, 1981.

Benjamin Franklin:
Clark, Ronald W. *Benjamin Franklin: A Biography*. New York: Random House, 1983.
Franklin, Benjamin. "Way to Wealth." *Poor Richard's Almanac*, 1757.

Alfred C. Fuller:
Fuller, Alfred C. *A Foot in the Door*. New York: McGraw-Hill, 1960.

Samuel Goldwyn:
Berg, A. Scott. *Goldwyn: A Biography*. New York: Alfred A. Knopf, 1989.

Conrad Hilton:
Hilton, Conrad. *Be My Guest*. Englewood Cliffs, NJ: Prentice-Hall, 1957.
Current Biography Yearbook, 1949. New York: H. W. Wilson, 1949.

Steven Jobs:
Cocks, Jay. "The Updated Book of Jobs." *Time*, January 3, 1983.
Schlender, Brent. "Steve Jobs' Hollow Deal." *Fortune*, September 8, 1997.
Sculley, John, with John A. Byrne. *Odyssey*. New York: Harper & Row, 1987.
Stross, Randall E. *Steve Jobs and the NeXT Big Thing*. New York: Atheneum, 1993.

John H. Johnson:
Johnson, John H., with Lerone Bennett, Jr. *Succeeding Against the Odds*. New York: Warner Books, 1989.
Sobel, Robert, and David B. Sicilia. *The Entrepreneurs: An American Adventure*. Boston: Houghton Mifflin, 1986.

Andy Kessler:
Kessler, Andy. "Getting the Wind at Your Back," October 1996.
Kessler, Andy. "The PEP Fortune Teller." *Forbes*, October 24, 1994.

Victor Kiam:
Kiam, Victor. *Going for It! How to Succeed as an Entrepreneur.* New York: William Morrow and Company, 1986.
Much, Marilyn. "Would You Buy a Shaver from this Man?" *Industry Week,* August 24, 1987.

Philip Knight:
Current Biography Yearbook, 1997. New York: H. W. Wilson, 1997.
Lane, Randall. "You Are What You Wear." *Forbes 400,* October 14, 1996.
Strasser, J. B., and Laurie Becklund. *Swoosh: The Unauthorized Story of Nike and the Men Who Played There.* New York: Harcourt Brace Jovanovich, 1991

Henry R. Kravis:
Bartlett, Sarah. *The Money Machine.* New York: Warner Books, 1991.
Current Biography Yearbook, 1989. New York: H. W. Wilson, 1989.

Edwin H. Land:
Chakravartry, Subrata N. "The Vindication of Edwin Land." *Forbes,* May 4, 1987.
McElheny, Victor K. *Insisting on the Impossible: The Life of Edwin Land.* Perseus Books, 1998.

Herman W. Lay:
Love, Albert, and James Saxon Childers, editors. *Listen to Leaders in Business.* New York: Holt, Rinehart and Winston, 1962.

Mark H. McCormack:
Braham, James. "From Tee to Green ($): Mark McCormack Shares his 'Street Smarts.' " *Industry Week,* November 12, 1984.
Feinstein, John. "The King of the Courts." *Tennis,* May 1995.
McCormick, Mark H. *What They Don't Teach You at Harvard Business School.* New York: Bantam Books, 1984.
Schmuckler, Eric. "Still the One." *Brandweek,* March 11, 1996.

Scott McNealy:
Schlender, Brent. "Javaman: The Adventures of Scott McNealy." *Fortune,* October 13, 1997.
"Scott McNealy's Rising Sun." *Business Week,* January 22, 1996.

Tom Monaghan:
Monaghan, Tom, with Robert Anderson. *Pizza Tiger.* New York: Random House, 1986.

Akio Morita:
Morita, Akio, with Edwin M. Reingold and Mitsuko Shimomura. *Made in Japan.* New York: E. P. Dutton, 1986.

Al Neuharth:
Neuharth, Al. *Confessions of an S.O.B.* New York: Doubleday, 1989.

501

Wolper, Allan. "Neuharth to Academics: Butt Out." *Editor & Publisher,* January 11, 1997.

Ken Olsen:

McLean, Bethany. "Ken Olsen's Search for Redemption." *Fortune Small Business,* March 16, 1998.
Rifkin, Glenn, and George Harrar. *The Ultimate Entrepreneur: The Story of Ken Olsen and Digital Equipment Corporation.* Chicago: Contemporary Books, 1988.

J. C. Penney:

Groner, Alex, and the editors of *American Heritage* and *Business Week. American Business and Industry.* New York: American Heritage Publishing, 1972.
Penney, J. C. "It Is One Thing to Desire—And Another to Determine." *American Magazine,* August 1919.
Penney, J. C. *The Man with a Thousand Partners.* New York: Harper & Row, 1931.

H. Ross Perot:

Mason, Todd. *Perot: An Unauthorized Biography.* Homewood, IL: Business One Irwin, 1990.

Kim Polese:

Current Biography Yearbook, 1997. New York: H. W. Wilson, 1997.
Fryer, Bronwyn. "The Next Bill Gates." *Working Woman,* March 1997.
"Time's 25 Most Influential Americans." *Time,* April 21, 1997.

Simon Ramo:

Louis, Arthur M. "The U.S. Business Hall of Fame." *Fortune,* April 2, 1984.
Ramo, Simon. *The Business of Science.* New York: Hill and Wang, 1988.

Arthur Rock:

Edwards, Owen. "Arthur Rock." *Forbes,* June 1, 1998.
Moritz, Michael. "Arthur Rock: 'The Best Long Ball Hitter Around.' " *Time,* January 23, 1984.

Anita Roddick:

"Anita Roddick." Let's Talk Business Network, Inc.: The Entrepreneur's Hall of Fame.
O'Byrne, Robert. "Jolly Green Giant." *The Irish Times,* November 4, 1997.
Roddick, Anita. *Body and Soul.* New York: Crown, 1991.

Colonel Harland Sanders:

"Colonel Sanders: Still a Formidable Presence." *Nation's Restaurant News,* December 15, 1986.
Sanders, Col. Harland. *Life as I Have Known It Has Been Finger Lickin' Good.* Carol Stream, IL: Creation House, 1974.

Howard M. Schultz:

Kim, Nancy J. "Daddy Starbucks Hot on Going Global." *Business Journal-Portland*, October 31, 1997.

Schultz, Howard M., and Dori Jones Yang. *Pour Your Heart Into It*. New York: Hyperion, 1997.

Frank A. Seiberling:

"Seiberling Comes Back at 71." *Business Week*, February 13, 1930.

"Seiberling: Rubber Industry's 'Little Napoleon' Reaches 75." *Newsweek*, October 13, 1934.

Irene Smith:

Smith, Irene. *Diary of a Small Business*. New York: Charles Scribner's Sons, 1982.

Dave Thomas:

Current Biography Yearbook, 1995, New York: H. W. Wilson, 1995.

Thomas, R. David, with Ron Beyma and Mary Maroon Gelpi. *Dave's Way*. New York: Berkeley Books, 1991.

Lillian Vernon:

Coleman, Lisa. "I Went Out and Did It." *Forbes*, August 17, 1992.

Vernon, Lillian. *An Eye for Winners*. New York: HarperBusiness, 1996.

Dr. An Wang:

Wang, Dr. An, with Eugene Linden. *Lessons: An Autobiography*. Reading, MA: Addison-Wesley, 1986.

Thomas J. Watson:

Rodgers, William. *Think*. New York: Stein and Day, 1969.

Watson, Thomas J., Jr., with Peter Petre. *Father, Son & Co.: My Life at IBM and Beyond*. New York: Bantam Books, 1990.

Joseph Wilson:

Jacobson, Gary, and John Hillkirk. *Xerox: American Samurai*. New York: Macmillan Publishing, 1986.

Kearns, David T., and David A. Nadler. *Prophets in the Dark*. New York: HarperBusiness, 1992.

Credits and Sources

"The Power in Commitment" from *The Power in You* by Wally Amos. Reprinted by permission of Wally Amos.

"Are You a Gunslinger" by Warren E. Avis. From *Take a Chance to Be First: The Secrets of Entrepreneurial Success.* Reprinted by permission of Simon & Schuster. Copyright © 1986 by Warren Avis.

"The American Museum" by P. T. Barnum, from *Struggles and Triumphs: Or Forty Years' Recollections.* New York: Penguin Books, 1981.

"If I Were Twenty-one" by Clarence Birdseye, from *The American Magazine,* February 1951.

"I Love Mondays" from *Bloomberg on Bloomberg,* by Michael Bloomberg with invaluable help from Mathew Winkler. Copyright © 1997 by Michael Bloomberg. Reprinted by permission of John Wiley & Sons, Inc.

"Risk Taking" by Richard Branson, from the *Journal of General Management,* Winter 1985. Reprinted by permission of the *Journal of General Management.*

"Diary of a Small Business Owner" from *Diary of a Small Business Owner* by Anita F. Brattina. Copyright © 1996 Anita F. Brattina. Reprinted by permission of AMACOM, a division of American Management Association International, New York, NY. All rights reserved.

"The Three Criteria for a Successful Business" by Norm Brodsky, from *Inc. Online,* April 1996. Republished with permission of *Inc. Online,* Goldhirsh Group, Inc., 38 Commercial Wharf, Boston, MA 02110. Reproduced by permission of the publisher via Copyright Clearance Center, Inc.

"To Win the Business Game Do What You Know" by Nolan Bushnell, from *Inc.,* August, 1979. Republished with permission of *Inc. Online,* Goldhirsh Group, Inc., 38 Commercial Wharf, Boston, MA 02110. Reproduced by permission of the publisher via Copyright Clearance Center, Inc.

"The Crucial Question" by Andrew Carnegie, from *Business,* a lecture delivered at Cornell University, January 11, 1896.

"10 Commandments for Building the Medium" by Steve Case from a speech delivered to the Jupiter Communications Annual Conference, March 5, 1998.

"Bagels, Ice Cream, or . . . Pizza?" from *Ben & Jerry's Double-Dip* by Ben Cohen and Jerry Greenfield. Copyright © 1997 by Ben Cohen and Jerry Greenfield. Reprinted with permission of Simon & Schuster, Inc.

"My Test of Good Management" by Marquis M. Converse, from *System: The Magazine of Business,* May 1924.

Credits and Sources

"Service Sells" by Michael S. Dell, from *Executive Excellence*, August 1993. Used with permission of Executive Excellence Publishing.

"The Discomfort Zone" by Barry Diller, from *Inc.*, November 1995. Reprinted by permission of Barry Diller.

"Mrs. Drucker Starts a Business" by Doris Drucker, from *Inc.*, October 1997. Reprinted by permission of Doris Drucker.

"Make the Camera as Convenient as the Pencil" by George Eastman, from *System: The Magazine of Business*, October 1920.

"My Style" from *One Smart Cookie* by Debbi Fields. Reprinted with the permission of Simon & Schuster. Copyright © 1987 by Debra J. Fields.

"Starting the Company" from *Men and Rubber* by Harvey S. Firestone. Copyright © 1926 by Doubleday, a division of Random House, Inc. Used by permission of Doubleday, a division of Random House.

"How I Made a Success of My Business" by Henry Ford, from *System: The Magazine of Business*, November 1916.

"Advice to a Young Tradesman" by Benjamin Franklin, from a personal letter, 1748.

"The Need for Controls" from *A Foot in the Door* by Alfred C. Fuller, 1960.

"You Can Always Do Better" by Samuel Goldwyn, from *The American Magazine*, July 1950.

"A Million Dollar Mountain and a Red Hat" from *Be My Guest* by Conrad Hilton, 1957. Reprinted with permission of Simon & Schuster. Copyright © 1957 by Conrad Hilton, renewed 1985 by Mary Frances Hilton, Constance F. Hilton, William Baron Hilton, and Erik Michael Hilton.

"When We Invented the Personal Computer . . ." by Steven P. Jobs, from *Computers and People*, July/August 1981.

"Breaking Through the Ad Barrier" from *Succeeding Against the Odds* by John H. Johnson. Copyright © 1989 John H. Johnson. Reprinted by permission of Amistad Press, Inc.

"Go Ahead—Jump!" by Andrew Kessler, from *Forbes ASAP*, February 26, 1996. Reprinted by permission of *Forbes ASAP* Magazine. Copyright © Forbes Inc., 1996.

"Remington's Marketing and Manufacturing Strategies" by Victor Kiam, from *Management Review*, February 1987. Reprinted by permission of Victor Kiam.

"Global Manufacturing: The Nike Story" by Philip Knight, from a speech delivered to the National Press Club Conference, May 12, 1998. Reprinted by permission of Philip Knight.

"LBOs Can Help Restore America's Competitive Edge" by Henry R. Kravis, from *Financier*, August 1989. Reprinted by permission of Henry R. Kravis.

"In the Creator's Mind" by Edwin Land. Reprinted from *How to Manage*, edited by Ray Wild, 1985. Reprinted by permission of Butterworth-Heinemann.

"Your Own Business" by Herman W. Lay, from *Listen to Leaders in Business*, edited by Albert Love and James Saxon Childers. Copyright © 1963 by Tupper & Love, Inc. Reprinted by permission of Henry Holt & Co., Inc.

"For Entrepreneurs Only" from *What They Don't Teach You in Harvard Business School* by Mark H. McCormack. Copyright © 1984 by Book Views, Inc. Used by permission of Bantam Books, a division of Random House, Inc.

"A Winning Business Model for the 90s" by Scott McNealy, from *Directors & Boards*, Fall 1995. Reprinted by permission of *Directors & Boards*.

505

Credits and Sources

"Bankers Are the Keepers of the Keys" from *Pizza Tiger* by Tom Monaghan. Reprinted by permission of Tom Monaghan.

"Moving Up in Marketing by Getting Down to Basics" by Akio Morita, from *The Conference Board Record*, December 1974. Reprinted by permission of The Conference Board.

"Showmanship and Salesmanship" from *Confessions of an S.O.B.* by Al Neuharth. Copyright © 1989 by Al Neuharth. Used by permission of Doubleday, a division of Random House, Inc.

"Digital Equipment Corporation: The First 25 Years" by Kenneth Olsen, from a speech delivered before the Newcomen Society, September 21, 1982, and reprinted in Newcomen Publication Number 1179. Reprinted by permission of the Newcomen Society.

"Why a Buyer's Market Hasn't Changed Our Plans" by J. C. Penney, from *System: The Magazine of Business*, February 1921.

"Change Is Fun" by H. Ross Perot, from *Executive Excellence*, 1996. Reprinted by permission of H. Ross Perot.

"A Tech Dream Comes True" by Kim Polese, from *Forbes ASAP*, December 1, 1997. Reprinted by permission of Kim Polese.

"The Technique of Anticipation" from *Century of Mismatch* by Simon Ramo. Reprinted by permission of Simon Ramo.

"Strategy vs. Tactics from a Venture Capitalist" by Arthur Rock, from *The Entrepreneurial Adventure*, edited by William A. Sahlman and Howard H. Stevenson. Reprinted by permission of Harvard Business School Press. Copyright © 1992 by the President and Fellows of Harvard College; all rights reserved.

"Four Letter Words" by Anita Roddick, from *Executive Excellence*, February 1998. Used with permission of Executive Excellence Publishing.

"The Making of a Colonel" from *Finger Lickin' Good* by Colonel Harland Sanders, 1974.

"The Best Way to Build a Brand" from *Pour Your Heart into It* by Howard Schultz and Dori Jones Yang. Reprinted by permission of Hyperion. Copyright © 1997 by Howard Schultz.

"Buying or Selling—Which Counts Most?" by Frank A. Seiberling, from *System: The Magazine of Business*, August 1920.

"Money: The Truth About Financing a Growing Business" from *Diary of a Small Business* by Irene Smith. Reprinted by permission of Scribner, a division of Simon & Schuster. Copyright © 1982 by Irene Smith.

"The Secrets of Sniffing Around" from *Dave's Way* by Dave Thomas. Reprinted by permission of Wendy's International. Copyright © 1991 by R. David Thomas.

"The Successful Entrepreneur's Toolkit" from *An Eye for Winners* by Lillian Vernon. Copyright © 1996 by Lillian Vernon. Reprinted by permission of HarperCollins Publishers, Inc.

"Going Public" from *Lessons: An Autobiography* by An Wang. Reprinted by permission of Boston University.

"To Make a Business Grow—Begin *Growing* Men!" by Thomas J. Watson, from *System: The Magazine of Business*, August 1926.

"The Product Nobody Wanted" by Joseph C. Wilson, from *Nation's Business*, February 1969. Reprinted by permission of *Nation's Business*. Copyright © 1969 by the U.S. Chamber of Commerce.

Chronology

Author Index

Companies Founded, Cofounded, or Managed by Authors

Subject Index